Hispanic/Latino Theology

Hispanic/Latino Theology

Challenge and Promise

ADA MARÍA ISASI-DÍAZ
FERNANDO F. SEGOVIA
Editors

Fortress Press   Minneapolis

HISPANIC/LATINO THEOLOGY
Challenge and Promise

Library of Congress Cataloging-in-Publication Data
Hispanic/Latino theology : challenge and promise / Ada María Isasi-
  Díaz, Fernando F. Segovia, editors.
     p.   cm.
  Papers originally presented at a conference held at the
Theological School of Drew University, April 15–17, 1994.
  Includes bibliographical references.
  ISBN 0-8006-2921-3 (alk. paper)
  1. Hispanic American theology—Congresses.   I. Isasi-Díaz, Ada
María.   II. Segovia, Fernando F.
BT83.575.H57 1996
230'.089'68073–dc20   96–4537
                                        CIP

Manufactured in the U.S.A.   AF 1–2921

3   4   5   6   7   8   9   10

To our Latino/Hispanic communities,
and to all aliens, everywhere

Contents

Part Two
LOCUS OF HISPANIC/LATINO THEOLOGY

Part Three
EXPRESSIONS OF HISPANIC/LATINO THEOLOGY

Preface

The present volume was first conceived by the editors in the early fall of 1992. It had become clear to us by then that the development of a Latino or Hispanic American theology—that is to say, a theology emerging from and addressing the social location of Latinos or Hispanics in the United States—was well on its way to a rich and sophisticated maturity. New voices were constantly coming to the fore; new contacts were being forged all the time; and new publications continued to see the light of day. The movement had simply become unstoppable. At the same time, it was also clear to us that too little dialogue and interaction were taking place between the theological voices from the dominant Catholic tradition and the theological voices from the smaller but rapidly growing Protestant tradition. Consequently, to facilitate and foster such contact and conversation among us, we planned a volume that would gather together the various theological voices of our communities, both Protestant and Catholic, so that we could all address, from our own respective backgrounds and traditions, questions and concerns common to all of us.

We further believed that it would be far better to bring together all of the various contributors not only in writing, in the proposed volume, but also face-to-face, by way of a national conference. Such a conference, we believed, would allow us a rare and wonderful opportunity not only to read one another's works and publications, in and of itself a most important task to be sure, but also to speak with one another, interact with one another, eat and drink with one another over the space of a few days. Such a conference, we further decided, would be held, if approved, at Drew University, given its proximity to New York City and the large number of Latinos and Hispanics of all colors and origins residing in the New York metropolitan area.

With the full and much-appreciated support of our respective deans, we approached the Lilly Endowment for funding. We did so through the person of Ms. Olga Villa Parra, then the officer in charge of all projects having to do with Latino or Hispanic socioreligious concerns. We were most fortunate. From the beginning she showed undivided support for the project, steered it wisely through the complex process of funding, and remained throughout a most valuable friend, counselor, and ally. In the end, our proposal, originally entitled "Aliens in Jerusalem: The Emerging Theological Voice of Hispanic Americans," was positively received and graciously approved for funding in the early spring of 1993. The project was then presented to Fortress Press—through the agency of J. Michael West, yet another esteemed friend, counselor, and ally—and it was immediately accepted for publication.

The conference itself, held at the Theological School of Drew University on April 15–17 of 1994, proved to be, as expected, a most exciting and successful gathering, not only for the participants themselves but also for the many people who attended from throughout the New York metropolitan area as well as from throughout the country as a whole. In the good tradition of our people, we talked at length, we shared at length, and we celebrated at length. Indeed, we believe that the conference not only served to bring us closer together but also provided further impetus and strength to our burgeoning theological movement and voice.

The present volume, then, contains most of the papers presented at the conference. Given their respective contents and orientations, a threefold division readily suggested itself for the overall organization of the volume: a first section would deal with the sources of our theology (the Bible, church history, cultural memory, literature, oral tradition, Pentecostalism); a second section would address the question of the locus of such theology (the urban barrios, the Puerto Rican experience, exile, liberation theology, the social sciences, feminism); a final section would be devoted to different expressions of this theology (*mujerista* and feminist theology, popular religion, postmodernism, social ethics, theological tradition, theopoetics). Needless to say, all papers addressed, in one way or another, every one of these different dimensions of the theological task, yet a dominant emphasis invariably emerged, thus accounting for their present classification and arrangement in the volume. The introduction by Fernando F. Segovia and the conclusion by Ada María Isasi-Díaz were written after the conference itself and in light of its presentations and proceedings.

Finally, the volume is meant as a further and important contribution to our continued quest for a voice in and from the margins, a voice that does not come any longer from strangers within the contemporary theological world—a world of profound and irreversible diversity, pluralism, and globalization. As such, we would like to dedicate it to our own communities of struggle and to all communities of struggle everywhere.

Acknowledgments

The editors express their profound gratitude to all those individuals and institutions who have made this volume possible.

First, to the Lilly Endowment for its strong support of the project and the generous funding that made it possible to bring together all these scholars from across the nation for the conference held at Drew University. Three individuals deserve special mention: Dr. Craig Dykstra, Vice-President for Religion; Sr. Jeanne Knoerle, S.P., Program Director; and, in a very special way, Ms. Olga Villa Parra, the officer in charge of the project, who backed it unconditionally from the very beginning, nourished it wisely during the long process of preparation, and saw it come to a most successful completion. To all three we are deeply indebted.

Second, to Dr. Joseph C. Hough, Jr., Dean of the Divinity School at Vanderbilt University, who gave the project his strong support in its early stages, and Dr. Robin C. Lovin, former Dean of the Theological School at Drew University, who graciously and wholeheartedly adopted it as his own.

Third, to Dr. Marshall D. Johnson, Editorial Director of Fortress Press, and J. Michael West, Senior Editor of Fortress Press, for their kind and unwavering commitment to the project, from the planning stages to the process of publication; and to Hank Schlau of ediType for his unparalleled editorial acumen.

Fourth, to all the students at both the Theological School and the Graduate School of Drew University whose kind participation and assistance proved invaluable during the course of the conference itself. Two deserve special mention: Ms. Nora O. Lozano-Díaz, of Drew University, who as administrative assistant played a crucial role in the overall preparation for and management of the conference; and Ms. Leticia Guardiola-Sáenz, of Vanderbilt University, who as research assistant undertook the task of editing and formatting the papers for publication.

Finally, to all our colleagues and friends who kindly accepted our invitations and whose contributions to the project grace the pages that follow. To them we are indeed specially indebted.

Contributors

Yamina Apolinaris, Executive Minister of the Baptist Churches of Puerto Rico, San Juan, Puerto Rico

María Pilar Aquino, Department of Theological and Religious Studies, University of San Diego, San Diego, California

Gilbert Cadena, Department of Sociology, Pomona College, Claremont, California

Ana María Díaz-Stevens, Union Theological Seminary, New York City, New York

Orlando O. Espín, Department of Theological and Religious Studies, University of San Diego, San Diego, California

Ismael García, Austin Presbyterian Theological Seminary, Austin, Texas

Francisco García-Treto, Department of Religion, Trinity University, San Antonio, Texas

Roberto Goizueta, Department of Theology, Loyola University of Chicago, Chicago, Illinois

Justo L. González, Columbia Theological Seminary, Decatur, Georgia

Ada María Isasi-Díaz, the Theological School, Drew University, Madison, New Jersey

Daisy Machado, Brite Divinity School, Texas Christian University, Fort Worth, Texas

Otto Maduro, the Theological School, Drew University, Madison, New Jersey

Sandra Mangual-Rodríguez, Seminario Evangélico de Puerto Rico, Río Piedras, Puerto Rico

Elena Olazagasti-Segovia, Department of Spanish and Portuguese, Vanderbilt University, Nashville, Tennessee

Ana María Pineda, Catholic Theological Union, Chicago, Illinois

Harold J. Recinos, Wesley Theological Seminary, Washington, D.C.

Jeanette Rodríguez, Institute for Theological Studies, Seattle University, Seattle, Washington

José David Rodríguez, Lutheran School of Theology, Chicago, Illinois

Fernando F. Segovia, the Divinity School, Vanderbilt University, Nashville, Tennessee

Samuel Solivan, Andover Newton School of Theology, Newton Centre, Massachusetts

Aliens in the Promised Land: The Manifest Destiny of U.S. Hispanic American Theology

_____ *Fernando F. Segovia* _____

In the last decade a new voice, a voice of liberation, has emerged and been heard on the global theological scene.[1] While closely related to other new theological voices from the non-Western world and in particular from Latin America—similar voices of liberation that have been making themselves heard for more than twenty-five years[2]—this new voice has come from within the West itself, being forged in the United States and, more specifically, within an ethnic minority group in the United States.[3] As such,

---

1. See Fernando F. Segovia, "A New Manifest Destiny: The Emerging Theological Voice of Hispanic Americans," *Religious Studies Review* 17 (1991) 101–9.

2. If one takes the original publication in Spanish of Gustavo Gutiérrez's classic work (*La teología de la liberación* [Lima: CEP, 1971]; Eng. trans.: *A Theology of Liberation: History, Politics, and Salvation* [Maryknoll, N.Y.: Orbis Books, 1973]) as a watershed in this regard, then a full two decades had already elapsed since the appearance of liberation theology on the scene (1971–1991). It should be recalled, however, that, while the appearance of this work marks a signal event in the development of liberation theology and non-Western theology in general, the liberation movement had much earlier roots; see, for example, Arthur F. McGovern, *Liberation Theology and Its Critics: Toward an Assessment* (Maryknoll, N.Y.: Orbis Books, 1989), esp. 1–19; Alfred T. Hennelly, ed., *Liberation Theology: A Documentary History* (Maryknoll, N.Y.: Orbis Books, 1990), esp. parts 1 and 2.

3. The expression "ethnic minority group" is a composite term, consisting of "ethnic group" and "minority group." A word of explanation is in order. The terms "ethnic group" and "racial group" as well as "minority group" and "majority group" are taken from the study of intergroup relations; see in this regard the helpful introduction by J. R. Fegin (*Racial and Ethnic Relations* [3d ed.; Englewood Cliffs, N.J.: Prentice-Hall, 1989] 4–19), with whose social definitions of these terms I find myself in agreement. On the one hand, "ethnic group" and "racial group" are terms applied to social groups singled out as such for social interest, whether good or bad, either from inside or outside the differentiated groups, on the basis of certain cultural or physical characteristics, respectively. On the other hand, "minority group" and "majority group" are terms that imply the presence of ethnic or racial stratification. As such, these labels are not just descriptive classifications but also evaluative categories. At times, the terms "dominant group" and "subordinate group" are preferred in the literature, in order to reflect the fact that a "minority group" in terms of stratification may actually be a "majority group" with respect to numbers. My own use of the term "minority group" with respect to the U.S. Hispanic American population implies both numbers and stratification, and thus I use the term "subordinate group" interchangeably as well.

its closest analogue is undoubtedly black theology, already long in existence.[4] The voice in question is, of course, that of U.S. Hispanic Americans, a growing segment of the population to which I belong. Elsewhere I have used the label Hispanic Americans, whom I defined as people of Hispanic descent, associated in one way or another with the Americas, who now live, for whatever reason, on a permanent basis in the United States.[5]

The contours of this voice can be described in terms of a number of distinctive and recurring concerns or themes that have been articulated through a broad spectrum of dialects and idiolects—each with its own vocabulary, grammar, and pronunciation. First, this is a voice that subscribes to the basic tenets of liberation theology, given its self-definition within a context of pervasive and sustained discrimination and oppression from the dominant culture. Second, from within such a perspective, this is a voice engaged in a profound critique of both the religious (institutional) and theological (educational) establishments of the country—whether liberal or conservative, Catholic or Protestant—which it generally perceives as provincial and uncritical in cultural outlook, attitude, and policy. Lastly, this is a voice with a clear sense of mission: to serve as a reminder that no one culture represents the sole and superior embodiment of the Christian tradition and to affirm the richness that cultural diversity represents for church and academy alike.

My earlier analysis of this movement was written on the eve of the quincentenary of the fateful encounter, actually much more of an *encontronazo* (clash) than an *encuentro* (encounter), between the peoples and cultures of Europe and the peoples and cultures of what would later come to be known as "the Americas." I concluded with a prediction that this new theologi-

---

4. For the origins and development of black theology, see the recent anthology by James H. Cone and Gayraud S. Wilmore, eds., *Black Theology: A Documentary History* (2 vols; Maryknoll, N.Y.: Orbis Books, 1993); see esp. 1:1–11 and 2:1–11, the general introductions to each volume.

5. In formulating this definition, I had a number of specific goals in mind. First, the prepositional phrase "of Hispanic descent" was meant to distinguish the group in question from other ethnic groups living in the United States who also traced their origins to the Americas, such as the French-speaking Haitians, the Portuguese-speaking Brazilians, and the English-speaking West Indians. Second, this particular phrase was also meant to be comprehensive enough to include the wide variety of subgroups within the group, such as Mexican Americans, mainland Puerto Ricans, and Cuban Americans—its three main components in terms of numbers. Third, the appositional adjectival phrase "associated in one way or another with the Americas" was further meant to distinguish the group as "New World" and thus as different from individuals tracing their origins directly to Spain and the Iberian Peninsula. Fourth, the relative clause "who now live . . . on a permanent basis in the United States" was meant to point specifically to the group's present and definitive location in the United States, whether as citizens, born or naturalized, or aliens, legal or illegal. Finally, the brief prepositional phrase within the relative clause, "for whatever reason," was meant to account for the enormous variety of reasons behind the group's presence within the country: from birth as descendants of groups taken over by the United States in its long process of national expansion; to birth as the children of immigrants, whether first-generation or more; to immigration on account of economic and/or political reasons.

cal voice would only grow stronger with time and ultimately evolve into a new "manifest destiny." In the years that have elapsed since that prophetic dictum of mine, the movement of U.S. Hispanic American theology has gone on to show vigorous growth indeed, way beyond any expectations I or anybody else entertained. In fact, it is entirely appropriate to speak, despite a number of undeniable disappointments and reverses,[6] of a U.S. Hispanic American theological boom. A number of developments in this regard deserve special mention.

1. The Academy of Catholic Hispanic Theologians of the United States (ACHTUS), founded in 1988, has continued apace its important task of theological reflection and discussion within the Roman Catholic context, primarily by way of its annual meeting and colloquium. Given its restriction of full membership to Roman Catholics with a doctoral degree in any of the classical theological disciplines, ACHTUS has witnessed steady but limited growth in numbers. This is, without doubt, an organization that will continue to serve as a major forum for U.S. Hispanic American theology in the years to come.[7]

2. In 1991 a new theological organization was launched, the Association for Hispanic Theological Education (AETH: Asociación para la Educación Teológica Hispana). Although open to Catholics, AETH actually functions as more of a counterpart to ACHTUS in the Protestant tradition.[8] Given its focus on theological education, however, its reach is enormous, bringing

---

6. Two such reverses come readily to mind. First of all, in 1992 the Community of Hispanic American Scholars of Theology and Religion (CHASTR), an academic organization of ecumenical character, open as it was to Catholics and Protestants from all theological disciplines, collapsed on its own, really for no other reason than lack of leadership at the top. Its demise has left a definite vacuum in our theological voice, since it was the only space where Catholics and Protestants could come together in significant numbers for dialogue. Then, a year later, in 1993, the Pew Charitable Trusts, after generous support for a good number of years, let it be known that it would not renew its financial commitment to the Fund for Theological Education, funding that had been used to support U.S. Hispanic American students in both graduate and ministerial studies. From an academic point of view, this was a heavy blow indeed. For years, such funding had made it easier for the best and the brightest in the group to pursue doctoral work, with nothing short of resounding success, as a look at its list of awards recipients readily indicates, many of whom are either already playing or beginning to play a prominent role on the national scene. For a recent reorientation of funding practices on the part of Pew, see n. 9 below.

7. In 1995 ACHTUS held its eighth annual meeting and colloquium in conjunction with the annual meeting of the Black Catholic Theological Symposium (BCTS). As a result of this joint gathering, both organizations have agreed (*a*) to hold joint annual meetings on a regular basis in the future; (*b*) to schedule related sessions within the framework of the Catholic Theological Society of America (CTSA) convention, where both groups convene annual sessions; and (*c*) to extend an invitation for dialogue to Asian American Catholics. Such intercultural discussions will only serve to strengthen the level of discourse and external influence of all the groups in question, including ACHTUS itself.

8. Its statement of purpose defines its concept of membership as follows: "While the *Asociación* is conceived in terms of responding to specific needs and goals in Protestant theological education, membership and participation is open to all Christians who share in the goals and aims of the *Asociación*." Thus, in effect, while de jure open to all, unlike ACHTUS, de facto it is a Protestant organization. In this respect, the demise of CHASTR

together individuals and groups from the whole spectrum of Protestant-ism, both in terms of denominations (from evangelicals and Pentecostals to the mainline or historical churches) and educational institutions (from newly established Bible institutes to long-standing seminaries and divinity schools). As a result, AETH not only has experienced remarkable growth in its brief period of existence but has also in its purview a broad range of programs meant to foster and strengthen the theological education of U.S. Hispanic Americans across the board.[9] There is every reason to believe that this organization will continue to experience rapid growth in membership as well as increased solidity in its programs and offerings.

3. In 1992, ACHTUS, under the active leadership of its then president, Orlando O. Espín, applied for and received a generous grant from the Lilly Endowment to launch, with the close cooperation of the Liturgical Press, a scholarly journal devoted to the theological concerns and issues of U.S. Hispanic Americans, the *Journal of Hispanic/Latino Theology*.[10] Although obviously Catholic in orientation, the journal was conceived as resolutely catholic in reach, open to contributions from U.S. Protestant His-panic Americans as well as from non-U.S. Hispanic Americans. Similarly, although clearly theological in character, the journal was further conceived

---

(see n. 6 above) has been especially noticeable, leaving no organization to bring the two traditions together with an open agenda.

9. In a recent issue of its newsletter, *Encuentro* (3:4, winter 1994), it was announced that the association had just received a major grant from the Pew Charitable Trusts through Columbia Theological Seminary (Decatur, Ga.). This grant, in the amount of $420,000 and for the space of three years, is meant to finance such projects as the following: meetings of members by disciplines; technical assistance to biblical institutes and colleges; scholarships for research and publication; the development of educational resources for the U.S. His-panic American community; regional meetings as well as national meetings. It was further announced in the same issue that the Pew Charitable Trusts had also funded a major re-search project entitled "The Future of Hispanic Graduate Theological Education: A Study of Successful Strategies for Access, Retention, and Development of Hispanic Religious Leaders and Scholars," to be conducted by Edwin I. Hernández of Andrews University, whose main goal would be to produce a document with specific recommendations to funding agencies, seminaries, and universities on how best to recruit, train, and develop religious leaders and scholars. It would seem from such recent developments that the Pew Charitable Trusts, after its withdrawal from the Fund for Theological Education, has been rethinking its funding for U.S. Hispanic American theological programs and turning to AETH as a main venue in this regard. Indeed, it has recently been announced as well that Pew will initiate a new and extensive funding program for U.S. Hispanic American students at both the ministerial and the graduate level, to be based at Emory University and headed by its own coordinator and board of directors. Needless to say, this is a major boon to the future of U.S. Hispanic American theological education and scholarship.

10. The editorial statement of the first issue (*Journal of Hispanic/Latino Theology* 1 [1993] 3–4) explained the need for such a journal as follows: first, as a forum for a his-torically excluded voice, insofar as the voice of Hispanic Americans, although reflecting the faith and realities of the oldest Christian communities on the continent, had been excluded as insignificant in mainstream U.S. theology; second, as a forum for a distinct voice, dif-ferent from both that of Latin America and that of Euro-America; finally, as a forum for a marginalized voice, experiencing enormous difficulty in making itself heard in the North American theological dialogue.

as broadly open to theological contributions in dialogue with the social sciences. Now in its third year of publication, the journal has been well received and has fulfilled its goals in eminent fashion, providing an exemplary and much-needed forum for the U.S. Hispanic American theological voice in all of its many expressions and inflections. More recently, the journal has established a new and distinguished board of contributing members, drawn from both the national and the international scene, with the aim in mind of becoming ever more "catholic" by expanding the dialogue among theologians of different cultural backgrounds and traditions, although to be sure with a continued and primary focus on the U.S. Hispanic American reality and experience.[11]

4. Since 1991, when I undertook my review-of-the-literature article mentioned above, the theological production of U.S. Hispanic Americans has continued to burgeon. Such literature encompasses a variety of fields and disciplines—biblical criticism,[12] feminist ethics and theology,[13] pastoral theology,[14] and social ethics;[15] a number of collections of essays have also appeared.[16] This corpus will continue to expand significantly in the years to come, with at least five manuscripts scheduled for publication in the near future.[17]

5. In terms of research and publication, special mention must be made of three important projects involving working groups of scholars. Two of these have to do with the history of the U.S. Hispanic American church

---

11. An editorial statement (*Journal of Latino/Hispanic Theology* 2 [1994–95] 3–4) explained the move as follows: in keeping with its original aim of expanding the North American theological conversation by giving voice to a tradition largely bypassed in mainstream U.S. theology, the journal wished to promote even greater "catholic" dialogue by setting up a board of contributing editors whose geographic, cultural, denominational, and methodological composition would reflect such "catholicity."

12. C. Gilbert Romero, *Hispanic Devotional Piety: Tracing the Biblical Roots* (Maryknoll, N.Y.: Orbis Books, 1991); Pablo A. Jiménez, ed., *Lumbrera a nuestro camino* (Miami: Editorial Caribe, 1994); Justo L. González, *Santa Biblia: The Bible through Hispanic Eyes* (Nashville: Abingdon Press, 1995).

13. María Pilar Aquino, *Our Cry for Life: Feminist Theology from Latin America* (Maryknoll, N.Y.: Orbis Books, 1993); Ada María Isasi-Díaz, *En la lucha/In the Struggle. A Hispanic Women's Liberation Theology* (Minneapolis: Fortress Press, 1993); Jeanette Rodríguez, *Our Lady of Guadalupe: Faith and Empowerment among Mexican-American Women* (Austin: University of Texas Press, 1994).

14. Harold J. Recinos, *Jesus Weeps: Global Encounters on Our Doorstep* (Nashville: Abingdon Press, 1992).

15. Eldin Villafañe, *The Liberating Spirit: Toward an Hispanic American Social Ethic* (Lanham, Md.: University Press of America, 1992).

16. Allan Figueroa Deck, ed., *Frontiers of Hispanic Theology in the United States* (Maryknoll, N.Y.: Orbis Books, 1992); Roberto S. Goizueta, ed., *We Are a People: Initiatives in Hispanic American Theology* (Minneapolis: Fortress Press, 1992); Justo L. González, ed., *Voces: Voices from the Hispanic Church* (Nashville: Abingdon Press, 1992); Fernando F. Segovia, ed., *Hispanic Americans in Theology and the Church*, special issue of *Listening: Journal of Religion and Culture* 27:1 (winter 1992).

17. All forthcoming from Orbis Books and in the field of theology: Arturo Bañuelas; Orlando O. Espín; Eduardo Fernández; Alejandro García-Rivera; Roberto Goizueta.

in its Catholic and Protestant dimensions, respectively. While the former project has already resulted in a comprehensive, three-volume work on the history of U.S. Hispanic American Catholicism in this century,[18] the latter has yielded a first and important step in the study of U.S. Hispanic American Protestantism.[19] A third project, under the leadership of the Program for the Analysis of Religion among Latinos (PARAL), has taken upon itself to examine the religious practices of U.S. Hispanic Americans from the perspective of the social sciences.[20]

I would only emphasize that such developments, important as they are, represent but a part of the theological production taking place among U.S. Hispanic Americans. Moreover, it has become quite clear to me in recent years that this theological boom actually forms part of a much larger one involving not only a variety of academic disciplines but also literature. Wherever one looks nowadays—be it fiction or poetry,[21] the humanities

---

18. The volumes, involving twenty scholars in all, were the result of a project carried out under the auspices of the Cushwa Center for the Study of American Catholicism at the University of Notre Dame and entitled "Hispanic Catholics in Twentieth Century U.S." As a whole, the work is entitled *The Notre Dame History of Hispanic Catholics in the U.S.* (Notre Dame, Ind.: University of Notre Dame Press, 1994) and consists of the following volumes: Jay P. Dolan and Gilberto M. Hinojosa, eds., vol. 1, *Mexican Americans and the Catholic Church, 1900–1965;* Jay P. Dolan and Jaime R. Vidal, eds., vol. 2, *Puerto Rican and Cuban Catholics in the U.S., 1900–1965;* Jay P. Dolan and Allan Figueroa Deck, eds., vol. 3, *Hispanic Catholic Culture in the U.S.: Issues and Concerns.*

19. Daniel R. Rodríguez-Díaz and David Cortés Fuentes, eds., *Hidden Stories: Unveiling the History of the Latino Church* (Decatur, Ga.: AETH, 1994). This volume, involving thirteen scholars in all, grew out of a conference held at McCormick Theological Seminary under the auspices of the then recently formed Academy for the Study of Latino Church History (APHILA), whose basic mission was to recover and document the history of U.S. Hispanic American Protestantism. The conference was meant to function as a watershed in this regard, with the following aims in mind: the creation of a network of individuals working on U.S. Hispanic American Protestant church history; the exchange of information; an assessment of needs; and the planning of future steps. Subsequently, APHILA decided to disband as a separate organization and to join forces instead with AETH (the Association for Hispanic Theological Education) as a way of strengthening the future of the U.S. Hispanic American church history project.

20. Out of this program, based at the Bildner Center for Western Hemisphere Studies of the Graduate School and University Center of The City University of New York, four volumes have emerged in all: Anthony M. Stevens-Arroyo and Ana María Díaz-Stevens, eds., *An Enduring Flame. Studies in Latino Popular Religiosity* (New York: PARAL, 1995); Anthony M. Stevens-Arroyo and Gilbert R. Cadena, eds., *Old Masks, New Faces: Religion and Latino Identities* (New York: PARAL, 1995); Anthony M. Stevens-Arroyo and Andrés Peréz-Mena, eds., *Enigmatic Powers: Syncretism with African and Indigenous People's Religions among Latinos* (New York: PARAL, 1995); and Anthony M. Stevens-Arroyo, *Discovering Latino Religion: A Comprehensive Social Science Bibliography* (New York: PARAL, 1995).

21. From the point of view of literature, three examples stand out, all directly associated with the University of Houston. The first is *The Americas Review,* formerly known as the *Revista Chicano-Riqueña,* a journal that has long served as a venue for U.S. Hispanic American literature. The second is Arte Público Press, a publishing house dedicated exclusively to the publication of established figures as well as beginning authors of U.S. Hispanic American literature of all genres; its catalog provides more than ample evidence regarding the high level of U.S. Hispanic American literary production in the United States. The third is the national project entitled "Recovering the U.S. Hispanic Literary Heritage," whose aim is

or the social sciences[22]—there is a steady stream of works by or about U.S. Hispanic Americans. The recent growth in theological production, therefore, represents but one facet of a much larger literary and academic boom in U.S. Hispanic American circles.

In light of such developments, it is the specific aim of the present volume to contribute to this ongoing theological movement by bringing together in conversation voices from both the Catholic and the Protestant tradition—a much too rare and yet much-needed occurrence nowadays, given the widely reported and rapidly expanding "Protestantization" of the U.S. Hispanic American church, not so much in terms of the mainline or "historical" churches (as they are called in Latin America: *las iglesias históricas*) but rather in terms of the Pentecostal and evangelical churches. Thus, scholars from both traditions address themselves hereby to a number of fundamental issues and themes of U.S. Hispanic American theology, grouped around the following three basic categories: sources, loci, and expressions. The result is a splendid ecumenical and kaleidoscopic overview of the field of U.S. Hispanic American theology, quite in keeping with the enormously diverse nature of Hispanic American reality and experience in the United States.

By way of introduction, I should like to pursue a number of general issues pertinent to the project as a whole that I have already brought to the fore in the title. I begin with the question of sociopolitical matrix ("the promised land"); then turn to the question of our status and role as "others" (as "aliens," thus raising the matter of manifest destiny); and conclude with the all-important but ultimately elusive question of nomenclature (the term "U.S. Hispanic American").

Sociopolitical Matrix: The Promised Land

Our present and permanent residence in the United States, our sociopolitical matrix, can be characterized in terms of "the promised land." This characterization has recourse to a long-standing tradition in the country and self-conception of the country, in effect, a national mythology: a deeply ingrained and much-cherished belief that the United States has been blessed and hence marked in a very distinctive and unique way by God (the Christian God). Consequently, the mythology continues, the country also has a

---

to recover the literary legacy of U.S. Hispanic Americans from colonial times through 1960, with critical editions to be published by Arte Público Press.

22. Quite indicative in this regard is the recent launching of a quarterly journal, the *Latino Review of Books: A Magazine for Critical Thought and Dialogue*, sponsored by the Center for Latino, Latin American, and Caribbean Studies (CELAC) of the State University of New York at Albany; the journal is devoted, as the title indicates, to the whole spectrum of U.S. Hispanic American studies. Given its focus on the Hispanic American population of the United States and the traditional connections between the diverse immigrant groups and their respective countries of origin, its basic aim is to keep abreast of research, publications, and issues presently shaping the field.

very distinctive and unique mission in the world: a duty to spread the good news of the "kingdom of God" (in itself a combination of Christian religious beliefs and republican forms of government) to the rest of the world, so that the blessings of God can be extended thereby to all other peoples and nations.[23]

Given the Protestant background of the dominant and majority group of the country and the centrality of the Bible for this group, such a belief—what has come to be known as "American exceptionalism"—has traditionally been given expression in strong biblical terms. Drawing on the "Old Testament," for example, the United States is seen as a present-day counterpart to ancient Israel: a promised land given by God to a chosen people and hence not only a chosen nation but also a "light to the nations." Likewise, drawing on the "New Testament," the country is further seen as a counterpart to the early Christian church: a beginning presence of the kingdom of God in the world with a duty to extend the message and confines of the kingdom to "all the nations."

Now, I doubt very much whether U.S. Hispanic Americans ever regard or refer to their present homeland, the United States, in such biblical terms as "promised land," "chosen nation," "chosen people," "light to the nations," or "kingdom of God." In these matters, however, one needs to be as concrete as possible, and thus I draw on my own personal experience. From the particular perspective of exile and the diaspora that I represent— my point of reference for all the comments that follow—I for one do not recall ever having used or having heard such expressions during my early years in Cuba, nor, I would add, have I ever heard or used such expressions in my thirty-some years in the United States: not within my family; not among our circle of friends; not even in our public sphere. In and of itself this is not all that surprising, since such biblical imagery never formed part of the standard linguistic or semiotic repertoire of those of us in the Catholic tradition, although I would also have to say that I have never heard such terms used in U.S. Hispanic American Protestant circles.[24]

---

23. The literature on this topic is ample; see, for example: Ernest Lee Tuveson, *Redeemer Nation: The Idea of America's Millennial Role* (Chicago: University of Chicago Press, 1968 [Midway reprint: 1980]); and Robert T. Handy, *A Christian America. Protestant Hopes and Historical Realities* (New York: Oxford University Press, 1971). On the ideology of national chosenness in the West as a whole, see William R. Hutchison and Hartmut Lehmann, eds., *Many Are Chosen: Divine Election and Western Nationalism* (Harvard Theological Studies 38; Minneapolis: Fortress Press, 1994).

24. A good barometer in such matters is the work of Justo L. González (*Mañana: Christian Theology from a Hispanic Perspective* [Nashville: Abingdon Press, 1990] esp. 21–30). First, speaking from the perspective of Protestants as a religious minority in Latin America, González describes their belief in the United States—a belief brought to and instilled in them by the early missionaries—as a society that was more Christian and more advanced than their own, a society where a mixture of Protestantism and culture accounted for its technological, political, and economic triumphs. Then, speaking from the perspective of Protestant Hispanic Americans in the United States, González points to a continuing sense of loyalty to

Yet, as I look back now, it is clear to me that, while we may not have called upon such terminology and symbolism, our image of our neighbor to the north, *al norte,* was not that far removed from such lofty heights of biblical rhetoric. To be sure, I remember quite vividly as well, painted all over the streets of La Habana, even before the *revolución* came to power and the subsequent adoption of a Marxist-Leninist form of government, the many signs—whether whitewashed, fading, or freshly painted—bearing the curt political message, "*¡Yanqui, Go Home!*" By and large, however, it seems to me, such feelings were confined to a small but committed—and, needless to say, persecuted—left.[25] Most people felt great admiration for the United States as a nation and world power, even when they deplored, as many did, the way in which it threw its weight around in the rest of the Americas and above all in the Caribbean, which had gradually become a sort of imperial *mare nostrum,* where military interventions could and did take place at will and where local governments, even when duly elected and progressive governments, could be and were deposed and replaced by the most regressive and repressive of dictatorships.

In other words, while the United States may not have been cast in the biblical imagery and vocabulary of divine election and mission as such, it was nonetheless widely seen in terms of exalted progress, liberty, and justice, especially against the background of our own reality and experience at home, marked as these were by widespread poverty and sharp inequalities, never-ending social and political upheavals, and profound governmental corruption and abuse of power. Such conditions, many believed and affirmed, simply did not exist and would not be allowed to exist in the United States.[26] Such visions and expectations of the country, I was to learn later on, closely matched those of so many others from around the globe who looked upon the United States in the highest of utopian terms, both from a material and a moral perspective.[27]

From a material point of view, there was no doubt whatsoever regarding

---

the country and its culture, so that any criticism of U.S. society is looked upon as disloyal to both their adopted nation and their religion. At no point, however, does González describe such attachments and feelings along the biblical lines of election.

25. On the Latin American left, see Jorge Castañeda, *Utopia Unarmed: The Latin American Left after the Cold War* (New York: Knopf, 1993).

26. I would thus argue that Justo González's description of the attitude of the Protestant minority in Latin America (see n. 24 above) was not all that different from that of the Catholic majority, except for the fact that we did not, as I recall, look upon the United States as a more "Christian" nation. This is not to say that we looked upon it as a less Christian nation: it was simply a Protestant nation. In other words, the view of the United States as the apex of modern civilization did not admit of religious boundaries, though it might have been more pronounced among the Protestant minority, given their views on the Christian character of the nation.

27. For reflections on the country on the part of immigrants from a broad variety of ethnic and racial contexts, see Wesley Brown and Amy Ling, eds., *Imagining America: Stories from the Promised Land* (New York: Presea Books, 1991); idem, *Visions of America: Personal Narratives from the Promised Land* (New York: Presea Books, 1993).

the economic superiority of our neighbor. Many did indeed believe that, in sharp contrast to our own situation, the streets in the United States were "paved with gold" and took the representation of the country in film and television as incontrovertible evidence. Besides, there was the ample evidence available in our own shops and stores, fields and streets, where U.S. products not only predominated but were also considered of the highest quality. For many, therefore, the United States represented progress at its very best—craftsmanship, reliability, comfort, innovation. From a moral point of view, its civil superiority stood equally unmatched. The material progress and well-being of the nation were taken to be readily accessible to all sectors of the citizenry: poverty was out of the question; work was plentiful and well recompensed; labor conditions were marked by principles of justice and dignity. All the basic civil liberties we generally lacked and yearned for, it was widely believed, were not only available to all but guaranteed as well—freedom of speech; freedom of the press; freedom of assembly. Political conditions were further seen as governed by regularity and stability, with the right to vote and the right to dissent holding a dear place in the society.

In sum, the United States was in a very real sense "the promised land," not so much perhaps in religious terms but certainly in terms of progress and modernity. Of course, to anyone familiar with the discourse of imperialism and colonialism, such visions and expectations on our part only reflect the mentality typical of colonial subjects and neocolonial subalterns. It is a mentality that operates within a binomial framework of center and margins, in which the margins are taught and come to think that they represent the very opposite of the center: the civilization, enlightenment, and sophistication of the center are directly matched by their own backwardness, ignorance, and primitiveness. For such a mentality, the center emerges as flawless and immaculate, a paragon of virtue and uprightness, while the margins remain invincibly flawed, inescapably mired in their own decay and corruption. For such a mentality, therefore, there is really but one option, strongly reinforced by the center: to put aside its natural tendencies and traditional expressions and to adopt those of the center. It is thus in the very nature of things for the center to lead, to show the way, and for the margins to follow, leaving their own ways behind.

It was with such visions of peace and serenity and such expectations of justice and opportunity that many U.S. Hispanic Americans have, in the long course of the century, left their respective homelands and arrived on these shores—whether by plane, barge, raft, train, car, tunnel, or some other means; whether by walking, climbing, riding, wading, swimming...[28]

---

28. I cannot stress enough the fact that I speak primarily for the experience of exile and the diaspora; I simply cannot speak for the visions and expectations of those born in the country, either as children of immigrants or as descendants of those whose territories came under the dominion of the country. How such other U.S. Hispanic Americans approach the

What many of us ultimately found upon arrival, however, was not quite what we had envisioned, but then utopian expectations are in the end impossible to satisfy and ultimately lead to practices of demythologizing and deconstruction, from the most minor to the most radical. The "promised land" did have its blemishes and imperfections, and some of those concerned us directly.

Social Status and Role: Aliens and Manifest Destiny

I have referred to our social status as an ethnic minority group in the country as being that of "aliens"—that is to say, "outsiders" or "strangers," seen as such not only by the dominant group and culture but also by ourselves. In other words, many of us not only feel but are made to feel that we do not quite belong in the "promised land," not in the way some others do anyhow (not all others, to be sure, for we are not quite unique in this regard, either from a historical or a contemporary point of view). I have also referred to our social role in the country in terms of a "manifest destiny"—that is to say, a call not to remain intimidated or silent in our status as "aliens" in the "promised land" but to embrace such status as our own and to raise our voice, as we have already begun to do, in light of our own reality and experience. In other words, just as the members of the dominant group and culture defined their mission for a long time in terms of a "manifest destiny," so we should define our own role and mission as a "manifest destiny"—but with a twist.[29]

I turn first to the question of our social status as "aliens." Again, what many of us found upon arrival in the country was altogether surprising, given our previous visions and expectations. From a material point of view, there was no question regarding the projection of money—"the almighty dollar," as the common expression has it—as a core value of the society. At the same time, not all streets, we found, were "paved with gold," nor were the accouterments of progress and modernity, the consequences and benefits of money, openly, let alone equally, available to all citizens. From a moral point of view, there was also no question regarding the projection of the individual and individual rights—"every *man* for *him*self," as the popular expression puts it—as another core value of the society. Nevertheless, here too we made a number of unexpected discoveries: there was

question of "the promised land," if at all, is simply beyond my knowledge and competence, and yet it would be a fascinating topic to explore.

29. "Manifest destiny" may be seen as a historical label for the mission of the country as "chosen" and "kingdom of God." The literature on manifest destiny is extensive; see, for example, Frederick Merk, *Manifest Destiny and Mission in American History: A Reinterpretation* (Westport, Conn.: Greenwood Press, 1963); Reginald Horsman, *Race and Manifest Destiny: The Origins of American Racial Anglo-Saxonism* (Cambridge, Mass.: Harvard University Press, 1981).

poverty, sometimes much poverty, as well as sharp inequalities in the distribution of wealth; work, while on the whole plentiful, could be brutal,
all-demanding, and all-consuming, with wages and benefits much lower
than imagined; labor conditions often left a great deal to be desired and
at times were downright appalling and exploitative; not everyone possessed
the same freedoms, or to the same extent; criticism and dissent were not exactly revered and could have untoward consequences; corruption seemed,
given the numbers involved, rampant and overwhelming; violence and the
fear of violence were by no means strangers to the society; and loneliness,
sometimes great loneliness, proved incredibly common, whether in the enclaves of suburbia or in the very midst of the city. Indeed, it seemed that,
as core values, the pursuit of money and individualism could easily override and subdue, with their great power and allure, all other values of the
society. Of course, there could be no comparison by and large with conditions in our own home countries;[30] it was just that our visions of the
United States did not have and did not allow for a more somber side. The
resultant cultural shock was thus in many ways overpowering: the promised land, while plentiful in many respects, seemed so strangely wanting in
so many others.

Most unexpected perhaps was the existence of ethnic and racial stratification within the chosen people and the promised land. To be sure, such
stratification was by no means unknown to us in our home countries,
where the following social pyramid generally held sway: at the top, a small,
"white" elite; below, the "white" middle classes, never very extensive; next,
the "white" lower classes along with the mulatto and mestizo middle and
lower classes; and at the bottom, the "black" and "Indian" lower classes.
It was just that we did not expect to find any such system in the promised
land. We never thought of the United States in terms of Indian massacres,
displacements, or reservations; of segregation of blacks, discrimination, and
ghettoes; of nativism, anti-immigrant fervor, and anti-Asian, anti-Catholic,
anti-Slavic, and anti-Jewish crusades. This was the face of the promised
land that many of us had never seen, heard about, or thought possible.

Yet there it was and with a passion, and, within such a system of ethnic
and racial stratification and its concurrent forms of prejudice and discrimination, we did not fare all too well. And for obvious reasons. Unlike most
of the waves of immigrants who had preceded us into the country, we
were not from the European continent, not even from its more questionable
southern, Mediterranean regions or eastern, Slavic lands. Our basic frame
of reference was not Western but Latin American, and, if we looked to Europe at all, we did so primarily through Spain—a Spain, however, that has

30. For a sharp comparison of the United States as a mass society and Latin America as a
traditional society, with a focus on Mexico, see Jorge G. Castañeda, "Ferocious Differences,"
Atlantic Monthly 276:1 (July 1995) 68.

never really formed part, with the single exception *perhaps* of Miguel de Cervantes Saavedra and his *El ingenioso hidalgo Don Quijote de la Mancha,* of the image of the West and Western civilization operative in the West. Most of us, moreover, were not exactly "white," for even the "whites" among us had any number of variations or shades of that particular skin color that pointed unmistakably to racial mixture of some sort or another in the background. Most of us, to boot, were Catholics of "Hispanic" descent, not only the children of quintessential Counter-Reformation magic and superstition but also hopelessly implicated in syncretistic practices and beliefs involving, of all things, the native religions of Africa and Amerindia. We were, in sum, the children of the South—the colonized world, the "underdeveloped" world, the Third World. And we carried with us that particular cultural "skin color"—that certain look and that certain demeanor unmistakably pointing as well to cultural mixture of many sorts in our past—so well captured by the Puerto Rican expression *la mancha de plátano* (with reference to the stain of the green plantain, almost impossible to remove). We were indeed aliens—foreigners and strangers—in the promised land. Again, the cultural shock involved was tremendous: the "promised land" was a land of promise for some but not for all.

To be sure, there had been strong indications and premonitions of such a view of us on the part of the dominant group and culture of the United States; again, many of us had always been aghast at the ways in which the United States had historically treated its own neighbors, our home countries, in the hemisphere. This had always remained a sore spot, a soft underside, in the overall visions and expectations of the country as a promised land. Then, as we settled into the country, we began to learn more and more of the ways in which our home countries had been used, time and again, by our new country with its own economic, military, and geopolitical interests in mind. In fact, it became increasingly clear that such policies had been and continued to be in large part responsible for present conditions, whether economic or political, in our home countries. Again, it seemed that, as core values, the pursuit of money and individualism could easily overwhelm and subdue all other values not only at the national level but also at the international level.

More recently still, with the demise of the Soviet Empire and the end of the Cold War, new revelations have begun to trickle out regarding the shameful if not sinful role played by the United States in Latin America during the days of the ideological war between East and West: a role that involved all levels of government, from national agencies in Washington to local embassies in the field; that brought the country to associate closely with and directly back the most repressive and repugnant sectors of our former societies; that implicated the country in repeated and widespread acts of brutality and terrorism, both at the personal and the social level; and that violated so many of the principles and ideals on and for which the country claims to stand.[31] As these revelations continue, and continue they shall, and the trickle turns into a torrent, what will emerge in the end is a national disgrace of unbelievable and unthinkable proportions, a sacrifice of much that the country holds dear and a sacrifice directly involving our own home countries. As a result of such knowledge and revelations, the cultural shock becomes even more profound: the promised land, whose self-appointed mission was to civilize and enlighten all others, can and does act in the most unpromising and barbaric ways.

Such, then, proved to be our cumulative experience as we gradually settled into the country: we witnessed its more somber side; we encountered its apparatus of ethnic and racial stratification; and we became keenly aware of its geopolitical wheelings and dealings. The reaction was as predictable as it was inevitable. On the one hand, sheer unbelief and corresponding erosion—a promised land that was no more. On the other hand, a struggle for survival as aliens. On one side, a world of broken visions and expectations; on the other, a world of determined struggle and survival. Yet, within the latter, a world of enduring hopes and dreams as well. After all, for many of us there was far more work and opportunity, far more peace and tranquility, far more freedom and stability in the United States than we could ever hope for in our respective home countries. Out of this complex world of ours, where disappointment and disillusion walked hand in hand with a thirst for justice and well-being, sooner or later silence was bound to break into voice, especially given our growing numbers. We then began to tell and write our stories—including our stories of the otherworld, of this-world, and of the relationship between such worlds—in our own voices. With time, this flux of many voices began to turn into a boom, the ongoing and expanding boom we are presently witnessing. In effect, the aliens were becoming "strangers no longer."

---

31. Not unexpectedly, the revelations have begun with Central America. See, for example, Sam Dillon and Tim Weiner, "In Guatemala's Dark Heart: C.I.A. Tied to Death and Aid," *New York Times,* 2 April 1995, nat. ed., A1; Eric Schmitt, "School for Assassins, or Aid to Latin Democracy?" *The New York Times,* 3 April 1995, nat. ed., A5; and Clifford Krauss, "Guatemala's War: Ideology is the Latest Excuse," *New York Times,* 9 April 1995, nat. ed., E7. It is enlightening to note in this regard the reaction to these revelations by the well-known conservative columnist of the *New York Times* and self-proclaimed civil libertarian William Safire ("Bashing the Spooks," *New York Times,* 6 April 1995, nat. ed., A15). First, Safire points out, the revelations have their roots in two generations of "liberals" frustrated by the U.S. support of anticommunist regimes in Central and South America, with a C.I.A. committed to stopping the spread of Cuban communism in "our" neighborhood. Then, Safire goes on, because of such policies, the United States was able to win—"often messily, sometimes undemocratically, on occasion scandalously"—the Cold War, defeating Soviet-Cuban hegemony in the hemisphere and preventing a much worse situation for democracy and human rights. While good ends do not justify evil means, Safire concludes, when thousands of lives are at stake, dirty tricks gain "some moral coloration." In other words, this distinguished libertarian seems to argue that, for the sake of democracy and human rights, it is necessary sometimes to subvert human rights and democracy! As the victims of such subversion, many of us would passionately disagree.

Within the discourse of imperialism and colonialism, such mutual reactions of center and margins toward one another within the locus of the center itself are rather typical. From the point of view of the margins, travelers to the center of whatever sort find it difficult to believe—despite the obvious signs of civilization and progress that abound—that certain conditions not only exist but are allowed to exist. From this point of view, the cultural shock in question is more of a structural shock, along the lines of the emperor-has-no-clothes reaction. The system of binomials at work in the traditional center-schema margins is stark and so rigid that, in the light of disconfirmation, the entire construction cannot but give way to a process of erosion, involving not only deconstruction and demythologization but also conscientization and self-determination. From the point of view of the center, the presence of the colonial subjects or neocolonial subalterns—the children of the South—in its very midst, especially if of the long-lasting or permanent variety, is always regarded as an imposition, given the operative view of all such people as fundamentally inferior, that is, as backward, ignorant, and primitive. For the center, it is one thing to take the mission of progress and civilization to other lands and countries, far from home, and quite another to have the new converts in one's own land and country, especially in growing numbers. The result is an immediate consignment of all such travelers, much to the surprise and consternation of the latter, to the lower rungs within the system of ethnic and racial stratification as well as outrage regarding any criticism whatever of the system.

For the margins several aspects of this structural encounter prove particularly shocking. One is to find that the freedom traditionally thought to reside in the center is deeply compromised by this concomitant system of ethnic and racial stratification—to find that one's language and tradition, one's reality and experience, are looked down upon as inferior. Another is to find that the knowledge traditionally associated with the center is deeply compromised by its sheer lack of knowledge, its ignorance as well as its insouciance, with regard to the margins—to find that one knows (and has been required to know) far more about the center than the center ever knows or cares to know about the margins. Yet another is to find that the tolerance traditionally thought to prevail in the center is deeply compromised by the center's sharp dislike of any sort of criticism—to find that those who never failed to criticize others at will, even in their own lands and countries, proved curiously resentful when such criticism is directed at them in their own land and country. A final one is to find that the justice traditionally associated with the center is deeply compromised by the policies undertaken by the center with its own and exclusive self-interest in mind—to find that the universal principles of justice and well-being, freedom and dignity, so often preached by the center unto all are often applied by the center in a highly selective and self-serving fashion.

I turn now to the question of our social role as a "manifest destiny." A word of clarification is immediately in order. It is certainly not my intention to claim that we have ceased to be seen as "aliens" or that we have stopped seeing ourselves as "aliens" in the country. That, I am afraid, is quite unlikely to happen in the foreseeable future, especially in light of our present political context at the turn of the century, when nativism, riding triumphantly on the crest of a new fundamentalist wave, just as it did at the turn of the nineteenth century and well into the twentieth, has made a powerful and boisterous comeback. Aliens we are, and aliens we shall remain. What I do mean to say is that we have ceased to behave as aliens, keeping our place and struggling for survival in silence; instead, we have embraced our place as aliens, found our voice as aliens, and lifted that voice up as aliens. It is this particular development that I refer to as our manifest destiny: a call to speak out of our place and status as aliens on behalf of liberation, not only our own but that of all others. As such, as I intimated before, it is a manifest destiny *with a twist*—not the manifest destiny of colonialism and imperialism, of a promised land and a chosen people in reverse, but a manifest destiny of justice and well-being, freedom and dignity, for all.

For us, given our reality and experience in our home countries and in our new country, there can be no illusions of a promised land and a chosen people. Not here, not where we came from, not anywhere. Not now, not ever. Yet for us there are persistent hopes and dreams—for ourselves, for our new country, for our home countries, and for the world as a whole—that the world can and must be made a better place to live; that the principles of justice and well-being, freedom and dignity, can and must function as core values; that such principles can and must be extended to all human beings regardless of race or ethnicity. With such dreams and hopes, I would add, our devotion and commitment as U.S. Hispanic Americans to the highest ideals of our new country and the deepest yearnings of our home countries are firmly established and beyond reproach. That, I believe, is the fundamental challenge of U.S. Hispanic American theology—the challenge of aliens who wish to be strangers no longer.

From the point of view of the discourse of colonialism and imperialism, such a subsequent reaction on the part of the margins vis-à-vis the center is rather typical as well. Once the process of erosion has been triggered into motion and the binomials of the system yield to the inevitable practices of deconstruction and demythologizing, the margins no longer look to the center as the supreme ideal, in the face of which their own natural tendencies and traditional expressions are to be left behind, but rather begin to look to themselves and do so, in part, with the very tools and ideals of the center: recovering their own places; embracing such places as their own; giving expression to such places in their own voices; analyzing what the center has done not *for* them but *to* them; and positing a different future altogether for both center and margins. In so doing, the margins embark on a process of fundamental decentering, of decolonization and liberation. The center, on the other hand—short of repression and violence, to which it can and does resort, but which in themselves represent a profound violation of its own ideals and principles—finds itself totally nonplussed and unable to stop any such movement, although it will try in one way or another, whether by tightening the controls on any further entrance of the margins into the center, blaming the margins for the largely self-inflicted problems of the center, or reinforcing the system of ethnic and racial stratification in force. Such measures, in the end, only serve to increase the resolve of the margins to speak forth, appealing once again to the very principles and ideals of the center and hence making for a quite uncomfortable and deeply embarrassing situation. After all, who can stand in the end in the way of a program based on justice and well-being for all?

Nomenclature: U.S. Hispanic American Theology

The adjective that I have used throughout to name our theological voice, "U.S. Hispanic American," represents for me a slight but important change of mind and usage, the result of careful reflection and considered argumentation. I should like to explain the rationale for this change in terms of the ongoing and rather complex discussion regarding appropriate nomenclature for the ethnic group as a whole.

To begin with, a close reading of the theological production of U.S. Hispanic Americans would indicate—as is the case in the present volume—the use of three different and recurring appellations for the group as a whole: (1) "Hispanic Americans" (adjective: "Hispanic American"), which I believe to be the most common; (2) "Latinos/as" (adjective: "Latino/a"), not as common but quite common nonetheless; and (3) "Hispanics" (adjective: "Hispanic"), the least common in my opinion and a term usually though not exclusively employed in conjunction with and as an abbreviation for "Hispanic Americans." Such variations in nomenclature permeate our literature, theological and otherwise. Such variations have also been for some time now the subject of considerable and sometimes rather sharp debate within the group.[32]

This state of affairs should not be at all surprising. The question of labeling or nomenclature—what we call ourselves, what others call us, what we

---

32. For a helpful analysis of the discussion from the perspective of the social and behavioral sciences, see Gerardo Marín and Barbara VanOss Marín, *Research with Hispanic Populations* (Applied Social Research Methods Series 23; Newbury Park, Calif.: Sage Publications, 1991) 18–23. It should be noted that the authors specifically point to the question of labeling as the first concern of the researcher in describing the participants or searching for data in archival research (18). What is true of social and behavioral research is certainly true as well, in my opinion, of religious and theological research. In other words, as theologians or religious scholars, we need to be as clear as possible about exactly whom we claim to analyze and represent.

would like to call ourselves and have others call us—constitutes, as with any other ethnic or racial group, a most important and highly sensitive question.[33] After all, names or labels are neither self-evident nor unchanging concepts, grounded as it were in the natural order of things, but social constructions with historical and ideological connotations.[34] In our particular case, a number of factors or subtexts play a significant though subtle role in the discussion.

It should be clear from my choice of label that I subscribe to none of the three options listed above. In what follows, therefore, I should like to explain such a decision on my part by bringing to the surface the various underlying subtexts and factors at work in the discussion.

1. A first factor has to do with the official name of the country where we presently make our permanent abode, "the United States of America." Although its inhabitants occasionally refer to the country as "the United States" and to themselves as "U.S. citizens," the preferred designations by far are "America" and "Americans," respectively. Now, in and of itself, such usage, with its recourse to the last component of the official name, is quite understandable and indeed not without parallel in the rest of the Americas. A word of explanation is in order. While the great majority of the other countries in the Americas either have a single official name or include the term "republic" within the official name,[35] a number of exceptions can be readily found.[36] Of these, two should be noted in particular,

33. This is so whether the group in question happens to be a majority or minority group. In my own experience, for example, I have found that U.S. citizens of European birth or origin oftentimes express vigorous opposition to any classification as "European Americans" or its abbreviation, "Euro-Americans," on such grounds as the following: (*a*) a self-conception as "Americans" and not as "hyphenated Americans"; and (*b*) the argument that European Americans are quite distinct from one another, ranging from the dominant Anglo-American group to such later immigrant groups as the Irish Americans or the Greek Americans, who experienced pervasive and sustained discrimination in their own time at the hands of the dominant group. While the first argument reflects a strong sense of "New World" assimilationism and nationalism (the we-are-all-the-same position), the second points to the enduring realities and consequences of "Old World" nationalisms in the "New World." In the end, I believe, the term is as valid and as applicable as a number of other similar ethnic umbrella terms—such as, for example, African Americans, Arab Americans, Asian Americans—labels that are frequently used by European Americans themselves without similar preoccupations or scruples regarding common identity as "Americans" or diversity within the group in question.

34. Marín and VanOss Marín (*Research*, 19) argue that the labels human groups assign to themselves are much more meaningful than the names given to other objects and go on to point out the findings of psychological research to the effect that different group labels produce differential attitudinal responses among those who use them.

35. Examples of the use of the single name: Antigua and Barbuda; Barbados; Belize; Canada; Jamaica; Saint Vincent and the Grenadines; Santa Lucia. Examples of the use of "Republic": (*a*) all the countries of Spanish-speaking Latin America, whether by way of adjective, as in the Dominican Republic (República Dominicana) or the Argentine Republic (República Argentina), or substantive (with Uruguay as the "Eastern Republic of Uruguay" [República Oriental del Uruguay]); (*b*) the Republic of Haiti (République d'Haïti); (*c*) the Republic of Suriname (Republiek Suriname); and (*d*) the Republic of Trinidad and Tobago.

36. A variety of other sociopolitical categories may be found as part of the official name:

given the similarities to the case of the United States: on the one hand, Mexico, whose official name is Estados Unidos Mexicanos, or the "United States of Mexico"—an explicit reference to the union of thirty-one states and a federal district; on the other hand, Brazil, with the official name of República Federativa do Brasil, or the "Federal Republic of Brazil"—an implicit reference to the union of twenty-six states and a federal district. In both cases, the citizens of these countries also refer to their country by the last component of the name, whether "Mexico" or "Brazil," and to themselves as "Mexicans" or "Brazilians."

In the case of the United States, however, the problem lies in the fact that the latter part of its official name, "America," is also the name used for the "New World" as a whole—what is often referred to as "the Americas," comprising two continents (North and South America); an isthmus (Central America); and an archipelago (the Caribbean). Thus, when citizens of the United States refer to themselves as "Americans" and to their country as "America," as they regularly do, they are in effect appropriating for themselves, via the common rhetorical figure of synecdoche, a much broader semantic designation and excluding as a result, quite unconsciously for the most part, from such a label all other inhabitants of the Western Hemisphere.[37] In fact, within the United States as such, the terms "America" and "Americans" are rarely if ever used with reference to the countries and inhabitants of the Americas as a whole, unless an individual is trying to make a specific point in this regard.[38] Not only is there little if any con-

---

(*a*) "commonwealth," as in the Commonwealth of the Bahamas and the Commonwealth of Dominica; (*b*) "state," as in the State of Grenada; (*c*) the Cooperative Republic of Guyana; and (*d*) "federation," as in the Federation of Saint Christopher and Nevis.

37. The issue comes up in a recent editorial in the conservative Spanish daily, *ABC*, reproduced in its weekly international edition ("Pesca ilegal en la lengua española," *ABC*, 28 June/4 July 1995, int. ed., 3), where Jesús López Pacheco returns, within the context of the recent dispute between Canada and Spain regarding fishing rights in the North Atlantic, to a line of argumentation presented years earlier in the same daily ("El imperialismo lingüístico de 'América' y el país sin nombre," *ABC*, 27 July 1985). López Pacheco, in effect, accuses the United States of linguistic piracy with respect to the name "America" on the grounds that, as a country, it lacks a true name, given the fact that, on the one hand, "America" refers to the hemisphere and, on the other, "United States" represents nothing but a descriptive and provisional phrase for the colonies that had rebelled against England. Eventually, he continues, this temporary formula became a proper name, although, even as late as the nineteenth century, there were various proposals to change it (for example, "Columbia" and "Freedonia"). Indeed, he points out, there were other attempts, but without success, to develop a label derived from "United States," with such examples as the following: "United Statesian"; "Ustatsian"; and "Usian." It is clear, therefore, that the problem we face as U.S. Hispanic Americans is a long-standing one, though now largely ignored in the country.

38. See, for example, Peter Winn, *Americas: The Changing Face of Latin America and the Caribbean* (New York: Pantheon Books, 1992), the companion volume to a 1992 PBS series entitled *Americas: Latin America and the Caribbean*. Winn, professor of Latin American history at Tufts University, begins by observing that many "North Americans"—in itself an incorrect usage, given the fact that "North America" also includes Canada as well as Mexico—forget that they share "America" with thirty-three other sovereign nations and

sciousness regarding the broader reach of these terms, but also such usage, I suspect, would not be at all kindly looked upon by many people; indeed, not a few would regard such a practice as distinctly "un-American."

To be sure, the more restrictive usage of these terms is not confined to the United States alone but is quite common as well in the rest of the Americas, especially with regard to the term for the inhabitants themselves, "Americans" or *americanos*.[39] This is not to say that *americanos* is never employed with reference to the inhabitants of the "New World" as a whole but rather that this term tends to be used as a designation for U.S. citizens in particular.[40] Indeed, I well remember as a child growing up in my native Cuba the widespread use of the term *los americanos* to refer to citizens of the United States. Such usage remains standard to this day.

At the same time, a number of other labels are also available, all of which may ultimately be seen as attempts to narrow the focus from the hemisphere to the country as such. Some of these are politically neutral, such as *norteamericanos,* or "North Americans" (Norteamérica/North America), and *estadounidenses,* or "U.S. citizens" (los Estados Unidos/the United States), with the latter much more common as an adjective than as a substantive. Others are politically ambiguous and may actually convey highly negative connotations, as in the case of *yanquis* or *gringos*. In the end, in my opinion, *estadounidenses* (U.S. citizens) proves most proper and accurate: it is a distinctive term, insofar as it is never employed by Mexicans; it is derived from the official name for the country; and it avoids the problematic identification between country and hemisphere.[41]

---

nearly half a billion people. He further points out, in a highly ironic vein, how the name "America" first appeared on sixteenth-century maps with respect to *South* America, whose northeast coast had been explored by Amerigo Vespucci, and how it was only with the founding of the United States of America as a nation that the term began to be used for the northern part of the "Western" Hemisphere as well. Interestingly enough, dictionaries of the English language invariably list the broader meaning of "America" and "American" prior to the more restricted meaning with reference to the United States and U.S. citizens in particular; see, for example, *Webster's Ninth New Collegiate Dictionary* (Springfield, Mass.: Merriam-Webster, 1987) and *The American Heritage Dictionary of the English Language* (Boston: American Heritage Publishing Co., and Houghton Mifflin, 1975).

39. In point of fact, no one would ever refer to the United States as América, whether from a personal or a national point of view. For example, no one would ever speak of a trip to América, when contemplating travel to the United States, or refer to the United States in terms of América in the context of international politics. Likewise, no U.S. Hispanic American immigrant would ever speak of his or her journey to the United States in terms of coming to América, not even the most assimilated within the group.

40. See, for example, María Moliner, *Diccionario de uso del Español* (2 vols.; Madrid: Editorial Gredos, 1975), where the first meaning of *americano/a* listed is that of a person from the New World or the Americas, with the self-designation adopted by the citizens of the United States given only as a fourth meaning. In my experience, however, this latter usage is far more common than the former in the everyday parlance of the people.

41. While certainly less restrictive, the terms "North Americans" and "North America" prove just as problematic, insofar as the latter consists of three sovereign nations (see n. 38 above)—and indeed more, if one takes into account, as well one should, the various "Native American" nations. Such usage would not be distinctive, encompassing as it does both the

From this point of view, the label "Hispanic Americans" and its corresponding adjective, "Hispanic American," prove unsatisfactory: all Hispanic Americans, whether born in the country or not, are Americans in the sense of being from the New World or the Americas.[42] That is to say, we were already Americans (*americanos*) and lived in America (América) before we or our ancestors ever became part of the United States. Furthermore, there is no label other than "Americans" that can serve as a proper designation for all the inhabitants of the Americas, from the northernmost reaches of Canada and the United States to the southernmost territories of Chile and Argentina. As such, this most common of labels is not sufficiently precise for our identity; in our case the synecdoche simply collapses.[43]

2. A second factor concerns the various collective names in use throughout the Americas in addition to those of "America" and "Americans." Several such terms come readily to mind.

Some have a decidedly ethnic or cultural/linguistic orientation: (*a*) "Latin America" and "Latin Americans" (Latinoamérica and *latinoamericanos*), applied to the countries, individuals, and characteristics of those whose language is ultimately derived from Latin, the language of ancient Rome; (*b*) "Iberian America" and "Iberian Americans" (Iberoamérica and *iberoamericanos*), terms rarely used in English, with reference to countries and individuals associated with the two nations that make up the Iberian Peninsula, Portugal and Spain; (*c*) "Hispanic America" and "Hispanic Americans" (Hispanoamérica and *hispanoamericanos*), denoting countries and individuals associated with Spain. Others have a clearly geographical basis: (*a*) "South America" and "South Americans" (Suramérica and *suramericanos*), referring to the countries and inhabitants of the southern

---

citizens of Canada and the citizens of Mexico; would not be derived from the official name of the country; and would amount to an identification of the country with a continent, with a resulting exclusion of all the other inhabitants of North America from the label. I should point out that this is precisely the issue behind the editorial mentioned in n. 37 above: López Pacheco is responding to a letter from a Canadian scholar, John Stone of the University of Barcelona, to a Toronto daily ("How to Be Invisible in Spanish," *The Globe and Mail*, 25 April 1995), in which the latter argues that Canada is not seen as part of "North America" in Spanish and thus remains "invisible." The problem, López Pacheco counters, is not with the Spanish or the Catalan language, but once again with the linguistic piracy of the United States. López Pacheco concludes by pointing out that Professor Stone himself has apparently forgotten that Mexico is also part of "North America"—not just Canada and the United States.

42. This is a meaning well captured by the official name for the political organization bringing together all the nations of the Americas (but Cuba): the Organization of American States (OAS)—Organización de Estados Americanos (OEA)—based in Washington, D.C.

43. As I have stated above, this is the designation for the ethnic group as a whole that I have employed in my writings up to this point. I found it to be not only more properly restrictive than "Latinos/as," given its specific reference to individuals of "Hispanic" origin or descent, but also very much in keeping with standard English usage regarding similar ethnic umbrella terms, like "African Americans" or "Euro-Americans," where ethnic designation precedes sociopolitical status. See n. 33 above.

continent of the Americas; (*b*) "Central America" and "Central Americans" (Centroamérica and *centroamericanos*), encompassing the countries and inhabitants of the isthmus connecting the two continents; and (*c*) "the Caribbean" and "Caribbeans" (el Caribe and *caribeños*), with reference to countries and individuals from the Caribbean archipelago, regardless of ethnic origin or language spoken.

To the best of my knowledge, there is no label that brings together as a whole the world of the non-Spanish-speaking Americas, or, for that matter, its anglophone or francophone worlds by themselves, that is to say, nations and individuals that trace their origin to Great Britain and France, respectively.

From this point of view, the terms "Hispanic Americans" and "Hispanic American" prove, once again, unsatisfactory: the label as commonly used in the United States to refer to an ethnic minority group is also used in the Spanish-speaking Americas to designate the dominant ethnic group and culture. In other words, we were not only Americans (*americanos*) but also Hispanic Americans (*hispanoamericanos*) before we or our ancestors ever became part of the United States. From yet another perspective, therefore, this most common of labels is likewise not precise enough for our identity.

3. A third factor has to do with the presence in the United States of individuals who trace their birth or origin directly to Spain, to the European mainland, rather than to Latin America, to the former territories and colonies of Spain in the New World. Given the accepted use of the term "Hispanic" (*hispano/a*) to refer to individuals associated with Spain, in keeping with the Latin name for the Iberian Peninsula as a whole (Hispania), such individuals can be appropriately classified as Hispanics and ultimately, of course, by extension as Hispanic Americans.[44] In point of fact, it should be mentioned in this regard that in 1978 the Office of Management and Budget officially adopted the label "Hispanics" to refer to all persons "of Mexican, Puerto Rican, Cuban, Central or South American or other Spanish culture or origin, regardless of race."[45]

Needless to say, however, there is a world of difference, cultural and otherwise, between such individuals and those with ties to the Spanish-

44. From the point of view of English, see, for example, *The American Heritage Dictionary of the English Language,* ad loc.: (*a*) "Of or pertaining to Spain, its language, people, and culture"; (*b*) "Having cultural origins in Iberia." From the point of view of Spanish, see Moliner, *Diccionario,* s.v.: *"español."* Yet cf. *Webster's Ninth New Collegiate Dictionary,* ad loc.: "of or relating to the people, speech, or culture of Spain, Spain and Portugal, or Latin America."

45. See Marín and VanOss Marín, *Research,* 20–21. This is the label adopted by these authors on the grounds that there is no better label at this point than the OMB definition (23), which they accordingly define as follows: "We have chosen to use the label 'Hispanic' in this book to refer to those residents of the United States who trace their family background to one of the Spanish-speaking Latin American nations or to Spain" (18).

speaking Americas. Indeed, no U.S. Hispanic American would ever refer to such individuals as *hispanos* or "Hispanic" but rather would use the terms *españoles* or "Spaniards."[46] In fact, such individuals should really be classified, first and foremost, under the label "European Americans," and, secondarily, as a subgroup thereof, as "Spanish Americans."

From this point of view, the terms "Hispanics" and "Hispanic" are also unsatisfactory: these are official terms introduced by an agency of the U.S. government with the goal of bringing under one category all individuals of "Hispanic" descent, whether connected directly with Spain or indirectly by way of Latin America. Moreover, their rather common use in conjunction with and as an abbreviation for "Hispanic Americans" and "Hispanic American" already represents a restrictive use of these labels, by means of which individuals of Hispanic American origin or descent are separated from individuals of Spanish origin or descent in the United States. Consequently, this particular label also fails to be sufficiently precise for our identity.

4. A fourth factor involves the enormous diversity to be found within the ethnic group itself and the ramifications of such diversity. On the one hand, there is no self-designation for the group as a whole that emerges either naturally or historically from the group as a whole, although certain segments within the group have argued strongly on behalf of "Latinos/as" (adjective: "Latino/a") as a comprehensive and proper label. On the other hand, the group has traditionally tended to express itself in largely nationalistic terms, whereby members of the group, whether actual immigrants into the country or born in the country, think of themselves primarily in terms of their countries of origin or descent, as Cubans or Cuban Americans, Puerto Ricans, Mexicans or Mexican Americans, and so on.

From this point of view, then, there is simply no one term that all of us can truly call our own, no term that we have chosen for ourselves, and no term that we have willingly embraced—not "Hispanic Americans"; not "Hispanics"; not "Latinos/as." The first two have been bestowed upon us by the dominant group. On the one hand, "Hispanic Americans" follows, once again, common linguistic usage. Indeed, this term forms part of a linguistic tradition for labeling that we ourselves follow whenever we use, as we very often do, the term "European Americans" or proceed to use the expression "Anglos" as a synonymous abbreviation, with specific reference to the language spoken, the language of the Anglo-Americans. On the other hand, "Hispanics" represents the result of a bureaucratic decision. The third term, "Latinos/as," does arise from the group as such but not

---

46. Indeed, no Spaniard would ever refer to himself or herself as an *hispano* or *hispana*, nor would any individual from the Spanish-speaking nations of America ever refer to a "Spaniard" in terms of *hispano* or *hispana*. Yet the adjective is widely used to refer to things of "Spanish" origin or descent; the noun, however, is used by and large as an abbreviation of *hispanoamericanos* and thus pointing to the Americas.

from the group as a whole, nor is it warmly received and appropriated by all members of the group, in large part, I believe, because it sounds rather foreign, even artificial, to the ears of many.

5. A fifth and final factor has to do with the term "Latinos/as," the one label that is, despite its varied reception, autochthonous. Its proponents have argued for it on various grounds: (*a*) it reflects more accurately the political, geographical, and historical links present among the various Latin American nations; (*b*) it preserves the national origins of the group as a significant characteristic; (*c*) it is culturally and racially neutral; and (*d*) it is the least objectionable of all possible ethnic labels.[47] A sharp version of this position was once offered in my presence by a "Latino" social scientist who insisted on the sociopolitical connotations of the label. I would paraphrase it as follows: while "Hispanic Americans" privileges the European dimension of the group, because of the modifying Eurocentric adjective, "Latinos/as" does not, insofar as it substantivizes the adjective "Latin" found in Latin America, which in turn stands for all the different races represented in the Southern Hemisphere.[48] The term, however, is neither without difficulties of its own nor as restrictive as claimed.

To begin with, both "Hispanics" and "Latinos/as" are labels ultimately derived from the Latin language and thus *equally* highlight the European component of the group. Both refer, in effect, to areas or territories of the Roman Empire: Hispania, for example, was an ancient name given to the Iberian Peninsula and adopted by the Romans upon their conquest of large portions of the land at the very end of the third century B.C.E.; similarly, Latium was an ancient name for the central region of the Italian Peninsula surrounding the city of Rome, a name also ultimately adopted by the Romans. Thus, from an etymological point of view, the label "Latinos/as" is by no means culturally or racially neutral, or, to put it another way, it is

---

47. I have adopted this summary of the argumentation from Marín and VanOss Marín, *Research*, 21–23. Among its proponents, see D. E. Hayes Bautista and J. Chapa, "Latino Terminology: Conceptual Bases for Standardized Terminology," *American Journal of Public Health* 77 (1987) 61–68; E. J. Pérez-Stable, "Issues in Latino Health Care," *Western Journal of Medicine* 146 (1987) 213–18.

48. For a similar version of this argument from the point of view of literary criticism, see Alberto Sandoval Sánchez, "La puesta en escena de la familia inmigrante puertorriqueña," *Revista Iberoamericana* 59:162–63 (January–June, 1993) 345–59, esp. 358 n. 31. In this study on the portrayal of the Puerto Rican immigrant family in drama, the author specifies that he uses the term "Latino" to refer to all the races of Latin America in the United States and the term "Hispanic" to refer to Spain in particular, since the latter is a Eurocentric term that excludes the Indian and African populations as well as the marginalized cultures of Latin America. The author adds two other arguments. First, while "Latino" is used by immigrants from the proletarian class, "Hispanic" is preferred by those who have received a university education as well as those from the elite classes who identify a priori with Euro-Spanish culture. Second, "Latino," unlike "Hispanic," is a Spanish word and thus forces the dominant group to pronounce a word in Spanish.

no more and no less Eurocentric than the label "Hispanic."[49] Both point directly and unmistakably to Europe.

Next, the term "Latin" or "Latino/a" commonly refers—as in the case of "Latin America" or "Latinoamérica," for example, where it comprehends French-, Portuguese-, and Spanish-speaking countries of the Americas, but not the English-speaking nations and peoples of either Central America (Belize) or the Caribbean—to countries and peoples using Romance languages, that is, the linguistic descendants of vulgar or spoken Latin, which include not only the three languages named above but also such others as Catalan, Italian, Rhaeto-Romanic, Provençal, Rumanian, and Sardinian. As such, it preserves the historical, geographical, and political links among some nations of the Americas but not all, and it does not preserve the national origin of the ethnic group as a significant characteristic, insofar as it includes a variety of such origins, both inside and outside "Latin" America. In this regard, the term "Hispanic" or *hispano/a* proves much more restrictive, insofar as it refers to the Spanish-speaking peoples and countries of "Latin" America, thereby differentiating them from other countries and peoples of "Latin" origin, with both "Franco" and "Luso" as linguistic counterparts in this regard.

Finally, given the fact that it is a Spanish word and thus always gendered, the substantive "Latinos/as" and its corresponding adjective, "Latino/a," would always be in need of an additional signifier, such as a slash, the usual preference, or parentheses ("Latinos[as]" or "Latino[a]"), in order for it to be rendered properly inclusive—a rather cumbersome practice, to say the least. There exists, of course, a common English usage in matters ethnic or political involving a neuter adjectival form ending in the vowel *o* (as in, for example, Anglo-American or Italo-American); however, this particular form is not at all applicable in this case, since it is used only as an adjective, never as a substantive, and then always followed by a hyphen. Consequently, an inclusive use of the label, whether in the singular or in the plural, would always be in order, no matter how cumbersome. It is amazing to me how many of those who argue for the racial inclusivity of "Latinos" end up using the label only in its masculine form and thus engage—quite unconsciously—in a different and systematic practice of exclusion altogether.

From this point of view, the quite common terms "Latinos/as" and "Latino/a" prove unsatisfactory as well. Despite explicit claims to the contrary, these terms point directly to the European component of the group,

---

49. See also F. M. Treviño ("Standardized Terminology for Hispanic Populations," *American Journal of Public Health* 77 [1987] 69–72). Thus, to claim that "Latinos/as" refers to all the races of "Latin" America and not just the Spanish or European is to bestow a new and rather different semantic definition on the term. In itself, to be sure, this is not an objectionable move, since ethnic labels are again not grounded in "nature"; however, it is a problematic move, given the long-standing meaning and application of this term.

what one might call its Euro-Latin dimension; in so doing, moreover, they posit a much wider semantic reference regarding national origins as well. The label is thus not precise enough for our identity.

•

In sum, no term currently in use to designate the ethnic group is ultimately satisfactory. More specifically, there is no label that I find sufficiently restrictive to designate the ethnic group as such. To recapitulate: first, "Hispanic Americans" (*hispanoamericanos*) ultimately fails to differentiate between those who live in the United States and those who reside elsewhere in the Americas. Second, "Latinos/as" does not distinguish between those who trace their birth or origin to Spain and those who do so to other Latin countries of Europe, such as Portugal and France. Finally, "Hispanics" (*hispanos*) fails to differentiate between those in the country with direct roots in Spain and those with direct roots in the Americas. A decision on behalf of any of these terms is thus inherently problematic. With the present study, therefore, I have opted for a new label: "U.S. Hispanic Americans" (adjective: "U.S. Hispanic American"). While the change in question may seem minor, consisting of the placement of the initials "U.S." before the appellation "Hispanic Americans," I consider the end result to be more precise with regard to our identity and hence more satisfactory.[50] My reasons are as follows.

First, the abbreviation itself points to our present and permanent residence in the United States. It does so, moreover, without raising the problem of synecdoche in the identification of country and hemisphere. Fuller versions of the label would be either "Hispanic Americans in the United States" or "U.S. citizens of Hispanic American birth or origin."[51]

Second, the modified substantive points to the national origins of the group, whether immediate (by birth) or remote (by origin), in Latin America and, more specifically, in Hispanic America. In so doing, following common usage in Hispanic America as well (*hispanoamericanos*), it effectively separates those with ties to the Spanish-speaking Americas and those with ties to Spain and Europe, the Spanish Americans as a subset of European Americans. The label further distinguishes the group, given

---

50. It is a label that covers, in effect, all that I have wanted to convey by my definition of "Hispanic Americans" in the past but that does so in a more explicit and appropriate fashion; see n. 5 above.

51. Cf. the interesting use of the combination of the initials "U.S." and the adjective "Latino" in the title of a recent volume by Marc Zimmerman (*U.S. Latino Literature: An Essay and Annotated Bibliography* [Chicago: March/Abrazo Press, 1992]). The addition of the initials, however, does not resolve the difficulties inherent in the label "Latino": for example, any literature produced by Haitian Americans can be properly included under such a label; similarly, any literature produced by Italian Americans can be included as well; finally, the label, which includes a word in Spanish, fails to be inclusive from the point of view of gender.

its reference to its colonial ties—cultural, historical, and otherwise—with Spain, from other "Latin" or Latino groups in the United States, including other groups from "Latin America," such as the Haitians and the Brazilians, with similar ties to France and Portugal, respectively.[52]

Third, the label preserves, even though it uses the word "American" in a different sense, as pointing to the hemisphere rather than to the country, the established pattern in American English for ethnic umbrella terms. As such, the term would encompass such subgroups as Cuban Americans, Dominican Americans, Mexican Americans, Puerto Ricans, and so on.

Finally, the label, though perhaps a bit more cumbersome, is inclusive and thus avoids the need for the far more cumbersome use of the double termination.

I should like to conclude this discussion by making it clear that I by no means consider this label to be ideal. It certainly continues to highlight the Spanish and European roots of the group over against its African, Amerindian, and Asian components. Given the options available, however, it is a term with which I find myself much more at ease. I would only add that, in highlighting the Spanish-European origins of the ethnic group, the aim is not to privilege this one dimension of our mixture but to acknowledge the fact that—by way of culture, history, and language—it has proved dominant for our reality and experience in the Americas.[53] Besides, there is no term presently in existence that can equally point to and encompass all these dimensions of our reality and experience.

As a postmodernist at heart and by conviction, I should also emphasize that, while seeking adequate terms for purposes of classification and analysis, as indeed one must, I also find such a complex and resistant *mezcolanza* rather to my liking. While one should certainly try to make clear whom one claims to analyze and represent, it should be clear as well that the ethnic group as a whole, its reality and experience, is so fluid and elusive that no label or appellation can ever wholly capture or express it. Thus, while I find "U.S. Hispanic Americans" to be a more precise term than the others, I would also readily acknowledge that it leaves much to be desired. I should further emphasize that it is not my desire to propose this label for universal use or to impose it, even if I could, on anyone. In this respect, I believe, the wishes of those who opt for one particular label or the other must be honored, even if one should disagree with the labels in question. I am not at all averse, therefore, as the present volume readily testifies, to

---

52. Indeed, one could readily argue for "U.S. Latin Americans" as an ethnic umbrella term that would cover all of these groups.

53. Yet the following observations should be kept in mind at all times: (a) there are many in "Hispanic America" who trace their origin first and foremost to the "native Americans" and whose first language is not any variation of Spanish; (b) there are other groups whose first and only language may be Spanish but who trace their origin to Africa or Asia rather than to Spain; and (c) there are many members of the group who either are fully bilingual or have turned to English as their first and perhaps only language of communication.

the continued use of the other labels. My main desire, aside from satisfying my own search for a more specific and precise label, is to contribute to a discussion that is in the end all-important but also ultimately elusive.

Concluding Comments

I should like to conclude, much as I did in my earlier overview of the movement, still very much in its nascent stages at the time, with a prediction. Now more than ever, in light of what has taken place since then and of what I see taking place at present, I believe that the future augurs well for U.S. Hispanic American theology. Our voice has not only emerged: it has gone on to develop deep foundations and to mature and flourish as well. The theological boom presently at work among us will continue, both alongside and within the general boom evident in U.S. Hispanic American studies in general. As a result, the envisioned "manifest destiny" of our voice will become an ever-greater reality as well. In so doing, we may not ever cease to be aliens, but we shall gradually cease to be strangers in the promised land. First, because for us there is no promised land—only dreams and hopes of promise. Second, because we refuse to accept our assigned role as aliens—speaking instead with a sense of manifest destiny. Third, because such speaking on our part is not for ourselves alone but for all, based on the principles and ideals of the nation—justice and well-being, freedom and dignity. Finally, because we thereby refuse to accept the notion of any system of ethnic and racial stratification, at home or abroad, in our home countries or in the rest of the world. In so doing, we remain intensely loyal to our present homeland, the United States, and intensely faithful to our traditions in the margins of Hispanic America. In so doing, we remain, as aliens, strangers no longer—and that is, once again, the fundamental challenge of our theology.

Part One

Sources of
Hispanic/Latino Theology

1

Judith Ortiz Cofer's *Silent Dancing*

The Self-Portrait of the Artist as a Young, Bicultural Girl

Elena Olazagasti-Segovia

Women's Autobiographies and Autobiographical Fiction

Over the last two decades feminist criticism has devoted itself to the reappraisal of the theoretical assumptions of male-centered criticism, to the rescue of the work of women that had been ignored, and to the re-visionism of the work of both men and women. Women's autobiographies and autobiographical fiction have been traditionally favorite objects of derision on the part of male literary critics. Writing an autobiography, making the private public, represents the ultimate display of self-knowledge, self-esteem, and self-affirmation. Domna Stanton—who has even coined a new term, "autogynography," to refer to autobiography written by a woman—assigns to it "a global and essential therapeutic purpose: to constitute the female subject.... The *graphing* of the *auto* was an act of self-assertion that denied and reversed woman's status. It represented . . . the conquest of identity through writing."[1] It is no wonder then, given the status of women in society, that female autobiography has been considered at the very least shocking, if not altogether intolerable; it is also not surprising that feminist critics have devoted their efforts to a systematic analysis of the genre. Elizabeth Winston charts the development of the genre and finds that while women autobiographers writing before 1920 wrote in an apologetic manner, trying to justify their untraditional behavior, later in this century, as stereotypes became less rigid, they affirmed their achievements without apology.[2]

On comparing several autobiographies written by both men and women, critics have found that there are certain traits that appear consistently in autobiographies written by women that set them apart from those written by

---

1. Domna C. Stanton, "Autobiography: Is the Subject Different?" *The Female Autograph* (ed. D. C. Stanton; Chicago: University of Chicago Press, 1987) 14.
2. Elizabeth Winston, "The Autobiographer and Her Readers: From Apology to Affirmation," *Women's Autobiography: Essays on Criticism* (ed. Estelle C. Jelinek; Bloomington: Indiana University Press, 1980) 93–11.

men.[3] However, these differences should not be viewed as a flaw, as they have been in the past, but rather as a direct consequence of the particular conditions of a woman's life. First, according to Estelle Jelinek, women's autobiographies share a fluid structure: "Irregularity rather than orderliness informs the self-portraits by women. The narratives of their lives are often not chronological and progressive but disconnected, fragmentary, organized into self-sustained units rather than connecting chapters."[4] Suzanne Juhasz agrees with Jelinek's characterization when she points out that "women's lives tend to be like the stories that they tell: they show less a pattern of linear development towards some clear goal than one of repetitive, cumulative, cyclical structure."[5] Second, the focus of the autobiographical narrative is different: "Women's autobiographies rarely mirror the establishment history of their times.... They concentrate instead on their personal lives—domestic details, family difficulties, close friends, and especially people who influenced them."[6] In this respect a woman's autobiography is but a manifestation of what psychologists Nancy Chodorow[7] and Carol Gilligan[8] have found in their research.

Jelinek also points out that there are two traits that both men's and women's autobiographies share, although with some differences. First, the portrayal of intimate memories:

Neither men nor women are likely to reveal painful and intimate memories, excluding specifically siblings, children, mates, and romantic attachments.... The major exception to this reticence to discuss close family members is the subject of parents. The pattern is to emphasize one, often to the exclusion of the other one. Women are less likely to focus on their mothers than men are.[9]

Second, their portrait of childhood: men view their childhood "as idylls of innocence and redemption..., [which] results in the projection of a self-image of confidence, [while] women's life stories reveal a self-consciousness and a need to sift through their lives for explanation and understanding."[10]

---

3. See, for example, Estelle C. Jelinek, "Introduction: Women's Autobiography and the Male Tradition," *Women's Autobiography,* 1–20; Suzanne Juhasz, "Towards a Theory of Form in Feminist Autobiography: Kate Millett's *Flying* and *Sita;* Maxine Hong Kingston's *The Woman Warrior,*" *Women's Autobiography,* 221–37; and Mary G. Mason, "The Other Voice: Autobiographies of Women Writers," *Life/Lines: Theorizing Women's Autobiography* (ed. Bela Brodzki and Celeste Schenck; Ithaca, N.Y.: Cornell University Press, 1988) 19–44.
4. Jelinek, "Introduction," 17.
5. Juhasz, "Theory of Form," 223.
6. Jelinek, "Introduction," 7–8.
7. Nancy Chodorow, *The Reproduction of Mothering: Psychoanalysis and the Sociology of Gender* (Berkeley: University of California Press, 1978).
8. Carol Gilligan, *In a Different Voice: Psychological Theory and Women's Development* (Cambridge, Mass.: Harvard University Press, 1982).
9. Jelinek, "Introduction," 10–11.
10. Ibid, 15.

Judith Ortiz Cofer's *Silent Dancing*

This essay focuses on a book of memoirs written by the Puerto Rican author Judith Ortiz Cofer, *Silent Dancing: A Partial Remembrance of a Puerto Rican Childhood,* which I would like to examine in light of the preceding comments and propose as a testimonial source of a particular family of "aliens in the Promised Land."[11]

The book consists of thirteen essays and eighteen poems interspersed among them; the latter function as a sort of tight synthesis of each preceding essay by underscoring its main point, although in a conversation with the author she confirmed that the poems preceded the essays sometimes by as many as eight years.[12] They actually functioned as a sort of launching pad for each essay. The time remembered roughly comprises fifteen years, from 1952 to 1967, actually the first fifteen years of the author's life, spent between Hormigueros—a small town in the Southwest of Puerto Rico, her birthplace and home for both her mother's and her father's families—and Paterson, New Jersey.

The book does exhibit the "anecdotal and disruptive characteristic"[13] observed by Jelinek in women's autobiographies, the "repetitive, cumulative, cyclical structure" described by Juhasz.[14] Each essay is indeed independent, truly a "self-sustained unit," and the connection between them is loose, to the extent that five of the essays were previously published separately in several literary journals. They are arranged in chronological

---

11. In the past seven years Ortiz Cofer has justly attracted the attention of publishers and readers with a consistent literary production, which up to this point comprises (*a*) six books of poetry: *Latin Women Pray* (Fort Lauderdale: Florida Arts Gazette Press, 1980), *The Native Dancer* (Bourbonnais, Ill.: Lieb/Schott Publications, 1981), *Among the Ancestors* (n.p., 1981), *Peregrina* (Golden, Colo.: Riverstone Press of the Foothills Arts Center, 1986), *Terms of Survival* (Houston: Arte Público Press, 1987), and *Reaching for the Mainland,* in *Triple Crown: Chicano, Puerto Rican, and Cuban American Poetry* (ed. Gary D. Keller; Tempe: Bilingual Press/Editorial Bilingüe, 1987), 64–120; (*b*) a novel, *The Line of the Sun* (Athens: University of Georgia Press, 1989); (*c*) a book of memoirs, *Silent Dancing: A Partial Remembrance of a Puerto Rican Childhood* (Houston: Arte Público, 1990); and (*d*) a book in which she combines prose and poetry, *The Latin Deli* (Athens: University of Georgia Press, 1993). She is currently working on a book of short stories and on a second novel. Numerous awards attest to the quality of her work: in 1981 she received a fellowship in poetry from the Fine Arts Council of Florida; in 1985 her book *Peregrina* won the Riverstone Press International Poetry Competition; in 1987 she was awarded the poetry fellowship from the Bread Loaf Writers' Conference; in 1988 she received a grant from the Witter Bynner Foundation for Poetry and was chosen for the Georgia Poetry Circuit Tour; in 1989 she received a fellowship from the National Endowment for the Arts, and her novel became the first original novel published by the University of Georgia Press; and in 1991 her book of memoirs was awarded the PEN/Martha Albrand Special Citation for Nonfiction and was selected for the New York Public Library's Best Books for the Teen Age.

All page references to *Silent Dancing* will be given in parentheses in the main text.

12. Fifteen of them appeared in *Reaching for the Mainland.*

13. Jelinek, "Introduction," 19.

14. Juhasz, "Theory of Form," 223.

order, although at times the narrative follows a sort of tidal flow, moving forward and backward. Since they can be read separately, when one reads all of them together, one finds numerous repetitions. As Jelinek and Juhasz have pointed out, one should assume that this disconnection and fragmentation are related to the particular situation of the author: the fact that this is a self-portrait of a bicultural childhood, whose constant feature for fifteen years was mobility between the island and the mainland, and once in the mainland, between the world crafted by her mother at home and the world outside.

However, despite the aforementioned independent character of the essays, it is possible to group them together into four thematic nuclei. The first one, made up of the first seven essays ("Casa," "More Room," "Talking to the Dead," "The Black Virgin," "Primary Lesson," "One More Lesson," and "Tales Told under the Mango Tree"), refers to her life in Puerto Rico: the setting, the characters, and the two institutions that made the strongest impression on her—the church and the school. The next two essays ("Silent Dancing" and "Some of the Characters"), about her life in the United States, constitute a second part. There are three essays that share the theme of being an adolescent or the discovery of sexuality in a bicultural context ("The Looking-Glass Shame," "Quinceañera," and "Marina"); these constitute a third grouping. The last essay ("The Last Word") needs to be considered separately because it is a reflection on the act of looking back.

In the book's preface, "Journey to a Summer's Afternoon," the author explains the genesis and purpose of the book. The book was born, on the one hand, "out of a need most of us feel at some point to study ourselves and our lives in retrospect; to understand what people and events formed us (and, yes, what and who hurt us, too)" (11). On the other, it was also fostered by her desire "to trace back through scenes based on my 'moments of being' the origins of my creative imagination" (12). The phrase "moments of being" is borrowed from Virginia Woolf, whom she acknowledges as her literary role model for this particular undertaking and who provided her with the method that she will be using. Like Woolf, she will be searching for "the tracks left by strong emotions" (13), because not everything can be or is worth being included.

She is aware of the dangers of looking back: the temptation to delete the painful memories, to foreground the joyful ones, even to embellish them. Woolf is also a good source of support in this respect because she too had confronted "the problem of writing truth from memory" (11), which she solomonically solved by coining the term "poetic truth" to refer to the end result. For her part, Ortiz Cofer conveniently remembers and reminds us that the name in Spanish for the vehicle that she will be using for her explorations, the essay, is *ensayo,* which can mean " 'a rehearsal,' an exercise or practice" (12), in sum, nothing definite.

Her warning about what the book is not reminds us of the second trait observed by Jelinek in women's autobiographies. Ortiz Cofer writes:

I am not interested in merely "canning" memories. . . . [The book's] intention is not to chronicle my life—which in my case is still very much "in-progress," nor are there any extraordinary accomplishments to showcase; neither is it meant to be a record of public events and personal histories. (13)

However, when she focuses on her personal life, looking for the people who formed her, she underscores three of her relatives, three portraits within the self-portrait: her father, her mother, and her maternal grandmother. The one close relative absent from the picture is her brother, who is only mentioned several times in passing. As to the events themselves, she foregrounds her father's decision to move to the United States. At this point it is important to consider the title of the book, also the title of one of the essays, which refers to an old family silent movie shot at a family party. That movie proved especially helpful in her quest for digging into her memory for more insight about her family and her own life (95). In the book the reader is given the same chance: she now handles the camera and parades before us those people and events that attained special significance both for her personal life and also for her professional life, since, as she states at the end of the book, Puerto Rico and its people are the major focus of her writing (153).

The very first thing that she lets us know is that her parents got married very young. Her mother was not yet fifteen years old,[15] while her father was eighteen and had just graduated from high school. They belonged to two very different families. Her mother's relatives came originally from Italy and were all farmers (39); her father's came from Spain "bringing tales of wealth and titles," although her paternal grandfather had been disinherited by his relatives because of his dissolute lifestyle. As was to be expected, their offspring were very different too, in fact, opposites that attracted: "My father was a quiet, serious man; my mother, earthy and ebullient" (39). Ortiz Cofer compares them to ice and fire, respectively.[16]

In 1951, just a few months after the wedding and prompted by the need to support his wife and a child on the way, her father joined the U.S. Army and was sent to Panama.[17] Ortiz Cofer would be two years old before she would meet her father for the first time. Similarly, when her brother was

---

15. Ortiz Cofer stresses this by using the phrases "teenage mother" (42) and "teenage bride" (45) to refer to her mother as well as "baby doll" (46) and "rubber doll" (47) to describe her mother's relationship to her at first.

16. Interestingly, she chooses the name Marisol, literally "Sea-and-Sun," for the narrator of her novel, quite certainly her alter ego, and in so doing places herself as the harmonious synthesis of both worlds.

17. As Jorge Rodríguez Beruff (*Política militar y dominación: Puerto Rico en el contexto latinoamericano* [Río Piedras, P.R.: Huracán, 1988] 155) points out, Puerto Rico has suffered from a subtle form of mandatory recruitment, since the high level of unemployment has forced a great number of young people to enter the U.S. Army. These people bene-

born in 1954, growing economic pressures made her father join the U.S. Navy. The following year, 1955, the family moved to the States because her father had been assigned to the naval base at Brooklyn Yard. Beginning in 1958, every six months or so her father would be sent to Europe, and the family would go back to Hormigueros until he returned to the States. This "gypsy lifestyle" (52) was to be the pattern until 1967, the last time she went back to Puerto Rico as an adolescent. She returned years later, already married, and still goes back but not on a regular basis.

Ortiz Cofer thinks of her father as a victim of the economic situation in Puerto Rico at the time.[18] She remembers him as "a sensitive, intellectual man whose energies had to be entirely devoted to survival" (129). He never regretted his decisions, for he felt that he had done what he had to do in order to support his wife and family, and there was no nostalgia for what could have been. Had he stayed on the island, he would have probably ended up working in the sugarcane fields, which had just come into the hands of North American owners.[19] In fact, Ortiz Cofer recalls the house of "the American," the manager of Hormigueros's sugar refinery, where the majority of the town's men worked (76).

Puerto Rican Immigrants in the United States

In emigrating to the mainland her father was not alone. His drama was the drama of thousands and thousands of other compatriots. It is well-known that Puerto Ricans had been emigrating to the United States before 1898 for political reasons, namely, to plot against the Spanish government. After the American invasion of the island, a series of measures taken by the military governor, Guy V. Henry, brought about major changes in the economy. One of the immediate effects was the expropriation of lands and the subsequent displacement of workers, who in turn sought a solution to their unemployment by emigrating to the States. In addition, Puerto Rican workers were actively recruited by U.S. companies established in Hawaii and on the mainland.[20] However, as can be clearly seen in the statistics provided by Adalberto López, the great Puerto Rican emigration began after World

---

fit from medical services, grants, and so on, all of which generate support of the colonial relationship.

18. Ortiz Cofer's father was not the only member of her extended family who migrated to the States. She remembers how much her maternal grandmother enjoyed reading the letters that her daughters and other relatives who were working in New York and New Jersey would send her. One of her sons was the victim of a scam when he was recruited as a farmworker, not unlike the cases encountered by Luis Nieves Falcón (*El emigrante puertorriqueño* [Río Piedras, P.R.: Editorial Edil, 1987]) during his research. Ortiz Cofer recalls how her paternal grandmother would do all sorts of penances in exchange for the safe return of her two sons who were fighting in Korea.

19. See Manuel Maldonado Denis's *Puerto Rico y Estados Unidos: Emigración y colonialismo* (Mexico City: Siglo Veintiuno Editores, 1978) for an analysis of the transformation of the Puerto Rican economy in the 1940s and 1950s.

20. See ibid., 71.

War II: In 1951, over 50,000 Puerto Ricans moved to New York; in 1953, the process reached its peak with 69,124 immigrants; in 1955, Ortiz Cofer's family was among the 45,464 Puerto Ricans who emigrated to the States.[21] As Rita Maldonado points out, unlike previous waves of immigrants who had come to the United States looking for political and religious freedom as well as economic opportunity, the Puerto Rican immigrants came solely for the latter reason.[22] According to Ransford W. Palmer, "Emigration in search of job opportunities has been an enduring feature of the economic history of the [Caribbean]."[23] Emigration to the mainland has thus been explained as a result of what the economists call "push and pull forces"[24]— that is to say, while unemployment was growing in the island and income was low, in the mainland income was growing and unemployment was decreasing. However, one has to agree with Clara Rodríguez's analysis that in the particular case of Puerto Rico the roots of these forces are to be found in the colonial relationship between the island and the United States.[25]

When Ortiz Cofer's father went to the States, where he already had some relatives, he first found an apartment in Paterson, New Jersey, one of the four states with the largest concentration of Puerto Rican immigrants.[26] It was in a tenement building that had originally been inhabited by Jewish families but was now occupied by Puerto Ricans, who appropriately called it "El Building" (87). He was not happy there because he had not moved from Puerto Rico to end up in an even worse situation, so he decided to find another place outside the barrio.[27] In the meantime, he instructed

---

21. Adalberto López's article ("The Puerto Rican Diaspora: A Survey," *Puerto Rico and Puerto Ricans: Studies in History and Society* [ed. Adalberto López and James Petras; New York: John Wiley and Sons, 1974] 316–46) provides a succinct and excellent analysis of the causes of emigration, the profile of the immigrant, the pattern of settlement in the States, the problems confronted by the emigrants in the States, and the possible solutions. See also Clara Rodríguez, *Puerto Ricans Born in the U.S.A.* (Boulder, Colo.: Westview Press, 1989); Virginia Sánchez Korrol, *From Colonia to Community: The History of Puerto Ricans in New York City, 1917–1948* (Westport, Conn.: Greenwood Press, 1983); and José L. Vázquez Calzada, "Demographic Aspects of Migration," *Labor Migration under Capitalism* (History Task Force, Centro de Estudios Puertorriqueños; New York: Monthly Review Press, 1979) 223–36.

22. Rita Maldonado, "Why Puerto Ricans Migrated to the United States in 1947–73," *Monthly Labor Review* 99:9 (September 1976) 7.

23. Ransford W. Palmer, "Caribbean Development and the Migration Imperative," *In Search of a Better Life: Perspectives on Migration from the Caribbean* (ed. R. W. Palmer; New York: Praeger, 1990) 3. See Maldonado Denis (*Puerto Rico*) for an analysis of the causes and consequences of this phenomenon.

24. Palmer, "Caribbean Development," 7.

25. C. Rodríguez, "Economic Factors Affecting Puerto Ricans in New York," *Labor Migration,* 197–221. For the role of the government as a decisive force encouraging migratory movement to the United States, see A. López ("Puerto Rican Diaspora") and Maldonado Denis (*Puerto Rico*).

26. See Maldonado ("Why Puerto Ricans Migrated," 7–8), who refers to this factor as the "chain effect of cumulative migration."

27. They were not living in Spanish Harlem, however. For a poignant presentation of what life was like in the barrio in the 1950s, though from the perspective of an outsider,

his family not to form any bonds with the place or with the people who lived there. He even bought them a television set so as to keep them entertained inside the apartment. He finally got an apartment on Park Avenue, after convincing the Jewish owner that they "were not the usual Puerto Rican family" (63). There were to be even more rules than before, since they "were expected to behave with restraint . . . to defeat the stereotype of the loud, slovenly tenement-dweller" (119). Ortiz Cofer remembers the ritual of removing their shoes at the door of the apartment and walking around in socks: "We were going to prove how respectable we were by being the opposite of what our ethnic group was known to be—we would be quiet and inconspicuous" (64). His father's behavior was clearly that of the colonized man, as described by Albert Memmi: "He has assumed all the accusations and condemnations of the colonizer. . . . He is becoming accustomed to looking at his own people through the eyes of their procurer."[28] In time, he became more and more of an introvert, especially after the six months that he spent on a ship circling Cuba at the time of the Cuban Missile Crisis; he was now absent even when he was home. Although there is only an allusion to it in one of the poems (123), we know that he suffered a nervous breakdown and had to retire from the navy after fourteen years of service.[29]

Her mother, however, did not share her husband's feelings. In fact, her attitude was completely the opposite. She also did what she had to do as a young woman of the time, namely, follow her husband, but she accepted that life only as a temporary state of affairs, although it lasted twenty years. Ortiz Cofer says that several times her mother felt she was "doing time" away from her homeland, that she lived in "exile," and she calls her a "Penelope-like wife, . . . always waiting, waiting, waiting, for the return of her sailor, for the return to her native land" (152).

Fortunately for her, her husband understood her feelings and made it possible for her to spend time with her family in Hormigueros during the months when he was away. During the time that she did have to be in the

---

see Dan Wakefield, *Island in the City: Puerto Ricans in New York* (New York: Corinth Press, 1957). For an insider's view, see Piri Thomas, *Down These Mean Streets* (New York: Alfred A. Knopf, 1967); Jesús Colón, *A Puerto Rican in New York and Other Sketches* (New York: International Publishers, 1982); Edward Rivera, *Family Installments: Memories of Growing Up Hispanic* (New York: William Morrow, 1982); and César Andreu Iglesias's edition of *Memorias de Bernardo Vega. Contribución a la historia de la comunidad puertorriqueña en Nueva York* (Río Piedras, P.R.: Huracán, 1988).

28. Albert Memmi, *The Colonizer and the Colonized* (trans. Howard Grenfeld; New York: Orion Press, 1965) 123.

29. See *Short Fiction by Hispanic Writers of the United States* (ed. Nicolás Kanellos; Houston: Arte Público Press, 1993) 176. Interestingly, the article "Hospitalization Rate of Puerto Ricans for Mental Disorders Said to Be High" (*The New York Times,* 26 March 1970, 36) lists the "stress from migration, including uprooting [and] adjustment to a new way of life," as one of the possible factors for the high percentage of mental disorders among Puerto Rican immigrants.

United States, she also did her best to survive. In her case this meant living a Puerto Rican life vicariously, in effect acting out another role of the colonized person: the countermythology.[30] Her husband's concern about displaying un–Puerto Rican behavior to counter the generalized stereotypical image was balanced by her ultra–Puerto Ricanness, a true nightmare for the enforcers of the "melting pot." She wore the same bright and colorful clothes and spike heels she would wear in Hormigueros; kept her house as "a reasonable facsimile of a Puerto Rican home" (152); never learned English; "never learned moderation in her emotions, or restraint for her gesturing hands and loud laughter" (127); prepared only Puerto Rican food; constantly shared her memories of the island and her mother's house with her children; listened to Puerto Rican songs (Daniel Santos, of course); and read only material in Spanish: the novels of Corín Tellado, popular magazines such as *Buenhogar* and *Vanidades,* and above all over and over again the letters from Puerto Rico. Accustomed to living in a single-family home, it was hard for her to get used to sharing a building with so many people, with whom ironically she was not supposed to have any contact. But even with that obstacle, she managed to structure her life in such a way that she could partake of familiar sounds and smells. Although the family would go shopping at the large department stores, she was able to get her husband's authorization to buy the groceries at La Bodega. This place not only provided her with the basic ingredients for her Puerto Rican meals but also and above all served as a meeting place where she could speak to her female neighbors, thus cleverly going around her husband's prohibition against establishing personal relationships with the neighbors (91). It all worked in the end: when she finally returned to Puerto Rico for good, after her husband's death, she had no uprooting to do, since she had kept her roots in the air, and no catching up either.

During her husband's absences, she remained his loyal lieutenant. She actually received instructions from him by mail. Ortiz Cofer recalls "the intense fear for our safety that our father's absences instilled in her. In order to keep us from harm when father was away, mother kept us under strict surveillance. She even walked us to and from Public School" (18). The high school Ortiz Cofer attended was only a few blocks away from their apartment, and if she was not home in fifteen minutes after school was out, her mother panicked and came after her (126). Her mother would only relax and let the children go wild in Puerto Rico...until they were called back to New Jersey: "I remember mother's frantic packing, and the trips to Mayagüez for new clothes; the inspection of my brother's and my bodies for cuts, scrapes, mosquito bites, and other 'damage' she would have to explain to father" (63).

---

30. Memmi, *Colonizer,* 139.

Finding a Role Model

Indeed, her grandmother's house meant freedom. Ortiz Cofer first went back when she was nearly six. She remembers being "stunned by the heat and confused by a houseful of relatives" (75). Her grandmother had five children, plus three who died at birth or in early infancy. In fact, she was pregnant when Ortiz Cofer's mother got married. At the time of that first summer back in Hormigueros, there were still two aunts and one uncle living there, the latter about Ortiz Cofer's age.

At her grandmother's house, with so many children around her, Ortiz Cofer learned to be a kid: to run, to play, to scream, to be in contact with nature. But most of all—and this is important because one should not forget that one of her purposes in writing this memoir is to look for the roots of her creativity—she now realizes in looking back that she learned to observe other people, to listen, and to become fascinated by the power of words through a family ritual: the telling of stories. This was the daily counterpoint, but for her truly the high point, of a day full of activity. These stories were told by the women, usually the grandmother, and to the women of the family, the daughters and granddaughters. They were based on real-life situations, with the added personal touch of the narrator, and always involved a lesson to be learned. The main topic was "what it was like to be a woman, more specifically, a Puerto Rican woman" (14); the moral: a woman's life was a mixture of self-denial and work, hard work and work for others. She learned, among other things, about the dangers of sex, the perils of love, the trials and tribulations of married life and child-bearing. It was not hard to look around and find examples, even in her own family, of women abandoned by men, before or after being married; young women surrounded by children; girls learning to be mothers at a very early age, helping out their mothers as a result of the many children in the family; women abused by their husbands, but survivors nonetheless.[31]

Her grandmother was admittedly Ortiz Cofer's female role model, the embodiment of the primeval Mother. It seems only natural that everybody would just call her "Mamá." She was Ortiz Cofer's source of warmth as well as stability in a time characterized by mobility and detachment. Nevertheless, she is aware of her grandmother's role in perpetuating the status quo of the women, which she explains as follows:

It was not that Mamá endorsed marriage as the only choice for women; it was just all she had been brought up to expect for herself, her daughters, and now, her granddaughters. If you did not get married, you became a nun, or you entered "la vida" as a prostitute. Of course, there were some professions a woman could practice—nurse, teacher—until you found a man to marry. The worse fate was to

---

31. Her paternal grandmother, for example, experienced great relief when her embittered husband, a gambler and a drunkard, died (40).

end up alone (by that she meant no more children, rather than no man) in your old age. (141)

She learned from her to be strong, to be determined, to take charge, to take advantage of the possibilities of turning a difficult situation into one's benefit, to be caring and giving but within reasonable limits. For all practical purposes her grandmother was the head of the house.[32] In fact, several times Ortiz Cofer uses the words "queen" and "throne" to refer to her and her room. Her grandfather assumed a policy of laissez-faire that was mutually convenient: he would go about his business (building and painting houses, offering spiritual counseling, and composing poetry), and his wife would be free to get things done the way she wanted. Ortiz Cofer's favorite anecdote about her grandmother, one that appears several times in the book, has to do with her grandmother's "bloodless coup" (26), when she rebelled against her husband by throwing him out of her bedroom after the birth of their eighth child and actually forced him to build a separate room for himself. Still, Ortiz Cofer explains this move more as a result of her grandmother's belief that her duty as a woman was to deny herself and give herself to others, at that point her children, than as a measure to achieve freedom and control.

Her grandmother's knowledge of all sorts of natural remedies fascinated her. She introduced her to the world of popular religiosity as well. The "room of her own" was decorated with an imposing crucifix, and the Bible had a place of honor on her dresser. From her as well as from the other women of the town, she learned that there was also the possibility of making secret alliances with that most powerful woman of all, the Virgin. It should be remembered that the sanctuary of Our Lady of Montserrate in Hormigueros has always been the pilgrimage center par excellence in Puerto Rico. As Ortiz Cofer acknowledges, women have always felt very comfortable and very confident addressing Our Lady of Montserrate because "being a woman and black made Our Lady the perfect depository for the hopes and prayers of the sick, the weak and the powerless" (44).[33]

Her grandmother was also—though unwittingly so—the author's literary mentor. Her stories inspired her granddaughter to wish to create stories of

---

32. For a profile of husband-wife relations in the Puerto Rican family, see Sidney W. Mintz, "Puerto Rico: An Essay in the Definition of National Culture," *The Puerto Rican Experience: A Sociological Handbook* (ed. Francesco Cordasco and Eugene Bucchioni; New Jersey: Rowman and Littlefield, 1973) 61–65.

33. Besides the nightly praying of the rosary, Ortiz Cofer remembers that *promesas* (vows) and *hábitos* (religious garments) were very popular with the women of the town, especially in times of war. Many families had relatives fighting in Korea at this time, as was the case with Ortiz Cofer's paternal family. This was a fairly common occurrence. According to Héctor Andrés Negroni (*Historia militar de Puerto Rico* [Madrid: Ediciones Siruela, 1992] 447), more than 43,000 Puerto Rican men enlisted to fight in Korea and over 3,000 died. In fact, from a proportional point of view, Puerto Rico had 100 percent more deaths than the United States: one out of every 660 inhabitants, instead of one out of every 1,125 inhabitants. In addition, one out of every 42 casualties was Puerto Rican.

her own, to become herself the narrator instead of just the narratee. Her influence is also noticeable in the undeniable oral quality of Ortiz Cofer's prose. Her stories are not only easy to read but also easy to tell. They are actually best appreciated when read aloud.

The Power of Language

Ortiz Cofer was in Puerto Rico at the time when she was supposed to begin school. She did not want to see the freedom attained during her visit with her grandmother come to an end; therefore, she tried to convince her mother that the idea of going to school in Puerto Rico would not please her father. He wanted his children to speak "good English" (53), and attending school in Puerto Rico was not the way to go about achieving that goal. Her mother was not taken in by her argument, and so she was exposed to the Puerto Rican public school system. She recalls being impressed by the power of the teacher inside and outside the classroom, but she especially foregrounds her memory of her first English lesson, when students were asked to learn basic vocabulary by means of a bilingual song, the well-known "Pollito—Chicken."[34] At this time, 1958, ten years had already passed since English had ceased to be the teaching medium and had become instead a required second language, taught as an additional subject.[35] Her class was conducted entirely in English, as required, but by a teacher who probably had never been to the United States and whose knowledge of the language was deficient. It took the children a while to realize that they were supposed to repeat the verses after the teacher until they learned them by heart. Ortiz Cofer was able to figure it out because she had been exposed to the language before; she also realized that it was a "heavily accented English" (55).

Attending school in the States for the first time could not have been more traumatic. The building itself was a striking contrast to the school in Puerto Rico:

The school building was not a welcoming sight for someone used to the bright colors and airiness of tropical architecture. The building looked functional. It could have been a prison, an asylum, or just what it was: an urban school for the children of immigrants. (65)

---

34. This song was and still is widely known. The Puerto Rican writer Ana Lydia Vega has used its first verse as the title of a story in which she makes fun of a woman whose discourse is an example of code-switching taken to hyperbolic extremes ("Pollito Chicken," *Vírgenes y mártires* [3d ed.; ed. Ana Lydia Vega and Carmen Lugo Filippi; Río Piedras, P.R.: Editorial Antillana, 1988] 73–79).

35. For a brief outline of the concerted effort on the part of the U.S. government to Americanize Puerto Rican children through the public school system, see Kal Wagenheim, "Puerto Rico: A Profile," *Puerto Rico and Puerto Ricans*, 102–3. For a thorough study of the period between 1900 and 1930, see Aida Negrón de Montilla, *La americanización en Puerto Rico y el sistema de instrucción pública 1900–1930* (Río Piedras, P.R.: Editorial de la Universidad de Puerto Rico, 1990).

More importantly, the uselessness of the Puerto Rican government's policy of teaching English as the second official language of the island was made evident when she was unable to communicate with her English-speaking classmates in the States. This linguistic problem even proved dangerous as, for example, when a teacher physically assaulted her because she could not understand a simple message written in English on the blackboard. This experience is presented in the book as a moment of awakening. It is her initiation into the world into which she had been transplanted, a revelation of her place in it. She learned painfully that language can either give or take away power: "I instinctively understood then that language is the only weapon a child has against the absolute power of adults" (66). However, she does not seem to be aware of the fact—or at least she does not say so explicitly—that it was not a matter of possessing *any* language. We are talking here about two types of diametrically opposed languages: the language of the powerful and the language of the powerless, the language that gives one access to control and the language that keeps one away from it, actually under it.[36] She did possess a language when she attended school in the States for the first time, but it was not the "right" language.

Her determination to master English was born not only out of her desire for revenge but also out of another and far more practical as well as immediate need: since her mother had not learned English as one of her ways of resisting assimilation, in her father's absences the young girl had to step into his shoes and become the interpreter of the world outside (103). Language empowered her to the point that she went from being just a daughter to assuming the responsibilities of a parent. It conferred upon her the dubious privilege of being considered an adult when she was still a child. Her self-imposed reading regimen was in effect not only a good form of escape, substituting for the forbidden outdoor activities, but also a great means of self-education in the language. Upon her father's return, when her services were no longer needed, she was free to go back to her books. Of course, this was not easy: "At times, I resented his homecoming, when I would suddenly be thrust back into the role of dependent which I had long ago outgrown—and not by choice" (104).

Spanish remained the language spoken at home, almost exclusively to her mother and at her grandmother's house, a fact that made her consider it "the language of fun, of summertime games" (52). Not surprisingly, the book is sprinkled with many words from Spanish that make their way into the narrative, the English translation always appearing next to them. These words are usually related to the spheres of food (*café con leche, asopao, adobo, pasteles*) or social and religious life (*casa, pueblo, cuentos, macho, promesa, alma de Dios, santeros, facultades, pruebas, luto, Navidad, los Reyes, misa del gallo, quinceañera, novelas*). Translation takes care of the

---

36. For the tension between these two languages, see Memmi, *Colonizer,* 107–8.

literal meaning of each word, but it is of no use in transmitting its emotional component. Given that this is a book of memoirs, it is important that the evocative strength of the word not be lost. Here more than ever the word names a reality as well as re-creates it.[37]

Trying to Find a Place

Things do not get any better when she attends Catholic schools. The author's indictment of the Catholic school system is pointed, in part because of the irony involved. We learn that the usual distrust of the Puerto Rican immigrant was alive there as well: "I was the only Puerto Rican student, having gotten in after taking a rigorous academic test and after the priest visited our apartment to ascertain that we were a good Catholic family" (125). Discrimination was very much in place, as can be further observed in the anecdote regarding the reenactment of a Roman banquet at the end of the school year. There was a need to choose a senator and his lady, and the nun in charge chose a red-haired young man who happened to be the best basketball player in the school and a recently arrived Polish immigrant girl whose blond hair and classical beauty outweighed the fact that she could not yet speak English well. Although Ortiz Cofer had the highest average in the class in charge of the production, she was only assigned the role of a Roman citizen, along with all the other students in the class.

Appearance, then, not just language, was considered of primary importance. It is no wonder, therefore, that she admits to being ashamed of both her mother and father because of their looks. She was too much aware of the fact that they were aliens, and it seemed to her that her parents were displaying their differences in too noticeable a way, precisely when she was learning how important it was to fit in, to blend in, that is, to be invisible. Early in the book we learn of her concern about being normal, given the fact that she felt she belonged nowhere:

I was constantly made to feel like an oddball by my peers, who made fun of my two-way accent: a Spanish accent when I spoke English; and, when I spoke Spanish, I was told that I sounded like a "Gringa." Being the outsiders had already turned my brother and me into cultural chameleons, developing early the ability to blend into a crowd, to sit and read quietly in a fifth story apartment building for days and days. (17)

To her chagrin, her mother "carried the island of Puerto Rico over her head like the mantilla she wore to church on Sunday" (127),[38] and her

---

37. For her comments on the role each language plays in her life and her writings, see her interview with Rafael Ocasio, "Puerto Rican Literature in Georgia? An Interview with Judith Ortiz Cofer," *Kenyon Review* 14:4 (fall 1992) 43–50.

38. When Ortiz Cofer's father went out looking for a place to live away from the barrio, he would take the children with him but not his wife. He was well aware that "her Latin beauty, her thick black hair that hung to her waist, her voluptuous body which even the winter clothes could not disguise, would have been nothing but a hindrance to [his] plans" (63–64).

father would always wear his "phosphorescent white Navy uniform" (134) everywhere he went.

Growing up in a bicultural milieu, therefore, gave rise to a number of other tensions besides bilingualism. It was obvious that her family was not the all-American family and that the place she lived was not the all-American home she was used to seeing on television. However, perhaps the hardest time of life in this bicultural context was when she was coming of age. For one thing, while her female classmates were enjoying greater freedom than ever before, her mother was enforcing more than ever the restraints dictated by her father. She was a Puerto Rican girl, and she was to be brought up as she would have been brought up in the island, "where an adolescent girl was watched every minute by the women who acted as if you carried some kind of time bomb in your body that might go off at any minute; and, worse, they constantly warned you about your behavior around men" (139–40). But such restrictions and warnings did not come with any information about what was going on, what it was that the older women seemed to be protecting her from. Ironically, although it was not so in her case, most of the time this linkage of prohibitions and ignorance led precisely to the undesired end. In addition, while in Puerto Rico, she began to resent having to spend time in what now seemed crowded quarters, because she had gotten used already to her privacy in New Jersey. Asking for privacy in Hormigueros was considered rude.

Being an outsider became an even greater obstacle when she fell in love. It brought to the fore the bearing that ethnic origin and class had on her life precisely at the moment when she was more able to understand; it hurt her deeply. It so happened that the boy in question was Italian and rich, both reasons she did not belong to his sphere of life. Fortunately for her, he worked at his uncle's supermarket, around the block from Ortiz Cofer's apartment (130–31). Despite the tragic nature of the situation, some of the funniest pages in the book are the ones in which she remembers the ingenious strategies she devised to be able to go to the store more frequently than usual, just to get a glance of him.

The ultimate impact of her bicultural upbringing was to be felt later in the choices she made for her own life (152), choices that did not exactly match her mother's expectations. It was hard for her mother, whom she calls her "loving adversary" (153), to accept that her daughter had a career that, among other things, demanded that she be away from home, but above all that her daughter's husband willingly—and adequately—shared the responsibilities for being a parent and keeping a household, in sum that her daughter would be leading a life opposite to hers when she was her age. This discrepancy in their perceptions is also obvious with regard to their recollections of the past; thus, for example, at the end of the book Ortiz Cofer confronts her mother regarding one of these anecdotes and gets a different explanation of it. In this respect the book comes full circle, and a component of its subtitle, "a partial remembrance"—therefore, incomplete, as well as personal and subjective—is underscored.

Concluding Comments

As the remainder of the subtitle also indicates, Ortiz Cofer's memoirs focus more on the Puerto Rican part of her childhood. This is so, on the one hand, as a result of the method she acknowledges as choosing, that is, to look for the "tracks left by strong emotions." Given her secluded life in the States,[39] her Puerto Rican experiences had a stronger impact on her. On the other hand, it can also be a manifestation of what feminist critics have observed in women's autobiographies: they tend to foreground the happy memories. Ortiz Cofer prefers to hint at the bitter moments rather than dwell on them. In her essay, Jelinek also addresses this point, insofar as she has noticed that

in place of glowing narratives [like the ones written by men], women tend to write in a straightforward and objective manner about both their girlhood and adult experiences. They also write obliquely, elliptically, or humorously in order to camouflage their feelings.[40]

Moreover, Ortiz Cofer's matter-of-fact way of referring to sensitive issues and situations that could otherwise give rise to a polemical discussion may be seen as a consequence of her awareness that she will be read not only as a woman[41] but also, and most importantly, as a Puerto Rican woman. If it is true that "women's life stories reveal a self-consciousness and a need to sift through their lives for explanation and understanding,"[42] it is more poignantly so when gender is compounded by ethnic origin and class. A woman's position of double marginality—hence, of dual oppression—causes her to be doubly careful.

However, it does not escape Ortiz Cofer that her childhood, despite the limitations she faced, was a privileged one. Her story is definitely not that of all Puerto Rican immigrants, not even the majority of them. To begin with, her father was a high school graduate; the family never lived in Spanish Harlem; and they even managed to get out of the New Jersey barrio. Her mother did not have to work outside the home because the money earned by her husband was steady and abundant. They could afford buying

---

39. It is interesting that we get to know only three other individuals, all of whom happen to be neighbors (Vida, Providencia, and Sal), and that all three were in one way or another victims of their sexuality.

40. Jelinek, "Introduction," 15.

41. Nancy K. Miller has pointed out that this self-awareness makes all the difference at the time of self-disclosure. She has observed ("Writing Fictions: Women's Autobiography in France," *Life/Lines,* 57–58) that "reading [women's] lives is rather like shaking hands with one's gloves on [because] the determination to have their lives make sense and thus be susceptible to *universal* reception blinds them."

42. Jelinek, "Introduction," 15.

clothes at department stores; the mother even received jewelry as presents from her husband; the family owned a television set; and the children attended private schools. They were able to go periodically to Puerto Rico, and there they were also looked upon as privileged. Her father's family was well known, and his job gave him and his family a sort of honorable status.[43] Still, despite all of this, they too had to pay a price.

By the end of her novel *The Line of the Sun,* Ortiz Cofer states that "the only way to understand a life is to write it as a story, to fill in the blanks left by circumstance, lapses of memory, and failed communication" (290). *Silent Dancing* is obviously her personal attempt to do that. As I have pointed out, the book does exhibit the main characteristics of the female autobiography though with modifications, insofar as it reflects not only the author's gender but more importantly her biculturalism.

Women have been telling their stories for a long time, but wide audiences have not until recently paid serious attention to those stories. Latina writers have had an even harder time, due to their double marginality. Sadly enough, there are still very few Puerto Rican women writers in the United States. Ironically, the literature produced by Puerto Rican men, like Piri Thomas and Ed Rivera, has not helped their sisters. The life portrayed by Thomas in *Down These Mean Streets* and Vega in *Family Installments* has been taken as the typical life of Puerto Ricans in New York. In this respect it is interesting to recall the experience of Nicholasa Mohr the first time she submitted an article for publication, an article that she had in fact been asked to write. In her interview with Roni Natov and Geraldine DeLuca,[44] she recalls that the manuscript was rejected because the editor "wanted something more sensational, something with sex and violence." In an interview with Edna Acosta-Belén,[45] she goes on to say that what the editor wanted was "a female version of *Down These Mean Streets.*" She does admit that she has read Puerto Rican male writers such as Thomas, but specifies that while "these books are ... about men who have suffered, have been traumatized and have fought for survival in Harlem," her own books are written "from a woman's point of view," and her experiences have not been traumatic in the typical way: "I have never been in jail, nor have I ever been a prostitute or been raped. I've never been involved in drugs." She concludes that she believes that "most Puerto Rican women have not gone through these experiences either. Puerto Rican women in El Barrio have had to cope with other situations although we are all brothers and sisters who have also shared certain collective experiences."

---

43. Ortiz Cofer recalls the time she was chosen for a school show because her parents had money (58).

44. "An Interview with Nicholasa Mohr," *The Lion and the Unicorn* 11:1 (April 1987) 116–21.

45. Edna Acosta-Belén, "Conversations with Nicholasa Mohr," *Revista Chicano-Riqueña* 8:2 (spring 1980) 35–41.

Literature has long been thought of as a mirror in which we can see our reflection: who and how we are; how other people see us; who and how we would like to be; who and how we should be. Any study of any given group, thus, must take literature into account. This study, by using Judith Ortiz Cofer's book, should serve as a reminder that we are called to listen to what Latina writers in general and Puerto Rican women writers in particular have to say.

2

Kingdom Building in the Borderlands

The Church and Manifest Destiny

Daisy L. Machado

The Borderlands of the southwestern United States have been described by Texican writer Pat Mora as *nepantla,* which means "place in the middle" in Nahuatl, one of Mexico's indigenous languages.[1] Mora tries to put into words what it is like to live in that "place in the middle," that place so familiar to millions of Latinas and Latinos who live there. The Borderlands are a geographical reality that one can find on a map, but they are also a lot more than that. The U.S. Borderlands are *that* place where Latinas and Latinos live, struggle, love, fight, and strive to define who they are in the midst of a society that has for centuries kept them an invisible mass, a footnote in the homogenizing historical process of an entire nation. In this broader sense the Borderlands have no geographical boundaries and are both a symbol and a reality, not just for Mexican Americans but also for the millions of other Latinas and Latinos who currently make up the new diaspora.

In response to the daily struggle for life in the Borderlands, Mora raises her voice to protest the patterns of dominance and repression, the false notion of a "common culture" created by a "melting" of people, so that their languages, cultures, and selfhood are shed and lost. These same patterns and notions have been bred by the concept of manifest destiny, the multilayered doctrine that reworks the religious images of a chosen people, God's redeeming nation, religious and moral superiority, and the religious right to conquer and subjugate, in order to create the national mythology that underlies the civil religion of the United States and that has fueled the historical movement of this country since the Revolutionary War of 1776. Mora writes:

No race, sex, religion, or ethnic group can transform the United States, can whisper wisdom that will instantly cure our ills, but there has been a goal in this country

---

1. Pat Mora, *Nepantla: Essays from the Land in the Middle* (Albuquerque: University of New Mexico Press, 1993).

63

to create a national culture.... This desire for a "common culture" is based on obfuscation, cultural destruction and repression of difference. We more critically need to examine the issues of power.... We need to consider, for example, Professor Renato Rosaldo's intriguing notion of the inverse relationship between "full citizenship and cultural visibility." Citizenship in the broadest terms, in the sense of full participation in the nation's public life, need not require melting in, shedding, or forgetting a part of ourselves. Citizenship should affirm, not deny, identity.[2]

The thesis of this essay is that the desire for a common culture found in U.S. society was also adopted and legitimized by the church in its missionary efforts, beginning in the mid-1800s and continuing well into the twentieth century, among Latinas and Latinos in the Borderlands. This push for a homogenized worshiping community, a mirror of that idealized, newly forming "melting-pot" nation adopted by the establishment Protestant denominations, was further sustained by attitudes of race based on the same social and political interests of the mid–nineteenth century. These attitudes toward race in turn had an impact on the philosophy of mission developed by the Protestant church in the U.S. Borderlands.

This essay will focus on only one state in the Borderlands, Texas, and on one Protestant denomination, the Christian Church (Disciples of Christ), which began its missionary activities to Mexicans in Texas in the late nineteenth century. While other Protestant denominations in the Borderlands share a similar history,[3] this essay will concentrate on how this one particular "frontier," "American born-and-bred" denomination had its mission theology shaped by the national forces of the time, particularly that of manifest destiny, as it played itself out in unique fashion in Texas.

The Borderlands Defined

The term "Spanish Borderlands" has become a historical commonplace, yet it goes unrecognized by most people who have been educated in the United States. Despite the fact that the phrase was first coined in 1921 and attributed directly to the historical research of Herbert Eugene Bolton,[4] over seventy years later it still goes unmentioned in almost all high school and introductory history courses. Bolton proposed a "broader approach to

---

2. Ibid., 17.

3. See R. Douglas Breckenridge and Francisco García-Treto, *Iglesia Presbiteriana: A History of Presbyterians and Mexican Americans in the Southwest* (San Antonio: Trinity University Press, 1987). For a historical overview of the attitudes toward Latinas and Latinos in the Roman Catholic Church in the Borderlands, see Moisés Sandoval, *On the Move* (Maryknoll, N.Y.: Orbis Books, 1991).

4. Herbert Eugene Bolton's essay "The Epic of Greater America," one of four of his essays collected in his *Wider Horizons of American History* (New York: Appleton-Century, 1939), gives an idea of how controversial this concept was for North American historians. This essay was his presidential address before the American Historical Association, delivered in 1932.

American history, one which was not simply Anglo-oriented or limited to the study of the thirteen colonies."[5] Bolton was attempting to create a historical space for the writing of a North American history that would be more than an "unhistorical Anglo epic."[6] He argued that the nearly three centuries of Spanish presence in the southwestern half of the United States could not continue to be ignored by North American historians. Borderlands history was for Bolton the recognition that the writing of U.S. history had been done in "isolation, apart from its setting in the history of the entire Western Hemisphere, of which the United States are but a part."[7]

Geographically defined, the Borderlands north of the Rio Grande include what is today Georgia, Florida, Texas, Arizona, Colorado, New Mexico, and California. South of the Rio Grande, the Borderlands encompass those lands that made up the defensive and colonizing outposts of the Spanish Empire in New Spain (colonial Mexico). For Bolton this was of particular importance because these Borderlands territories not only made up a particular geographic zone but also shared a unique history with clearly identifiable tensions and problems, of which the foremost was race.

It was in these Borderlands that most Euro-American settlers moving east to west, as the United States sought to expand its national borders, first encountered the people and culture that were unique to this area. According to Bolton, the problems first arose with these initial encounters because the Borderlands were not really representative of the empire Spain had developed to the south in Mexico and into Latin America. As Bolton saw it,

Anglo-American writers concluded that Spain did not really colonize, and that, after all she failed. The fallacy came, of course, from mistaking the tail for the dog, and then leaving the dog out of the picture. The real Spanish America, the dog, lay between the Rio Grande and Buenos Aires. The part of the animal lying north of the Rio Grande was only the tail.[8]

The image Bolton uses of the Borderlands as a "tail" is really multilayered and multivocal. If seen as the end piece of a larger whole, this "tail" was important yet not important, belonging yet not really belonging, Spanish but not really Spanish. From this initial phase we can already see some of the inherent tensions and ambiguities found in Borderlands life. The Borderlands people of New Spain north of el Río Grande were not really living within the Spanish Empire and its thriving cities like Lima, Mexico City, and Buenos Aires but were instead a part of the crown's periphery. These Borderlands people were technically Spanish but had also intermarried with

---

5. John Francis Bannon, *Bolton and the Spanish Borderlands* (Norman: University of Oklahoma Press, 1964) 3.

6. Ibid.

7. Herbert Eugene Bolton, "Significance of the Borderlands," *Wider Horizons of American History,* 56.

8. Ibid., 57.

Indians and with Africans and were in a sense very different people from their "pure blood" Spanish descendant sisters and brothers to the south. They were under the supposed protection of the Spanish military forces but more often than not were at the mercy of Apaches and Euro-American settlers hungry for land.

Bolton's pioneering research in the as yet unexamined Mexican archives of the time, undertaken in the early part of this century, showed that these northern Borderlands territories were settled by the Spanish crown with a specific purpose and a deliberate method. Bolton describes the use by Spain of what he calls "pioneering agencies."[9] He identifies these agencies as the *presidio* (military garrison), the *villa* (civilian settlement), and the *misión* (religious mission). This is significant to note because it points to the creation of a new society, economic system, culture, and religion that were indeed on the fringes of the Spanish world that helped to create them. Spain wanted the Borderlands to serve as a buffer against the military aggressions of foreign powers aimed at the rich silver mines of the South. This was the primary purpose of the Borderlands, and as long as this was carried out the people who inhabited these lands were left on the fringes. They were in a very real sense an invisible or marginal part of New Spain's politics, economy, religion, and society. This marginality had become so much a part of the Borderlands reality that it helps to explain why Mexico, after its independence from Spain, was willing to open its northern territories with such few restrictions to the Euro-American settlers. The paradigm for an ambiguous existence began to be created over four centuries ago in the Borderlands of the Spanish crown. Unfortunately, this paradigm is still very real in the Borderlands of the twentieth century in the United States.

The Issue of Race

The issue of race became one of the main components of the Borderlands paradigm and still influences the lives of today's Borderlands Latinas and Latinos. To examine how this issue played itself out, I will analyze its development and impact in the Borderlands state of Texas. Most whites who first met Tejanos in the 1820s had never had prior experiences with Mexicans.[10] Yet the significant issue is that, despite the fact that Mexicans as a people were so new to the Euro-American settlers of the Borderlands, "their reaction to them upon contact was contemptuous, many thinking Mexicans abhorrent."[11] How and why did this happen?

Southwestern historian Arnoldo De León gives a number of persuasive reasons for the importance of race in the Borderlands paradigm. For ex-

---

9. Ibid., 55–106.
10. Arnoldo De León, *They Called Them Greasers* (Austin: University of Texas Press, 1983) 1.
11. Ibid.

ample, he points to the English religious suspicion of and contempt for Spaniards, which can be traced to King Henry VIII's break with Rome. He also cites the Elizabethan distaste for the racial mixing to be found in the Iberian Peninsula between Spaniards and Moors. For De León the result of these historical influences was that Mexicans were seen as doubly suspect: they were not only heirs to Spain's Catholicism but also, to make matters worse, they were a mixed people. The racial issue was intensified because the English saw the Mexican native peoples as "degenerate creatures: un-Christian, uncivilized and racially impure."[12] Mexicans were a racial mixture of Spanish ancestors, Mexican natives, North American natives, and African slaves, and that fueled a racism among the Euro-American settlers that led to crucial political and religious decisions. These decisions changed life on the Borderlands forever and opened a new historical chapter for this region.

De León does a thorough job of examining the newspapers of the mid-to-late nineteenth century, which made public the racial attitudes of the early Euro-American settlers.[13] However, it is the rhetoric of the founders of what was to become the Republic of Texas in 1839 that best reflects the mentality that would become dominant in this Borderlands state. It seemed that in Texas all the elements of manifest destiny fused into a single nationalist movement,[14] within which were echoed the sentiments being expressed in the newly expanding nation. Stephen F. Austin clearly stated the agenda of the Euro-American settlers to be imposed on the Borderlands. He declared, "My object, the sole and only desire of my ambitions since I first saw Texas, was to redeem it from the wilderness—to settle it with an intelligent, honorable and interprising [sic] people."[15] Austin's ideas were echoed by another Texan hero, Sam Houston. In an 1835 speech to the citizens of Texas, who were contemplating the creation of a new republic, Houston addressed the worries about the Mexican population. In so doing, he provided a very clear statement revealing the racial demarcations found in the minds of these settlers. He said, "The vigor of the descendants of the sturdy north will never mix with the phlegm of the indolent Mexicans, no matter how long we may live among them."[16] In essence, then, the voices of these early Euro-American settlers in Texas were very much synchronized with those being raised in the Congress of the United States and in major newspapers like the *Washington Union,* which boasted, "The march

---

12. Ibid., 5.

13. De León's *They Called Them Greasers* is a well-documented source for examining the racial attitudes of the Anglo settlers in Texas, using primary source material from the nineteenth century. De León also examines other effects of these attitudes in his *Tejanos and the Numbers Game* (Albuquerque: University of New Mexico Press, 1989) and *Mexican Americans in Texas* (Arlington Heights, Tex.: Harlan-Davidson, 1993).

14. Norman A. Graebner, *Manifest Destiny* (Indianapolis: Bobbs-Merrill, 1968) xxvii.

15. De León, *Greasers,* 3.

16. Cited in ibid., 7.

of the Anglo-Saxon race is onward. . . . They must accomplish their destiny, spreading far and wide the principles of self-government."[17]

While we must keep in mind that North America's mission to humanity was not a new concept, the generation of the 1840s "was the first to attach to it territorial expansion,"[18] and this meant that the Euro-American settlers had to deal with those people already inhabiting the lands they sought to conquer. For the early settlers of the territories of northern Mexico, the racial differences between the peoples of Texas were clearly marked, as evidenced by the writings of Austin and Houston. Even more specifically, Austin's mission statement provides a plan of action: before him lay a wilderness to be conquered and tamed by a more enterprising, more intelligent, racially pure, and divinely chosen Christian people; a wilderness that had been, until the arrival of the Euro-American settlers, untamed and mismanaged by a people who were "religious pagans, purposelessly indolent and carefree, sexually remiss, degenerate, depraved, and questionably human."[19] That is why "what removed all taint of injustice and oppression from the Texas question was the knowledge that the vast majority of Texans [meaning the Euro-American settlers] favored annexation to the United States."[20] Mexicans' capacity for self-government was questioned by both Washington and the new settlers, which meant that the determining cry calling for annexation would not be in Spanish.

The Role of the Church

Like the Spanish before them, the Euro-American settlers in the eighteenth-century Borderlands brought the church with them as an agent of conquest. Further, the Protestant church of these new colonizers not only supported the racial component of the Borderlands paradigm but also adopted it in its mission work. The Christian Church (Disciples of Christ) was one Protestant denomination in Texas that can serve as an example of what such a philosophy for mission among Borderlands peoples looked like.

The historical primary source material regarding the Disciples of Christ in Texas is scant but very revealing. In 1888 a Disciples Mexican mission was started with the hope that it might spread the Disciples movement into Mexico.[21] This tells us that right from the start the idea was not to evangelize the Tejanos of San Antonio but to move into Mexican territory. The Mexican population found in Texas was not a focus for the mission the Disciples were undertaking. Instead, the Mexicans of Texas were pushed aside,

17. Cited in Graebner, *Manifest Destiny*, xix.
18. Ibid., xix.
19. Cited in De León, *Greasers*, 15.
20. Graebner, *Manifest Destiny*, xxxii.
21. Carter E. Boren, *Religion on the Texas Frontier* (San Antonio: Naylor, 1968) 292.

thus perpetuating the marginality of church life that had existed under Catholic Spain and that would continue under the Protestant United States.

In the first thirty years of the Disciples' work in Texas, the development of Latino congregations was slow, intermittent, and haphazard. Records show that, despite the fact that between 1904 and 1927 eleven new Mexican American churches were started, more than half were then closed due to lack of autochthonous leadership. It was to be another eighteen years between the founding of the church in McAllen (1927) and the next new church in Brownsville (1945). One cannot but wonder how much the attitudes of Euro-American Disciples working with Mexican Americans caused such slow and uneven growth. In his book about Disciples in Texas, Charles Boren says:

The seasonal occupational migrations of the Mexican population have always made the work of organized religion among [Mexicans] a tenuous process. [Yet] a larger factor explaining the insignificant progress of the Texas Disciples has been a lack of social concern for the Mexican population, the absence of a liberality in financial support and failure to appreciate the philosophy of missions.[22]

While Boren does not explain what this "philosophy of missions" among Texas Disciples was, the 1928 report of the United Christian Missionary Society to the denomination contains some very clear and explicit statements that can provide some clues. In this report the understanding of Disciples mission work in Texas with the Mexican American population was termed the "Mexican Problem." The report states:

The "Mexican Problem" is ever present with us. It is inescapable. The border line between Mexico and the United States is 1,833 miles long. It is a political rather than a natural barrier and is therefore artificial and easily crossed.... The Mexican population [1928] in the United States is easily 1,500,000 [with] fully 400,000 of these living in Texas.... The Christianization and Americanization of this large body of alien people is a task for the whole church.[23]

The language used by those in the Texas mission field, those who described the work as a "Mexican Problem," must be carefully considered when analyzing the failure of the Disciples in Texas to develop large and numerous Mexican American churches. A connection can be made between the attitudes De León identifies as prevalent in Texas in the mid–nineteenth century and the attitudes found later among Euro-American Disciples leaders involved in church work in Texas. What we find in this denominational publication are the same ideas held by the Anglo settlers of the state. The church, like the early settlers, felt it had before it an inferior people who in the words of one missionary were "ignorant, superstitious and with a low

---

22. Ibid., 295–96.
23. United Christian Missionary Society, *Survey of Service* (St. Louis: Christian Board of Publication, 1928) 128, 129.

standard of morals."[24] This meant that the ultimate goal of the Disciples as they dealt with this "Mexican Problem" was to "Christianize and Americanize." It was to remake the recipients of the mission into the image of the missionary.

Yet the church did not take this "task" seriously, as shown by the fact that no materials or supplies in Spanish were produced and especially by the fact that there was never any intentional recruitment of Mexican Americans for the ministry. The mentality prevalent here favored a philosophy of mission that perceived church work with such a population group as destined for failure, even perhaps as a waste of resources. These ideas in turn fostered an obvious lack of interest and commitment of human and monetary resources by the denomination, which only served to help keep a people, and the few Mexican American Disciples congregations that did exist, in the margins of the church's mission.

These Mexican American Disciples congregations were never embraced by denominational structures or processes, and they began to form the "tail" of what was a thriving and growing denomination of the American western frontier at the turn of the century. The Mexican American Disciples churches in Texas were further isolated because church starts in the other Borderlands states of Colorado, New Mexico, California, and Arizona were (and remain to this day) almost nonexistent. The only change occurred in California, which had its first Latino Disciples church start in the mid-1970s.

The Impact of Culture and Society on Faith

The inability of Disciples in Texas to reach Mexicans and to nurture numerous, thriving congregations stands in stark contrast to the denomination's immense national growth in the nineteenth century. The Disciples grew at twice the rate of the nation's population in the post–Civil War era. Beginning with a base of 22,000 in 1832, they grew to 188,000 by 1850; 350,000 by 1870; and 1,120,000 by 1900.[25] What must be considered in looking at these statistics is that this growth was almost all in rural areas and that it followed the nation's western frontier expansion. The church represented a very "American" religion in that it spoke a culturally relevant message to a clearly defined group of people living in the United States. The Disciples were only 6 percent urban in 1890[26] and had also failed, in comparison to other denominations, to develop any significant European-language ministries to the millions of European immigrants entering the United States during this same time period.

---

24. Ibid., 127.
25. See Winifred E. Garrison, *Religion Follows the Frontier* (New York: Harper and Brothers, 1931) 199–201.
26. Ibid., 199.

So it would seem that from its beginnings the denomination carried within it the national self-perceptions that were being fostered on the frontiers of the United States as the nation moved westward and invented itself. The ideas that fed this national self-image included: a divinely chosen people called to help the inferior, racially mixed races; a homogeneous people who "melted" together to form a new nation, God's new Israel; a faith (Protestant) that was the true religion as opposed to false religions (that is, the Catholic faith); a divine right to conquer, settle, and develop land that was being wasted by an inept and nonindustrious people.

These concepts were part and parcel of that great national North American myth of the nineteenth century, the myth of manifest destiny, that took on special meaning in the 1840s, 1850s, and 1860s. The phrase "manifest destiny" itself was coined in 1845 by a magazine and newspaper editor, John L. O'Sullivan, but it had been present in the national ethos since the Revolution of 1776. O'Sullivan, with an eye to national glory, joined the terms "manifest" and "destiny" into one phrase in newspaper articles in which, when urging the annexation of Texas, he wrote of "our manifest destiny to overspread the continent allotted by Providence."[27] The idea of a manifest destiny encompasses a variety of ideologies, including nationalism, imperialism, and expansionism, that became rationalizations and justifications for the political decisions being taken by the U.S. government. This was particularly real in the administrations of John Tyler and James Polk, when in "fewer than one thousand days, Tyler, Polk and their supporters pushed the boundaries of the United States to the Rio Grande, the Pacific, and the forty-ninth parallel."[28] The Indian Removal Bill of 1830 and the war with Mexico of 1846–48 were in many ways fueled by the cry of a nation's manifest destiny. It was a self-assured cry that made native peoples and Mexicans strangers in their own lands. It was a cry in which racial factors were interwoven into national policy, often supported by a religious rhetoric that was at its core racist. It was a belief that the God of the New Israel taking shape on the North American continent had no use for red and brown people.

These notions formed the base of the culture and society in which the Disciples flourished in the late nineteenth and early twentieth centuries. Once that is realized, the reluctance by the Disciples to work with people who represented all they were not can be better understood. This reluctance promoted the invisibility of Mexican Americans in Texas, which in turn led to a policy of no support of missions, no recruitment of Mexican Americans for the ministry, and no development of materials and supplies in Spanish for religious education.

---

27. Charles H. Brown, *Agents of Manifest Destiny* (Chapel Hill: University of North Carolina Press, 1980) 16.

28. Thomas R. Hietala, *Manifest Destiny: Anxious Aggrandizement in Late Jacksonian America* (Ithaca, N.Y.: Cornell University Press, 1985) 2.

This inability to see a people, to recognize the legitimacy and validity of their difference, led the Euro-American Disciples to create a philosophy of mission that was nuanced with the cultural values and national self-image of their day and age. It was a mission that sought to remake a people in the image of the missionary. It was a mission in which the national myths of the culture were infused with the theological concepts of "divine mission" and "chosen people," in which Christianization meant Americanization. It was a philosophy of mission that has created, almost a century later, a Hispanic church with a dearth of ministerial leadership, poor funding, and haphazard and uneven growth. As the Hispanic Disciples face the next century, their task will be to use the lessons of the past with the skills of the postmodern world to open the way to greater participation within the denomination so that their voice will no longer be ignored or denied its right to speak their story.

3

The Lesson of the Gibeonites

A Proposal for Dialogic Attention as a Strategy for Reading the Bible

Francisco O. García-Treto

I

> *But as for the towns of these peoples that the Lord your God is giving you as an inheritance, you must not let anything that breathes remain alive. You shall annihilate them—the Hittites and the Amorites, the Canaanites and the Perizzites, the Hivites and the Jebusites—just as the Lord your God has commanded, so that they may not teach you to do all the abhorrent things that they do for their gods, and you thus sin against the Lord your God.*
> —Deut 20:16–18

That the Bible has been seen to foster xenophobia, to justify oppression and persecution of "the other," or even to promote genocide cannot surprise anyone acquainted in the most general way with the history of the use of the Bible from the very beginnings down to our own time. Those of us whose histories and cultures are rooted in the encounter of the Iberian and the native American worlds, which for some was discovery and for others conquest, can amply attest to that. In 1513, a conclave of Spanish theologians gathered in Valladolid heard Martín Fernández de Enciso compare the papal donation of the Indies to the divine grant of the promised land to the Jews. As Lewis Hanke puts it, Fernández de Enciso concluded that

the king might very justly send men to require those idolatrous Indians to hand over their land to him, for it was given to him by the pope. If the Indians would not do this, he might justly wage war against them, kill them and enslave those captured in war, *precisely as Joshua treated the inhabitants of the land of Canaan.*[1]

---

1. Lewis Hanke, *All Mankind Is One: A Study of the Disputation between Bartolomé de Las Casas and Juan Ginés de Sepúlveda in 1550 on the Intellectual and Religious Capacity of the American Indians* (De Kalb: Northern Illinois University Press, 1974) 35; emphasis added.

The product of that conclave was the *Requerimiento,* a legal ultimatum that was to be read to the Indians, informing them (in Spanish) that the pope had, with divine authority, granted their lands and persons to the Spanish monarchs, to whose rule they must immediately submit or be subjected to the horror of total war. The cynicism with which the *Requerimiento* was applied by the conquistadores does not diminish its importance as a theological, or, one might say, an exegetical, artifact: it is simply the first product of the equation of the conquering Europeans (whether Spanish Catholics or English Protestants) with the Israelites of the biblical conquest, God's chosen people to whom God has granted the promised land,[2] an equation that indelibly shaped the historical experience and culture of America. Of course, as Fernández de Enciso made explicit, that equation also cast the Native Americans in the sad role of the Canaanites, a role involving subjection to slavery, oppression, and genocide which also forms part of our historical experience.

It is not enough, however, to fault simply the conquistadores or the Puritans (or proponents of apartheid, white supremacists, and so on) for an arrogant reading of the Bible. The real problem lies in the undeniable presence of a core of problematic materials in the Bible where the obliteration of "the other" is put forward as a divine command. Simply to ignore these passages is not enough. I propose to take a step toward developing a method for dealing with them by taking up the scene presented in Joshua 9, where in the narrative context of the Deuteronomic idealization of the conquest the requirement of the "ban" is successfully subverted by the Canaanite inhabitants of Gibeon. I shall argue that the ruse of the Gibeonites is one of many places where the astute reader can hear not one single and oppressive monologic discourse but a dialogizing voice that subverts and simultaneously opens up the meaning of the text.

The judgment that the Deuteronomic authors' ideal of the *herem,* or "ban," of the entire Canaanite population of Israel is "utopian and is indeed unheard of in the historical accounts of Israel" is practically a commonplace of Old Testament scholarship, most recently restated by Moshe Weinfeld.[3] The "ban" as an ideological construct derives from circles involved in the intensely nationalistic patriotism of the Hezekiah-Josiah era and reflects, according to Weinfeld, not so much a true picture of historical reality as "the bitter struggle with the Canaanite religion and culture" of the ninth to the sixth centuries B.C.E. in Israel, a struggle that Wein-

---

2. Lewis Hanke (*Aristotle and the American Indians: A Study in Race Prejudice in the Modern World* [Chicago: Henry Regnery, 1959] 100) quotes the following resolutions passed by a New England assembly in the 1640s: "1. The earth is the Lord's and the fullness thereof. Voted. 2. The Lord may give the earth or any part of it to his chosen people. Voted. 3. We are his chosen people. Voted."

3. Moshe Weinfeld, "Deuteronomy, Book of," *The Anchor Bible Dictionary* (6 vols.; ed. David Noel Freedman; New York: Doubleday, 1992) 2:179.

feld calls a *Kulturkampf*.[4] While in basic agreement with this judgment, I would like to append two observations to it, which become basic for setting the direction of this essay. The first is that, utopian ideology or not, it is precisely the "Deuteronomic theology" emerging from that struggle that played perhaps the single most important role in shaping the biblical traditions, and—as a corollary to it—that a vision of a God whose command encourages genocide is not at all foreign to the biblical traditions. The second is that there are passages, in several instances within the conquest traditions, that betray a profound sense of embarrassment at the "survival" of the Canaanites, a survival that by the ideological standard cited above was an impossibility.[5] Contemporary archaeology and linguistics, to mention only two of the relevant disciplines, take, on the other hand, as a matter of course the difficulty, if not the impossibility, of distinguishing "Israel" from "Canaan" in material culture or language. And yet the biblical tradition has to deal with facts such as that of the "survival" of major Canaanite urban populations within Israel in the account of the aftermath of the conquest in Judg 1:27–36. There the traditionists, in a very distinctive strategy, extenuate the survival by explaining that those populations were subsequently enslaved (submitted to forced labor). Of particular interest in this respect is the treatment of the Gibeonites, specifically in the story of their successful deception of Joshua and the men of Israel in Joshua 9, by means of which they obtain a covenant that protects them, albeit reduced to the status of "hewers of wood and drawers of water" for the congregation of Israel.

A further complication arises when the ideological construct of the "ban" is itself seen over against the universalistic stance of biblical monotheism, which produced, in passages such as Gen 1:26–29, expressions of the lofty ideal of seeing (all) human beings as created in the image of God and thus free, as J. Severino Croatto says, "in their ontological radicality and in their projection onto the world, in their essence and in their vocation."[6] Croatto points out the contradiction implicit between this passage and Joshua 9 when he uses them both to indicate the existence of a gap between ideology and implementation in the social praxis of ancient Israel:

The Pentateuch tells us that the Hebrews did not practice slavery among themselves—surely as a reflection of the theology of the Exodus, lived at the level of the

---

4. Ibid. For a fuller treatment of this subject, see also Moshe Weinfeld, *The Promise of the Land: The Inheritance of the Land of Canaan by the Israelites* (Berkeley: University of California Press, 1993), esp. 76–98.

5. "There was in any case an embarrassment about the Gibeonites living in the midst of Israel," say Robert G. Boling and G. Ernest Wright, *Joshua* (Anchor Bible 6; Garden City, N.Y.: Doubleday, 1982) 279.

6. J. Severino Croatto, *Exodus: A Hermeneutics of Freedom* (Maryknoll, N.Y.: Orbis Books, 1981) 35.

people. Even when a Hebrew sold himself as a slave to another, the latter had to free him in the seventh year (legislative texts in Lev. 25:39ff. and Deut. 15:21ff.). Curiously, the acquisition or retention of slaves "from among the nations that are round about you" (Lev. 25:44; cf. Jos. 9:23, 27) was quite permissible. In this case the "vocation to freedom," to "be more," claimed for all people in the ideological passage of Genesis, was not implemented in Israelite social praxis. It always happens that praxis draws inspiration from an ideal or a worldview, but it never attains their total actualization.[7]

That is to say, the discourse in Joshua 9, as in many places in the Bible, is conflicted: it betrays by its moments of embarrassment the gap between ideology and praxis, as well as the tension between incompatible ideologies. Danna Nolan Fewell has referred to what she describes as "a subversive descant fostering ambiguity about identity"[8] in chapter 9 and other instances in Joshua (the story of Rahab in chaps. 2 and 6 in particular), where the Deuteronomistic program's clear-cut definitions of "insider" and "outsider" (along with their brutally simplistic outcomes) are overturned by "outsiders" who become "insiders." In these stories, "fluid identity boundaries render nationalistic categories ambivalent and call into question the [Deuteronomic] obsession with annihilating outsiders."[9] In a literary study of the Book of Joshua, L. Daniel Hawk rightly points to the intertextuality that shapes the narrative of the Gibeonite covenant, saying that it "deconstructs the plot of obedient Israel, so recently affirmed by the victory over Ai and the ceremony at Mounts Ebal and Gerizim," and intertextually creates "an ominous mood" by "appropriating themes and motifs of Moses' speech during the covenant renewal on the plains of Moab (Deut. 29:1–29)."[10] While fully agreeing with Hawk both on the importance of intertextuality for the framing of this narrative and on the evident echo of the Deuteronomic voice heard in Moses' speech on the plains of Moab, this essay will suggest that the narrative of the Gibeonite covenant is intertextually more complicated than that and also that it approaches being polyphonic and dialogic, in a Bakhtinian sense.[11]

---

7. Ibid., 36.

8. Danna Nolan Fewell, "Joshua," *The Woman's Bible Commentary* (ed. Carol A. Newsom and Sharon H. Ringe; Louisville: Westminster/John Knox Press, 1992) 63.

9. Ibid., 66.

10. L. Daniel Hawk, *Every Promise Fulfilled: Contesting Plots in Joshua* (Louisville: Westminster/John Knox Press, 1991) 88.

11. For an excellent discussion of these terms, see Gary Saul Morson and Caryl Emerson, *Mikhail Bakhtin: Creation of a Poetics* (Stanford, Calif.: Stanford University Press, 1990), esp. 231–68. It is well known that Bakhtin applies those terms, strictly speaking, only to the work of F. Dostoyevsky and that, again strictly speaking, they "belong" only in criticism of the modern novel. It is also clear that Bakhtin's categories are useful far beyond the strict bounds to which he chose to limit them and that their application to biblical narrative is a fruitful area only beginning to be explored. See most recently Walter L. Reed, *Dialogues of the Word: The Bible as Literature according to Bakhtin* (New York: Oxford University Press, 1993).

II

But he said, "Your brother came deceitfully, and he has taken away your blessing."

—Gen 27:35

If indeed, as Hawk points out, Joshua 9 reverberates intertextually with echoes of Deuteronomy 29,[12] these are not the only echoes the reader senses. Were that the case, the story would bear an exclusively monologic stamp and follow one of two inevitable alternatives to a conclusion where either the Gibeonites are exterminated or Israel is punished for temporizing with the draconian terms of the Mosaic covenant. The first surprise is that the narrative in Joshua 9 refuses to follow either path and leads instead to a compromise in which, while neither side comes off unscathed, both survive. The monophonic drone of the exclusive covenant, which defines the inhabitants of the Land as objects of genocidal "ethnic cleansing" as a matter of principle, has indeed been overlaid by Fewell's "subversive descant" as the Gibeonites take for themselves the role of subjects of their own survival. The time has come to identify the notes that make up that descant.

Susan Niditch describes the folkloric character of "the trickster" as "a subtype of the underdog" who "brings about change in a situation via trickery," a type of folk hero well attested in many world cultures and particularly well documented in Native American and West African folk traditions.[13] Like their West African counterparts, Niditch points out,

biblical tricksters...display some of the same ambiguities in motivation and realization of goals. They never gain full control of the situation around them and often escape difficulties in a less than noble way. Their tale does not end with unequivocal success, but they survive to trick again—and, indeed, are survivors par excellence.[14]

The archetypal (though by no means the only) trickster in the biblical traditions is Jacob, and the signal example of the trickster tale is in Genesis 27, where Jacob, by deceit and disguise, steals the primogeniture from his brother Esau by deceiving blind Isaac on his deathbed. Niditch identifies in this tale an instance of a morphological pattern (another example of the same pattern is Gen 12:10–20, where Abraham tricks Pharaoh by pretending that Sarah is his sister) whose elements she details in figure 1,[15] which I have slightly adapted.

---

12. Hawk, *Every Promise,* 88–90.

13. Some well-known trickster figures in the folklore of the Americas are the Afro-Caribbean Annancy, Afro–North American Brer Rabbit, Pedro Ordemalas (Urdemalas) in Hispanic North America, and Coyote in the Native American traditions of the southwestern United States.

14. Susan Niditch, *Underdogs and Tricksters: A Prelude to Biblical Folklore* (San Francisco: Harper and Row, 1987) xi.

15. Ibid., 100.

Figure 1

Morphology	*Typology in Genesis 27*
Marginal status:	Younger son is not meant to receive blessing; his father plans to give it to the elder son.
Deception:	Younger son disguises himself to make his father think he is the elder.
Improved status:	Younger son receives blessing.
Deception uncovered:	He is found out.
Return to outsider status:	Younger son flees and performs a new series of tricks.

While the connection of the motif of the Gibeonites' ruse in Joshua 9 with the patriarchal trickster stories is not lost on modern commentators, not much is usually made of it, as for example, by Robert Boling in the Anchor Bible, who limits himself to observing that "the trickery motif was a favorite in the formation of the patriarchal heritage: Jacob and Esau (Genesis 27), Jacob and Laban (Genesis 30), Shechem and the sons of Jacob (Genesis 34)."[16] I propose a closer look, taking in order each of the categories of Niditch's morphological pattern.

Marginal Status

In the Jacob story, the central issue is primogeniture, that is, the preeminence of one brother over the other as successor to the father as head of the family and possessor of its property and customary prerogatives, grazing rights or the use of certain wells, for example. The impending death of Isaac and his announced intention of conferring the blessing on Esau precipitate the critical situation for Jacob and for Rebekah, who prefers Jacob and who in fact functions in this story as the intellectual author of the deception of her blind husband, just as her son Jacob is the actual perpetrator of the trick. Genesis 27, then, presents the reader with a compound trickster, a conspiracy of deceit between two (at least) members of the family group who refuse to accept the paternal determination of status and set out to subvert it.

Joshua 9 also begins with the de facto announcement of an imposed fate, as the inhabitants of Canaan become aware of the Israelites' hostile intentions and apparent invincibility, which they intend to counter rather unimaginatively by all-out war (vv. 1 and 2), an approach that the reader

---

16. Boling and Wright, *Joshua,* 263.

of Joshua knows to be doomed to failure. The inhabitants of Gibeon, on the other hand, see an alternative that will permit their survival: like Jacob and Rebekah, they set out in concert to subvert the oppressive project that marginalizes and threatens to annihilate them by *stealing* the covenant, much as the patriarch had stolen the blessing. The text of verse 4 denotes their activity (*vayya'asu gam-hemma be'e'orma*) in very significant terms. First, *gam-hemma* (they also) refers to the activity of Joshua in the victories of Jericho and Ai, both of which had been won by unconventional methods, the latter in particular by deceit and cunning after a more conventional direct approach had failed (see chaps. 7 and 8). "They also" then, deciding that the pragmatic way that gets results is best, desert their neighbors of the Canaanite coalition and resolve to "act with cunning" (*vayya'asu . . . be'e'orma*). The meaning of the latter term ranges in English translation from "treachery" (for example, Exod 21:14) to "shrewdness" (for example, Prov 1:4) to "prudence" (for example, Prov 8:5)[17] and is closely related to *'arôm,* the term used in Gen 3:1 to describe another archetypal trickster (the snake) as "crafty." But, as Niditch also points out in her analysis, by placing the archetypal figure of Joseph the wise alongside that of Jacob the trickster, there is, for trickster and wise man, "a boundary where the two roles meet."[18] The use of the same verb to denote the *craftiness* of the trickster and the *prudence* of the wise is neither accidental nor trivial. For the Gibeonites, unwilling to accept the Israelite project that would marginalize them literally out of existence, the only open alternative is to subvert that project, to steal a covenant they could not otherwise have obtained and, in doing so, to follow the way of the trickster to the most prudent goal of the wise, that of survival. Does not Qohelet, that quintessential expression of pragmatic wisdom, after all say: "But whoever is joined with all the living has hope, *for a living dog is better than a dead lion*" (9:4)? Significantly, the narrative of Joshua 9 makes place for the Gibeonites' voice, actively claiming the right to their human existence, no matter what the God of Israel has said or what that God's followers have proposed to do. They thus join the chorus of other survivors, both wise and crafty, with whom the biblical tradition is replete: with Jacob and Joseph stand also the likes of Rahab, Ruth, and Esther, among many others.[19]

---

17. As translated in the NRSV. I will return to "prudence" as a significant term in the latter part of this essay.

18. Niditch, *Underdogs,* 120. See her entire fourth chapter, "Jacob and Joseph: Patterns and Content, Digging Deeper."

19. The trickster motif has been put forward most recently by Claudia Camp, "Feminist Theological Hermeneutics: Canon and Christian Identity," *Searching the Scriptures,* vol. 1: *A Feminist Introduction* (ed. Elisabeth Schüssler Fiorenza; New York: Crossroad, 1993) 154–71. Camp suggests the strategy of "reading as a trickster" or "reading as a strange woman" as one of three complementary models for the reconceptualization of biblical authority (the other two are the "dialogical authority" and the "metaphor" models). Reading as a trickster/strange woman, for Camp, entails "first, claiming identity with those at the

Deception

In both cases the form of the deception is a claim to be someone else (Esau or people "from a far country")—that is, someone who is either entitled to the blessing or not excluded from the covenant—and significantly in both cases the means of the deception involve food and clothing that are represented as being other than they are. Blind Isaac will be taken in by the taste of Rebekah's faux game stew, by the smell of Esau's clothes worn by Jacob, by the feel of goat hair on the smooth-skinned trickster's hands. Joshua and the leaders of the congregation are similarly fooled by the sight of worn-out (the adjective *balim/balot* appears four times in vv. 4 and 5) clothing, shoes, sacks, and wineskins and by the dry and moldy provisions the sacks and wineskins contained, provisions that they taste as well (v. 14). There is a certain irony in this when one remembers that Gibeon was in fact an agricultural center renowned for its production of fine wine. But more significantly, these elements serve to remind the reader that the primary issue in the narrative is economic, that it is over possession of the bountiful land that the children of Israel are prepared to commit genocide. The Gibeonites, by their choice of deception—instead of, say, pretending to be non-Israelite (for example, Kenite) Yahweh worshipers—demonstrate their grasp of the issue. They set out to convince Joshua and the elders of the congregation that, as travelers from a distant land, they pose no threat to Israel's claim to the conquest of Canaan. Their project sets out not only to subvert the children of Israel's goal of extermination but also to undermine the stated "religious" rationale for it by successfully laying bare its economic roots, the appropriation of the "vineyards you did not plant," an expression that Deuteronomic discourse often uses as a stereotyped reference to the bounty of the conquest.

Improved Status

By stealing his father's blessing, Jacob, the second son, becomes irrevocably invested with the right of the firstborn: "Be lord over your brothers, and may your mother's sons bow down to you" (Gen 27:29). It is important to note that the blessing, once given, is not susceptible to being recalled, even if it was obtained by deception, as Isaac has to explain with dismay to Esau: "Your brother came deceitfully, and he has taken away your blessing" (Gen 27:35). Whatever happens now—and Jacob finds himself in danger for his life as soon as his father dies—the blessing is his, as well as the status it confers. Similarly, the Gibeonites cheat their way into a guaranteed survival among the Israelites by obtaining a covenant under the pretense that

margins and, second, willingness to read against the text, to read subversively." The resulting "hermeneutics of strangeness teaches us to tell the sameness, to undercut the apparently absolute opposition between good and evil; to illuminate instead their paradoxical, but experientially validated, unity; to affirm the disorder that energizes our struggle against unjust order" (167).

they are travelers from far away. They say to Joshua: "Your servants have come from a very far country. . . . We are your servants; come now, make a treaty with us" (vv. 9, 11); and they succeed in deceiving him: "And Joshua made peace with them, guaranteeing their lives by a treaty; and the leaders of the congregation swore an oath to them" (v. 15). Once again, the improved status—in this case the improvement is from designated victims of genocide to excepted survivors—is irrevocable, even when the deception that obtained it is uncovered. In the case of the Gibeonites, this narrative element functions as a sort of etiology of survival, a post facto explanation of a historical reality whose existence contradicts the ideological construct and that demonstrates the historical failure, or the nonexistence, of the "ban."

Deception Uncovered

The trickster is, characteristically, discovered because trickster stories are not, as Patrick Taylor has said, "romance stories."[20] Not only does the trickster "hero" operate by employing forms of villainy unthinkable in the action of the romantic hero, but the trickster's victory is tragic, often Pyrrhic, and never unmixed. Taylor concludes: "The trickster tale, though it may conclude with a temporary restoration of equilibrium, manifests a tragic ordering of existence: the hero is also a villain, and equilibrium always remains shaky."[21]

Jacob's trick is discovered almost immediately, as soon as Esau returns to Isaac's bedside with the game stew he had dutifully prepared: "Then Isaac trembled violently, and said, 'Who was it then that hunted game and brought it to me, and I ate it all before you came, and I have blessed him?— yes, and blessed he shall be!'" (Gen 27:33). The Gibeonites' deception becomes obvious to Israel when, after only three days' journey, they reach the territory of the people who had falsely claimed to be "from a very far country": "So the Israelites set out and reached their cities on the third day. Now their cities were Gibeon, Chephirah, Beeroth, and Kiriath-jearim" (Josh 9:17).

Return to Outsider Status

In classic trickster-story form, the conclusion of each of these tales is ambiguous (or, as in the words of Taylor cited above, "tragic"). That is to say, in a narrative that deals with the resolution of a conflict of status, the winner ends up with a new but still ambiguous status. Jacob is now the heir, the bearer of the irrevocable blessing, but he is also the fugitive, the exile

---

20. "In some European fairy tales, villainy is liquidated by a virtuous hero (the good prince kisses the poisoned Snow White). A romantic narrative resolves the contradiction (villainy) in a sequence of events leading to a harmonious ending (equilibrium)" (Patrick Taylor, *The Narrative of Liberation: Perspectives on Afro-Caribbean Literature, Popular Culture, and Politics* [Ithaca, N.Y.: Cornell University Press, 1989] 144).

21. Ibid.

who must flee from his brother, who intends to murder him. The Gibeonites have eluded extermination but have done so at the price of becoming an "accursed" group within Israel, destined to slavery and to becoming "hewers of wood and drawers of water" for Yahweh's sanctuary, or in modern parlance, an oppressed minority within the people of Yahweh.

III

Yes, and blessed he shall be!
—Gen 27:33

If these stories are considered by themselves, it is perhaps enough to say that they conclude with the establishment of something like Taylor's "shaky equilibrium" and to recall that they resound with Fewell's "subversive descant" to the oppressive monophony of their dominant tone. Hawk, for his part, sees in the stories of Rahab and of the Gibeonites "a plot of disobedience" that, besides subverting the "symbols of obedience" (among them the *herem*), "tells the story differently."[22] Hawk, however, goes no further than to acknowledge that the stories are told in such a way as to "elicit sympathy" for Rahab and the Gibeonites,[23] even though he has already observed the amazing fact that even Yahweh becomes involved in saving the Gibeonites. The miraculous stopping of the sun and moon at Joshua's command (Joshua 10), in fact, takes place in the battle in which Yahweh joins Israel in defense of the Gibeonites.[24]

In his book *Dialogues of the Word*, Walter L. Reed applies the Bakhtinian concept of the "chronotope"—which he prefers to call instead a "paradigm of communication"—to characterize the three basic categories of genre that make up the Hebrew Bible: law, prophecy, and wisdom.[25] In the paradigm of law, Reed says, "God meets with his people personally and continuously," eliciting in dialogue a response of assent and obedience. Even in that paradigm, however, "there are significant moments when God allows his purposes to be shaped, even changed, by human objections to the way he has initially presented them."[26] The second paradigm, that of prophecy, presents an Israel "in perennial crisis." It is a paradigm formed by an ethos of separation, whose emblem is the drawn sword. Through the prophetic proclamation of "God's terrible divisions of the nation," a remnant of Israel is being preserved to serve as the basis for Israel's regeneration as a whole.[27] The third paradigm, that of wisdom, is by far the

---

22. Hawk, *Every Promise*, 92.
23. Ibid., 93.
24. Ibid., 91.
25. Reed, *Dialogues*.
26. Ibid., 53.
27. Ibid., 56.

most universal and inclusive, says Reed, as well as the most secular. Wisdom is learned from aliens, from women—even personified as feminine, as in Proverbs 8 and 9—and prefers to focus on the order of creation rather than on the history of a people, preferring the context of civil order to that of the conflict of power as its arena. "Wisdom," says Reed, characteristically "celebrates and advocates a human responsiveness deeply rooted in general human experience and the order of nature."[28] Besides identifying "chronotopes" (Reed's "paradigms of communication"), Bakhtin went on to point out that, in works such as the novel, different chronotopes interact in various ways:

Within the limits of a single work...we may notice a number of different chronotopes and complex interactions among them, specific to the given work or author; it is common moreover for one of these chronotopes to envelope or dominate the others....Chronotopes are mutually inclusive, they co-exist, they may be interwoven with, replace or oppose one another, contradict one another or find themselves in ever more complex interrelationships....The general characteristic of these interactions is that they are dialogical (in the broadest use of the word).[29]

Bringing these insights to the case of Joshua 9 and 10, we can say that the narrative of the Gibeonites' ruse and its results effectively dialogizes what would otherwise have remained monologic: Deuteronomic prophetic discourse is altered by the interjection of the pragmatic wisdom discourse of the crafty/wise trickster. That the Gibeonites' survival agenda succeeds in subverting the genocidal project the Deuteronomic Yahweh promulgated, and Israel was engaged in carrying out, is in fact a saving grace: the outsider, the "other" first defined as an undesirable alien to be exterminated from the promised land, has been heard and once heard can no longer be denied humanity or the consequent right to exist. The covenant has been changed by the challenge: while, on the one hand, the survival of the Gibeonites—and others, notably Rahab and her family—is indeed a subversion of the prophetic ideal of an exclusive covenant between Yahweh and Israel, it is, on the other hand, an extension of that covenant toward an inclusive vision that would save the God of Joshua from merciless despotism and the people of that God from unspeakable inhumanity.

In his 1991 Gifford Lectures, James Barr proposed that the neglect of natural theology—and natural theology is present throughout the Hebrew Bible—by the biblical theology movement has produced a disability of interpretation, which he illustrates at length by means of its extreme instance of the *herem*.[30] The image of a God who requires the wholesale extermina-

---

28. Ibid., 63–64.
29. M. M. Bakhtin, "Forms of Time and the Chronotope in the Novel," *The Dialogic Imagination: Four Essays by M. M. Bakhtin* (ed. Michael Holquist; Austin: University of Texas Press, 1981) 252.
30. James Barr, *Biblical Faith and Natural Theology* (Gifford Lectures for 1991; Oxford: Clarendon Press, 1993).

tion of a people "cannot be justified as the picture of a moral deity," says Barr, but "biblical theology, through its general, if not universal, ignoring of natural theology, has led to a position where the issue is not raised at all, and where it would seem wrong even to raise it at all."[31] Not only does that stance hamper interpretation by making it ignore what is otherwise an evident moral problem in the depiction of God, but, as Barr goes on to say,

The attitudes engendered by attempts to justify consecration to destruction spill over into wide areas of religion: into the invention of a sort of racial wickedness of which there is no real evidence, into the production of views that "wickedness" justifies mass destruction, into non-discrimination between innocent and guilty, into the perception of a sort of racial guilt, and above all into the belief that religious commands override morality and that it is good for us that this should be so.[32]

There can be no doubt of the truth of Barr's observation for us, as people who live within the history that began with the conquest of the American continent by Europeans[33] and whose consciousness has been formed by the bitter ultimate consequences of monologic readings of the Bible such as that espoused by the Valladolid conclave. Clearly, cultural and religious arrogance is what led some of our sixteenth-century ancestors to oppress others in the name of God, but the passage of four centuries has not seen the passing of that arrogance. Current debate in North America over the value of cultural diversity does not lack the voices of those who call "biblical" the values of one or another religious subculture and who "prophetically" call for what amounts to a *herem* of cultural difference, seeking to suppress whatever does not meet their narrow standards. As I have suggested, a monologic reading of the Bible is neither the only nor the best one possible, and the assumption that the prophetic paradigm of communication is the only one present in the biblical text is likewise flawed and limiting. Paying attention to the dialogic moments in the biblical text itself, which subvert monologic pretensions as they appear, and to the presence there of a wisdom paradigm in which the ethical claims of a common humanity assert themselves successfully against the monologic exclusiveness of the "people of God" opens a space for new and nonoppressive readings of the Bible.

Lest this essay leave the impression that I propose that close attention to the dialogization of monologic discourse applies only to the Old Testament, let the story of Jesus' meeting with the Syrophoenician woman, particularly in its Markan version (Mark 7:24–30), serve as a coda. Jesus, surprisingly, is the one who learns a lesson in that story. He starts out by xenophobically denying the woman's desperate request for help (his help is for "the children") and instead hurling an ethnic slur at her: "dog." That,

31. Ibid., 212.
32. Ibid., 218–19.
33. See Luis N. Rivera-Pagán, *A Violent Evangelism: The Political and Religious Conquest of the Americas* (Louisville: Westminster/John Knox Press, 1992).

however, does not end the matter. Craftily/wisely, she uses his own worst word to press her claim and gracefully forces him to acknowledge her humanity and her claim: "Sir, even the *dogs* under the table eat the children's crumbs." Unlike the Matthean version, where her "great faith" is the reason given for the grant of her request and where therefore one may read the whole story as an elaborate (and, one could say, heartless) "test" of her faith, Mark has Jesus answer, "For saying that [literally 'because of that word'], go—the demon has left your daughter." It is precisely because she refuses to let the scene remain monologic, because she inserts the word that asserts her humanity and its claims upon him and that turns his rejection into dialogue, that both are helped: she with healing for her child, and he with a new and more inclusive vision of the meaning of "the children." Close attention to the many instances in which the Bible presents a similar dynamic may open the door to healing and inclusive readings for us as well.

4

In the Image and Likeness of God
Literature as Theological Reflection

Ana María Díaz-Stevens

Years before it became fashionable to use *cuentos* (stories) as a culturally sensitive psychotherapy for children[1] or as a basis for theological or philosophical reflection, my mother would gather us around the kitchen fire and, as she prepared food for our bodies, enkindle in our imaginations wondrous worlds of adventure, beauty, and goodness. Since then and after countless years of formal schooling and scholarly reflection, I have come to realize what she seemed to have known instinctively. And that is that storytelling is an art. Like other art forms, storytelling serves to express and to shape our longings and inner emotions because it speaks about the spirit and to the spirit. However, art also transcends the personal worldview to reflect the values upon which a society is either maintained or transformed.

Lukács and Reification

The century in which we live has been one of rapid research and progress in technology, accelerating thereby contact between peoples of divergent cultures and ways of life. In the process, there has been ample opportunity for reciprocal influence among societies, cultures, and worldviews as well as for diversification and proliferation of products, including those related to the world of art. Were one to judge on the basis of sheer number or quantity of production alone, there would be no doubt that modern technological advances have enhanced the literary, musical, and artistic expression of world populations competing for geographic, political, and economic turfs. Yet some argue that the essence of creativity has been lost because rampant technology has rendered artistic productions mere commodities to be packaged, bought, and sold at public auction, while others hold fast

---

1. Giuseppe Constantino, Robert G. Malgady, and Lloyd H. Rogler, *Cuento Therapy: Folktales as a Culturally Sensitive Psychotherapy for Puerto Rican Children* (Hispanic Research Center Monograph no. 12; Maplewood, N.J.: Waterfront Press, 1985).

to the notion that art still offers humanity comfort and solace as a means for securing continuity for our longings, aspirations, and quest for inner meaning.

This apparent controversy is not new. The inherent dangers of a world where the commodified object becomes more important than its originator or the person for whom it was intended were underlined by Karl Marx. Introducing the concepts of commodity fetishism and alienation, Marx analyzed the individual's inability to recognize that the forces binding him or her to unsatisfying labor are predicated upon human relationships that are not necessary. For the Hungarian thinker Georg Lukács, poems, plays, novels, and the like are the consumable items of culture and may also prove alienating, if the human activities that produce them are "made part of a second...nature impervious to human control."[2] Thus, Marx's commodity fetishism and its correlate, alienation, were pushed into a wider realm, and new concepts were introduced to include all cultural activity and other facets of human life into that world of social relations that Marx had defined.[3]

For Lukács, "reification" is the cultural analog to economic alienation, and *Aufhebung* is the process through which a situation of social freedom is attained. However, more optimistic than Marx, Lukács believed that artists, writers, and poets also had the power to offer society a way of escaping from a world in which only the status quo was perceived as rational. Precisely because they had to manipulate the abstract relationships to bring forth their creations, they had to understand somehow that the world they described was not necessary to itself but could in fact be *remade* into a

---

2. Cited in Andrew Arato and Paul Breines, *The Young Lukács and the Origins of Western Marxism* (New York: Seabury Press, 1979) 177. Paul R. Messbarger (*Social Uses of American Catholic Literature, 1884–1900* [Boston: Boston University Press] 19) refers to the "deliberate fabrication for non-artistic purposes,...a phenomenon to which we are sensitive in an era of the industrial production of mass entertainment." He cautions that "even in earlier ages such a phenomenon was not unknown; the hack is a perennial figure in the world of art. Without attributing complete cynicism to such a person, one can at least note that he works from a certain awareness of what has immediate currency, and he manipulates his materials to exploit that condition." However, Messbarger also points out that these works are not without value in a cultural-historical analysis: "Our new understanding of the ability of the dream merchants not only to satisfy but to create a market, makes it apparent that innovation and change are as likely to result from industrial and technological factors as from a simple competitive reach for a piece of the market. The entertainment industry, for all its competitiveness, requires a degree of rationalization in order to produce pre-tested elements which can then be put together in a variety of ways to suit an ever more standardized, if ever more whimsical, public" (20). An interesting example from Puerto Rican literature of how literature can act to "keep people in their place" or "liberate them" is found in Jesús Colón's short story "Kipling and I" (*A Puerto Rican in New York and Other Sketches* [New York: International Publishers, 1982] 19). One night, in effect, the author realizes that the piece of paper with Kipling's poem on it is only good to make himself a small fire where he can warm his freezing fingers.

3. See Cornel West, *The Ethical Dimensions of Marxist Thought* (New York: Monthly Review Press, 1991). See also Arato and Breines, *Young Lukács*, 203.

more just reality. That is, the same process of *Aufhebung* by which a particular historical agent acquires increased self-consciousness and overcomes alienation from reified socioeconomic circumstances can be used to negate, preserve, and transform present sociocultural circumstances and attain a situation of social freedom.[4] It should be noted, however, that the capacity of artists for recasting the molds of society is often beyond their own expectations and transcends time. Their production may speak to their time and place or hold universal messages and lasting repercussions beyond their geographic, political, and historical setting.

Goals of This Essay

In this essay I have recourse to Lukács's concepts of reification and *Aufhebung* as well as his understanding of the role of artists in society in order to cast light on religious reflections embodied in some samples of Hispanic literature. My focus in this regard is twofold: on the one hand, the mode in which the written production constructs a vision of ourselves, the divine, and our relationship to others and to the Creator; on the other hand, the language used to convey this vision and how such language approximates a theological source.

Writing from a sociological perspective and drawing on concepts from the other social sciences, literature, philosophy, and theology, I do not include literature with a parochial purpose[5] or literature that is inherently of a religious nature. Thus, for example, I will not be concerned with the works of such writers as Teresa de Ávila, Juan de la Cruz, Sor Juana Inés, and others whose lives and literary expression were directly tied to their vision of religion and the church. In addition, my interpretation is also based on certain sociological assumptions regarding literature and human relations, such as the following: human beings are social agents, influencing and being influenced by others; no human action can be completely divorced from other human activity.

While acknowledging that art for the sake of art is possible, I—along with the Peruvian José Carlos Mariátegui—see art as having something concrete to say about the state of affairs of a particular people and something to contribute beyond the purely aesthetic in ways even unperceived

---

4. Of course, as with many other human activities, in art we may have a double-edged sword, insofar as it can be used to enslave or to set the spirit free, to pit one group against another by distorting rather than interpreting reality, by being exclusive or alienating. Lukács was well aware of this and lamented this ill-inspired use of certain genres and literary movements. However, since artistic inspiration is not the exclusive realm of any one group in society, it can also offer a space for group- and self-identification as well as a common meeting ground for many, not only lessening social distance but also creating a new and more equitable environment. For the "theological role" of literature, see T. R. Wright, *Theology and Literature* (Oxford: Basil Blackwell, 1988); see also West, *Ethical Dimensions*, 155–60.

5. See Messbarger, *Social Uses*.

by the author. Art can often function as a far-reaching commentary on the author's reality as well as a springboard for new conceptions: it can not only interpret reality but also help to reconstruct it. Thus, Paul Messbarger believes that artifacts as records of society are "consciously fashioned to serve at least partially [a] spiritual purpose" and constitute "a rich source of investigation for the social historian."[6] Furthermore, he contends that the more conventional as well as the most accomplished workers have the capacity of combining in varying proportions that which is public and private, personal and communal, so that the artistic expression is not the exclusive domain of a few:

An artifact, considered as a cultural document, must be treated as an "event" in the sense that it is rooted in time and place. The tool, the building, the poem, are not completely meaningful in themselves; the act begins with the person of the fabricator and his environment and ends only with its impact on a community.[7]

As with the first creation (that of the cosmos and the human species), once creations have come into being no one should be deprived of them. Everyone should be free to enjoy, accept, be inspired by, or even reject them. Furthermore, a creation often exhibits a power and a life beyond that of its creator. At times, art seems even to resist manipulation and control. Beyond the superficial beauty and the immediate impression, to the keen observer there are layers of meaning, subtle messages, and assumptions that at first glance may be unrecognizable even to the creator. This is so because every artist and writer has been conditioned to one degree or another by his or her world—and that world includes many variables, such as gender, age, nationality, culture, language, historical period, socioeconomic condition, religious formation and religious beliefs, and so forth. All that the artist is—that which took place toward the construction of the present in which he or she lives and creates; what is unfolding before his or her eyes; all the dreams, aspirations, hopes, and plans for the future he or she may have—will be reflected in the artistic production. Not drawn from a vacuum or fashioned only from a people's personal experiences but derived from collective history and consciousness, the artist's creations are cast into an imaginative mold of ideas, color, and sound and laden with multiple layers of meaning and subtle messages. Thus, following the first creation, every creative act is one of interpretation, rearrangement, and recasting.

Although artists have been "regarded as more fully attuned to the present and the particular, the world of the concrete and ephemeral, than [their] contemporaries," Messbarger believes that they are also capable of transcending the ideology of their own culture to free themselves from the ethnocentrism of their social environment.[8] This allows artists to function

---

6. Ibid., 17.
7. Ibid.
8. Ibid.

prophetically in their own milieus, using their music, dance movements, or other artistic expressions to tell of or call attention to the need for a new story of humanity. While music and the plastic arts have had lasting effects upon human history in the world of art, I believe it is the *word,* written or spoken, that has had the most profound and pervasive impact.

The Power of the Word

In his *Questiones disputatae de mysterio Trinitatis,* Bonaventure speaks of the creation of the human species as being the first book, a book in which every creature is either a vestige of God or an image of God.[9] Contemporary "geologian" Thomas Berry reflects on the need for a *new story* that will bind humanity together in one mind and goal.[10] David Avalos adds a prerequisite: *everyone* must articulate his or her own story so that out of many voices will come one harmonious story of humanity.[11] Notwithstanding the differences in background, time, and orientation among these authors, I find in their assessment of humanity's quest for authenticity and purpose a common thread that coincides with my own interpretation. A reading of these works reveals a clear recognition of—almost a reverence for—the creative and empowering force inherent in the articulation of the word.

La palabra (the word) as a concept has special meaning in the Hispanic world. For example, *dar palabra* (giving one's word) supersedes all other legal arrangements: one is worth as much as one's *palabra.* Similarly, *no tener palabra* (having no word) is tantamount to weakness and hypocrisy. Further, not to be given in vain, words are meant to shed new insights. So the saying goes, "Hablando se entiende la gente" (Talking to one another brings about understanding). Finally, *la palabra* is also prophetic because, besides providing new understandings, it has the power to cause movement and change.

Oral tradition and literature as well as the other arts can convey a partial yet faithful expression of the "look, sound, and texture of life." At the same time, they can also help to develop implicitly "a structure of thought, a set of attitudes . . . that reveal not only the conventional *Weltanschauung* (worldview) but also a criticism of these same values."[12] This is often articulated in terms of a positive nostalgic vision of the past, which serves to emphasize all the more contemporary shortcomings, or an attempt to give a

---

9. Cited by Jonas Barciauskas, "Leaves of Light: The Textual Journeys of Dante and García Márquez," *Cross Currents* 43 (1993) 214.

10. A member of the Passionist Order, Berry is the director of the Riverdale Center for Earth Studies. He has been characterized as a "geologian" because his theology is based on an understanding of and appreciation for the ecology of the planet; see his *The Dream of the Earth* (San Francisco: Sierra Club Books, 1990).

11. D. Avalos, "Multicultural and Gender Inclusive Education in the Service of Transformation," *Latino Studies Journal* 2 (1991) 3–18.

12. Messbarger, *Social Uses,* 18.

futuristic vision of how things might or ought to be. Rather than romanticizing the past, the *nostalgia* (homesickness) evoked can serve as a point of departure to rescue moral and cultural values that are in danger of extinction and deemed paramount in reconstructing the future. *Nostalgia,* which in our literature is so imbued with religious images and symbols of the creation, a lost Eden, and a need for redemption, becomes a creative force rather than self-deception or a clever disguise for one's sense of impotence before the harsh realities of the present.

Hispanic Literary Production

Hispanic literature and art abound with images of God and the spirit world, salvation and damnation, virtue and sin, desire for the divine and its rejection, humanity reflecting on the sufferings of Jesus and Christ's divinity. Other themes also abound: the incapacity of human beings for total understanding;[13] the comparison of one's homeland to paradise;[14] the journeying beyond one's land to a foreign country as exodus;[15] the cleansing through celestial or ground waters or fire;[16] ostracism or separation as punishment or in order to claim a pristine condition or transcend a corrupted present state.[17]

Furthermore, no one can deny that Christian values related to the individual, family, or community are exalted in our music and poetry. In the Puerto Rican *décimas* (popular songs with several stanzas of ten lines each),[18] for example, the *trovadores* have for centuries given us their vision of creation and the Creator; Jesus' birth and passion, which interestingly are often fused together as two sides of the same reality; Mary's sacrifice in the history of salvation; the Christian role of the father and mother in the society; and so on.[19] In addition, our vernacular and oral tradition is replete

---

13. See, for example, the work of the Chilean poet Gabriela Mistral, a Nobel laureate.

14. See, for example, the poetry of Puerto Rican José Gautier Benítez: *Cantos a Puerto Rico* (ed. Luis Hernández Aquino; San Juan: Instituto de Cultura Puertorriqueña, 1967); and *Poesía Puertorriqueña* (ed. Carmen Gómez Tejera, Ana María Losada, and Jorge Luis Porras; Mexico City: Editorial Orión, 1957).

15. A common theme in many writers, such as Pedro Juan Soto, René Marqués, José Luis González, and Gabriel García Márquez.

16. On cleansing through water, see, for example, Manuel Zeno Gandía, *La charca* (San Juan: Instituto de Cultural Puertorriqueña, 1975). On cleansing through fire, see, for example, the works of Enrique Laguerre, Rosario Ferré, René Marqués, and Gabriel García Márquez.

17. See, for example, the works of Pedro Juan Soto and Gabriel García Márquez.

18. See Pedro and Elisa Escabí, *La décima: Vista parcial del folklore de Puerto Rico* (Río Piedras, P.R.: Editorial Universitaria, 1976).

19. *Décimas* sung by Ramito, a well-known Puerto Rican folksinger, often deal with the themes of God's creation, the social evils of delinquency as direct consequence of the loss of Christian moral values in the family, and the love of parents, wife, husband, and children as a reflection of God's love in our lives. See also Marcelino J. Canino Salgado, *La canción de cuna en la tradición de Puerto Rico* (San Juan: Instituto de Cultura Puertorriqueña, 1970).

with references to God and divine intervention in our lives: "si Dios quiere" (God willing); "con el favor de Dios" (by the grace of God); "El hombre propone y Dios dispone" (Humanity makes plans and God ordains); "¡Virgen, sálvanos!" (Mary, save us!); "Quien a Dios busca, a Dios encuentra" (Whoever looks for God, finds him). Many of our *cuentos* (stories) begin with the phrase "Cuando Jesús aún andaba por el mundo" (When Jesus still walked this earth) and conclude with "y vivieron felices y en gracia de Dios" (and they lived happily ever after and in the grace of God).[20]

In fact, from Miguel de Cervantes to Gabriel García Márquez, the personification of the main character as a Christlike figure recurs in our short stories, dramas, and novels.

Miguel de Cervantes

Such seemingly mundane figures as Sancho and Don Quijote have been used as images of the inner soul of the Hispanic people in their quest for identity and meaning. In that duality and complementarity they portray— and in that coincidence of opposites are reflected—the Spanish psyche and worldview. More important in my estimation is that such identification has transcended the Iberian world to embrace a more inclusive Hispanic reality.[21] This may not sit well with those among us who would rather forget that along with our indigenous and African roots there is much that is Spanish in us, those who look upon Spain not as *la madre patria* (the mother country) but as the evil empire of *la leyenda negra* (the black legend). For others, however, as for the author of *Yo soy Joaquín*,[22] it is precisely this seemingly contradictory mixture that we carry within that makes us Latinos, a unique and rich people. Thus, we can no more negate the Sancho and the Don Quijote in us than we can negate the Cantinflas, the Periquillo, the Juan Bobo or the Pedro Animala, the Tres Patines or Chapulín Colorado.[23]

---

20. See Ricardo E. Alegría, ed., *Cuentos folklóricos de Puerto Rico* (n.p., 1969).

21. See Eduardo Ordoñez, *Quijotismo puertorriqueño* (Monterrey, Mexico: Imprenta Universitaria de Nueva León, 1967).

22. This poem by Rodolfo Gonzáles (*Yo soy Joaquín* [New York: Bantam, 1972]) traces the history and experience of the *mestizaje* of the Mexican American people.

23. "Cantinflas" is a fictional character of the Mexican cinema played by the now deceased actor Mario Moreno. Cantinflas is well known throughout the entire Hispanic world and, though a fictional character, is regarded with affection. Like Don Quijote, Cantinflas has acquired a personality and life of his own. These personalities are better known to the general public than those of the author, Miguel de Cervantes, or the actor, Mario Moreno. Indeed, just as in the Spanish language people have coined words to refer to a mode of behavior that is distinctive of Don Quijote and Sancho, the same has been done for Cantinflas. Thus, we say: "Hacer las de Sancho Panza"; or "Quijotear"; or "Hacer cantinfladas" ("To act like Sancho Panza"; or "To be quixotic"; or "To act like Cantinflas"). "El Periquillo Sarniento" is a picaresque fictional character created by the Mexican writer Joaquín Lizardi in a book by the same name. "Juan Bobo" and "Pedro Animala" are, respectively, the Puerto Rican folk hero and antihero. "Tres Patines," a Cuban fictional character, and "El

Furthermore, rather than just a trickster or pathetic fool, Don Quijote represents a messianic figure. His story is a journey into the human soul, a sign of hope in a world that needs to be shocked out of its state of complacency by being confronted with his own precarious situation—a madness that often appears more sensible than the behavior of his compatriots, certainly more sane than the social institutions of his time.[24] In Don Quijote the world of the imagination and the spirit (his desire to bring about righteousness through his sword) and pragmatic everyday reality (the windmills) clash. What "ought to be" is counterpoised to what people say "should be" or in fact "what is." Ultimately, Don Quijote's supposed madness is nothing compared to the madness of those who, having sold their souls for a piece of bread, for the pleasures of the flesh, for acceptance and power in society, have lost their way to righteousness and their sense of dignity.

Don Quijote represents the quest not only for new meaning but also for revelation. Reminiscent of the three falls of Jesus in Jerusalem and the three journeys of Paul, three times the knight undertakes to venture away from the comfort and security of his own home. On these erratic expeditions through open roads and narrow paths that seemingly lead nowhere, Don Quijote also undergoes a continuous and circular process of self-awareness, identification, and transformation. Although inspired by the obsolete literature of chivalry, his quest becomes a personal one for purpose in life and for more noble aspirations. Thus, he speaks to peoples of all ages because noble aspirations are not the exclusive domain of his own time or his own people.

Cervantes has recourse to biblical concepts to narrate the genesis of Don Quijote.[25] The call to mission begins with the awareness of a new self and a change of name. No longer Quijano, but Don Quijote de la Mancha, he proceeds to rename his old steer and his "lady-in-waiting" as well. Before his eyes everything and everyone takes on new meaning: Don Quijote assumes the right to vest each with a new name that speaks of a personal or particular purpose. Every completed step toward the preparation for the *journey* is marked with a pause for contemplation and an emphatic declaration to the effect that "it is good." Such an unlikely hero has as his mission the bringing back of order to chaos. Don Quijote has to straighten out a world that has gone astray, to re-create a place where things are not what they appear to be. He is compelled to share his own vision, to make

---

Chapulín Colorado," a Mexican fictional character, are of more recent vintage and belong to the world of radio and television.

24. This artistic and literary device is used also in the common parlance of Hispanic people. In Puerto Rican usage, for example, the *campesino* (peasant) often makes reference to his or her own ignorance—"Yo, como no sé nada, . . . pero aún así . . . " (I really know nothing, . . . but even so . . .)—only to underline his or her opponent's own ignorance.

25. Carlos Fernández Gómez (*Vocabulario de Cervantes* [Madrid: Real Academia Española, 1962]) reveals that in the *Quijote*, the word "God" is used 510 times, the word "heaven" 242 times, the word "Christian" 179 times, and the word "Catholic" 24 times. Many references can also be found to the church, the Virgin Mary, and the saints.

the blind see, and thus to restore a paradise that has been lost due to greed, cruelty, and lack of justice and imagination in humankind.

Thus, Don Quijote is both a trickster and a Christ figure. By playing the fool, he reveals the absurdities of his compatriots' behavior. By serving as an object of ridicule and rejection, he creates the possibility of a new vision. In a busy world, where the need for everyday survival and physical needs have rendered all capacity for imagination and lofty aspirations impractical, he makes others stop, even if for a brief moment, by his sheer presence and tenacious insistence to consider the possibility of another more noble reality. In the imaginations and hearts of those who dare to dream and transcend their immediate reality, the antihero has been enthroned as the hero because what was first thought to be a foolish dream has proven to be illuminating.[26]

Miguel de Unamuno and Antonio Machado

The concept of the dream is also very important in the Hispanic world, and this too is reflected in our literature. From the lowly *curandera* (female healer) to the illustrious philosopher we have heard over and over again that dreams are revelatory. Turn-of-the-century authors Miguel de Unamuno and Antonio Machado often use this concept of the dream to speak to us about their notion of the divine.

Miguel de Unamuno. Recognizing that oftentimes the fictional entity attains a life of its own, Unamuno has Augusto Pérez, the main character in one his stories, literally jump out of the pages of the book and appear in person before Unamuno to argue for his existence.[27] To Unamuno, who often talks of humanity as being the product of a dream of God (a God that had to be kept asleep and dreaming to assure our continuance), this conversation with his fictional character is indeed revelatory. The question before him is, "Why have you gone to the trouble of inventing me, giving me existence and a desire to go on existing, if in the final analysis you are going to impose your will and do away with me?" This fictional character echoes Unamuno's preoccupation with immortality, evident throughout his writings. Thus, it is no longer Unamuno's fictional character who speaks to the writer, it is the writer himself who questions his own Creator. This is made clear when Augusto, having pleaded with Unamuno and having been denied continuation of his existence, remarks to his author that a similar fate awaits Unamuno. Unamuno, too, and all of Unamuno's readers, says

---

26. Because he is a prophetic figure, Don Quijote has been at times both maligned and exalted by the same person, as was the case with Miguel de Unamuno. What survives is not the pathetic image of the fool but rather the image of someone who, despite many odds, had sufficient imagination and courage to dream and strive to make his dream a reality. See Miguel de Unamuno, *Vida de don Quijote y Sancho* (Madrid: Espasa-Calpe, 1966).

27. Miguel de Unamuno, *Niebla* (Madrid: Espasa-Calpe, 1971).

an irate Augusto, will also perish. All created life, sooner or later, will come to an end. If in fact there is a "tragic sentiment or feeling for life,"[28] it is because life is finite, though the soul longs for immortality. Yet no assurance is given other than this longing for immortality—and the longing for strengthened faith so that one may believe. Hope lies only in the ability to believe beyond life. The biblical passage "I believe; help my unbelief" (Mark 9:24) resonates in this author's writings, but with one change: "I want and need to believe; help my unbelief."

The issue of faith is central to Unamuno's philosophy and literary production. In *San Manuel Bueno, Mártir,*[29] his most autobiographical work, this dream of immortality is presented through a flashback.[30] The author uses a woman as narrator. It is the priest, however, whose "agonizing"[31] life she recalls, who is Unamuno's soul mate. Don Manuel's life is but a revelation of that doubt/faith journey so characteristic of Unamuno's own life. As in *Don Quijote,* there is an inner quest as well as an outer commitment. However, while Don Quijote was driven onward by his conviction that he could indeed save the world, Don Manuel pushes onward only through his conviction that, if he doubts, the world of faith he has helped to create for his followers would come apart. Operative here is that sense of *el deber del deber* (duty as duty) concerning which the Puerto Rican educator and sociologist Eugenio María de Hostos speaks in his *Moral Social.*[32] Forsaking personal needs and doubts, the priest must convince his people that there is salvation in believing. Like Unamuno, Don Manuel fears dying and not dying;[33] death could be the end of all, but it also could be the "resurrection of the body." The articulation of this phrase of the Apostle's Creed is avoided by Don Manuel during his daily Mass, perhaps because saying these words would be tantamount to *giving God his word* to the effect that he in fact believes.[34] Only in death can an answer to the afterlife be found. Certainly, death would put to rest his fear of causing harm to others, if in a moment of weakness the revelation of his doubts should occur. When death finally

---

28. Miguel de Unamuno, *El sentimiento trágico de la vida* (Madrid: Espasa Calpe, 1971).

29. Miguel de Unamuno, *San Manuel Bueno, Mártir* (Madrid: Alianza Editorial, 1971).

30. Unamuno often expresses a sort of envy toward women because they are capable of "creating life" through motherhood and thus, in his estimation, have a greater claim than men to immortality. A careful reading of Unamuno, however, reveals a concept of motherhood that transcends biological motherhood. Thus, for example, he speaks of *maternidad del alma* (spiritual motherhood) and the ability of the wife to *prohijar al esposo* (engender her husband).

31. Unamuno uses the adjective *agónica,* from the verb *agonizar* (to agonize).

32. Eugenio María de Hostos, *Moral Social* (New York: Las Américas, 1964).

33. This "dying and not dying" can be seen as either counterposing or paralleling Saint Teresa's *muero porque no muero* (I die because I do not die).

34. Unamuno himself laments the fact that in his time too many words were being said with little or no consequence. In his estimation people seemed to have been losing the importance of the spoken word; therefore, intentional actions that would accompany what was articulated were an imperative.

comes, Angela Carballino, the narrator, remembers a lake with its deep dark waters: a mirror of God's glorious heavens; a reminder of the abysmal "dream of God"; a reflection of Don Manuel's troubled soul.

Antonio Machado. Antonio Machado, a contemporary of Unamuno's, also employs the imagery of dreams in his poetry.[35] Machado, unlike Unamuno, is not afraid to awake God:

> It was last night that I dreamt
> that God was shouting: Alert!
> Later on, God was asleep
> and I was crying: Awake![36]

"Dios viene por el sueño" (God comes through dreams), he says, and God speaks to us from *la nada* (nothingness),[37] which is not an empty vacuum of nonexistence. As creation of God, *la nada* encompasses the possibility of newness and revelation. The *word,* God's instrument of creation, is paramount in the quest of discovery. It may resound from the midst of *la nada.* Thus, we must be alert at all times, if we are to hear God's voice:

> Love? Forgiveness? or Charity?
> Jesus Lord, which was your word?
> All your words can be reduced
> to only one: Watchfulness.[38]

We must be watchful because God is at the same time the eternal other, elusive and incomprehensible, yet part of our very existence. We search for God, knowing full well God is beyond us. Yet God also walks with us:

> Everywhere I seek your presence
> which nowhere is to be found,
> and in all places I find you
> merely by seeking you out.[39]

This intriguing God that cannot be attained is always "there." In fact, there is a realm of our existence in which we create God to our own image and likeness, just as God has created us:

---

35. See Manuel Tuñón de Lara, *Antonio Machado, poeta del pueblo* (Barcelona: Editorial Nova Terra, 1967). Also José María González Ruiz, "La teología de Antonio Machado," *La religiosidad popular: Antropología e historia,* vol. 1 (ed. Carlos Álvarez Santaló, María Jesús Buxó, and Salvador Rodríguez Becerra; Barcelona: Anthropos, 1989) 246–56.

36. "Anoche soñé que oía / A Dios gritándome: ¡Alerta! / Luego era Dios quien dormía / y yo gritaba: ¡Despierta!" All quotes from Machado's poetry are taken from Tuñón de Lara, *Antonio Machado,* but the translations are mine.

37. González Ruiz, "Teología," 249.

38. "¿Cuál fue, Jesús, tu palabra? / ¿Amor? ¿Perdón? ¿Caridad? / Todas tus palabras fueron / una palabra: Velad." Notice that a more accurate translation for *Velad* would be the two English words: "Be watchful."

39. "En todas partes te busco / sin encontrarte jamás, / y en todas partes te encuentro / sólo por irte a buscar."

> The God we all have within us,
> the God whom we all create,
> the God who is sought by all
> yet by no one is attained.
> Three gods or three persons are
> of the one True God proclaimed.[40]

Thus, in the journey toward God and the quest for meaning, the journey itself is worth the effort, even when there is no road map and no clear assurance as to where it would lead, not even the possibility of a return.

> Sojourner, your footprints lead the way,
> and that is all;
> only by walking will you make the path
> or not at all.
> And so the journey opens up new pathways,
> though looking back, you'll understand,
> never again shall the same steps trace
> the path that's left behind.[41]

Despite the uncertainties of life and the ultimate uncertainty of what lies after death, Machado is able to underscore his faith in God and life:

> In liberty and hope I do believe,
> and in a faith reborn
> by seeking God though he'll not be attained.
> The God within myself, the one I do create.[42]

This faith is there in the most critical periods of the poet's life, as for example, at the time of his wife's death. And when that faith is tested by the fire of death and despair and still persists, then a miracle is possible, bringing forth new life out of decay. Then, the poet can write:

> Stroked by lightning, already half-decayed,
> with April showers, and sun shining in May,
> the old elm tree, green leaves has sprouted again.
> ...And thus, my heart only awaits
> a springtime miracle of light
> turning my life ablaze.[43]

---

40. "El Dios que todos llevamos, / el Dios que todos hacemos, / el Dios que todos buscamos / y que nunca encontraremos. / Tres dioses o tres personas / del sólo Dios verdadero."

41. "Caminante son tus huellas / el camino, y nada más; / Caminante, no hay camino, / se hace camino al andar. / Al andar se hace camino / y al volver la vista atrás, / se ve la senda que nunca / se ha de volver a pisar."

42. "Creo en la libertad y en la esperanza, / y en una fe que nace / cuando se busca a Dios y no se alcanza, / y en el Dios que se lleva y que se hace."

43. "Al olmo viejo, hendido por el rayo / y en su mitad podrido, / con las lluvias de abril y el sol de mayo / algunas hojas verdes le han salido. / ...Mi corazón espera, / también hacia la luz y hacia la vida / otro milagro de la primavera."

These three writers (Cervantes, Unamuno, and Machado), like many others in the Spanish-speaking world, created artistic expressions that reflect their particular historical period and society. Widely read in the Hispanic and non-Hispanic world, their works have transcended their native lands and times and continue to speak to us today. In addition to reflecting prevalent values, symbols, and social preoccupations of each epoch, they also point the way toward a process of negation, preservation, and transformation whereby reified sociocultural circumstances can be freed. Their probing of life's ultimate meanings touches upon theological themes with which we struggle in our own time. But rather than be bound by the limits of formal theology, these writers have used artistic form as their genre for discourse.

Gabriel García Márquez and René Marqués

The quest for meaning and a higher plane of existence in the guise of an exodus (into the future or the past) is likewise reflected in the works of Hispanic writers such as Julia Álvarez, who is from the Dominican Republic; Esmeralda Santiago, René Marqués, Pedro Juan Soto, and Edward Rivera, all Puerto Ricans; Gabriel García Márquez, a Colombian; and others.[44] Often they depict a conflictive world where things are not what they appear

---

44. Julia Álvarez, *How the García Girls Lost Their Accents* (New York: Penguin Books, 1992). Esmeralda Santiago, *When I Was Puerto Rican* (New York: Addison-Wesley, 1993). René Marqués, *The Oxcart (La carreta)* (trans. Charles Pilditch; New York: Charles Scribner's Sons, 1969). In *Los soles truncos,* also by Marqués, as in *Cien años de soledad,* by García Márquez, the end is marked by the destruction by fire of a small world that has been created but that ultimately cannot survive. In Marqués's play, that world has been reduced to "la casa vieja señorial," the old family house of bygone years whose existence in the present is anachronistic. In García Márquez's novel, the creation is not a throwback to a world of yesteryear, nor can we claim with assurance that it is a world in the future. It seems a world suspended in time or in a time dimension unknown to us. In both works, however, the reader at times may feel immersed in a dreamlike reality. Pedro Juan Soto, *Hot Land, Cold Season* (New York: Dell Publishing Co., 1973). Edward Rivera, *Family Installments: Memories of Growing Up Puerto Rican* (New York: William Morrow, 1982). At the end of the story the protagonist goes back to Puerto Rico to search for his grandfather's resting place as well as for "memories" of his personal identity. Gabriel García Márquez, *Cien años de soledad* (Buenos Aires: Editorial Sudamericana, 1967). A recent book by Cristina García (*Dreaming in Cuban* [New York: Knopf, 1992]) brings together the idea of *nostalgia* (dreaming) and journeying back to the homeland as part of that quest for meaning and identity. Dreaming and *nostalgia* for the homeland are also intimately connected in the common expressions of Hispanics even when a return seems improbable. A well-off Cuban living in Miami, for example, is reported to have told David Rieff, author of *The Exile: Cuba in the Heart of Miami* (New York: Simon and Schuster, 1993): "We Cubans are realists. None of us are going back, you'll see, no one but a magnate here and retiree there will go back. But our dream gave us strength when we needed it, and if we can't quite let go, is that really so terrible?" (cited in the *New York Times Book Review,* 12 September 1993, 14). In *Growing Up Latino: Memoirs and Stories* (Boston: Houghton Mifflin, 1993), Harold Augenbraum and Ilan Stavans provide a good sampling of Hispanic writers in the United States as well as a good bibliography of suggested readings.

at first sight. Shortness of space dictates that I choose but two examples here. The drama *La carreta* (The oxcart) written by René Marqués, is now a classic of twentieth-century Puerto Rican literature. In *La carreta,* Luis is not who he appears to be. He is not Doña Gabriela's son, although he does not know it, nor is he the son of her late husband, though the latter went to his grave ignorant of the fact that Luis was not his own but the offspring of his mistress and another man. In *Cien años de soledad* (One hundred years of solitude), García Márquez paints a picture of an illusive world beyond reality, where human beings are preoccupied with deciphering mysterious parchments. Both end with what seems to be destruction, but upon closer examination, this destruction can be interpreted as purification.

Gabriel García Márquez. Jonas Barciauskas argues that in García Márquez "there is no indication of joy, fulfillment of healing," and questions if the moments he creates in his writings "bring us to an awareness of higher possibilities in our lives."[45] In *Cien años de soledad* one might be led to think that García Márquez is a seeker. However, it is only in *Amor en tiempo de cólera* (Love in the time of cholera) that "the profound importance of the Other, an importance only intermittently suggested in *One Hundred Years,*" is given relevance. Although he believes that each of the author's novels "is another essay into the darkness, another raid into the unspeakable," Barciauskas concludes that each time "García Márquez emerges with a richer sense than most of what life is all about." "Too dark and individualistic" to provide the new story of which Thomas Berry speaks, Márquez's work "may offer a glimpse of what a great narrative could do to rekindle the postmodern imagination."[46]

García Márquez's work, I believe, may not explicitly define a transcendent dimension,[47] but the very act of portraying the real and the imagined in such starkness reveals a need to continue the search in that direction. One is often reminded of Don Quijote, half-blinded by the splendor of his own lofty quest, yet moving on into unknown and uncharted territory for the sake of the quest. After all, as Machado reminds us, the quest itself is worth the effort. I am also reminded of Unamuno's agonizing and questioning faith as well as Machado's conception of *la nada,* that pure and deep vastness where nothing and everything exist because it is the realm of God. Indeed, if there is an uncharted territory to raid or conquer, it is this one. If there is a place for faith to be tested, it is here.

Most of all, however, I am reminded of the "illusive God," playing "hide-and-go-seek" with humankind and yet letting him/herself be

45. Barciauskas, "Leaves of Light," 226.
46. Ibid., 226, 226, 227.
47. See ibid., 226.

"caught," not only in cataclysmic explosions but also in the common realities of everyday life. It is, then, not only what García Márquez says but
the way he says it that speak of a distinctive quest. His stark portrayal of
the real and the imagined points the way; here are the *huellas* (traces) that
open up the path if not to a higher dimension at least to the need for it, a
dimension that he dares not define. Like Unamuno's Don Manuel Bueno,
García Márquez cannot bring himself to articulate certain words. "García
Márquez cannot commit himself to any particular set of metaphysical or
ethical principles that would provide a map to the arche of our existence,"
says Barciauskas.[48]

René Marqués. Although it may not be true of all his writings, in *La carreta* Marqués does what García Márquez fails to do. There he predicts
signs of a new dawn. A note of *nostalgia* rather than pessimism marks
this work.[49] When Doña Gabriela and the grandchildren leave the small
mountain farm in their quest for a better life in the city, Don Chago returns to La Cueva del Indio (the Indian's Cave). Rather than venture into
"unknown territory," the old grandfather seeks the past by going back to
live his last days among the ancestral spirits. The family's migration trek
is a *via dolorosa.* They lose not only their traditional livelihood but also
the symbols of their religiosity and family life. When Doña Gabriela, the
mother, loses the wooden image of St. Anthony, the old *santo de palo*
(wooden image of the saint), she loses not only a family heirloom but the
object of her religious veneration. When the young daughter, Juanita, is
robbed of her virginity by a man she does not even know, she also loses
her sense of self-worth. In giving up the farm, Luis, the eldest child, loses
his self-respect. He gives up his skills as a farmer to become an insignificant hired hand who tends to rich people's gardens in San Juan. Chaguito,
the youngest, loses his innocence and freedom, ending up in jail as another
juvenile delinquent. In New York, Luis continues his agonizing quest for
meaning. His faith in technology is literally swallowed up by the reality he
sought to understand, when he is mangled by malfunctioning equipment in
the factory where he works. Only the two women remain at the end: Doña
Gabriela, *mater dolorosa,* with the mangled body of the child that technology has crucified; Juanita, the rebellious young woman turned prophet.[50]
Tested by their personal and family tribulations at what seems the darkest

---

48. Ibid.

49. This *nostalgia,* which I have elsewhere explored and analyzed, is present in many
Hispanic writers, notably so in the literature produced in the United States.

50. It is interesting to note that in Marqués's production, as in the work of other Puerto
Rican writers, women appear to be more spiritual, wiser, and stronger than men. The impli-
cation of this for theological analysis and for concrete praxis in relationship to theologizing
within the Puerto Rican context is a subject that requires serious consideration far beyond
the limits of this essay.

hour, they are strengthened in the realization that there is a tomorrow and a return to the land is possible.[51]

The exodus has come full circle. The return signifies not defeat but a new beginning in a place that has been transformed, not in itself but in the hearts of the two women. The spilling of Luis's blood has cleansed the family. They now understand what he could not, that the quest for meaning lies not outside but within the self and that no outer resource can fulfill the needs that inner strength demands. From remnants of the past, full realization of the present, and hopes for the future a new story is made possible. This story and its telling incarnate the resurrection and salvation for the people as promised by Juanita's word at the end when she declares, "And I shall tell my children things they will not find in schoolbooks." The old story having ended, the new one begins with a sense of optimism (hope) and intentionality (deep commitment).

Concluding Comments

Beyond this essay lies a feminist interpretation of the literary production of Hispanic men and women. It remains to be seen if in the stories told by Hispanic women the characters are indeed Christlike, if both men and women are cast in this role or if only women are ascribed the role of the *mater dolorosa*. At issue also is whether there is a U-turn for *la carreta*, since in fact many Puerto Ricans and other Latinos in the United States are here to stay. What the U-turn means is in part revealed in the works of Hispanic/Latino writers in the United States. It is certainly not a negation of their cultural and ethnic roots, but a new way of being Hispanic. Nor is it a negation of the fact that—as Puerto Ricans, Cubans, Dominicans, and Central and South Americans—both the theme of going back ("Volver, volver, volver" [Return, return, return], as the words of the well-known song would have it) and the experience of migration are what set us apart. We are always returning to "a previous existence," to "the land of our origin," "the land of our dreams," as our poets and musicians remind us. Thus, with the Panamanian singer Rubén Blades in "Todos vuelven" (They all come back), we affirm our need to return; with the Puerto Rican *tríos* from New York, we are invited to dream "En mi Viejo San Juan" (In my old San Juan); and with the traditional Cuban "Guantanamera," we revive

---

51. Avalos ("Multicultural and Gender Inclusive Education," 16) reminds the reader that it is not actually the machine that devoured or ripped Luis apart, but "the system of this country . . . because . . . it gave him no sense of being sacred, of being centered in himself as a human being." But providentially, through his death, "the repressed feminine in Latino culture," which he equates with "the return of the principle of liberation," emerges: a return to ancestral lands "where one can bury the hands in the red earth" signifies a "return home," to one's self, to that sacred space central to each one of us.

our hopes of seeing Cuba once again. Such is the hope and longing reflected in our popular saying "De la esperanza vive el cautivo" (Hope gives life to the prisoner).

Elsewhere I have analyzed the feeling of *nostalgia* and the maintenance of the Spanish language in our literature in this country as creative agents in our quest for ethnic identification and a reconstruction of our reality as a distinct people in the United States. Likewise, in the transition from Spanish to English, I have seen, rather than defeat or a loss of our own language, a desire to make our story known to a larger audience. Added to this, however, and perhaps more important, is the strong tendency to transform the medium of expression itself, so that English becomes, rather than a means toward amorphous assimilation, one more empowering tool in the recasting of the Latino people in the United States.

The authors chosen in this essay present an interpretation of a reality that is rich and complex. Don Quijote's vision finds echo in Miguel de Unamuno's agonizing search for immortality and in Antonio Machado's declaration of faith that *la nada* calls us forward into an ever more engaging quest, that both quest and encounter are but two facets of the same reality, that each revelation is a new challenge to a new mystery, and that the sojourn is never completed. In keeping with this imagery, René Marqués describes a desire for a new beginning, a reorientation of *la carreta* of our lives. There may be no guidelines, yet there is much room for creative responses.

In *Cien años de soledad,* the looseness of the parchment leaves—the fact that they are not bound into a volume—reflects a simple though not always obvious truth: our personal and collective memories are unstable, changing, and difficult to record with precision, not unlike dreams themselves.[52] If, as Gabriel García Márquez reminds us, life is not a well-bound book, then it does give us, as a loose-leaf binder, the freedom to subtract and add, to cast away and re-create. As in the case of dreams, our personal and collective memories, our actual reality, and our hopes and aspirations have a power for revelation not to be neglected. The greatest compliment we can pay to any of our writers is to recognize that "the means and goals of [their] quest,...the stuff of [their] richly textured fiction,...are opened to interpretation." Truly, the world our writers and artists portray for us is a "world...indeed enchanted," yet one where "a spiritual journey is still possible" because in it we can "relive the disappearance and reemergence of an awareness of the spiritual dimension permeating our everyday existence."[53] The writer's message about a world that was created with many defects contains a hint that liberation may yet take place. As with Lukács's notion of reification, the artistic expression of a world in need of redemp-

---

52. Barciauskas, "Leaves of Light," 227.
53. Ibid., 228.

tion is the beginning of just such a redemption. To construct for us such a niche from the "ashes" of previous experience, to believe when there is little cause for hope,[54] has been in great part the mission of our writers and artists, and within that niche we can certainly begin to write the first draft of our new story.

---

54. In fact, the Puerto Rican poet Tato Laviera has written a poem whose title is "The Carreta Made a U-Turn."

5

The Oral Tradition of a People

Forjadora de rostro y corazón

Ana María Pineda

> *Here is what you are to do, what you are to realize: It is that which is guarded, that which is bound; the secret knowledge that the old men, the old women, those who go white-haired, those who go white-headed, those who go emaciated with age, our forefathers, left as they departed.... You are their off-spring; from them you descended. Regard them; look them in the face. And their memory, their torch, their mirror, that departing, they left: take, place, set the mirror before you. See therein how you are; compare your way of life, your being.*
>
> —Miguel León-Portilla, *Native Mesoamerican Spirituality*

The "discovery" of America in the sixteenth century opened doors to previously unknown worlds, worlds that proved to be intoxicatingly different from anything else that the Spaniards had previously experienced. The reports that arrived in Spain from the "New World" described the lands and their inhabitants in vivid detail. Christopher Columbus even displayed his findings in public by bringing back to Spain a group of natives—Taínos— whom he paraded through the streets of Seville during the Palm Sunday celebration of 1493.[1] The Palm Sunday event would prove to be the exception, offering the gathered crowd firsthand experience of a reality that until that moment had been primarily communicated through the letters and journals written by conquistadores and missionaries as mandated by the Royal Crown. In fact, the task of keeping detailed written accounts describing everything that pertained to the behavior, customs, tradition, and religious practices of the people would produce an invaluable body of information of great historical importance.

Amid the numerous details that were recorded, frequent mention was made of the observable fact that the "indians lacked an alphabet and

---

1. See Helen Rand Parish, ed., *Bartolomé de las Casas: The Only Way* (Mahwah, N.J.: Paulist Press, 1992) 12.

writing and preserved all their past history in the form of pictures."[2] Various accounts document the existence of painted characters that extensively recorded the life of the people.[3] These painted histories or accounts were often referred to by the chroniclers as "books," "manuscripts," and "codices."[4] These terms, however, were inaccurate, since the Spanish language did not possess a vocabulary that could describe the large sheets of "paper"[5] on which the pictographs or drawings were painted. In fact, these painted pages constituted only one part of a system of communication radically different from that employed by the European conquerors. Rather than a system of writing based wholly on phonetic symbols, the communications system of the inhabitants of the New World was based on the inherent power of the spoken word.

The meaning encoded in these painted books needed to be interpreted for the community by men specially entrusted with this sacred task. The *tlamatinimes*, or wise ones, constituted the second part of this oral system of communication. Both the painted books and the *tlamatinimes* were constitutive components of the oral system of communication of the indigenous world. The depository from which the system of communication drew was the accumulated oral tradition of the people, which had been faithfully preserved from one generation to the next through the medium of the *tlamatinimes* and the painted books.[6]

Diego de Durán, a Dominican friar who lived in the New World in the sixteenth century, noted in his written work that the collective history of the people of these lands was *written*[7] and painted in books and on sheets of paper.[8] Regrettably, the majority of these rich sources of history were destroyed during the military conquest by Spain. Others were destroyed after the *conquista* by many of the missionaries in their attempt to abolish

---

2. Alonso Zorita, *Life and Labor in Ancient Mexico* (New Brunswick, N.J.: Rutgers University Press, 1963) 86.

3. See Fray Diego de Durán, *Book of the Gods and Rites and the Ancient Calendar* (trans. Fernando Horcasitas and Doris Heyden; Norman: University of Oklahoma Press, 1975).

4. See José Alcina Franch, *Códices Mexicanos* (Mexico City: Editorial MAPFRE, 1992) 22.

5. The sheets of "paper" were made from the bark of the amate tree and/or deer skin, which was folded over lengthwise in booklike fashion.

6. The Mesoamerican people belonged to cultures of orality in contrast to cultures of literacy. A culture that has no knowledge of the written word relies on the oral transmission of knowledge. In recent years, studies exploring orality and literacy have indicated that the use of a specific medium (orality or literacy) shapes the consciousness of a society in a manner distinct from the other type of societies. See Walter Ong, *Orality and Literacy* (New York: Methuen, 1982).

7. The word "written" was used by Durán to refer to the drawings of figures and artistic representations that were painted on the sheets of amate paper or deer skin. Again, the Spanish vocabulary did not have a word that could describe the production of the works found in the indigenous world.

8. See Durán, *Book of the Gods and Rites*, 65, 395–96.

every manifestation of what they considered to be idolatry. A large number of codices simply disappeared, hidden or buried by the indigenous people, who did not want the sacred tradition of their ancestors to be confiscated by the Spaniards. In the end, the massive destruction of the painted codices impoverished the evangelization endeavor of the missionaries while effectively undermining the historical identity of the people themselves: what could have been a source of information for the missionaries in their encounter with the people was reduced to ashes; what could have helped the conquered people to maintain a link with their collective history was eliminated.

In the ensuing years, some of the missionaries would come to recognize the value of the painted books and the system that was employed, but the vast bulk of these primary sources was irretrievable. The few painted codices that were not destroyed were dispersed and preserved either as exotic gifts or museum pieces.[9] With the passage of time, a number of scholars embarked on serious research, intent on discovering the interpretive key that would unlock the treasures of the painted manuscripts. Notable work by scholars such as Ángel María Garibay K., Miguel León-Portilla, Alfredo López Austin, G. Aguirre Beltrán, Charles Gibson, W. B. Taylor, and Nancy M. Farris has greatly advanced the understanding of the significance of the painted codices and the role of the *tlamatinime* in the institutionalized system of communication in the Mesoamerican world.

The modern world is indebted to the research efforts undertaken by these scholars and others. The historical patrimony of Mesoamerican culture has been made accessible thereby to others and in particular to the offspring of that conquered culture. In fact, the mestizo offspring, the Hispanic/Latino people, are the heirs to the treasury of the oral wisdom of the old men and women of yesterday. The secret knowledge left behind by the elders rests in the power that oral tradition has in transmitting the history of a people and in serving as a viable medium in forging the present identity of a people. As such, the practice of oral tradition in the U.S. Hispanic/Latino communities can be explored as the continuation of the cultures of orality of our ancestors. It is precisely the Hispanic/Latino oral tradition that needs to be understood as an authentic medium that orients the people morally. The oral tradition provides the people with a record of their origins and with a sense of their identity and historical relevance.

In this study I will examine the dynamics of the oral tradition of the Mesoamerican world in order to suggest ways in which oral tradition continues to play a vital role in the forging of the U.S. Hispanic/Latino identity. Oral tradition lives on in narrative and symbolic form and is used today by

---

9. See Franch, *Códices Mexicanos,* 24. Hernán Cortés sent painted books along with other gifts from the New World to Charles V in Spain. These codices are identified today with the names *Códice Vindobonese* and *Códice Fejervary-Mayer.*

teachers, artists, poets, and theologians in U.S. Hispanic communities. In fact, the power that can be unleashed by attending to oral tradition can be a major factor in the ongoing creation of a Hispanic American theology.

Revisiting Our History: Oral Tradition

In revisiting the history of Mesoamerica, it becomes evident that oral tradition played a significant role in the life of its *pueblos* (peoples). In a culture where the principal medium of communication was the spoken word, the preservation of the oral history of a people became paramount. It was through the oral transmission of knowledge that each generation was able to maintain a sense of its history and its identity. Oral tradition not only continued to keep the stories of the people alive; it also continued to make present the memory of the ancient ones. It was important for the community constantly to utter anew the words of wisdom that its ancestors had spoken in its lifetime for the community's edification. This *palabra antigua,* this word of the elders, assisted the people as well in knowing what principles of good conduct were to be followed in order to lead a morally upright life.

The Oral System of Communication

In a culture where writing was nonexistent, the task of preserving the *palabra antigua* was important. Initially, the Mesoamericans, like many other peoples in other different cultural contexts, spontaneously committed to memory what is now labeled as their cosmic myths, epic poems, legends, accounts about the past, sacred hymns, songs, poetry, and other various forms of discourses.[10] In time this task became specialized. In the case of the Mesoamerican world, as I have already mentioned, this need to store the history or memory of its people resulted in a twofold systematization of the oral transmission in terms of the *tlamatinimes* and the "codices."

In the Nahuatl culture the task of passing on the oral tradition was assigned in a specialized way to the *tlamatinime,* or wise one.[11] Information provided by the *Códice Matritense de la Academia* and the *Colloquies of the Twelve* points out that the preservation of the oral tradition of the people of Mesoamerica resulted in the diversification of tasks. The functions needed for this task were many and consequently "more than thirty

---

10. Miguel León-Portilla, ed., *Native Mesoamerican Spirituality* (New York: Paulist Press, 1980) 30.

11. This is confirmed in such contemporary accounts as those of Bernardino de Sahagún, Inca Garcilaso de la Vega, Don Fernando de Alva Ixtililxóchitl, Fray Diego de Durán, Fray Gerónimo de Mendieta (Motolinia), as well as by modern-day experts such as Ángel María Garibay K., Miguel León-Portilla, and Alfredo López Austin. In addition, the figure of the *tlamatinime* appears in the painted codices that remain from that period.

distinct classes of priests" existed.[12] Each had a specific function that contributed to the preservation of the oral tradition of the community. This
diversification of tasks would lend support to the awesome task assigned to
the *tlamatinime* and give shape to the painted narrative of the codices.

The Tlacuilo, *Artist of the Codices*

One of the primary tasks was assigned to the artist, the *tlacuilo*. The artist
had the responsibility of painting the codices on long strips of amate paper.[13] A person was destined to be a *tlacuilo* or artist if he[14] was born on the
dates favoring artists. But this destiny had to be carefully nurtured by the
tlacuilo. Such nurturing involved a lifelong process of striving to be worthy
of the task and learning how to speak to his heart. In the Nahuatl religion,
the heart symbolized the source of dynamism in human will,[15] and for that
reason it was believed that God resided in the human heart. Therefore, the
artist had to commune profoundly with his heart in order to faithfully draw
the history of the people. This disposition of centering himself in the heart
was also accompanied by the need to possess the knowledge of the different
kinds of Nahuatl symbolism.

It was crucial that the *tlacuilo* know the symbols of mythology and tradition. For the Nahuas, as for other traditional cultures, myth fulfilled an
indispensable function. "They [the myths]... [could] be expected to eluci-
date the entire religious life of a community, shedding light especially on
the ritual acts and sacred objects that by themselves... [did] not speak
at all, or certainly not often, and not as clearly."[16] The myths revealed
something of the society in which they were formulated, and consequently
the *tlacuilo* needed to possess profound knowledge of the Aztec-Nahuatl
culture. The codices were the painted books that reflected the collective
wisdom of the people. The colors red and black represented wisdom and,
consequently, the expression "red and black" became a symbolic metaphor for the painted wisdom of the codices. The paintings/codices served
as a visual code with the power to convey the mythology of the Nahuas.
The paintings were intimately connected to the truth that the Nahuas

---

12. See Miguel León-Portilla, *Aztec Thought and Culture* (trans. Jack Emory Davis;
Norman: University of Oklahoma Press, 1963) 134.

13. See *El universo del amate* (Mexico City: Museo Nacional de Culturas Populares,
1987), a work that describes the actual uses of amate in some of the popular sectors of
Mexico.

14. See Miguel León-Portilla, *Trece poetas del mundo azteca* (Mexico City: Universidad
Nacional Autónoma de México, 1984) 157–69. According to León-Portilla, during the time
of the Nahuas, women were counted among the known poets and painters. However, this
does not seem to have been a general practice, with the women who occupied this role
coming from the noble class.

15. León-Portilla, *Aztec Thought*, 114.

16. Roy Wagner, *Symbols That Stand for Themselves* (Chicago: University of Chicago
Press, 1986) 23.

characterized as *flor y canto* (flower and song). The paintings/codices synthesized both the visual-graphic and the verbal accounts of the history of the Nahuas as it had been lived from one generation to the next.

The *tlacuilo* was the master of the visual communication of the communal history of the *pueblo*. Like the *tlamatinime,* the artist was constantly required to ponder the stories of the people in order to transfer that divinely inspired wisdom onto the amate paper of the codices. The artist followed in the tradition of the Toltecs, a people who had gained the reputation of being the master artists of the truth. The *tlacuilo* strove to become a good painter following in the tradition of the Toltecs. He would have attained a high degree of artistic perfection when others could say of him:

> The good painter is a Toltec, an artist,
> he creates with red and black ink,
> with black water....
> The good painter is wise,
> God in his heart.
> He puts divinity into things;
> he converses with his own heart.
> He knows the colors, he applies them and shades them.
> He draws feet and faces,
> he puts in the shadows, he achieves perfection.
> He paints the colors of all the flowers,
> as if he were a Toltec.[17]

The Tlamatinime, *the Caretaker and Interpreter of the Painted Codices*

The *tlamatinime* was the master of the oral transmission of the tradition of the people. The *tlamatinime* was the master of the word and was credited with the title of *tlamatinime* because he was "the one who knew something,"[18] who meditated on human and divine realities. The *tlamatinime* was the guardian of the oral history of the people as well as the caretaker and interpreter of the painted books.[19] Fray Diego de Durán testified to the fact that everything was recorded in the numerous painted manuscripts of the Mesoamerican people. Durán reported that the paintings contained their laws and descriptions of their ancient history, their wars and victories, their experiences of hunger and illnesses, as well as their times of prosperity and adversity.[20] Nothing that occurred to them as a people went unremem-

---

17. León-Portilla, *Aztec Thought*, 172–73.

18. León-Portilla explains (*Trece poetas,* 40) that the *tlamatinime* was called "el que sabe algo."

19. As in the case of the *tlacuilo* (see n. 14 above), there is evidence that there were some women present among the *tlamatinimes*. Once again, however, it seems not to have been a general practice, with the women who occupied this role coming from the noble class. More research is required in this area to ascertain the extent to which women shared in this role.

20. Fray Diego de Durán, "Comienza el calendario antiguo," *Historia de las Indias de Nueva España y Islas de Tierra Firme* (3 vols.; Mexico City: Editora Nacional, 1951) 2:247–305.

bered or unrecorded. It was the sacred responsibility of the *tlamatinime,* the wise one, to articulate faithfully all that comprised the narrative (oral) and symbolic (painted codices) tradition of the Nahuas.

As the *tlamatinimes* "turned"[21] the sheets of amate paper, a sound was produced that in time became easily associated with the image of the *tlamatinime.* They were referred to as those who noisily turned the pages of the illustrated manuscripts. They were "the guardians of the black and red ink,...writing and wisdom."[22] The wise one, the *tlamatinime,* was perceived as guide, possessor, and guardian of centuries of accumulated wisdom passed down from the beginning through generations of wise men. Similar to the declaration of the successful artist cited above, the statement of the successful *tlamatinime* would be:

> I sing the pictures of the book
> and see them propagating,
> I am a graceful bird
> for I can make the books speak
> within the house of the painting.[23]

The *tlamatinimes* were given to search deeply for the meaning contained in the painted codices; they were given to inner questioning in the pursuit of the truth. They boldly inquired into the whole of reality and investigated it with insatiable curiosity. Often their answers emerged in the composition of songs and poetry. It was said that to the *tlamatinime* belonged the black and red ink—symbolic metaphors for "writing" and wisdom. They read and interpreted the painted manuscripts and were perceived by the community as the teachers of truth. It was their task to place before the community the "mirror"[24] of tradition as a way of making it prudent and cautious. The *tlamatinime* passed on the traditional wisdom, the fruit of the wisdom of generations of the elders. It was that traditional wisdom that was constantly set before the community as a mirror, a mirror that allowed each person to perceive his or her personality or *rostro y corazón* (face and heart)[25] in relationship to the deposit of wisdom that had been proven through time. It was the sacred responsibility of the wise men to forge the *rostro y corazón* of the members of the community. It was that traditional wisdom that could faithfully continue to reproduce in each generation the face (*rostro*) of a people. It was the duty of the *tlamatinimes* not

---

21. We would say, "read" the sheets.
22. León-Portilla, *Aztec Thought,* 10.
23. León-Portilla, *Native Mesoamerican Spirituality,* 33.
24. A metaphor that stemmed from the Nahuatl idea of what it meant to be human and how the process of humanization took place. The educator, the teacher in the Nahuatl culture, had a principal role in making wise the countenances of others. In this way, it was the responsibility of the teacher to hold up the wisdom of the community as one does a mirror.
25. León-Portilla (*Aztec Thought,* 114–15) describes at length the meaning of the phrase *rostro y corazón,* relating it to the Nahuatl philosophy of education.

only to explore the mysteries of the paintings of the codices but also to interpret and teach the songs and poetry of the tradition to the people. In this manner, they attempted to orient the people morally and juridically, while they also preserved the record of their origins, their successes and failures.

Education: The Humanization of a People

Education occupied an important place in the social organization of all Mesoamerica. In Mexico-Tenochtitlán each neighborhood (*capulli*) was required to have a school. The educational system combined the religious and academic/social dimensions, resulting in a *templo-escuela* (temple-school) institution. The *templo-escuela* was primarily a place where young boys and girls were expected to render service to the titular god. In them Mesoamerican youths were given moral and religious instruction and were taught how to be contributing members of that society. This system of education encouraged the young to be involved in the production of goods based on the division of labor and hence responded to the needs of the social organization of the Nahuas; thus, for example, young men might be trained as farmers, construction workers, warriors, or priests.[26]

The Nahuas also established institutions of higher learning. The *calmemac* was the educational institution designated for the future *tlamatinime*. The wise one was trained from his earliest years to commit the tradition of his people "to heart" (memory). The writings of Fray Bernardino de Sahagún provide valuable information regarding the training given to the young males who were destined for the *calmemac*. According to Sahagún, shortly after birth the male child was offered to the teachers: "Lords, chieftains or old men (wise men) offered their sons to the house which was called *calmemac*; it was their intention that they should be educated there in order to become ministers (priests) of the idols."[27] Fifteen rules formed the framework of their education, all geared toward teaching them the truth that would make them capable of making others bear a wise countenance. The Nahuas had two words for education: *tlacahuapahualiztli*, which meant the art of strengthening or bringing up members of the community, and *neixtla machiliztil*, which signified the act of "giving wisdom to the face."[28] For the Nahuas education had the purpose of drawing the individual into the life of the community; the elders saw this as a priority in the education of the young.

However, the very act of "giving wisdom to the face" could be achieved only if the collective wisdom of the elders of the community was preserved.

---

26. See Alfredo López Austin, *La educación de los antiguos Nahuas* (2 vols.; Mexico City: Ediciones El Caballito, 1985).

27. Fray Bernardino de Sahagún Ribeira, *Historia general de las cosas de Nueva España* (Mexico City: Editorial Porrúa Larios, 1969) 30.

28. Cited in León-Portilla, *Aztec Thought,* 134–35.

This collective wisdom constituted the foundation upon which the educational system was established: education was to transmit "truth." High value was placed on the word of the elders, as is demonstrated in the following excerpt:

You who are my son, you who are my youth, hear the words, place, inscribe in the chambers of your heart the word or two that our forefathers left departing; the old men, the old women, the regarded ones on earth. Here is that which they gave us, entrusted to us, entrusted to us as they left, the words of the old men, that which is bound, the well-guarded words.[29]

To go against that which pointed out the path of proper living was to make mockery of the wisdom of the community embodied in the teachings of the wise ones. This good counsel applied to both male and female members of the community and was given by teacher and parent alike. The *palabra antigua* was spoken in order to educate the young with the message of wisdom that had been transmitted from one generation to the next. It was a word that was applied to a variety of life circumstances, ranging from the good counsel of parents to the governing task of the rulers.[30] While the cultural roles as determined in Nahuatl society shaped the application of the *palabra antigua,* all were held by the same general principle. To fail to listen to the *palabra antigua* would be to

give a bad name to our forebears, to those of the lineage that gave you birth. You will scatter dust and dung on the books of paintings in which their history is preserved. You will make them figures of fun. It will end forever, the book of paintings in which your memory was to be preserved.[31]

La Palabra Antigua and U.S. Hispanics

The oral tradition of the Mesoamerican world serves as a rich and humanizing inheritance for U.S. Hispanics/Latinos. Returning to these sources reveals the authoritative power that belongs to teachers, artists, poets, and theologians in the Hispanic community. The power of oral tradition persists in multiple ways throughout the Hispanic community in the United States. A striking example of the passing on of our history, *el hacer memoria* (the making of memory), is apparent in the development of a new visual language that has its root in the pre-Columbian painted codices.[32] This new visual language is expressed in the countless murals that can be

---

29. León-Portilla, *Native Mesoamerican Spirituality,* 78.

30. See Librado Silva Galeana, *Huehuehtlahtolli: Testimonios de la antigua palabra* (Mexico City: Secretaría de Educación Pública, Fondo de Cultura Económica, 1991).

31. Cited in León-Portilla, *Native Mesoamerican Spirituality,* 70–71.

32. See Eva Sperling Cockcroft and Holly Barnet-Sánchez, *Signs from the Heart: California Chicano Murals* (Venice, Calif.: Social and Public Art Resource Center, 1990) 1.

found throughout the diverse Hispanic/Latino neighborhoods in the United States.[33]

The resiliency of their symbolism witnesses to the persistence of a people's determination to transmit a historical identity to present and future generations of Hispanics/Latinos. Inevitably, the paintings combine symbols of the past, such as the architectural wonders of the temples intermingled with mythical figures of ancient gods, with scenes of current Hispanic/Latino reality—the life of factory workers, the plight of the undocumented, the mechanization of modern society, the need for education, the Hispanic family. Other murals portray modern historical figures, such as César Chávez, Emiliano Zapata, "La Adelita," Father Miguel Hidalgo, John F. Kennedy, Martin Luther King, Rubén Salazar.[34] The murals also document historical events and personalities[35] that have contributed significantly to the making of today's history and the current forging of the *rostro y corazón* of the Hispanic personality. While the murals depict the rich history of the past as well as the present struggles of the Hispanic community, they also evoke the memory of a strong religious heritage that continues to mark the intuitive religious spirit of today's Hispanic. Guadalupe appears in many neighborhood murals, often as a symbol of liberation and resurrection. The broken body of the crucified Jesus serves as an important religious symbol in mural art, whether it be at sites where gang violence has claimed the lives of youth or as a force behind such political struggles as that of the United Farm Workers (UFW). The images of the saints provide ample inspiration for muralists—vivid "embellished depictions of favored images such as El Sagrado Corazón de Jesús (The Sacred Heart of Jesus), El Santo Niño de Atocha (the Holy Child of Atocha), La Virgen de San Juan de Los Lagos (the Virgin of San Juan of the Lakes), and myriad others."[36]

The public nature of mural art "provides society with the symbolic representation of collective beliefs as well as a continuing re-affirmation of the collective sense of self."[37] It is an art form that belongs to the people and as such is available to everyone in open, public, neighborhood spaces. This kind of art is "popular" and accessible to everyone regardless of economic or social possibilities. The art of the murals makes it possible for marginalized communities to take claim of their rightful place in society by publicly manifesting the diverse aspects of their life. It is a vehicle of communication that educates, challenges, and inspires communities toward the ongoing appropriation of their dignity and cultural heritage.

---

33. Murals can be found in cities with significant Hispanic/Latino populations, such as Chicago, Los Angeles, Miami, San Francisco, and San Antonio. They can also be found in areas that have a smaller Hispanic presence.

34. Cockcroft and Barnet-Sánchez, *Signs from the Heart,* 29.

35. An example of this type of mural can be found on the campus of Stanford University in Palo Alto, California.

36. Cockcroft and Barnet-Sánchez, *Signs from the Heart,* 58–59.

37. Ibid., 5.

In many respects, therefore, the role of the *tlacuilo* is continued by the countless artists, often anonymous, of neighborhood murals, who take on the arduous commitment of constantly pondering the stories of the *pueblo* in order to communicate them faithfully in the mural paintings. These modern-day *tlacuilos* are challenged by their vocation as artists to master the symbolism of the people—the red and black ink of wisdom. It is imperative that they read in the collective social, economic, and political reality of the *pueblo* all the brush strokes of its history. The artist must be able to place before the community paintings that record its journey through the use of the rich symbols of its mythology and tradition. Following in the ancestral tradition of the Toltec master artists, the mural artists strive to apply the colors until perfection is achieved.[38] In order to be successful, the artist must strive to know the colors of all the flowers,[39] as did the Toltecs.[40]

In similar manner, the role of the *tlamatinime,* the wise one, continues to be actualized in today's Hispanic/Latino communities. The historical context has been altered by the consequences of the *conquista,* and the *calmemac* as an educational institution no longer exists. Nevertheless, the role continues to be realized by the wise persons present in the communities. Their credentials lie in the depth of wisdom earned in the process of living and validated by the trust that others in the community have placed in them. Often these roles are carried out by the elderly, the old women[41] and old men who faithfully transmit the wisdom they have guarded throughout their lives, a wisdom they learned from their grandparents and parents. They draw from a rich collection of stories, proverbs, and *dichos*[42] that synthesize in a few words advice based on the experience of the community. This good counsel is for the edification of young and old alike; it serves as a mirror wherein the forging of *rostro y corazón* can take place. This wisdom orients the people morally and judicially, as previous generations have attempted to do.[43]

The faithful transmission of the history of the people is guarded and

---

38. See León-Portilla, *Aztec Thought,* 172–73.

39. It is important to keep in mind that the Nahuas used the metaphor "flower and song" to mean "truth." In this context, the word "flower" is equivalent to "truth."

40. This is the same description given in ancient times for the *tlacuilo* of the Mesoamerican world. Miguel León-Portilla (*Aztec Thought and Culture,* 172–73) does a masterful job of detailing the task of the *tlacuilo.*

41. The importance of women in this regard must be stressed. In the Hispanic communities it has been the spoken word uttered by the grandmothers and mothers that has taught the young about the cultural and religious heritage that belongs to them. It has been the advice of these women that has directed and guided many of the young into adulthood and beyond.

42. Common sayings used to convey popular wisdom that can be applied to a given social situation.

43. See examples of wise counsel given to others in the Nahuatl world in the book written by Librado Silva and Natalio Hernández, *Flor y canto: De los antiguos Mexicanos* (Mexico City: El Día en Libros, 1990).

communicated by these modern-day *tlamatinimes*, and, just as in the days of old, this includes the religious customs and realities of the culture. It has often been said that the women in the Hispanic/Latino communities have functioned as the teachers of the faith. This they do for the most part by transmitting orally many religious traditions, customary prayers and rituals as well as the teachings of the faith. An example of the religious traditions passed on orally is the *posada*, a ritual repeated during the nine days preceding Christmas in which the community reenacts the search of Joseph and Mary for lodging. This reenactment is a very effective teaching technique, emphasizing the Christian imperative of hospitality to the stranger and sharing what we have with others. The oral transmission of faith, carried on by and large by Latinas, has sustained the faith in communities even in the midst of persecution and the absence of church ministers. By telling stories from the Bible, these women have often communicated the oral wisdom of the faith in ways that repeat anew the practice undertaken by their grandmothers and mothers when they were young. It is a word that gives and sustains life.

Another dimension of the *tlamatinime* and the *tlacuilo*—parallel to what today is called a theo-poet—is continued in the community by those Hispanic/Latino theologians who have committed their lives to the "articulation of the faith experience of United States Hispanics."[44] It is a commitment that requires the theologian to emulate the example set by the *tlamatinime* in assuming the role of the teacher and faithful communicator of the "song and poetry" (truth) of the *pueblo*. This is attempted in the same manner in which the original *tlamatinime* undertook the task of "giving wisdom to the face," that is, through constantly striving to commune with one's heart, where the divinity resides. This clearly entails a lifelong process that calls for the theologian to accompany the Hispanic people in order to be able to discern the movement of the Spirit in the unfolding of its historical journey.[45] The theologian must become knowledgeable in the "painted chronicles" of that journey and learn how to interpret both the "shadows and the lights" that are reflected in the lives of the U.S. Hispanic/Latino communities.

Following the example of the *tlamatinime*, the theologian must grapple with the lived reality of the community and then attempt to give voice to the challenges and religious understandings that it raises. In the tradition of the *tlamatinime* the theologian must learn to sing the songs that reveal the faith-experience of the *pueblo* in the full diversity of its socioeconomic, political, and cultural contexts and manifestations.[46] It is a daily

---

44. This phrase is taken from the mission statement of the Academy of Catholic Hispanic Theologians of the United States (ACHTUS). ACHTUS was founded in 1988 and currently has over sixty members.

45. See ibid.

46. Ibid.

pursuit in which the truth of a people's religious tradition and wisdom can be continuously reclaimed and proclaimed. This endeavor should enable the theologian not only to orient the people morally but also to reproduce in each generation the *rostro* of a people. This is a significant contribution that Hispanic/Latino theologians make to the ongoing historical task of our communities of forging our own *rostro y corazón,* our own identity within the United States.

Our identity as U.S. Hispanics is one of the serious theological issues our community must pursue. This preoccupation is reflected in the theological works of Hispanics that address primary concerns of justice, culture, and identity.[47] These modern *tlamatinimes*—the theologians—struggle in their attempts to make a significant contribution to the forging of a people's *rostro y corazón.* We are called to converse with our own hearts, where the deity resides. Only in this manner will the *rostro y corazón* of our Hispanic communities become an authentic revelation of their historical identity and personality. Only in this manner will the *rostro y corazón* of our people include the religious understandings that constitute an intrinsic part of our culture.

The rich oral tradition that is part of our culture can be a very valuable source for the development of U.S. Hispanic/Latino theology.[48] The roles of the *tlamatinime* and the *tlacuilo* are just as vital today as they were for our ancestors. We must look constantly in the face of the old women and the old men of our communities in search of wisdom. We must always set before ourselves their wisdom as a mirror. Therein we will see what we need to know to find our own *rostro y corazón.*

---

47. Arturo Bañuelas, former president of ACHTUS, has attempted to systematize the recurring themes evident in the work of Hispanic theologians; see "U.S. Hispanic Theology," *Columbus and the New World: Evangelization or Invasion?* (ed. Stephen Bevans and Ana María Pineda; special issue of *Missiology: An International Review* 20 [1992] 275–300).

48. Walter J. Hollenweger, "Flowers and Songs: A Mexican Contribution to Theological Hermeneutics," *International Review of Mission* 60 (1971) 232–44. The author suggests that the philosophical concept of *flor y canto* could offer another theological hermeneutics to the theological categories used by the Western world.

6

Sangre llama a sangre

Cultural Memory as a Source of Theological Insight

_____ *Jeanette Rodríguez* _____

For some time now I have been struggling with the question of how to identify and describe the notion of cultural memory. I see two experiences as crucial sources for my interest in cultural memory: my early discovery of Jewish origins within my family and my later research regarding the sixteenth-century phenomenon of Our Lady of Guadalupe in colonial Mexico.

The first experience took place during my college days in New York. I was a religious studies and philosophy major at a college where 80 percent of the students had their roots in Jewish culture and tradition. I am a "cradle" Roman Catholic and a New York Latina. My parents and brothers immigrated from Ecuador into the United States in 1952. Given my own bilingual and bicultural background, I cannot remember a time when I did not live in creative tension. This particular period, however, was one of intense struggle, as I wrestled with questions of religion and meaning in the twentieth century. Key to this *angst* of mine was my exposure to and understanding of the Holocaust. I thought that anyone in touch with their humanity would be outraged by the Holocaust. I was. Yet many of those around me and certainly our own American culture seemed blasé about this catastrophic tragedy. My own affective reaction included youthful indignation and a commitment that this should happen "never again." At home I attempted to regain inner peace.

One night while at the dinner table with the other members of my family, my father and I entered into a discussion about why I was so "obsessed" with the Holocaust. I suggested that perhaps I identified with a group that yearned to know their God and maintain their culture. As I became more visibly emotional in the discussion, my mother turned to my father and said, "Sangre llama a sangre" [Blood cries out to blood]; it is time to tell her." My father then began to tell me his story. He said his family had Jewish roots. As he spoke movingly of his origins, his discourse seemed vague and confused. While he spoke, several memories began to make sense

117

to me: how my father would drop us off at church on Sundays and then take off—I had thought it was simply a Latin American thing for a man to do; the yarmulke (a skull cap worn by observant Jews) I had seen in one of his drawers when I was in high school—he had explained that he kept it so that he could attend the prayer services of his employer, who was Jewish; how all of my cousins on my father's side in Latin America wore yarmulkes—I had always thought this very strange during my trips there; his swaying back and forth at prayer when he did come to church with us.

"Sangre llama a sangre" is an expression that connotes something in the blood that allows one to access the affective, "intuitive level." It surges up without any rational trappings. It has its own truth.

The second experience has to do with the image of Guadalupe. In the course of my doctoral research, I found that although second- and third-generation Mexican Americans have affective attachments to the image, they are unable to explain who she is or articulate what her message is about. I found it very curious indeed that they should be affectively attached to something that they could not explain. Nevertheless, it was clear to me that *something* was passed on to them, whether a feeling of comfort, a sense of security, or a family treasure. Whatever it was, it manifested itself at the affective level.[1]

In this essay, then, I should like to pursue this concept of cultural memory, of blood calling out to blood, by focusing on the image of Our Lady of Guadalupe as a salient example of this *something* that allows one access to the affective level, that surges up without rational trappings, that bears its own truth. In what follows I begin by identifying and describing the notion of cultural memory and then proceed to analyze the image of Guadalupe as an example of cultural memory.

The Concept of Cultural Memory

Tradition and Cultural Memory

A colleague of mine explains that "tradition passes on a world of meaning" from generation to generation.[2] It carries all the experiences of a people: personal as well as communal experiences; implicit and explicit understandings; myths; stories; affectivities—anything that actualizes the potential of the human person. Concerning tradition, Charles Davis further writes:

A tradition is a way of responding to reality, including feelings, memories, images, ideas, attitudes, interpersonal relationships: in brief, the entire complex that forms

---

1. See my book on the impact of Guadalupe on the psycho-theological development of Mexican American women: *Our Lady of Guadalupe: Faith and Empowerment among Mexican-American Women* (Austin: University of Texas Press, 1994).

2. I owe this insight to Michael Raschko, theologian for the archdiocese of Seattle, who in conversation provided this definition of the function of tradition.

life within a particular world, a world bounded by a horizon that determines the particular sense of reality that pervades it.[3]

Tradition also has two distinct parts: (1) the process—the *traditio,* the actual handing on; and (2) the product—the *traditium,* the content. In other words, tradition can be seen both as a participle, "remembering," and a noun, "remembrance" or "memory." In fact, participle and noun represent two sides of the same coin. The same two elements can be found in cultural memory: it is both a remembering and a remembrance or memory. One side of cultural memory is the *traditio,* the process. Who remembers? It is a people, a society, a culture that carries a memory. How is it remembered? It is remembered in memory, raised in celebration, passed on orally, recorded in writings, designated to a sacred place. The other side is the *traditium,* the product. What is being remembered? Again, in this essay I focus on the image of Our Lady of Guadalupe. What does this memory do? What does it evoke? What are its manifestations? I would contend that what is remembered or evoked includes feelings or affectivities, modes of action, forms of language, aspirations, interpersonal relations, images, ideas, ideals, and so forth. These elements and more may be contained in a memory. (See fig. 1 below.)

Moreover, a memory or content is carried by a people in their historical, social, and political context. Thus, in any given culture it is the social group that carries on from generation to generation that which they choose to pass on and perhaps that which they are even not conscious of passing on. With regard to cultural memory, therefore, I would contend that the people carry a memory and that the memory itself is also a carrier. Thus, for example, in the case of Guadalupe, a memory is captured—her image and message carry the memory and its content—and this memory in turn evokes an affectivity that bonds individuals not only to Guadalupe itself but also to one another.

Any social group that defines culture does so in and through the contents of its traditions—its feelings, modes of action, forms of language, aspirations, interpersonal relations, images, ideas, and ideals. Thus, tradition reveals a variety of contents: doctrine, stories, myths, creeds, symbols, experiences, and everyday moral decisions. Cultural memory represents another such carrier of the tradition, one that I have not found analyzed as such anywhere else.

Symbol and Cultural Memory

Traditions also reflect a variety of theological typologies, as Charles Davis makes clear:

---

3. Charles Davis, *Body as Spirit: The Nature of Religious Feeling* (New York: Seabury Press, 1976) 151.

Figure 1

TRADITION
(a way of responding to reality)

TRADITIO
Process
Participle—remembering

TRADITIUM
Content
Noun—remembrance

A. Who remembers?	B. How is it remembered?	C. What does it evoke?
– a people	– in memory	– feelings, biases
– a society	– in celebration	– modes of action
– a culture	– orally	– forms of language
	– in writings	– aspirations
		– interpersonal relations
		– images, ideas, ideals

CULTURE - - - - - - - -> MERGE <- - - - - - - - MEMORY

CULTURAL MEMORY
(as manifested in Our Lady of Guadalupe)

A.	B.	C.
– A people carry a memory	– Image/Story	– Feelings
– Memory is also a carrier	– Celebration	– Aspirations
	– *Nican Mopohua*	– Devotion
	– Basilica of Guadalupe	– Direction
		– Hope

Theologies are not pure, uncontaminated intellectual enterprises; they are influenced by a variety of interests. They are not self-contained entities; they are parts of a wider whole. They cannot be intelligently studied apart from other writings coming out of the same tradition taken as a whole. To make complete sense, they have to be replaced in the economic, social, political, and artistic life of the social groups from which they sprang.[4]

In other words, we are all influenced by experience. Each person is the product of a complex of experiences collected over a lifetime. When a person or a people have had a significant or depth experience, it is often embodied and expressed in a symbol. The symbol can pull together all the aspects of one's life and elevate the experience to an encounter with the di-

---

4. Ibid., 159.

vine. Within the Mexican American Catholic experience, the image of Our Lady of Guadalupe functions as such a symbol. The cultural memory of the Guadalupe event is a dynamic diachronic carrier of meaning, symbolized in her image. Through her story, image, and affective influence, she carries, by means of cultural memory, the religio-cultural tradition of the Mexican American people. From generation to generation, the cultural memory of Guadalupe tells Mexican Americans who they are and to whom they belong.

A theology that raises questions of truth, meaning, and affectivity is imperative for understanding the power behind the story of Our Lady of Guadalupe. Her story has a threefold significance. First, it serves as the foundation of Mexican Christianity: that is, it manifests the conversion of the indigenous people. Second, it provides a connection between the indigenous and the Spanish cultures.[5] Third, the story anchors and supports a cultural memory, an unexplored dimension that I will develop in this essay.

Understanding Cultural Memory

Cultural memory bears similarities to both historical memory and myth. Like historical memory, cultural memory is rooted in actual events and in the surrounding and resulting alignment of images, symbols, and affectivity that turn out to be even more persuasive than "facts." There are many kinds of historical memories transmitted through texts, oral history, tradition, plays, and memory. Occasionally, there are historical memories that are so overwhelmingly important that they define the essence of a people and become imperative for their survival. Such is the case of the Holocaust. Thus, the Jewish people exclaim, "Never again!" They will survive meaningfully only as long as the historical memory of the Holocaust remains active and alive.

Unlike myth, cultural memory has a historical basis; however, like myth, it can be transformative. It has power to influence human life. Thus, Wendy Doniger O'Flaherty argues:

A myth is a story that is sacred to and shared by a group of people who find their most important meanings in it; it is a story believed to have been composed in the past about an event in the past, . . . an event that continues to have meaning in the present because it is remembered; it is a story that is part of a larger group of stories.[6]

Suggesting that a story is sacred immediately throws us into questions of religious meaning: questions about life and death, divine intervention,

---

5. See Virgilio Elizondo, *Galilean Journey: The Mexican-American Promise* (Maryknoll, N.Y.: Orbis Books, 1983); idem, *La Morenita: Evangelizer of the Americas* (San Antonio: Mexican-American Cultural Center, 1980).

6. Wendy Doniger O'Flaherty, *Other People's Myths* (New York: Macmillan, 1988) 27.

creation, human nature, culture, ultimate meaning. Religious and psycho-social themes are difficult to separate from cultural memory because the private and the public realms are closely intertwined. This transforming characteristic attributed to myth is also characteristic of what is carried on in the process of cultural memory. Thus, cultural memory transmits an experience rooted in history that has reached a culturally definitive, transformative status. As such, the myth/story of Guadalupe not only is a "master symbol . . . [because] it enshrines the major hopes and aspirations of an entire society"[7] but also has transformative potential as well.

Cultural memory need not emerge from a catastrophic tragedy; in fact, most often it arises out of events that prove transformative, that bring about recognizable shifts in the world of meaning of a people. Thus, cultural memory fulfills the need to transcend certain events or circumstances (for example, the Holocaust) and/or maintain a corporate identity, as in the case of historical events used to generate patriotism (the American patriots and the Boston Tea Party; Guadalupe and Mexican identity). This memory passes from generation to generation, from parent to child, from leader to follower, from church to adherent, through oral traditions, written accounts, images, rituals, and dramas. Cultural memory is evoked around image, symbol, affect, or event precisely because it keeps alive and transforms those events of the past that are not bound to the past but continue to give meaning to the present.

Guadalupe as Cultural Memory

Historical Background

The Guadalupe event is a historical occurrence. It is rooted in history. There is a given content to Guadalupe, not just whatever one wants to think about this event. Memory is carried in memory, like a couple who will never forget the beginnings of their relationship, yet whose relationship changes over time. It is "cultural" because culture is a living and dynamic reality. Memory does something about defining this culture. Carriers of culture put emphasis on the memory. This holding on to, passing on, and reinterpreting of the memory is not only an intellectual but also an affective process.

In this regard I am grateful for the insights and application of memory to be found in the practical fundamental theology of Johann Baptist Metz. Metz contends that memory can be an "expression of eschatological hope" and a "category of the salvation of identity."[8] He further states that

---

7. Eric R. Wolf, "The Virgin of Guadalupe: A Mexican National Symbol," *Journal of American Folklore* 71 (1958) 34–39.

8. Johann Baptist Metz, *Faith in History and Society: Toward a Practical Fundamental Theology* (New York: Crossroad, 1980) 184.

"memory is...of central importance in any theory of history and society as a category of persistence to the passage of time."[9] This understanding and application of memory provide a model for grasping the impact of the Guadalupe event. Our Lady of Guadalupe represents an eschatological hope for those who believe in her: she reveals that the world is not as it is meant to be. To uphold the memory of the Guadalupe event is to show "solidarity in memory with the dead and the conquered."[10]

To put it succinctly, cultural memory continues to exist because it feeds a basic need for identity, salvation, hope, and resistance to annihilation. The cultural memory of the Guadalupe event exists because there is a need for it. The story speaks of the restoration of human dignity in a voice once silenced and now restored. It speaks of the restoration of a lost language and a way of perceiving the divine. It speaks of accessing lost symbols and transforming them in a new time. Ultimately, it speaks and continues to speak of a shared experience of a people—a people that suffers. The Guadalupe event resurrected the Nahuatl cultural memory at a time when everything in the world of the Nahuatl people had been destroyed. By activating their cultural memory, Our Lady of Guadalupe empowered and renewed the life of that people.

How did she do this? What characteristics of Nahuatl cultural memory does the Guadalupe story activate? The following points from the story should be particularly noted in this regard. First, Guadalupe speaks not in the language of the conquistadores (Spanish) but rather in the language of the conquered, the oppressed, the marginalized, and the silenced (Nahuatl). Second, when she appears, she presents herself in the symbols of the people. She thus uses the symbols of the marginalized and at the same time transforms them. Third, by utilizing the names of the gods of the Nahuatl people, she identifies herself as *uno de ellos* (one of them). Consequently, Guadalupe resurrects the cultural memory of the people by entering into their history and incarnating their culture, symbols, and language. In so doing, she validates and gives them a place in the world. She dialogues with them and thus empowers them. She restores their dignity and facilitates their liberation by demanding that they participate in the reclaiming of their own voice. She shows "solidarity in memory with the dead and the conquered." This process of empowerment is played out in the person of Juan Diego, who represents the oppressed people.

The image of Guadalupe pervades the neighborhoods of over twelve million people of Mexican descent in the United States: whether as a statue or painting in a sacred corner of the home or as an image on T-shirts, on the sides of buildings, and even on business logos. Her name, Guadalupe, is not

---

9. Ibid., 184–85.
10. Ibid., 114.

only bestowed by parents on their children, both girls and boys, but also given to parishes and churches, streets and towns, rivers and mountains.

A fuller appreciation of the Guadalupe story as cultural memory can be gained by understanding the context in which it was first told and experienced. The analysis that follows is based on the research of Clodomiro Siller, a Mexican priest, theologian, and anthropologist. Siller combines his academic work in anthropology with extensive pastoral work among the indigenous peoples of Mexico.[11] His anthropological interest in indigenous peoples, particularly those who speak Nahuatl, as well as his theological work are based on liberation theology. The primary reason for using Siller's work is that he is among the very few who have attempted to understand the Guadalupe event from the viewpoint of the indigenous Nahuas rather than from the perspective of those who are too quick to Christianize the event. What follows, therefore, is a close reading of the narrative of the apparition with particular emphasis on its meaning within sixteenth-century Nahuatl culture.

The *Nican Mopohua* document that records the story of Our Lady of Guadalupe was written in Nahuatl. This language is highly symbolic: it is "much beyond words, much more profound, more significant, much more rich and full. It is a simple language, direct, smooth, precise, elegant, resounding, beautiful, profound, highly significant, and even sublime."[12] Two important aspects of the Nahuatl language are (1) the use of *disfracismos*— a way of communicating profound concepts by using two words or symbols instead of one; and (2) the use of numerology—the interpretation of numbers as having symbolic meaning; two numbers are particularly significant in the Nahuatl language and culture: the number four, which indicates completion, and the number five, which refers to the center of the world.

An understanding of Nahuatl cultural symbols and myth is essential for interpreting the *Nican Mopohua* narrative. According to Siller, an attempt to read the narrative with a Hebrew mentality would render it false.[13] Such a reading would impose a preconceived meaning on the symbols and, as a result, neglect the unique symbolic universe of the Nahuatl people. The Nahuas themselves must function as the principal spokespersons for telling other cultures about Nahuatl culture. As is true in all cultures, Nahuatl myths help determine the meaning and significance of their cultural symbols. These become multivalent over time. The flower, for example, represents for the Nahuas truth, beauty, and authenticity. Thus, Nahuatl mythology holds that the truth of all things was brought by the god Quetzalcoatl in the form of a flower so that humanity could live happily.

---

11. Clodomiro A. Siller, *Flor y canto del Tepeyac: Historia de las apariciones de Santa María Guadalupe* (Mexico City: Servir, 1981). All translations of Siller's work, which is unavailable in English, are mine.

12. Ibid., 12.

13. Ibid., 12–13.

Sources of the Narrative

Our Lady of Guadalupe appeared in 1531. Because her appearance dates from well before the age of newspapers and the mass media, it contrasts radically with later appearances, such as that of Lourdes, where the story was immediately carried around the world by rail and steamship. Further, Guadalupe emerged in a society with an enormous language divide. At Lourdes, everyone spoke the same language, and all pilgrims recited one and the same story, which revolved around the well-known person of Bernadette de Soubirou and the similarly well-known grotto by the river. At Tepeyac, however, a whole world separated the Indians, who thought in terms of Tonantzin (Our Mother) and their own traditions, and the Spaniards, who thought in terms of the old Marian shrine of Guadalupe in Extremadura (Spain), a well at the base of the hill, and in terms of other ancient Marian shrines of Europe and the whole Catholic tradition regarding the Virgin in general.

Although there are different positions with regard to the existence of an oral tradition concerning the Guadalupe event, there is evidence that such a tradition did indeed exist, including Juan Diego's own testimony for as long as seventeen years after the event itself:[14]

From Indian to Indian, from community to community, the word spread. What had happened to Juan Diego at Mount Tepeyac began to be told, along with his adventures in Mexico City, how the Virgin had cured his uncle, and the other marvels that took place in the presence of the Virgin of Guadalupe. Rapidly, the deeds began to enter the traditions of the people.[15]

In addition, the appearance of Our Lady of Guadalupe in 1531 is recorded in an ancient document entitled *Nican Mopohua,* a copy of which I was able to examine in the course of on-site research in March 1986 at the Institute for Guadalupan Studies in Mexico City. The oldest copy of the *Nican Mopohua* was written by the learned Indian convert Antonio Valeriano, sometime between 1540 and 1545.[16] It should be pointed out, however, that some scholars date this report much later, as late as the seventeenth century (1649), and attribute its authorship to Luis Lasso de la Vega, a chaplain at the shrine at Tepeyac.[17] In the first volume of the *Monumentos Guadalupanos,* there are two ancient copies of the Guadalupan account written by Antonio Valeriano. The paper is literally worn away in many places, especially the first page. The second copy, dated

14. See Thomas J. Ascheman, "Guadalupan Spirituality for Cross-Cultural Missionaries" (M.A. thesis, Catholic Theological Union at Chicago, 1983) 84.

15. Siller, *Flor y canto,* 11.

16. See Elizondo, *La Morenita,* 47–48; Mario Rojas, *Nican Mopohua: Traducción del Nahuatl al Castellano* (Huejutla, Hidalgo, Mexico: n.p., 1978); Siller, *Flor y canto,* 14. The translation of the quotations from the work by Mario Rojas are mine.

17. Martinus Cawley, *Guadalupe—from the Aztec Language* (CARA Studies in Popular Devotion, no. 2: Guadalupan Studies, no. 6; Lafayette, Oreg.: Guadalupe Abbey, 1984).

about forty years after the first, toward the end of the sixteenth century, is written in a far more careful literary style.[18] The earlier version has a spelling and writing style that is characteristic of the mid–sixteenth century. In addition, the vocabulary, language, sentence structure, and idioms of the two documents are different. The earlier document is written in a literary style that reflects the way the Indians spoke at the time.[19] The text used here is the one translated into Spanish by Don Primo Feliciano Velázquez in 1926.

The Text

A text is true to the extent that it leads one toward further meaning. In this section I shall describe and disclose the meaning of the text/narrative. The apparition narrative of Our Lady of Guadalupe in the *Nican Mopohua* begins with the historical context of the event. The Virgin Mary, mother of God, appeared in the setting of the *post guerra* (1531), ten years after the final conquest of the Aztec Empire by the Spaniards in 1521. Our Lady of Guadalupe appeared to Juan Diego at Tepeyac in what is today the northern part of Mexico City. At the time of the apparition, the Aztec nation was in a state of subordination, alienation, suffering, and oppression.

Guadalupe reveals herself as coming from "El verdadero Dios, por quien se vive" (The true God who gives us life). In Nahuatl this phrase served as the name of one of the gods. When the Virgin states that she is from the one true God, the God who gives life, the Nahuas would have recognized this God to be their God.[20] Moreover, Guadalupe's self-designation as "always Virgin" is Nahuatl for *doncella entera,* or "whole woman," in Spanish. Virginity was highly valued in Nahuatl culture by both men and women. Consequently, they would have looked upon Our Lady of Guadalupe as an embodiment of a preconquest value of their culture (27). Thus, her image represents values esteemed by the Nahuas themselves.

The *Nican Mopohua* text records Saturday, December 9, 1531, early in the morning, as the time of the apparition. In Nahuatl culture, *muy de madrugada* (very early in the morning) referred not only to daybreak but also to the beginning of all time. Thus, the image represents the beginning of something new. The Guadalupe event takes on the significance of a foundational experience equal in importance to the origin of the world and the cosmos (37).

The apparition account relates that, on his way to church, Juan Diego hears music. In the context of Nahuatl *disfracismos,* music represented one-

18. See Ernst J. Burrus, *The Basic Bibliography of the Guadalupan Apparitions (1531–1723)* (CARA Studies in Popular Devotions, no. 4; Guadalupan Studies, no. 4; Washington, D.C.: Center for Applied Research in the Apostolate [CARA], 1981).

19. Ibid.

20. Siller, *Flor y canto,* 32; references to this work in the following paragraphs appear in the text.

half of a dual way of expressing truth, beauty, philosophy, and divinity. Flower and song together manifested the presence of the divine. When Juan Diego hears such beautiful and enchanting music, he asks, "Have I gone into paradise? Can I be hearing what I am hearing?" The word *canto* (song or music) appears five times. As mentioned above, in Nahuatl cosmology, five was a symbol for the center of the world (38–39). The reference to *canto*, then, points to another way of experiencing, understanding, and conceptualizing contact with the divine. Similarly significant in the Nahuatl account is the use of the number four, which symbolizes cosmic totality or completion. In the text Juan Diego asks four questions: First, "Am I worthy to hear what I am hearing; perhaps I am dreaming?" Second, "I must awake from this dream. Where am I?" Third, "Perhaps I have entered the land of paradise that our ancient ones have told us about?" Finally, "Am I in heaven?" There is a moment of silence between the time Juan Diego hears the music and asks the questions. This silence, in conjunction with nighttime, represents another dual Nahuatl expression that serves to link the event with the origins of creation (40–41).

Upon hearing the music, Juan Diego looks to the east, the home of the sun and symbol of God. The sun rises in the east, the direction from which Guadalupe appears. Again, Guadalupe enters the Nahuatl reality in a way that the people can understand. She first addresses Juan Diego by the diminutive form, Juan Dieguito—a Nahuatl form of expression conveying maternal love, delicacy, and reverence (42). The *Nican Mopohua* does not emphasize Guadalupe's apparition to Juan Diego but rather his "encounter" with her. What is the nature of this encounter? There are two characters: Juan Diego and Our Lady of Guadalupe. Juan Diego, a fifty-two year old man, is a member of the oppressed and enslaved indigenous people. How does he perceive Our Lady of Guadalupe? He sees her as a woman of nobility. At this point, the text makes an important distinction. Our Lady of Guadalupe is standing up. Nobles, however, whether Aztec or Spaniard, would receive people sitting down, sometimes on a pedestal or in some other specific, designated place. Such a posture was meant to show not only that the individual in question presided over the people but also, given the experience of the conquest, that such an individual had dominion over the people. In the case of Guadalupe, however, the nobility that Juan Diego observes in this woman is not of the dominant sort (43). Unlike the conquistadores, Guadalupe does not treat Juan Diego as one of the conquered ones; on the contrary, she acknowledges and restores his dignity by her posture, her words, and her dialogue.

Guadalupe's presence also elicits a response from the earth. The flowers and the ground, the text reports, glow like gold. This encounter affects the world. Guadalupe, therefore, presents new life for the people and for the land. The text further describes the "Lady" as clothed with the radiance of the sun. In Nahuatl culture, a person's clothing, especially that of an important person, was dyed a certain color and adorned with objects or symbols that revealed who that person was, who had sent that person, or from where that person had come. The rays of sun emanating from behind Guadalupe informed the indigenous people, as represented by Juan Diego, that God formed part of her experience and personality (44). Virgilio Elizondo puts it as follows: "The Sun god was the principal god in the native pantheon.... She is greater than the greatest of the native divinities yet she does not do away with the Sun."[21]

One of the most important lines in the narrative is that in which Guadalupe reveals her identity: "Know and be assured, the smallest of my children, that I am the ever Virgin Mary, Mother of the true God, for whom one lives, the creator on which all depends, Lord of the heavens and the earth."[22] Thus, Guadalupe identifies herself as: (1) mother of God, who is the God of truth; (2) mother of the giver of life; (3) mother of the Creator; (4) mother of the one who makes the sun and the earth; and (5) mother of the one who is near. These titles coincide with names given the ancient Aztec gods. She refers to five names of gods known to the Nahuas. Guadalupe states who she is and where she is from using Nahuatl duality and phrases.

The Virgin tells Juan Diego that she wants a temple to be built for her, where she can bestow her *love, compassion, strength,* and *protection* on all those who come to her. She wishes her house to be at Tepeyac, a site of great significance.[23] Previously, it had been the shrine of Tonantzin, one of the major earth mother divinities of the Aztec people. One scholar argues that "it was very natural for the Aztec to associate Guadalupe with the pagan Tonantzin since both were virgin mothers of gods and both appeared at the same place."[24] Yet several major differences are noted between Tonantzin and Guadalupe:

The Virgin of Guadalupe was not a mere Christian front for the worship of a pagan goddess. The adoration of Guadalupe represented a profound change in Aztec religious belief.... Tonantzin was both a creator and a destroyer. The nature and function of the Virgin of Guadalupe are entirely different from those of the pagan earth goddess. The Christian ideals of beauty, love, and mercy associated with the Virgin of Guadalupe were never attributed to the Aztec deity. The functions of the Catholic Virgin are much broader and more beneficial to man than those of the Aztec nature goddess. Guadalupe protects her children (the Mexicans) from harm, cures their sicknesses, and aids them in all manner of daily undertakings.[25]

---

21. Elizondo, *La Morenita*, 85.

22. *A Handbook of Guadalupe* (Kenosha, Wis.: Franciscan Marystories Press, 1974).

23. Siller, *Flor y canto*, 50.

24. William Madsen, "Religious Syncretism," *Social Anthropology*, vol. 6, *Handbook of Middle American Indians* (ed. Manning Nash; Austin: University of Texas Press, 1967) 369–91.

25. Ibid., 378.

The text relates how Juan Diego, following the mandate of Guadalupe, goes to the bishop, only to be told to return at a more convenient time. Juan Diego returns to Guadalupe and despondently addresses the Virgin as "Señora, la más pequeña, de mis hijas" (Lady, the most humble of my daughters). By referring to the Virgin in this manner, he implies that she too is poor and despised, just as he is. Juan Diego tells the Virgin to send someone "who is of greater importance, who is known, who is respected, and who is esteemed." The use of four terms to describe the ideal envoy represents, in keeping with Nahuatl numerology, totality and completion. Juan Diego believes that he is not taken seriously because he is an Indian and that her mission would best be completed if a person of higher status were sent.

Juan Diego asks forgiveness from the Virgin for any pain he may have caused her by his failure to convince the bishop of her message. Juan Diego believes that it is his fault that he was not accepted.[26] This sense of self-depreciation and unworthiness reflects the tragic result of the conquest, whereby the Aztec people took on an "oppressed mentality," a "victim mentality," leading to a loss of their sense of self-worth. The Virgin absolutely refuses to choose another messenger. She reaffirms her desire that Juan Diego be her messenger, although she has "many servants and messengers" from whom to choose. She does not negate or deny the oppression that Juan Diego is experiencing, but she does insist on and begs for his involvement, using such phrases as "Con rigor te mando"; "Te ruego"; and "Mucho te ruego" (I command you; I beg you; I beg you very much).

The account portrays the conversation as a dialogue between equals. Guadalupe accords Juan Diego the dignity and respect of a person who has the freedom to choose (64–65). She concludes her conversation with Juan Diego as follows: "And once again, tell the Bishop that I send you, the ever Virgin, holy Mary, Mother of God, it is she who sends you." In response, Juan Diego reaccepts and reembraces this mission. His desire not to cause the Virgin any pain as well as his wish to make his commitment manifest are evident in his joyful and energetic response: "I will go and complete your order" (65).

Following this conversation, Juan Diego returns to the bishop's home in Mexico City. Once again, Juan experiences difficulties. He subjects himself to distrust, humiliation, and disbelief for the sake of the mission. When the bishop finishes interrogating Juan Diego, he states that he cannot build the temple on the Indian's word alone. He sends Juan Diego back to ask the Virgin for a sign. Siller makes an interesting observation with regard to the communication between Juan Diego and the bishop (68–69). When Juan Diego is speaking with the bishop, he refers to the Virgin as the "always

---

26. Siller, *Flor y canto*, 61; references to this work in the following paragraphs appear in the text.

Virgin, Holy Mary, Mother of Our Savior the Lord Jesus Christ." Siller
suggests that this is a theological reflection on the part of Juan Diego (69).
Guadalupe never refers to herself as the mother of our savior the Lord Jesus
Christ. Siller argues that with the return of the self (Juan Diego's restored
dignity) comes the ability and perhaps the freedom to theologize.

After agreeing to elicit a sign from the Lady so that the bishop may believe, Juan Diego returns home. When he arrives at his home, he finds that
his uncle, Juan Bernardino, is sick. His uncle asks Juan Diego to go to Mexico City and bring back a priest to administer the last rites. Juan Diego finds
himself caught in a dilemma. Is he to fulfill his uncle's request, or is he to
meet the Lady in order to receive the sign? The issue of death is paramount.
Juan Diego decides to go for a priest so that the last rites may be given:

> The sickness of the uncle came at a crucial moment in the mission of Juan
> Diego....For us perhaps it would have been more important if the mother or
> father of Juan Diego was sick,...but for most of the meso-American people, the
> uncle played a social role of capital importance....The uncle received the maxi-
> mum expression of respect that one could give an adult and he was the critical
> element in understanding the barrio and the people. (76)

On his way to Mexico City, Juan Diego decides to take an alternate
route so as not to have to "disappoint the Lady." However, as he is walking, he hears the Lady calling to him, asking him where he is going. Juan
Diego is convinced that the sad news of his uncle's mortal illness will cause
grief for the Virgin. He begins his conversation with her by saying, "I'm
going to cause you affliction" (79). Guadalupe's response to Juan Diego's
concern is expanded to include all sickness and anguish. She says, "No
temas esa enfermedad, ni otra alguna enfermedad y angustia" (Do not fear
this sickness, or any other sickness or anguish) (82). She further asks, "Am
I not here, your Mother? Are you not under my shadow and protection?
Am I not your fountain of life? Are you not in the folds of my mantle,
in the crossing of my arms? Is there anything else that you need?" Again,
there are five questions, indicating a reference to the center of the world.
In these questions, Guadalupe reveals herself as someone with authority.
For Mexicans a person with authority was a person who had the ability
to cast a shadow, precisely what Guadalupe does with her mantle: "Mexicans understood authority...as one who casts a large shadow...because
the one who is greater than all the rest must shelter or protect the great
and small alike" (83).

Juan Diego believes in Guadalupe's authority, and Juan Bernardino is
cured, giving rise thereby to the Virgin's first miracle. However, a greater
miracle occurs when the apparition of Guadalupe brings psychic healing
for Juan Diego and ultimately the whole Nahuatl people. The healing of the
uncle extends to Juan, who "felt much consoled and was left feeling con-
tented" (84). At peace with the knowledge that his uncle had been cured,

Juan Diego asks the Virgin to send him, with a sign, to the bishop. The Virgin orders Juan Diego to go to the top of Tepeyac and look for roses to cut, gather, and bring to her. She touches the flowers and makes herself present in them, thus remaining within the symbolic logic of the Indians, for whom flowers signified truth and divinity (86–88).

Juan Diego, filled with faith and resolve, goes to the bishop's palace. There he encounters disrespect and ridicule from the courtiers, yet he holds his ground and waits to see the bishop. Siller makes another interesting observation to the effect that such a scene is quite common whenever an Indian or a poor person is placed in the power of the dominant culture. In this particular case, the servants at the bishop's palace try to take away what Juan Diego is holding in his *tilma* (cloak), but Guadalupe had ordered him not to show the flowers to anyone except the bishop. Siller sees this attempt to take the flowers from Juan Diego as symbolic: it is an attempt on the part of the dominant culture to take away the Indian's truth. The conquerors and the dominant culture have already taken from Juan Diego and his people their land, their goods, their city, their form of government, and their reasons for being and acting. Now they want to take away Juan Diego's symbol of truth, that is, all he has left. Siller argues that, given the Guadalupe event, it is no longer possible to take the truth away from the indigenous people (93). Rather, it is Juan Diego, an Indian, who brings the truth to the Spanish bishop.

After having Juan Diego wait for a long time, the servants inform the bishop of his presence and allow Juan Diego to enter. Again, Juan Diego relates his story. He implies that by doubting him and asking him for a sign, the bishop is, in fact, questioning and demanding a sign from the Virgin. In the text, Juan Diego says that the Virgin "sent me up to this hill to get flowers, but I knew it was not the season, yet I did not doubt." After this statement, Juan Diego hands over the proof, the roses, and asks the bishop to take them. As the flowers fall from Juan Diego's *tilma,* the fifth apparition occurs. The image of Guadalupe appears imprinted on the *tilma.* When the bishop and those around him see it, they all kneel, admire it, and repent for their failure to believe.

Concluding Comments

What theological insights can be derived from this cultural memory of Our Lady of Guadalupe? To begin with, I would argue that Our Lady of Guadalupe represents far more than just compassion, relief, and a means for reconciliation between two different peoples. In fact, Virgilio Elizondo has already identified at least four powerful theological interpretations of this drama.[27]

---

27. Elizondo, *La Morenita,* 87–92.

First, by identifying herself as "mother of the true God through whom one lives," Guadalupe identifies herself with the supreme creative power, that is, the power of creative and creating presence.[28] Second, Guadalupe is a symbol of a new creation, a new people: "Only in an event that clearly originated in heaven could the conquest and rape of the people of Mexico be reversed and a people be truly proud of their new existence."[29] Third, Guadalupe responds to the deepest instincts of the Mexican psyche, which Elizondo identifies as an obsession with legitimacy, that is, anxiety about being an orphaned people.[30] I would go so far as to say that the drama addresses a deeper need for dignity, for restoration of self, a self made in the image and likeness of the Creator. Ultimately, the drama speaks of unconditional love and a place in salvation history. Perhaps most significantly, Guadalupe also suggests that the deeper need is to experience the maternal face of God. Fourth, Guadalupe symbolizes a reversal of power: "The reversal of power was not done through military force . . . but through the compenetration of symbols whose core meaning is somewhat mutually understood."[31]

To these four I would add the following four theological insights of my own. The first is that God does care: God is faithful to the covenant that promises that God is *our* God and that we are God's people. Guadalupe constitutes a further manifestation of that promise of God. Johann Baptist Metz writes, "Christian faith can be understood as an attitude according to which man remembers promises that have been made and hopes that are experienced as a result of those promises and commits himself to those memories."[32] Such is precisely the case with the devotees of Guadalupe. Through the process that carries cultural memory, the people remember the promises of compassion, help, and defense that Guadalupe has made. Because these promises have been made, the people experience hope—a hope carried through cultural memory. As a result of these promises, the people commit themselves to the Guadalupan memory and image—"that which can be read, touched, felt, seen, experienced."

The second insight is that Guadalupe represents a symbol of death and resurrection. In many ways she frees people to die to the old, destructive, and painful life and to believe in new life. I often tell people, when giving presentations on Guadalupe, that if they are unable to remember a time in their lives when they felt as if they were nothing, they will never be able to understand the Guadalupan story. To do so, we must remember where we came from, that we are dust, that we were slaves in Egypt, that we are oppressed, and that God has carried us and will continue to carry us to

28. Ibid., 88.
29. Ibid., 90.
30. Ibid.
31. Ibid., 91.
32. See Metz, *Faith in History and Society,* 200.

freedom. Cultural memory reminds us both of those who sought to control and dominate us and of those who led us to freedom.

The third insight has to do with the example of God, who, in order to enter into a divine-human dialogue, was willing to undergo an act of self-humbling, to come in human form. In the same way, Guadalupe also enters into the Nahuatl world, the Mexican world, the Mexican American world, the world of those who call out to her, believe in her, and trust in her. She comes in a way that the people can readily understand: clothed in their symbols and embodying their identity. She accesses and resurrects a memory in cultural stories and truths. She meets the people where they are and leads them to a deeper wisdom. She makes use of their symbols and leads them beyond the symbols.

The fourth and final insight is that Guadalupe's message of love and compassion, help and protection, cannot be frozen into a mere devotional experience. Rather, the message has to do with the affirmation of a people. Her image is a carrier of eschatological hope insofar as the people visit her, look upon her, and know that everything will be fine. Such knowledge, however, does not at all mean that nothing further is expected of them, since everything will be fine; on the contrary, she hears, affirms, heals, and enables them. Part of the healing, therefore, is a call for them to stand up for themselves.

There is so much more that could be passed on about this story, about the significance of affectivity, about carriers of culture, about cultural memory. However, given the constraints of the present essay, I should like to conclude with the following two comments. First, I find a quotation from Baba Dioum very much to the point: "In the end what will endure is what we love, and what we love is what we understand, and what we understand we are taught." Thus, it is my hope that the message and image of the power and the healing of Our Lady of Guadalupe will continue to be loved, understood, and taught. Second, although I have identified and described an image that speaks to a depth experience remembered within Mexican American culture, I believe that the Christian tradition is ample enough to be cross-cultural. Unfortunately, what we have done in our efforts to be Christian has been by and large to eliminate other cultures. Yet it is clear that the image of Guadalupe not only lies within Christian culture but also reclaims and honors the culture of the Mexican American. What would happen then if Christianity began to reclaim other cultural traditions—such as the Celtic, the African, and the Caribbean—that have been similarly eliminated? Perhaps then our brothers and sisters would no longer feel like aliens in the promised land.

7

Sources of a Hispanic/ Latino American Theology

A Pentecostal Perspective

Samuel Solivan

The Hispanic American Theological Locus

All Christian theological discourse draws upon a number of common resources for its task. At the same time, the various denominational, cultural, and ethnic dimensions of such discourse are operative not only in the identification of the sources in question but also in their interpretation and application. This must be kept in mind when analyzing Hispanic theologies. All of these theologies draw from the Scriptures, the history of the church, reason, and the experience of the faithful. Yet each variation employs these sources in the light of its own locus. Consequently, one's locus (context, milieu, *Sitz im Leben*) serves as the matrix that organizes and prioritizes the multiple sources and levels of interaction among them. This occurs in both an intentional and an unintentional manner. Theologians' awareness of their relationship to their locus and of the dynamic relationship of this locus to their implicit and explicit sources will have considerable impact on their critical constructive task.

In the case of North American Hispanic/Latino theology, a multidimensional matrix is required at various levels of its theological development. The Hispanic/Latino locus responds to what Virgilio Elizondo has called a *mestizaje* incorporating various cultural, racial, ethnic, historical, and theological streams.[1] Indeed, as one seeks to nuance a particular Hispanic perspective, it will be necessary to identify and describe a specific locus for each of its component parts. This task is further complicated when one considers the variety in denominational affiliation present among Protestant Hispanics, which is not to say that a similar variety is not present among Roman Catholics.

---

1. Virgilio Elizondo introduced this concept in his book *Galilean Journey: The Mexican American Promise* (Maryknoll, N.Y.: Orbis Books, 1983).

One must also recognize that one's locus is dynamic, always in flux, moving and being changed, as it responds to the dynamic variants of its larger global context. The task of locus identification is therefore complex and fluid, subject to a number of competing and at times conflicting factors always under consideration. Moreover, in identifying and articulating a Hispanic theological locus, one is also immediately confronted with the fact that the principal identifying tag, whether "Hispanic" or "Latino," is itself a disputed question among us.[2]

The Hispanic American theological locus is thus as varied as our people. Economic status, race, gender, theological perspective, denominational affiliation, ideology, and regionalism are but some of the factors that inform our diversity. One's self-consciousness about how context informs or misinforms one's theological and praxeological orientation directly influences how the other variables of our ethnicity interrelate and coalesce or conflict with one another. Quite often, the single variable that unites us is language, but even that is a problematic statement, since growing numbers of Hispanics are English-speaking monolinguals.

The issue of the location and context of a Hispanic theology is crucial insofar as one's starting point informs the overall perspective, direction, and history with which one works, to which one reacts, and by which one is informed. Thus, we often say that Hispanics/Latinos are like white rice— we are everywhere. Consequently, any identification of a Hispanic locus will be at best a generalization. Such an exercise is like trying to designate the precise location of a moving train. The Hispanic community is a fluid community; its locus changes daily and yet remains the same. In general, Hispanics, like other people, want to "move on up." This goal, however, is often frustrated, hampered, and undermined by the competing racist and sexist values of our society, often resulting thereby in stagnation, delay, and frustration. In what follows I list some of the generalizations that can be made in this regard.

We are by and large of urban character, located in the major cities of the country; of low income; predominantly Roman Catholic in affiliation; young; high school graduates; theologically conservative; and politically liberal or independent. We are also a people of color: our skin ranges from black to white; our eyes may be brown, green, or blue; our hair ranges from the straight to the curly. We are, in effect, a *mestizo* people. Our socioeconomic reality is well captured by the popular saying, "Estamos chabao pero no acabao; tenemos esperanza y coraje" (We may be down but not out; we are full of hope and courage).

Our overall situation can be described as displaced. As Justo González

---

2. See Fernando F. Segovia, "Hispanic American Theology and the Bible: Effective Weapon and Faithful Ally, *We Are a People! Initiatives in Hispanic-American Theology* (ed. Roberto S. Goizueta; Minneapolis: Fortress Press, 1992) 25–28.

has noted, we are a people on the margins, on the periphery of the dominant culture.[3] It is often from this location of displacement and disregard that we know and are known by others and ourselves. This dislocation from the center of power, definition, and control informs both the sources employed in our cosmovision and the manner in which they are employed. Thus, the sources that are used for the construction of a Latino theology will vary in accordance with the diversity of our locations and their relation to the center or dominant cultural forces.

Our cosmovision, therefore, is not only perspectival—that is to say, we not only make our universal claims from a particular constellation of relationships—but also peripheral, emerging from the margins as opposed to the center. This means that we appropriate and apply our sources in ways that draw upon both traditional and nontraditional interpretations and applications. Such a relationship to our sources can be characterized as both eclectic and conjunctive: eclectic, on the one hand, insofar as it brings together a variety of sources that might not often be placed together; conjunctive, on the other hand, insofar as we often hold together that which might be thought of as opposite.

Our relation to the center (that around which everything else revolves or is defined) as a community of the periphery greatly influences what we identify and use as resources and how we do so. Our imagination is informed by this location as well as by the potential for what we might become. This realization should alert us to the fact that, although a source we employ might seem similar to or the same as that used by other theological perspectives, often our understanding of its contents and our application of it will differ from its traditional use.

Sources of a Hispanic/Latino Theology: A Pentecostal Perspective

The sources or raw materials from which one draws in constructing a theology determine the particular shape and perspective such a theology will take. Again, a Latino theological perspective often draws upon sources shared with other theological perspectives, yet it is the use of these sources, how they are reshaped or interpreted, that ultimately results in a different perspective. Two important facts, which may be said to function as norms, provide this distinctive Hispanic *sazón* (seasoning).

Essential Norms of Hispanic/Latino Theology

First, a Hispanic theology is *of the struggling and suffering poor* and a theology *for the poor* and all others willing to listen to its insights. While other theologies speak of the poor and seek to interpret the world of the

---

3. See Justo González, *Mañana: Christian Theology from a Hispanic Perspective* (Nashville: Abingdon Press, 1990) 31–42.

poor and the marginalized, a Hispanic theology emerges from the margins and speaks on behalf of those on the periphery to those at the centers of power. The location of this perspective is essential in distinguishing it from other theologies that are in solidarity with the oppressed. This difference can be characterized as a worldview from a seashore as opposed to a worldview from a boat. It is an indigenous perspective as opposed to a colonial perspective.

Second, Hispanics/Latinos are a conjunctive community. We are a Hispanic/Latino people, different from both our historical and cultural parents. We are both Hispanic, whether Boricua or Chicano, and North American. Thus, for example, when we Hispanics/Latinos visit Puerto Rico to see our families, we are told that we are not true *puertorriqueños,* while back home we are told that we should return to the island where we belong. For both sides of our North American Hispanic reality, we are strangers, yet we know that we are greater than our parts, that we constitute a people known today as the Hispanic Americans. This amalgamation leads us to experience and interpret the world differently from both our families in the countries of origin and our neighbors in the United States. This multilingual, multicultural existence constitutes a powerful interpretive lens, absorbing and reflecting light in a highly distinctive manner. Our locus as a hopeful community of disregarded people and our struggle to define who we are as a new community represent our point of departure for doing theology.

The Hispanic/Latino Pentecostal Perspective

In addition to these existential norms, the Hispanic Pentecostal community also recognizes the Scriptures as divine revelation and primary norm, in light of which all other norms and sources are to be defined and employed. Yet the Pentecostal use of the Scriptures as primary norm should not be too easily confused with the fundamentalist understanding of biblical inerrancy or absolute inerrancy. Unlike fundamentalists, who posit a doctrine of biblical inerrancy and infallibility, Hispanic Pentecostals regard the authority of Scripture not as a theological proposition but rather as a transformational experience of the Holy Spirit. It is the transformative experience of conversion, that inner work of the Holy Spirit in one's life, that bears witness to the power and authority of Scriptures.[4]

Our experience as a marginalized people and our multifaceted identity as Hispanic Americans along with our high view of Scripture serve as norms to which the sources must be subject. These, to a great extent, are the constants through which the variable sources are mediated. It is this mix that

---

4. It was not until 1961 that the largest of the Pentecostal denominations, the Assemblies of God, introduced into its doctrinal statement an article on the authority of the Bible. Prior to that time, like other Christian traditions, it assumed the authority of the Scriptures and felt no need to argue for it.

produces *el sabor* (the taste) of a Hispanic American theology with a Pentecostal twist. The Pentecostal twist that further distinguishes this theology from other Hispanic/Latino theologies is the central role assigned to the Holy Spirit as interlocutor between the norms, the sources, and the people. It is this Pentecostal emphasis on the work and power of the Holy Spirit as the advocate, guide, and interpreter of the sources and norms that distinguishes the Pentecostal perspective. The people are not left at the mercy of their own rational or mystical predilections; rather, the Holy Spirit is seen as enlightening, directing, teaching, discerning, and empowering the people in this hermeneutical process of becoming and announcing.

The Holy Spirit is seen as given to the community of the disregarded and the dispossessed for the purpose of equipping them for the task of being signs of the reign of God in the world. Often, the individualism and privatism of U.S. culture influence and distort the work of the Spirit, reducing it to a radical religious individualism. Among Pentecostals, this is not its primary role. It is to the community as a holistic, organic body that the Spirit is given. As a result, both the norms and the sources are subject to the collective discernment of the community and not to the personal whims of individuals.

As I stated above, the task of articulating and examining the contents of a Hispanic theology is multidimensional. The present work is limited by time, space, and expertise in attending to the various aspects of the task. Other theologians, social scientists, cultural anthropologists, and practitioners will need to continue that which I merely introduce in this essay. In this essay sources are employed and interpreted through the particular lens of a Hispanic Pentecostal New Yorker. Other sources, interpretations, and applications are possible and even at times desirable, as we seek to construct a Hispanic theology of empowerment and transformation.

Appropriation of Sources in Hispanic/Latino Pentecostal Theology

The sources drawn upon by Hispanic Pentecostals vary depending on whether or not they are consciously or unconsciously appropriated. A critical appropriation will usually bring to the surface sources that might normally be rejected or at least held suspect. An uncritical appropriation usually narrows the scope of influence to those sources that correspond with the given theological or traditional teaching. In the case of most Pentecostals, the identification of sources, whether critical or uncritical, is done within the limits of a premodern approach or what Gerald Shepherd has called a submodern consciousness.[5] This submodern appropriation of sources creates problems as well as insights for a critique of modernity.

The negative aspects of this submodern approach to the identification and use of sources have to do with the limitations and, at times, even the

---

5. See Gerald Shepard, "Biblical Interpretation after Gadamer" (unpublished paper).

inability on the part of Pentecostals to appropriate the insights of modern theological, scientific, and historical inquiry. This situation often places undue authority on the sources and norms employed, while narrowing the scope and possibilities of both the questions asked and the responses given by one's theology. This premodern perspective also serves to place the community in a different set of relationships vis-à-vis the world and the Scriptures. This set of circumstances contributes to a cosmovision that is often at odds with modernity. This historical if not scientific dislocation often corresponds with the theological otherworldliness usually present among Pentecostals and other theologically conservative communities.

I would argue that this submodern or premodern worldview is not limited to or necessarily defined by a conservative theology. Indeed, a similar worldview is evident among most marginalized communities. Whether Pentecostal, Roman Catholic, or Baptist, most disenfranchised persons tend to use a premodern approach in their hermeneutical reflections, what could be categorized as a type of commonsense realism: that is, "What you see is what you get." This approach is often associated with the philosophical perspectives of conservative theology in general and is not necessarily obscurantist. Rather, it is defined by traditional science, drawing upon the likes of Bacon, Locke, and Newton, rather than Darwin, Einstein, or other modern scientists or philosophers.

What one finds among Hispanic Pentecostals, as among other poor people, should not be at all surprising. It is in keeping with the absence of the basic educational resources that are often denied the poor. This premodern worldview challenges some of the principles of theologies having to do with the poor. Two such principles particularly stand out: the preferential treatment of the poor and the hermeneutical advantage of the poor. If one were to truly support these dictums, one would have to admit, or at least recognize, that the very poor who supposedly receive preferential treatment hold worldviews and perspectives often at odds with those who claim to speak on their behalf. This premodern perspective often offends the ideological sensibilities of the elite who seek to liberate the poor.

The second popular dictum, the hermeneutical advantage of the poor, often flies in the face of most hermeneutical approaches employed by theologians. It can be argued that most poor people's hermeneutics run directly counter to those of their professional theological *compañeros* (confreres). A reading of most liberation texts gives the impression that the poor employ a modern hermeneutic. If the poor have a hermeneutical advantage, why is it then often rejected or ignored by those who make the claim? Or is it that the poor spoken of as being treated preferentially and as having this hermeneutical insight are some special group of economically poor people who possess an ideological perspective not unlike that held by a theological elite? If the poor truly possess a hermeneutical insight unavailable to the nonpoor, somehow it resides in the premodern or submodern cosmology held by most marginalized people. It seems to me that something can and will be gained from a premodern reading of the sources.

Sources of a Hispanic/Latino Pentecostal Theology

Among the sources drawn upon for understanding and articulating a Hispanic Christian theology, the following would be most evident: the experience of conversion; the Christian tradition acquired through the preaching of the gospel; Bible study; *coritos* (popular Christian songs and hymnody); church history in general; Hispanic national history in particular; faith; and, to some extent, reason, at least a commonsense version of it. I should like to examine more closely a number of these sources, exploring how and what implications arise from them that might be helpful in informing a Hispanic theology in general and a Hispanic Pentecostal theology in particular.

1. Hispanic/Latino Pentecostal Spirituality. The issues of sources and norms must be placed within the broader context of the ethos of a Hispanic Pentecostal spirituality. Hispanic Pentecostalism is a spirituality that incorporates elements of culture, religious experience, and Christian tradition within the daily reality of struggle—what Ada María Isasi-Díaz has called *la lucha.*[6] This spirituality to a great extent manifests the pietistic and Reformed heritage of Europe as well as the Catholic roots of its Spanish ancestors. These are often coupled with the spiritualist practices of our indigenous foreparents. This spirituality finds its center and clearest expression in the weekly *culto* or worship service.

The worship service is the place and the occasion where the sources and the norms that inform our theology come together. It is in the midst of the *culto* that we hear, see, feel, and reflect upon what God has said, is saying, and is calling us to be. Hispanic Pentecostal theology is incomprehensible apart from this experience of Holy Spirit–filled worship and praise. It is in this evangelistic service that one encounters the multidimensional character of the sources that inform our worldview. The event of the worship service brings together the world of passion and the world of reason. The reading, study, and proclamation of the Scriptures constitute a rational activity. Placed among the people at worship, the written word powered by the Holy Spirit speaks to their human condition at the point of its pathos. The word of life speaks a word of hope to those in the struggle. The living word calls into fellowship an oppressed and struggling people. Worship is the context, the event, where heart and mind are drawn holistically to praise, worship, and thank God for God's sustaining love. Passion lies at

---

6. Ada María Isasi-Díaz, *En la lucha—In the Struggle: A Hispanic Women's Liberation Theology* (Minneapolis: Fortress Press, 1993) 168.

the heart of this spirituality. This passion-centered rather than cognition-centered relationship to the sources of our understanding of God and the world gives Hispanic theology a different ethos.

Once again, although all theologies draw on common sources, the attitudes they bring to these sources are quite different. In contrast to modern theological approaches, where the world of the mind is central, Hispanic theology draws upon the wealth of knowledge and insight of human religious experience mediated through a commonsense philosophy. Hispanic Pentecostal spirituality should not be equated with its North American Anglo counterpart. Hispanic spirituality—whether Pentecostal or Methodist, Baptist or Presbyterian—is different from its North American expression. Although many of the sources are the same, their appropriation, interpretation, and application respond to a very different set of needs and expectations. Rather than drawing on some global insights, such spirituality works from the experience of its own particularity, which is what it really knows, and relates this experience to the world around it. Its world is not one of universal objectivism but rather one of particular subjectivism in light of its communal reality.

The experience of our community has taught us to be suspicious of the objective, rational, and scientific priesthood of the dominant culture. We have observed that the narrow cognitive fixation of the dominant culture is reductionistic and opposed to the holistic nature of humanity and creation. This objectivity and its denial of the world of passion are evident in the conditions placed on the sources and norms employed in the theologies of the dominant culture. The realm of passion (the body, our experience) is systematically divorced from rather than incorporated into the realm of the mind (cognition and critical objective analysis).

It seems to me that the Hispanic Pentecostal approach is similar to that suggested by Stephen Toulmin, who sees postmodernity as having introduced a process of reversal.[7] He argues that such a reversal is characterized by a shift from written to oral, universal to particular, general to local, and timeless to timely. These are, in effect, the very traits that characterize the handling of the sources that inform our Hispanic theology. Two important differences stand out nonetheless. The first is that, as regards Hispanic theology, such traits are not the result of having gone through a modern construct. Hispanic theology in general and Pentecostal theology in particular, I would argue, have been and continue to be, if not premodern, submodern.[8] Our approach is not a reversal of modernity, as posited by Toulmin, but rather a critique of modernity. The second important differ-

---

7. Stephen Toulmin, *Cosmopolis: The Hidden Agenda of Modernity* (New York: Free Press, 1990) 186–92. An insightful critique of the shifts occurring in the postmodern period is presented in Walter Brueggemann's *Texts under Negotiation: The Bible and Postmodern Imagination* (Minneapolis: Fortress Press, 1993).

8. See n. 5 above.

ence is the universal and timeless character given to the Scriptures as a hermeneutical norm.

The context of Hispanic Pentecostal worship, both in terms of place and event, is the *locus theologicus* of the community. It is the place where God is worshiped and praised and where the people commune most intimately with God. It is also the event of encounter between the people and God. It is private and public. It is the event of empowerment, fiesta, confession, and commissioning of the community to be light to the world and signs of God's shalom. It is the place and event where those who struggle are comforted and empowered, healed and sustained. *El culto* is the matrix that sustains and feeds the people in their struggle. This communal spirituality expressed in *el culto* or *el servicio* (worship service) is one of the principal expressions of the community's praxis. As noted in Roberto Goizueta's insightful critique and analysis of the development of the notion of praxis and its relation to the U.S. Hispanic community, this experience furnishes a new insight into the very meaning of historicity or praxis itself. He describes this aesthetic aspect of praxis in terms of popular religiosity:

> The fundamental goal of popular religiosity is the practical, performative, and participatory affirmation of community as the foundation of all human activity.... The community implicit in praxis is not, however, the modern Western community, understood as a voluntary association of atomic individuals; rather it is an organic reality in which the relationship between persons is not only extrinsic but, at a more fundamental level, intrinsic as well. In and through praxis, the intrinsic unity of person, community, and God is affirmed.[9]

Goizueta goes on to describe this Hispanic expression of praxis, music, dance, and ritual as aesthetic performance.[10] In so doing he has captured an aspect of praxis long present among U.S. Hispanics in general and Pentecostal Hispanics in particular. Yet, a more critical political critique is pending among Pentecostals, though already emerging, as evident both in the writings of Eldin Villafañe and in my own writings.[11] It is within this view of spirituality, community, and praxis that one should understand how and why the sources are used.

2. Personal and Communal Experience. Among Hispanic Pentecostals, experience, both personal and communal, serves as an important source for understanding and sharing the faith. The experience drawn upon for doing theology reflects two aspects, one secular or cultural and the other spiritual (that is, the experience acquired in and through the religious experience of

---

9. Roberto S. Goizueta, "Rediscovering Praxis: The Significance of U.S. Hispanic Experience for Theological Method," *We Are a People*, 62, 64.

10. Ibid., 67.

11. See Eldin Villafañe's impressive work in Pentecostal social ethics, *The Liberating Spirit: Toward an Hispanic American Pentecostal Social Ethic* (Grand Rapids: Eerdmans, 1992).

prayer, praise, and worship). Often these experiences spill over into one another, at times consciously and at other times unconsciously. Because of the often radical separation maintained between the secular world and the world of the holy, many creative and liberating aspects of our Hispanic culture are negated or rejected outright. This Christ-against-culture mentality forms part of the conservative theological worldview inherited from those who evangelized our community in the United States and in our countries of origin.

In spite of this theological denial of our culture, already there is evidence of an appropriation of our culture in new *coritos* (hymns and poetry) shared in our services. Pentecostal composers and singers such as Merrari Castro, Mike Díaz, and Carmen Sanabria have restored *la danza, el bolero, el le-lo-lai*—all traditional musical genres of Puerto Rico—to our expressions of praise and worship. They have, in effect, reintroduced *la sazón Hispana* (the Hispanic seasoning) into our Pentecostal community. This is a result of reconsidering the positive aspects of culture in light of the transformational nature of the Christian life and the belief that the Holy Spirit empowers the community to discern between that which is redeemable in the culture and that which is not.

The experience of life in the Spirit, grounded in the event of conversion and mediated through life in the community of believers, in song and Scripture, serves as the primary source for expressing the salvation event. This religious experience shared by all members of the community is described in terms of being born again. This experience is divided into three distinct stages with regard to both time and content: conversion or regeneration; sanctification; and baptism by the Holy Spirit.

Life in the Spirit is characterized by the exercise of a variety of spiritual gifts and the fruit of the Holy Spirit exhibited in one's daily life. Through the exercise of the gifts and ministries of the Spirit a voiceless and often powerless community regains its voice and power. In the event of worship, *el culto,* the disempowered and the voiceless exercise their power and share their insights. In *el culto* the maid and the dishwasher are given respect and opportunities to exercise their gifts and talents. In the event of the gathered community *la hermana* Carmen is regarded as an authority on the Scriptures and *el hermano* Carlito is sought for his administrative advice and leadership. Here the community experiences a transformation of roles, where women can be pastors and evangelists, prophetesses of God, and where disenfranchised men and women are affirmed and restored to the place of dignity intended by God. This transformational experience of community and affirmation in the power of the Holy Spirit colors all the other sources used by Pentecostals.

3. *The Scriptures.* The Scriptures constitute the highest norm, in the light of which one's religious experience is informed and interpreted. A His-

panic Pentecostal understanding of the authority of Scripture should not be confused with a fundamentalist literalist approach or an evangelical propositional approach to biblical authority. On the surface, for the uninitiated, such an equation might be tempting. However, Hispanic Pentecostals arrive at the conclusion that the Scriptures are the inspired word of God based on their personal and collective experience of transformation. It is often the event of healing, the resolutions of family and personal problems, and other answers to prayer that witness to the reliability and authority of the Scriptures. This is similar to what John Calvin in the *Institutes* spoke of when he argued that it was the internal witness of the Holy Spirit in our lives that bears witness to the authority of the Scriptures.[12] It is not a cognitive assent or affirmation that leads us to conclude that the Scriptures are divinely inspired. Rather, it is the incarnational power of the Scriptures that addresses us and localizes the I AM of God in ways that transform our daily lives. Together the Scriptures and the personal and collective experiences of transformation work as a source and a norm in further defining a Hispanic Pentecostal theology. Evidently, this circular argumentation and narrow scope of interpretation need to be enlarged in order to incorporate the insights of other factors.

Within the category of religious experience lies a potentially transformative truth that can serve to break open a whole new area of reflection and praxis. Our pneumatological emphasis and belief that the Scriptures teach that we are to examine all things, retain the good, ignore the bad, and be guided by the Holy Spirit in all truth (see, for example, 1 Thess 5:21 and John 16:13) hold the promise of a potentially revolutionary resource for attending to the issues with a new imagination. This teaching, coupled with an understanding of the power of the powerless, can and hopefully will lead Hispanic Pentecostals to assume a more responsible and realistic role in the daily politics of our community.

4. *Preaching, Pastoring, Teaching.* Another source for informing our worldview is the triad of preaching, pastoring, and teaching. These as well as the important role of music and song represent the most influential mediums for informing and directing the life and mission of the church.

a. Preaching is a powerful source informing our understanding of God, the world, and ourselves. This medium is particularly influential in that it draws from the strength of our oral tradition. Its power of invoking, affecting, and challenging the received truths of the community has been proven again and again by local and national evangelists who not only gain our attention but also receive our financial support. Preaching remains one of the most powerful mediums of information and persuasion. It is the preacher

_____

12. John Calvin, *The Institutes of the Christian Religion* (Library of Christian Classics, no. 20; Philadelphia: Westminster Press, 1973) 1.7.4.

who interprets and applies the Scriptures to daily life. It is the expositor of the word who has access to the masses of our people and is both heard and heeded. Often the preacher's spiritual and political worldview is received as being almost equal to the word of the Lord. As such, preaching is the most influential theological medium in the Pentecostal church. The preacher as theologian is the one who tells forth and interprets God's will in the community. It is the preacher in our churches who serves as the example against which other public figures are judged and measured. There is no comparable figure to the preacher in our community except for the local politician. Often, however, our preachers are more eloquent and respected than our politicians. If our preachers could be further empowered to broaden the scope of their worldview beyond the world of the "spiritual" to include critical tools of analysis—beyond a premodern understanding of the Bible, history, and science—the effect on the people's understanding of God's will for us as agents of liberation (a liberation that encompasses the whole of creation) would be quite positive indeed. Failure to articulate a critical sociopolitical ethics puts at risk the leadership potential and contribution of this growing and influential segment of the Christian church.[13]

b. The second member of this oral triad is the pastor. The pastor is the spiritual leader of the community, the interpretive link between God, the people, and the world. At the most influential times of our lives (births, death, marriage, confirmation, worship), the pastor is the one to whom the people turn in their times of sorrow as well as in their times of joy. The pastor as a source for theological construction and critique may function as the embodiment of a dependent model of ministry that serves to maintain the ecclesial and secular structures of oppression or as a source of support and action for overcoming the forces of injustice and dependence. The pastor in the Pentecostal tradition is the spiritual choreographer of the ministries and gifts of the Spirit in the local church. It is she/he who daily empowers or disempowers our people in a most direct way. Any movement of critical reflection in the local church, if it is to succeed, will require the support and leadership, at some level, of the pastor. It is crucial, therefore, that the pastor maintain a holistic tension between the role of spiritual leader and the role of the prophet of God who cries against injustice. Failure to do so undermines the credibility of the pastor before the community.

The pastor as community leader and personal counselor constitutes a most strategic venue for influencing the worldview of the community. Pentecostal pastors must break with the narrow worldview inherited from our millenarianism and our sectarian traditions. Pentecostalism must dare to believe what it preaches and teaches—that the Holy Spirit can and will lead us in all truth. It must dare to venture out and see what God sees and ex-

13. See Harvey Cox, *Religion in the Secular City: Toward a Postmodern Theology* (New York: Simon and Schuster, 1984).

periences, what God feels, in the lives of the marginalized and neglected. As a church of the poor, we often grow accustomed to the devastation around us. We often find excuses or even rationalizations for the existing state of the world. Our received theological schemes are used to support and justify the very oppression we experience. The pastor can serve as a critical hermeneutical key in redefining the questions, the tools, and the sources to be used in reconstructing a liberating response to the needs of our people.

An encouraging sign among Pentecostals has been and continues to be the inclusion of women as pastors. In the majority of Pentecostal denominations and independent movements, women are received as pastors.[14] They, like their male counterparts, play a crucial role in the church. Women are respected and followed and their experiences are heeded, while providing a different point of view from that of the traditionally male pastorate. The leadership of women as pastors and even bishops in our churches can potentially provide another entry point to new sources and insights for constructing a theological perspective that can better serve our Hispanic community.[15]

c. The third member of the oral triad is the teacher. Among Hispanic Pentecostals and Pentecostals in general, the Bible teacher is usually the individual in the Sunday school department. The formal notion of theologian is still very underdeveloped due in part to the premodern attitudes toward the world of scholarship. There has been some significant change in this regard, however, among English-speaking congregations of middle-class background. The local Bible teacher represents yet another important resource for informing our church's worldview. This is evident in the fact that the most influential training vehicle among Pentecostals is the evening Bible institute. These normally meet two evenings a week in a local church and draw students from several churches in the vicinity. It is estimated that 80 percent of Hispanic pastoral and lay leaders have received their theological training in Bible institutes. Literally thousands of Hispanic church leaders attend these evening Bible institutes weekly.

It is within this local, community-based, -led, and -funded theological model that one comes closest to the function of the Bible teacher as theologian in the Hispanic community. What is taught by these teachers becomes the daily staple of what is received as the sound doctrines of the gospel. The theological perspective taught is very often conservative if not orthodox in content and political orientation. The sources used—such as commentaries, theological textbooks, hermeneutics texts, and so forth—are all translated

---

14. See María González, *Latinas in Ministry: A Pioneering Study on Women Ministers, Educators and Students of Theology* (New York: New York City Mission Society, 1993).

15. Loida Martell, "Women Doing Theology: Una perspectiva evangélica" (unpublished paper, 1993). The paper contrasts evangelical Hispanic women's perspectives with Anglo and Catholic women's perspectives.

materials from English to Spanish. This often means that the materials in question are not directly germane to the daily issues and concerns facing the community.

In spite of these shortcomings, the teacher intuitively makes the connections with the issues facing the community and improvises both resources and strategies for attending to them. These Bible teachers often continue a primary if not the primary formal source of theological education for the Hispanic Pentecostal churches today. Often, as in my own case, students from these weekly Bible institutes are called and motivated to pursue further theological education, and some later return to teach in these institutes. This form of theological education serves to maintain the received theological perspective of our foreparents. The theological and biblical sources used are dated, and very little if any of the social science resources are utilized. This accounts for the narrow range of sources employed by Pentecostals. A high degree of biblical content is expected to be memorized by all students. Mastery of the Bible is stressed, along with its application in preaching and evangelism. Among the other strengths of this approach is the fact that institutes are sustained, directed, and defined by local Hispanic congregations. Yet their theological perspective continues to be defined by others. This inconsistency between the independent spirit of local leaders and their doctrinal dependency on others must be overcome if this vital resource and source for doing theology in the Hispanic community is to fulfill its promise as a local, grassroots theology.

It should also be noted that, unlike many of its denominational counterparts, the leadership in the Pentecostal churches—whether in preaching, pastoring, or teaching—comes from among the laity and not the clergy. This, I believe, is to a great extent the reason why we are often able to overcome the decontextualization present in so many of our teaching materials. The lay leader daily confronted with the common chores of *el obrero* (the blue-collar worker) is able to apply and identify the issues of the day to which the Gospels speak and that one is called to engage.

This intuitive, hermeneutical, or epistemological insight (what Pentecostals call *discernimiento* [discernment]) has led our churches to reach out to addicts, street people, and other disenfranchised individuals in our communities. This insight has led numerous congregations to violate immigration laws by taking in and harboring illegal aliens. This insight and direction of the Holy Spirit lead this so-called apolitical community to engage the principalities and powers with a message of hope and liberation in spite of the conditions of neglect and disregard they face in their communities. These churches remain in our urban ghettos when others flee to the suburbs for safety and comfort. This tenacity against what dehumanizes our people is contained in Pentecostals' worldview. It is not a political party or a partisan political agenda, but a struggle against the broader landscape of the presence and power of evil and sin.

5. The Holy Spirit. Finally, a Hispanic Pentecostal reflection on the sources that inform and empower theology must explicitly recognize the central role of the Holy Spirit as source and resource. The person of the Holy Spirit in its relation to both the individual and the congregation serves as the primary resource for identifying and employing the sources used. The Holy Spirit illuminates, directs, and discerns the sources used. Hispanic Pentecostals believe that if isolated from the ministry of the Holy Spirit, all resources and sources will be inadequate for informing and empowering us in overcoming the power of injustice in our communities.

The above-mentioned sources are those most frequently and consciously identified by Hispanic Pentecostals. Surely there are others, but the premodern stance assumed by Pentecostalism at times prohibits their appropriation, either explicitly, as in the case of politics and culture, or implicitly, as in the case of other extrabiblical sciences. Further exposure to and dialogue with other traditions will assist in self-consciously identifying and creatively appropriating other sources as well.

Concluding Comment

A Pentecostal perspective can be helpful and even informative insofar as it provides a window to the theological approaches often used by other Hispanics who are working with a premodern worldview. Pentecostal theology and hermeneutics function as a microcosm of what exists across denominational lines in the church of the poor. Our theology though submodern stands as a sign of hope that not everyone has sold out to the god of reason and the priesthood of atomistic scientism. Deep within, our people discern and have stood against the cult of oppressive objectivism and have retained the communal and spiritual vitality of their foreparents—standing, like them, in hope, *en la lucha,* as signs of God's ultimate victory over injustice and oppression.

Part Two

Locus of Hispanic/Latino Theology

8

Notes toward a Sociology of Latina/o Religious Empowerment

Otto Maduro

Hispanics already constitute over one-tenth of the population of the United States. Compared with other ethnic, linguistic, or cultural ingredients of the so-called "melting pot," we are a minority no more. Moreover, we are the fastest growing segment of both the entire population and the labor force of this country. Socioeconomic indices reflect, however, inequities as regards Hispanics: while overrepresented in both the hardest working segments of the population and the lower tiers of income, health, housing, and education, they are notoriously *under*represented in the higher levels of social, political, economic, or cultural decision making.[1] This alone would suggest that Hispanics are, in one way or another, at least partially *oppressed*. In other words, although fully capable of participating in the decision-making networks and processes that affect their own living conditions, Hispanics are not only consistently hindered from access to these networks and processes but also negatively affected in a systematic way by the decisions taken through the same networks and processes.

In terms of religion, Hispanics constitute the single largest and fastest growing ethnic slice of the U.S. Roman Catholic population. At the same time, we are also the single most important source of converts for the Protestant and other Christian denominations in the United States, in many of which we represent if not the largest, then certainly the single fastest growing portion of the constituency.

Are there any connections among these facts and trends? How does one's religious affiliation contribute to cushion, criticize, or change an oppressed position in the larger society? Does the social situation of Hispanics somehow influence our religious choices, changes, and conversions? Can processes in the religious dimension affect—both individually and collectively—the direction Hispanics take in the workplace, in politics, in the

---

1. See Frank D. Bean and Marta Tienda, *The Hispanic Population of the United States* (New York: Russell Sage Foundation, 1987).

151

life of one's own community? Are these inevitable mechanisms or, on the contrary, can these processes be altered by deliberate, premeditated human action on the part of Hispanics themselves? In this essay I will furnish a few elements of response to some of these questions. Specifically, I want to share some concepts, hypotheses, and modes of thought taken from the sociology of religions that, in my view, may prove stimulating, fertile, and thought-provoking in attempting to answer such questions.

Religion and the Empowerment of the Oppressed

Religion as a Dynamic Social Dimension

Religions may be seen from a variety of perspectives and understood in many ways. They can be seen, for example, as juxtaposed, discrete, static organizations, each with its own bureaucracy, belief system, moral code, and liturgical rules (where transformative interaction would seem more an accident than the norm). I would suggest instead, along the lines indicated by Pierre Bourdieu,[2] that one should think of any religion always as part of a given social "religious field," in analogy to the "energy fields" (magnetic, electric, and so on) of the physical sciences. In this sense, a "religion" would be an identifiable, relatively autonomous hub—and a very animated, shifting, and complex one for that matter—within the ever-changing domain of action, interaction, and friction of agencies striving to define what is sacred and to manage the relation to the sacred of a given community.

In this sense, a "religion" is never a reality defined once and for all but rather a multifaceted, vibrant reality in constant interaction with its environment, continuously exposed to both internal and external resources, limitations, tendencies, and pressures. At every concrete juncture of its history in a given society, a religion is—among other things—the singular outcome of the interaction between, on the one hand, its own distinctive traditions, factions, and constituencies and, on the other hand, the surrounding conventions, conflicts, demands, and pressures—each carrying a different weight.[3]

Furthermore, we should not persist in conceiving of religion as a preexisting, external, and unreachable realm in relation to human initiative.[4] Rather, we should approach the religious field as a social terrain, partially

2. See Pierre Bourdieu, "Genèse et structure du champ religieux," *Révue française de sociologie* 12 (1971) 295–334.

3. In *Religion and Social Conflicts* (Maryknoll, N.Y.: Orbis Books, 1982), I dealt extensively with these aspects, already under the strong influence of Pierre Bourdieu's essential article cited in n. 2 above.

4. As Leonardo Boff, among many others, has suggested (see esp. *Church, Charism and Power: Liberation Theology and the Institutional Church* [New York: Crossroad, 1985]), such a conception of religion need not be at all in conflict with an orthodox Christian stance: we might understand religions—including the Christian churches—as *human* attempts to respond to God's self-revelation, self-bestowal, and invitation. True, not all the-

similar to and different from other unique domains of human activity, such as the educational, military, or economic arenas. It is, as Alain Touraine would say, a mode of action of human society upon itself.[5] In this sense, the religious field would be a sphere of generation, discussion, communication, interchange, and modification of a specific type of human undertakings and bonds—those referring to transcendence, the divine, the sacred, God, and the ultimate meaning of human existence—involving, indeed, the very processes of discerning and delineating that which transcends, guides, and regulates human decision making and behavior in relation to each other, that is, the *ethical* realm.

Thus, religion—or, better, the religious field—could be sociologically conceived as the realm created through and for the human quest to respond to what is experienced by at least a sector of a community as entailing a transcendent urgency: the area, therefore, where the sacred is defined, re-defined, articulated, interpreted, celebrated, meditated, and translated into codes, organizations, and customary operations. A major component of the activity of the religious field is thus the endeavor to redefine continually what is its own specific domain—what is thus sacred or transcendent—and what are its location, scope, limits, demands, and implications. Churches, codes, creeds, clergy, and ceremonies are but a few among the myriad of concrete embodiments of such a quest, but so are also popular devotions, pilgrimages, processions, secret societies, feasts, and dances evoking the holy.

Religion may be thus envisioned as an extremely dynamic social dimension, one that we enter as soon as we are born into a community and where we participate, somewhat actively at least, in the ongoing conversation about what it is that transcends us and what are its implications for our lives.

Social Power and Empowerment under Oppression

Power, of course, may be understood in many ways, and recent feminist interventions in the debate have indeed transformed and enriched its meaning.[6] Consequently, I explicitly want to avoid the reduction of power to the idea of "power *over* others," which in fact would be only one modality of social power, the one usually alluded to with the words "domination," "oppression," and "exploitation," among others. Following conventional usage, let me define *power*—in a sociological sense—as the capacity of a

ologies would gladly embrace such a possibility—but such refusal would itself deserve a sociological analysis of its own possible roots in quite concrete human social conditions.

5. Alain Touraine, *Production de la société* (Paris: Seuil, 1973).

6. See in this respect the pioneering book by Ada María Isasi-Díaz and Yolanda Tarango (*Hispanic Women, Prophetic Voice in the Church: Toward a Hispanic Women's Liberation Theology* [San Francisco: Harper and Row, 1988]), which proposes a *mujerista* analysis and theology, that is, a theology and analysis that emerge from U.S. Hispanic women's struggles for their own liberation.

group (or an individual) to define its (his or her) interests and goals and attain the latter, including vis-à-vis other groups and persons. In this sense, nobody enjoys absolute power: our power is always partially defined *in relation to and limited by* the power of those with whom we interact as well as our finite faculties and restricted resources. Conversely, nobody lacks power entirely:[7] while we are alive, while we are still able to somehow move and communicate, we can influence—even if minimally—some of the processes affecting our existence. In this sense, we might understand social power as something simultaneously relational, gradational, and unstable. I should like to argue, therefore, that we are all constantly involved in a wide array of power relations and dynamics and that the perception we might have of these is part and parcel of those very same power relations and dynamics.

Oppression, domination, exploitation, and hegemony are among many names given to asymmetric power dynamics, where a human person or group exercises—on a more or less continuous, institutionalized basis— a disproportionate control *over* resources and behavior and *against* the interests of another human individual or group. We may perceive these dynamics in a variety of ways, for example, as indifferent, inevitable, eternal, intolerable, sacred, legitimate, wrongful, or natural. Each specific perception could diversely affect the very power dynamics of which it is part and parcel: it might contribute to make these dynamics invisible or bring them to public focus; it might question and subvert those dynamics or strengthen and expand them.

Within such power dynamics, then, a complex conflict is present—at sundry levels, including one's own innermost life—between, on the one hand, tendencies toward accommodation, consolidation of the status quo, private advantages, short-term benefits, inertia, or safety, and, on the other hand, inclinations toward solidarity with the weak and defenseless, equality, long-term benefits, defense of community, and identity. Such strife is carried on in the material world of homemaking, markets, or politics as much as in the spiritual realm of contemplation, critical reflection, mourning, or rejoicing.

Religion, understood as the energetic field of activities and institutions wrestling with the question of what transcends us and its exigencies, can hardly avoid becoming part and parcel of the conflictive processes inherent in such social dynamics of oppression. Among many other dimensions, religion also becomes both one more arena where the struggle among the different interests, tendencies, and perceptions of social oppression is waged and a terrain for further proliferation of specific forms of domination and, therefore, of struggles for empowerment.

---

7. See Rollo May, *Power and Innocence: A Search for the Sources of Violence* (New York: Dell, 1976).

Empowerment may be defined as the process of increasing one's own capacity, as a group or as a person within a group, to influence the decisions bearing on one's own lot. This process often involves the development of a wide array of resources, both "material" and "spiritual," such as networks, means, and modes of communication, educational tools, new forms of leadership, spaces for expression, healing, and so forth. Within relations of oppression, however, empowerment seems to involve some measure of checking—if not directly resisting, fighting, and diminishing—the power of those at the opposite side of such relations of domination. Those enjoying benefits and privileges of power *over* others tend to feel threatened by and thus lash back against the empowerment of the underdog. In this sense, empowerment can often be a conflictive process, especially when involving groups or persons marked by a long, deep history of suffering under subjugation. Here, it is not only the backlash of those in charge but also the "internalization of the oppressor" as well as the weakened self-esteem among the oppressed—individual as well as collective—that constitute major difficulties for creative empowerment against and *beyond* oppression.[8]

Religion as a Medium of Empowerment of Hispanics

Religion could be—besides and, at times, despite other functions—a possible medium, among others, for the articulation and proactive stimulation of a people's empowerment, that is, for the actualization of their capacity to transform their social environment in consonance with their own interests. This might be particularly true in the case of U.S. Hispanics, for whom all too often our religious traditions and institutions occupy a central place in our worldview, one of our scarce sources for self-identity as well as for the ethical assessment of our typically alien environment.

However, as I have already suggested above, processes of popular empowerment tend to emerge both amid and over against pressures in the opposite direction: pressures tending to weaken, hinder, and otherwise frustrate the yearnings for autonomy bursting among the oppressed. This is also true *within* religious traditions and institutions.[9] In the case of

---

8. This suggestion owes a great deal to the work of both Franz Fanon and Paulo Freire. For Fanon, see, for example, *A Dying Colonialism* (New York: Grove Press, 1967); *Black Skin, White Masks* (New York: Grove Press, 1967); *The Wretched of the Earth* (New York: Grove Press, 1968). For Freire, see, for example, *Pedagogy of the Oppressed* (New York: Herder and Herder, 1970); *Education for a Critical Consciousness* (New York: Seabury Press, 1978); *The Politics of Education: Culture, Power, and Liberation* (Hadley, Mass.: Bergin and Garvey, 1985).

9. See in this regard the historical examples of the role of Anglo Roman Catholicism recalled by Gilbert Cadena ("Chicanos and the Catholic Church: Liberation Theology as a Form of Empowerment" [Ph.D. diss., University of California Riverside, 1987]) and Alberto L. Pulido ("The Religious Dimension of Mexican Americans," *The History of the Mexican American People* [ed. Julián Samora and Patricia Vandel Simon; rev. ed.; Notre Dame, Ind.: University of Notre Dame Press, 1993] 223–34).

oppressed, impoverished minorities who share their religious institutions with the elites—as is more often the case than not with Hispanics—this lends specific obstacles, constraints, and opportunities to the processes of a people's empowerment through the religious field.

On the one hand, religious institutions where oppressed and oppressors share a common ground furnish the elites with a ready-made channel of communication with those who could have serious grounds for grievance and hostility toward them. As far as the elites enjoy a certain clout over and within those religious institutions, they might succeed in steering these to function as a medium for further *disempowerment* of the oppressed. The recent quincentenary remembrance of the European invasion of the Americas yielded many a study on the different ways in which the Christian churches—for instance through official condemnation of autonomous initiatives of the Native American, African American, mestiza/o, mulatta/o, or other disenfranchised groups in the Americas—actually functioned as such.[10] On the other hand—and this is a discovery that has been crucial in the current peacemaking processes of Central America—religious institutions where both the privileged and the disenfranchised partake can constitute for the latter an invaluable resource for gaining strength while challenging the authority of the elites.[11]

Historically, in fact, many Christian churches—Protestant as well as Catholic—allowed oppressed groups to produce their own specific religious organizations, by means of which they could develop their organizational skills while building legitimate, relatively autonomous spaces of expression, communication, and decision making. At times, some churches also undertook educational initiatives toward the oppressed, which in the long run helped to enhance the communicative abilities of people involved in movements of resistance, protest, or outright liberation. Last but not least, the preaching of equally divine origin, sacred dignity, and the love of God for each and every human being—sung and celebrated in the presence of both wealthy and poor—served to bolster the self-esteem and mutuality of many people living under oppression, strengthening their capacity both to acknowledge themselves as subjects of rights and to fight for such rights as well. All of these undertakings, as far as they are generated from within institutions that are deemed sacred by both the powerful and the weak, can enjoy a certain degree of legitimacy, which would be much harder to attain if emerging from institutions exclusively created by and for the oppressed.

Moreover, sharing the same religious space with the oppressed places the elites in a community of accountability with the former. At times, this might

---

10. See my "Nuestra variedad etnocultural," *SIC* (Caracas, Venezuela) 55:545 (1992) 217–21.

11. See in this regard the thought-provoking work of Daniel Levine, a political scientist specializing in religion and politics in contemporary Venezuela and Colombia: *Popular Voices in Latin American Catholicism* (Princeton, N.J.: Princeton University Press, 1992).

allow the oppressed to negotiate with, put pressure upon, and call the elites to task in ways that would be otherwise socially illegitimate, unthinkable, or clearly intolerable. Truces, releases from prison, new laws, resignations from office, prices, salaries, and scores of other demands have been settled through the mediation of religious institutions where both populace and ruling groups participate, although indeed never without the proactive initiative of those challenging the status quo.[12]

Religions are not only churches, however, nor are they always under the pervasive influence of the elites. Underneath, behind, around, within, and beyond the official religion of the established churches blossoms constantly the religious creativity of the common folk, especially when the weight of the mighty forces this creativity outside the public arena of official religion. What the official terminology attempts to disqualify as superstition, heresy, ignorance, witchcraft, or syncretism may thus often be read—at least partially—as semiautonomous efforts on the part of the oppressed to articulate their own original religious experience, including the grievances, yearnings, and exhortations that constitute the cry of the oppressed.[13] It may be here, in the realm of popular religion, that much of the empowerment of Hispanics actually takes place.

The Need for Specific Empirical Research

On the Inexhaustible Wealth of Actual Reality

At this point, a Weberian reminder is very much in order. Actual reality is always infinitely richer, deeper, more heterogeneous and variegated and hence far more dynamic, complex, and in flux than our perception could ever grasp. This applies as well to the actual reality of the U.S. Hispanic population. Mexican Americans and Puerto Ricans no longer exhaust the detail of U.S. Hispanics, as was the case until the early 1960s, and even the inner homogeneity of these major Hispanic groups can no longer, if indeed such was ever the case, be taken for granted. In fact, the number of different national and regional origins, ethnic and cultural mixtures and traditions, linguistic legacies, social, economic, and political backgrounds, and other forms of self-identification is at present constantly growing, and these factors are in constant flux and interaction, with their relative proportions and intertwinings also continuously changing.

---

12. This is an aspect that remained invisible for me until recently and is therefore absent altogether from my *Religion and Social Conflicts,* as is the importance of the so-called syncretisms in the processes of empowerment of the oppressed. For this last point, see Leonardo Boff (*Church, Charism and Power,* chap. 7) and Orlando Espín ("Tradition and Popular Religion: An Understanding of the *Sensus fidelium,*" *Frontiers of Hispanic Theology in the United States* [ed. Allan Figueroa Deck; Maryknoll, N.Y.: Orbis Books, 1992] 63–87).

13. Bourdieu ("Genèse") suggests that "sorcery" is but a disqualifying name given by the elites to the autonomous religions of the oppressed, while "religion" is the legitimating label the elites give to what could otherwise be interpreted as *their own brand* of "sorcery."

The same could be said for the religious reality of U.S. Latinas/os. The proportion of Roman Catholics—though not the actual numbers, given the factors of birthrate and immigration—is undergoing a marked reduction in these last decades of the century, while the percentages and numbers of mainline Protestants, evangelicals, Pentecostals, Jehovah's Witnesses, Mormons, and members of several other denominations seem to be constantly on the rise. At the same time, many religious traditions of Afro-Caribbean and/or Native American descent—heretofore commonly subjected to invisibility, clandestine existence, repression, and other forms of exclusion and marginalization—are of late coming out into the open, successfully recruiting adepts, interacting with other religious traditions and the wider society, gaining a larger degree of legitimacy, and undergoing a number of other significant innovations. Such is the case, for example, with Voodoo, Santería, Palo, Arará, Umbanda, Candomblé, the María Lionza cult, and the Mexica traditions related to the dead. More often than not, these popular religious traditions have been—and continue to be—in such a complex, creative interaction with Christian institutions that we may speak of a pervasive Hispanic reality of multiple religious affiliation, which defies and challenges not only the exclusiveness claimed by official definitions of most church authorities but also predominant conceptualizations of religion in the social sciences as well.

In addition, the experience of a growing "religious marketplace"[14] and the emergence of a multiplicity of "liberation theologies" within the major religious denominations—both phenomena that challenge, albeit in different ways, the exclusivity and legitimacy of current religious bodies and their authorities—complicate the real picture even further.

Theory and Empirical Research

As I have suggested elsewhere, theories may be fruitfully understood as maps for orienting ourselves in the midst of an unknown reality.[15] They are neither "copies" of actual reality nor simple illusions thereof. They are, as it were, compasses, lighthouses, guides—usually constructed on the basis of a certain familiarity with the sketched reality or with a reality that is deemed similar or analogous and, like any chart, supposed to be of help for the uninitiated to better navigate, understand, or manipulate novel territories. At best, theories are systems of signs trying to imitate and evoke one view—among many—of a few actively selected and creatively interrelated points of a certain domain. Thus, it makes more sense to speak of the comparative degrees of usefulness, productivity, and so forth of different

---

14. See Peter L. Berger and Thomas Luckmann, "Secularization and Pluralism," *Theoretische Aspekte der Religionssoziologie* (2 vols.; Internationales Jahrbuch für Religionssoziologie, nos. 2–3; Cologne-Opladen: Westdeutscher Verlag, 1966–67) 1:73–86.

15. See, for example, my book *Mapas para la fiesta: Reflexiones latinoamericanas sobre la crisis y el conocimiento* (Buenos Aires: Centro Nueva Tierra, 1993).

theories than to engage in a sterile—or counterproductive—classification of them as either "true" or "false." Theories are indeed indispensable in order for us to be able to simply "see" anything at all. The process of growing up, interacting with other human beings, learning a language, and internalizing a whole culture may in fact be interpreted as—among other things—an interiorization of the prevailing maps (that is, theories) of reality, which are meant to enable us to live "normally," that is, according to the norms of our community. It is a process of learning to find our way in a preexisting, prefabricated world. Such seems to be the case with scientific theories as well.

A certain difference may be suggested, however, between, on the one hand, most implicit, learned, and interiorized maps of reality in a human community and, on the other, so-called scientific theories. Scientific theories represent *deliberate* attempts, within a *specialized* body of "experts," to lay out *explicit* maps of predefined *segments* or dimensions of reality. In principle, scientific theories are open to discussion, correction, enrichment, transformation, refutation, and substitution, although we all know too well how this ideal may differ from the actual reality of discussions among scientific experts.[16] This difference, however, does not erase the commonalities between scientific theories and interiorized images of the world around us: both spring from the fact that without theories—without prefabricated maps of our environment—we can hardly know anything at all; help us avoid an overwhelming, chaotic, deranging impact of reality on our spirit by introducing some elements of selection, order, and orientation in the infinite wealth of our experience; and are liable to the temptation—and the danger—of substituting our conjectures for the reality around us.

Thus, we should always remind ourselves that, although we certainly *need* theories in order to know the reality of religion among U.S. Hispanics, no theory can ever exhaust the infinite wealth of reality; no theory can ever explain anything either fully or definitely; and no theorizing can ever substitute for continuous, renewed empirical research on our changing reality. On the contrary, theories are useful only insofar as they stimulate fresh questions, unconventional hypotheses, creative explanations. Theories are worthwhile if we take them as flexible, open, partial, provisional, limited tools. Thus, we should allow ourselves to utilize, question, complement, supplement, correct, transform, and substitute our theories according to the requirements emerging from the journey of our people, from our empirical research, and from our creative imagination, both individually and collectively.

---

16. See in this regard Paul Feyerabend, *Against Method* (2d ed.; London: Verso, 1980), and Thomas S. Kuhn, *The Structure of Scientific Revolutions* (2d ed.; Chicago: University of Chicago Press, 1970).

The "Research/Action/Evaluation" Circle

In the last decades of struggles on the part of our peoples—both in Latin America and the United States—we have produced many an innovation within and through our churches. One of these has been a homegrown blend of three European perspectives: two of them Christian in origin—the "hermeneutical" and the "see/judge/act" circles; the third, Marxist—the dialectical unity of theory and praxis. This methodological blend has been variously named and formulated in diverse milieus. Basically, it consists of conceiving the connections between social scientific research, political action, and ethico-religious concerns—especially in situations of injustice and violence—as something real, complex, and important, something to be faced with urgency, to get involved in, and to examine critically in a continuous fashion. I shall label it, provisionally, the research/action/evaluation circle.

In simple words, this approach entails the following: we need to pursue *research* on the past, the present, and the future perspectives of our communities in such a way as to enhance and correct the transformative *action* and struggles of these same communities. This, however, is not enough: we also need a continuous, critical *evaluation* in community of our research—including its theories, methods, and outcomes—and our actions. Through such continuous, critical evaluation in community we might enable ourselves to correct, enrich, and transform for the better both our research and our action—and, ultimately, our communities and our selves as well. At the heart of this process is life, active life in community unifying action and reflection, "matter" and "spirit."

I certainly do not mean to imply that this proposed circle exhausts the reality of human life or that there are neither other nor better ways of bolstering the life and views of our communities. Indeed, where then would we leave love, prayer, celebration, mourning, contemplation? Rather, all I wish to do is to call attention to a recent tradition of ours that could nurture our creative imagination in searching for new ways of looking at the Hispanic religious reality, ways that can hopefully serve to empower our communities, enabling them to attain greater degrees of durable solidarity, justice, and peace. Such a tradition—homegrown in our basic ecclesial communities—is that of linking socioreligious *research,* ethico-political *action,* and critical, communal *evaluation* of both in a circle of continuous reassessment and reciprocal sustenance of all the elements involved.

To give some flesh to this method, let me suggest an example. Say we are interested in the growth of Pentecostalism in the Hispanic population of our state. We might tackle the matter—depending on our expertise, feelings, location, and so on—from different points of entry. Whatever we do, it might be useful to go beyond mere impressions, word-of-mouth versions, or shared biases toward a systematic *research* regarding the actual reality of Hispanic Pentecostals. To this end, we could consult census data, databases, specialized publications, as well as experts on these and related fields. We might want to check and compare this information and discuss it with others versed in the area, including people with a different experience and perspective than ours on the subject. We may benefit, further, from doing direct field research ourselves: holding interviews, conducting surveys, recording life-stories, doing participant observation of Pentecostal congregations, scrutinizing relevant records, having meetings with leaders, and so on. In so doing, we may obtain a richer, deeper, more nuanced and sophisticated view of our subject, especially if we are open to expand our views and question our preconceptions. We could clarify, reinforce, and sharpen our images and attitudes, of course, but we might also, on the contrary, reconsider and even modify such conceptions and evaluations.

Whatever the case, our *actions*—whichever these were—in relation to Hispanic Pentecostals might be challenged and transformed as a result of our research. We could become more respectful, critical, appreciative, distant, attentive, involved, and/or cooperative toward them. This depends, indeed, on the way our research impacts our preconceptions and stance toward our subject, but it also depends enormously on how open and free we are not just to pursue a line of research that threatens to shake our biases but also to reassess and alter the direction of our actions. If the latter are revised even slightly—but also if persisting in old ways is accompanied by challenging surprises or frustrations—this might stimulate new experiences and questions, which, in turn, could fuel revision and invigorate our research.

As we can already sense, research and action are likely to stimulate and influence each other, and both might elicit and rejoin collective *evaluation* of their foundations, features, and direction. This appraisal, on the other hand, might help us grasp important aspects of Hispanic Pentecostalism that we might systematically overlook, thus fostering new research. It might help us spot bigotry or elitism, or, on the contrary, naïveté and favoritism underlying our actions in relation to Pentecostalism and thus contribute to sharpening and transforming our practice in this regard. As such, this methodology has at its heart the conviction that justice and peace are better served through a constant disposition to reassess—in democratic, pluralistic dialogue—anything pitting human beings against one another. The goal is not an impassive ethical relativism but rather a recognition that communication and change are essential traits of all forms of life and a consequent disposition to probe in community what has characterized our views and deeds thus far, if only eventually to reaffirm and deepen it.[17]

---

17. Or, to put it in other words, this methodology assumes that, willy-nilly, our future is shaped in the image of our relations to our subjects of research and action. If we relate to these in a dialogical, compassionate, patient, pluralistic, and democratic way, we will contribute to future communities with such traits. If, on the contrary, force, deceit, arrogance,

A Few Hypotheses for Future Research

Religion and the Reidentification of Hispanics

Long-range transformative action for the benefit of a disadvantaged people requires a deep, common identity within such a people. We are a people, but not quite yet. Our past identity would do only partially in our present circumstances. We are in fact realizing our need to deepen and reaffirm our identities, but we need to expand, enrich, and transform them as well. We need to further the already ongoing, creative, conflictive process of rei-dentification as a people—with common memories, symbols, values, and aspirations. This hypothesis could lead us to do research around questions like the following: Are there signs of processes of re-identification taking place among U.S. Hispanics? Where? How? Are there common traits among the Hispanic individuals and communities involved in such processes? What role do gender relations, ethnic differences, language, class and national origins, regional specificity, age, education, generation, religious affiliation, political sensitivities, and so on seem to play in these processes?

Religious beliefs, symbols, rites, values, and organizations often play a central role in the generation, sustenance, and expression of a people's identity. This seems to be the case with Latin American and Caribbean peoples as well, including Latinas/os who were born in or are immigrants to the United States.[18] Are there any signs of this in the denominations, congregations, and other religious groupings that we know? How do such signs affect those who feel their identities are not expressed in them?

Religious values, beliefs, bonds, and rituals are at the heart of the Hispanic communities. However, religious individualism, authoritarianism, and exclusiveness can weaken and shatter the already vulnerable and frail identity of Hispanics. Are these tendencies present in the Hispanic-attended congregations that we know? How do they manifest themselves? Is there a variety of responses among Hispanics toward those tendencies? Are there processes of explicit exclusion of dissenters, sacralization of assimilationism, and/or restraints to communication with "others"? Religious individualism, authoritarianism, and exclusiveness are very much present in our communities, as much as sexism, elitism, and racism. How are the latter expressed and sanctified through our religious congregations—in our explicit preaching or, more subtly, in our songs, theology, organizational and spatial arrangements, silences, gestures, and the like? Are there

---

inflexibility, and sectarianism prevail in the ways we view and deal with "others," such will be the future we are birthing.

18. See the groundbreaking essays gathered in three collections of U.S. Hispanic theological essays: Roberto S. Goizueta, ed., *We Are a People! Initiatives in Hispanic American Theology* (Minneapolis: Fortress Press, 1992); Deck, ed., *Frontiers of Hispanic Theology*; and Justo L. González, ed., *Voces: Voices from the Hispanic Church* (Nashville: Abingdon Press, 1992).

any initiatives—open or subtle, individual or collective—toward criticizing and overcoming these "isms"? If so, how are these initiatives differentially received? Are there any changes in that direction, even minimal?

A real, durable reidentification of Hispanics requires a communitarian, democratic, and ecumenical religious spirit—one where religious traditions serve to recall and nurture the best of our history: solidarity, hospitality, dedication, altruism; the ability to appreciate, nurture, enjoy, and celebrate life; family, home, barrio, land; the balance between work and fiesta. Do we perceive any efforts to foster such spirit? Where? Since when? By whom? Are there any significant differences between those who tend to get involved in these efforts and those who oppose them? And what about those "in be-tween"? What kind of denominations, congregations, and religious leaders seem abler to encourage those efforts? Which ones tend to reject them? Can we detect any significant effects of those different responses? How do local elites react to those efforts? Do they show any form of support—or, on the contrary, of deterrence—vis-à-vis such initiatives?

Religion and the Rebuilding of Hispanic Communities

Historically, Hispanic peoples have built their communities with sacred places, values, and bonds at their center. True, European invasions first and U.S. expansionism later have brought with them a novel way of do-ing religion: one where the folkways of the assailants have been forced on Hispanics as "the right way of doing religion," while our own ways have been bashed and crushed as "primitive and superstitious." Do we find any evidence in our Hispanic communities of a critical recollection of that his-tory of religious imposition? Any indication that some among us distinguish critically—or ironically, which might amount to the same thing—between "their" religious ways (that is, those of the Anglos) and "ours"? Are there indices of disdain for what could be termed "typical" Hispanic religious traditions? Did the quincentenary affect this in any way whatsoever?

When we have been left on our own with our own—be it at home or in exile, while being persecuted, neglected, or forsaken by our former tyrants, or while experiencing the yoke of a novel occupation—we have shown an uncanny ability to revive, adjust, and enhance our religious traditions (in-cluding those taken from the invaders), and, through this process, we have been able over and over again to rebuild our communities anew. What do we see of this in our current neighborhoods and families? Are there ini-tiatives to develop or explore ancestral religious traditions, often deemed "superstitious" or "satanic" by our elites? Do any of these labors—within or without our churches—contribute in any way to reinforce family and neighborhood bonds? How?

We are at a juncture in U.S. history in which our own existence—indi-vidual and collective, material and spiritual—is possibly more endangered than ever before. We seem to be at a unique point in which we need to gather all of our past and present resources in order to minimize the threat of our extermination or else be swallowed by the suicidal tendencies present in the prevailing culture. Above all, we need to rebuild our communities, not as isolated slums shamefully turned in upon themselves, but, on the contrary, as vibrant, energizing networks of persons and families nurturing their members and contributing a distinctive creativity and criticism to the larger community. We need to redo our barrios, our families, and our selves.

In this attempt to rebuild our communities, without which any Hispanic identity will hardly be anything other than an academic fiction, our religious traditions, networks, symbols, and values may be the preeminent resource. Do we perceive some ongoing experiments in reconstructing, strengthening, and enhancing Hispanic neighborhoods, for instance, through the renovation of buildings, the creation of neighborhood associations, the development of support for battered women and children, the improvement of local schools, the organization of block parties, the struggle against drug addiction, police abuse, unhealthy living conditions, and so on? Are there such experiments where the initiative has emerged from within the neighborhood itself? In any case, have religious networks, expressions, or motivations been at work in such experiments? How? Where has the support, if any, arisen from? And the opposition? What have been the results? Have there been any continuity and interconnection among those experiments? Has there been any systematic evaluation of the same? How do most people in the neighborhood view and relate to those experiments? Has there been any significant increase—or decrease—in the involvement of neighborhood dwellers in those attempts to improve life in their community? Any hints of the factors influencing those trends?

Religion and the National Hispanic Presence

We are a people in the making within a larger nation-state. Most of what we produce is taken beyond our reach, and we get back from the larger society much less than we contribute to it. In fact, what we get is useful only to buy things that, more often than not, we have not produced. Law and order are defined and imposed from outside of our culture, communities, and control. We cannot thus realistically expect to solve our problems and meet our needs by ourselves alone. We need to enhance our clout and our say in the larger U.S. society. We have to create a national Hispanic presence in unions, neighborhood associations, consumer organizations, taxpayers' coalitions, political parties, electoral campaigns, lobbies, and the like. Do we sense that this perception is somehow present among U.S. Hispanics? Or is this a complete misrepresentation of our reality? If such perception is present, then among whom and with what effects? Are there any religious bodies presently promoting a similar view? Which ones, and with what response? Is there any significant participation of Hispanics in associations like those listed? Is there in our religious congregations any stimuli, indifference, or disapproval toward such participation? What seems to be the impact of such participation on the people involved and on the neighborhoods they came from?

Such a presence—if it is destined to make a durable, promising contribution to ourselves and other peoples—cannot define itself in terms of submissive assimilation to U.S. society as it presently stands. It ought to entail as well a critical denunciation of systemic injustice as well as a witnessing annunciation of social, economic, and cultural democracy for this country. Our presence, though, cannot be reduced exclusively to confrontation and demands. It also needs to create bridges, dialogue, alliances, and coalitions: in the first place, with those who bear the heaviest brunt of systemic injustice in this country, namely, African American women, men, and children; but also with all women and children, regardless of ethnic background, especially those enduring poverty, violence, pain, and isolation. Are there any corporate protests and denunciations of injustice arising in the Hispanic communities we know of? Any demonstrations or mobilizations claiming our rights? Are these or other activities in our communities done in cooperation with other marginalized groups? How are our relations with the African American population—including their culture, organizations, struggles, and grievances? Are there conflicts between us? Who seems to benefit from such conflicts? Are there any coalitions and alliances between us? Who encourages these? And again: How do our religious bodies, values, traditions, leaders, and organizations affect these facets of our national presence?

In this multidimensional task—denouncing, witnessing, confronting, demanding, bridging, and networking—our religious traditions and institutions can be of paramount importance. Through them we may be able to break out of our marginalization and build a lively, creative national presence.[19] But is this happening yet? Which religious bodies and congregations seem to be more supportive of such a presence of Hispanics in the national scene? What is it in them that allows them to be supportive? Is it a matter of ethnic background, social location, theological tradition, and/or individual idiosyncrasy of a specific pastor? Or is it something else? What about those denominations that refrain from intervening in such "secular" affairs or that clearly discourage their members from such participation? What is it in them that elicits that attitude, particularly in what refers to Hispanics?

---

19. As is the case in literature, where the national presence of U.S. Hispanic writers is, quantitatively as well as qualitatively, currently experiencing a boom. Witness the reviews, publicity, sales, and ramifications of the works of Sandra Cisneros, Cristina García, Julia Alvarez, Victor Villaseñor, Danny Santiago, Pat Mora, Piri Thomas, Edward Rivera, Carmen de Monteflores, Luis Valdez, Luis Rodríguez, and a host of others.

Concluding Comments

In this attempt to contribute to an understanding of the actual and potential role of religious traditions in the empowerment of Latino/a communities in the United States, I have tried to combine some sociological insights and political orientations within an ethical option for the empowerment of U.S. Hispanics.

I began by presenting a few sociological perspectives on the relations between religion and the processes of empowerment of the oppressed, with the suggestion that, despite the hardships and ambiguities of religious initiatives under oppression, some of our religious traditions and institutions might serve as means of empowerment for the U.S. Hispanic communities of the present. Subsequently, I submitted some epistemological considerations. Starting with an emphasis on the infinite richness of socioreligious processes, I went on to suggest some ways of viewing theories and their role in the understanding of our socioreligious reality. After underlining the need to test and transform our theories through actual research on the tangible facts of the socioreligious life of our communities, I concluded by proposing one way among many of connecting research, action, and critical reflection for the socioreligious empowerment of our communities. Finally, I advanced a few hypotheses to nurture our research and struggles around the relation of religion to the empowerment of our Hispanic communities in the United States.

To be sure, what I have done here barely scratches the surface of some of these issues. It is my hope, however, that if not the strengths at least the shortcomings of this essay will serve to encourage others to pursue this quest much further.

9

The Social Location of Liberation Theology

From Latin America to the United States

_____ *Gilbert R. Cadena* _____

> *We definitely will not have an authentic theology of liberation until the oppressed themselves can freely and creatively express themselves in society and among the People of God, until they are artisans of their own liberation.*
> —Gustavo Gutiérrez

Liberation theology did not develop in a vacuum but came about as a result of a long historical process that fermented in the 1960s and 1970s. Religious, political, and economic forces contributed to its emergence. As a new way of doing theology, it involves a critical shift in the traditional imbalance of power between the church's hierarchy and its members. No longer accepting a subordinate class, ethnic, or gender status, Latin Americans and U.S. Latinos are calling the church to respond to the social condition of its members.

This essay grounds the current theological discourse of liberation theology within a sociohistorical context. I shall compare Latin American and U.S. Latino[1] theologies by briefly highlighting the social forces contributing to these theological movements. These forces are divided in terms of internal religious factors within the Catholic Church and external social factors. I argue that liberation theology emerged partly as a reaction to both traditional Catholic hegemony and conflicts in civil society. In addition, the interaction between progressive religious leaders and the laity contributed to its development. As liberation theology developed into a new paradigm of religious thought and practice, it influenced theologians worldwide. A link is now forming between Latin American and U.S. Latinos under a

---

1. This essay utilizes the terms "Latino" and "Latina" to refer to individuals of Mexican, Puerto Rican, Cuban, and other Latin American origins living in the United States. Specific terms such as "Chicano," "Puerto Rican," and "Cuban" are used when focusing on a particular group. "Latin American" refers to individuals and groups living in Mexico, the Caribbean, Central America, and South America.

pan-ethnic theology.[2] This theological relationship is dialectically related to particular group identities and a larger global consciousness. The formation of Latino pan-ethnic theology transforms these groups into political and mobilized populations.

By examining the Roman Catholic Church during the last three decades, we can trace social forces in order to identify how particular church sectors have contributed to socioreligious change. To understand how subordinate groups challenge the hegemony of religious and ruling elites, one must socially locate them within a particular context. The social location of liberation theology refers to the relationship between religious institutions, their members, and their social structures. According to Otto Maduro, every religion is "a situated reality—situated in a specific human context, a concrete and determined geographical space, historical moment, and social milieu."[3] Religious activity is limited and oriented by the local, national, and international contexts. The social context provides similarities and differences between Latin American and U.S. Latino theologies.

Latin American Liberation Theology

Latin American liberation theology came out of a milieu of extreme poverty, class conflict, military coups, and political turmoil in countries such as Brazil, Peru, Chile, Mexico, Nicaragua, and El Salvador. Progressive religious leaders began to recognize the powerful alliances between the church and the state while the vast majority of the population lived in poverty. As religious leaders participated in movements of dissent, they reacted to religious and social domination with a counterhegemonic theology. Liberation theology addressed the role of Christians in relationship to class oppression, the role of foreign multinational corporations, U.S. foreign policy, Latin American regimes, and military dictatorships. Gender and ethnic discrimination were viewed as secondary concerns and subsumed under class relations. Figure 1 summarizes the internal and external factors influencing the development of Latin American liberation theology. The following section discusses some of the tensions and contradictions within the church that led to liberation theology in the 1960s.

Internal Religious Factors

1. Class Struggle. Progressive church sectors recognized institutional class conflict during the 1960s. Theologian Gustavo Gutiérrez criticized the church's traditional stance as follows: "When the Church rejects the class struggle, it is objectively operating as a part of the prevailing system.

---

2. See Felix Padilla's *Latino Ethnic Consciousness* (Notre Dame, Ind.: University of Notre Dame Press, 1985) for a discussion of Latino pan-ethnic identity.

3. Otto Maduro, *Religion and Social Conflicts* (Maryknoll, N.Y.: Orbis Books, 1982) 41.

FIGURE 1

Social Forces Contributing to the
Development of Latin American Liberation Theology

Internal Factors	*External Factors*
1. Class struggle within the church	1. Class conflict and urbanization
2. Clerical church crisis	2. Failure of developmental reforms
3. Popular church movements	3. National revolutions
4. Christian student movement	4. Necessity of radical political action
5. Vatican II and Medellín Conference	5. Competition with external groups
6. Social change and institutional survival	6. State repression and persecution

By denying the existence of social division, this system seeks to perpetuate this division on which are based the privileges of the beneficiaries."[4] As proponents of liberation theology recognized the interconnection between their impoverished material conditions and capitalism, the church, and foreign imperialism, conflict arose within the church, a conflict that reflected the class struggle in society. Two antithetical forces, which I call the "traditional" church and the "liberationist" church, represented a struggle of ideology and class interests. While the traditional church generally supported the ruling classes (that is, oligarchy and dictatorships), the liberationist church generally supported popular social and political movements.

2. Clerical Church Crisis. A decline of clergy vocations and a decrease in church participation by the laity contributed to an institutional crisis in the 1950s and 1960s. The church's influence weakened in the countryside, where over 60 percent of the population resided. In some countries small increases in clergy could not keep up with large population increases. After 1965, the gap between priests and laity widened dramatically year by year. Between 1965 and 1970, over 8 percent of Brazil's clergy left the priesthood. Many countries relied on foreign priests, examples being Guatemala and Nicaragua, where 80 percent of the clergy were foreign-born. Among Catholic sisters, one-third of almost thirteen thousand sisters who made their vows in 1965 renounced them within three years.[5]

3. Popular Church Movements. Without clergy in many rural areas of Latin America, *comunidades de base* (CEBs), or base Christian communities, evolved. As small organized groups of Christians, CEBs interpret

---

4. Gustavo Gutiérrez, *A Theology of Liberation* (Maryknoll, N.Y.: Orbis Books, 1973) 275.
5. See Christian Smith, *The Emergence of Liberation Theology: Radical Religion and Social Movement Theory* (Chicago: University of Chicago Press, 1991), 127–29.

the Bible and Christianity in light of their material, political, and social conditions. Today over two hundred thousand such communities exist throughout Latin America. In Brazil alone, between eighty thousand and one hundred thousand CEBs exist with about one to two million participants. Many CEBs raise the consciousness of their members and organize to change the social and political structures.[6] Some are involved in labor movements; others in health and child care issues; and still others in housing and educational campaigns.

4. *Christian Student Movement.* In reaction to Marxist and conservative student movements within the universities, Christian student movements began to form in the early 1960s. Initially, these groups organized themselves under the auspices of the bishops, but when some students later began to advocate socialism and armed struggle, the church forced them out. In Brazil, the Juventude Universitária Católica (JUC—Young Catholic University Students) blamed the country's economic conditions on imperialism and capitalism. It called for the construction of a planned economy, the abolition of private ownership of the means of production, changes in the electoral system, and egalitarian relations with other nations.[7] In Nicaragua, many students left the university and joined the Sandinista insurrection.

5. *Vatican II and Medellín.* The papacy addressed world changes formally by means of the Second Vatican Council (1962–65). Vatican II led the way for the laity to assume a more productive role within the church and for the clergy to take a more active role in the parish community. The council advocated an "opening to the world" and recognized the new technological and historical changes that were taking place. In *Gaudium et Spes,* the council's final document, the church affirmed the validity of worldly concerns and called for social justice. At the 1968 Medellín Conference in Colombia, 130 Catholic bishops identified institutional forms of violence such as poverty, lack of education, and substandard housing. They criticized "developmental" solutions for Latin America and called for "revolutionary" ones. The documents on peace, justice, and poverty discussed the social situation of Latin America by condemning colonialism and denouncing unjust structures as "serious sins." For the first time, publicly, Latin American bishops reversed their traditional, often tacit support of the ruling class by siding explicitly and clearly with the poor.

6. *Social Change and Institutional Survival.* The momentum for social change taking place in Latin America suggested that people would struggle

---

6. Madeleine Adrience, *Opting for the Poor: Brazilian Catholicism in Transition* (Kansas City: Sheed and Ward, 1986).

7. Ibid.

with or without the church. Religious leaders recognized that for the church to be part of the future of Latin America and become relevant to the lives of the people, it would have to participate in the transformations taking place. If it did not, as in Cuba, it risked losing its significance with the majority of people. In contrast, because the Catholic Church participated in the Nicaraguan Revolution, it played an important part in the reconstruction of the country after 1979. As popular movements advocated anticapitalist and socialist revolutionary changes, religious leaders were forced to respond. Some liberationists supported socialist options; others condemned the exploitation of capitalism; while others felt that churches should not side with any particular system but rather provide constructive critiques of all governmental and economic abuses. These internal factors coincided with a number of external influences in Latin America.

External Social Factors

1. Class Conflict and Urbanization. In most Latin American countries, wealth, land, and power were concentrated within national oligarchies. In Central America, 2 percent of landowners owned two-thirds of arable land. In Ecuador, Brazil, and Honduras, the richest 10 percent earned over 50 percent of total income, while the poorest 40 percent shared less than 7 percent of total income. Approximately one-half of Latin Americans lived in poverty in 1970, with Honduras, Brazil, Colombia, Mexico, Peru, and Panama having the highest poverty rates.[8] New industries, foreign investment, multinational corporations, foreign debt, and high inflation polarized the urban classes. The capitalization of agricultural development produced a large, seasonal, low-wage workforce and pushed peasants off their lands. As a result, millions of peasants seeking employment migrated to the cities from the 1930s to the 1960s. Migrant populations concentrated in urban areas created social upheaval and movements of dissent. Class conflict and revolutionary conditions arose as a reaction to deteriorating labor conditions, governmental repression, and emerging social movements.

2. Failure of Developmental Reforms. Pressure from First World nations to develop led to extensive debt. Soon, many countries were paying over 75 percent of their export earnings to foreign banks. Free-market strategies benefited the oligarchy and small middle-class sectors, rather than the population as a whole. The church responded with programs and organizations focused on developmental social reforms. Christian democratic political parties and unions attempted to contribute to political reform, but their efforts ultimately failed because they did not address the root cause of poverty. Simultaneously, in the United States, President John F. Kennedy's administration promoted the Alliance for Progress policy as a

---

8. Smith, *Emergence of Liberation Theology,* 150–56.

way to promote U.S.-controlled capitalism. All these attempts reacted to a growing discontent throughout Latin America and sought to minimize the influence of Cuban socialism. For the next three decades, U.S. governmental and business interests, in the name of democracy, modernization, and developmental reforms, increased their "anticommunist" efforts by destabilizing legitimate governments and movements and supporting authoritarian regimes.

3. *National Revolutions.* The success of the Cuban Revolution in 1959 served as a watershed event in Latin American history. Throughout the 1960s, Cuba provided an alternative model to U.S. domination, old ruling-class alliances, and foreign dependency. Socialist ideology spread throughout Latin America among students, popular movements, workers, peasants, intellectuals, and Christians fighting for social change. For a brief period, Chile served as an example of a peaceful transition to socialism, until the U.S-backed coup in 1973 did away with all such possibilities. Later in the 1980s, the Nicaraguan Revolution served as a symbol of hope for Christian student organizations, Christian political organizations, and Catholic clergy and sisters.

4. *Necessity of Radical Political Action.* The failure of developmental reforms led liberationists to recognize the necessity of structural change. To fight military dictatorships, national security states, and U.S. military intervention, many CEBs, clergy, and church groups actively participated in political education, supporting popular movements and touring worldwide to gain support for national revolutions. In a Peruvian pastoral letter, the bishops wrote: "To construct a just society in Latin America and in Peru is to be liberated from the present situation of dependence, oppression and plunder.... This means that persons should have a real and direct participation in the revolutionary action against structures and oppressive attitudes and for a just society for all."[9]

5. *Competition with External Groups.* The missionary efforts of evangelical churches in Latin America concentrated on neglected rural peasants and urban slum dwellers. These churches attracted dissatisfied Catholics through their accessibility in the countryside and the creation of smaller congregations in the cities. Protestant denominations grew at a rate of 10 percent annually from 1925 to 1961. In the early 1920s, there were about 240,000 Protestants; by the 1960s, there were 7,710,000.[10] Many of the missionary activities were financed by U.S. churches. In addition, secular

---

9. In Alfred T. Hennelly, ed., *Liberation Theology: A Documentary History* (Maryknoll, N.Y.: Orbis Books, 1990) 127–28.
10. Smith, *Emergence of Liberation Theology,* 75–77.

political movements addressing injustices and foreign domination (for example, nationalist movements, socialist movements, political parties, trade unions, and student groups) attracted many young people, giving way to a further decline in church participation as well as new voices of critique toward Catholic hegemony.

6. *State Repression and Persecution.* As liberationist sectors challenged the state and church, their activities created a backlash and became a target for persecution. From the 1968 Medellín Conference to 1978, over fifteen hundred active clergy and lay leaders became victims of torture, arrests, threats, and murder. Many others disappeared or were forced into exile.[11] In Brazil, from 1964 to 1978, arrests included 183 religious leaders, 185 priests, and 2 bishops. The assassination of three priests and the expulsion of twenty-seven more revealed the treatment suffered by religious leaders.[12] International attention focused on El Salvador in the 1980s when three U.S. Maryknoll sisters and one lay woman were kidnapped, raped, and killed. The assassination of Archbishop Oscar Romero in the middle of a religious service along with the murder of six Jesuit priests, their housekeeper, and her daughter in the rectory of the Catholic University served to further increase the world's attention on the extreme violence in that country. This repression of particular sectors within the church caused further divisions within the traditional church-state alliance.

U.S. Latina and Latino Theology

As conscientious Latino religious leaders and laity in the United States paid attention to the course of events in Latin America, many priests and sisters traveled to Latin America to study in religious institutes and to work with theologians and CEBs. By the late 1980s a study on Chicano clergy revealed that the majority knew about liberation theology and felt that it influenced their ministry.[13] Access to Latin American theologians, like Gustavo Gutiérrez, Enrique Dussel, and José Marins, increased through summer programs offered at the Mexican American Cultural Center in San Antonio. By the time of the early writings of U.S. Latino theologians in the 1970s and 1980s, the shared experiences of powerlessness and poverty influenced their theological reflections. However, the legacy of racism in U.S. society and the church received primary focus.[14] As Latinas began to

---

11. See Penny Lernoux, *Cry of the People* (New York: Doubleday, 1980).

12. Scott Mainwaring, *The Catholic Church and Politics in Brazil, 1916–1985* (Stanford, Calif.: Stanford University Press, 1986).

13. Gilbert R. Cadena, "Chicano Clergy and the Emergence of Liberation Theology," *Hispanic Journal of Behavioral Sciences* 11 (1989) 107–21.

14. See Virgilio Elizondo, *Galilean Journey: The Mexican-American Promise* (Maryknoll, N.Y.: Orbis Books, 1983); Andrés G. Guerrero, *A Chicano Theology* (Maryknoll, N.Y.: Orbis Books, 1987).

write in the late 1980s and early 1990s, their experiences in confronting patriarchy and sexism as well as racism and classism influenced their theological contributions.[15] As in Latin America, internal and external factors influenced Latino-Catholic relations; figure 2 provides a summary of these factors.

FIGURE 2

Social Forces Contributing to U.S. Latino Theology

Internal Factors

1. Latino culture as a religious culture
2. Stratification within the church
3. Latino religious organizations and lay movements
4. Latino religious leaders and theologians
5. Latino institutionalization of pastoral centers
6. Latinization of the Catholic Church

External Factors

1. U.S. discriminatory social structures
2. The strength of Latino political movements
3. Vatican II and Medellín Conference
4. Influence of liberationist theologies and theologians
5. Competition with non-Catholic denominations
6. Increase of U.S. Latino population and urbanization

Internal Religious Factors

1. Latino Culture as a Religious Culture. Latinos have historically been a religious people. Today most consider religion to be an important part of their lives, with the majority affiliated with Catholicism. However, the number of Latinos becoming Protestants steadily increases. One estimate calculates that approximately sixty thousand Latino Catholics leave the Catholic church annually to join Protestant denominations.[16] For many Latino Catholics, popular religious expressions—such as home altars, pilgrimages, *promesas* and *mandas* (vows), and devotions to saints—play a significant role in maintaining the religiosity of their families.

2. Stratification within the Church. While most Latinos identify themselves as Catholic, the church has historically stratified Latinos by ethnicity, race, class, and gender. The church denied Latinos positions as bishops for more than a century. From 1848 to 1970 no episcopal appointments of

---

15. See Ada María Isasi-Díaz and Yolanda Tarango, *Hispanic Women, Prophetic Voice in the Church: Toward a Hispanic Women's Liberation Theology* (Minneapolis: Fortress Press, 1993); Ada María Isasi-Díaz, *En la lucha—In the Struggle: A Hispanic Women's Liberation Theology* (Minneapolis: Fortress Press, 1993); and María Pilar Aquino, *Our Cry for Life: Feminist Theology from Latin America* (Maryknoll, N.Y.: Orbis Books, 1993).

16. Andrew Greeley, "Defection among Hispanics," *America,* 30 July 1988, 61–62.

Latinos occurred. Since 1970, token appointments have not rectified their extreme underrepresentation in all aspects of church leadership: from bishops, priests, sisters, and deacons to theologians, college theology professors, administrators, and seminary professors. Roman Catholic teachings do not permit the ordination of women, further excluding Latinas from decision-making positions within the church. A significant number of Latinas serve as an unpaid labor force in numerous religious education programs. In California alone, an estimated two thousand Latinas support the church in this important aspect of pastoral ministry.[17] Opportunities for advancement remain minimal because women are also barred from becoming permanent deacons. Such restrictions maintain a church stratified by ethnicity and gender.

3. Latino Religious Organizations and Lay Movements. A flurry of organizations founded in the 1960s and 1970s promoted Latino consciousness, leadership building, and grassroots mobilizations. For example, Católicos por la Raza (Catholics for the Race) challenged the bishops of Los Angeles and San Diego, demanding the appointment of socially active Chicano bishops, funding for community programs, and changes in Catholic schools and hospitals so that they would become responsive to Chicano Catholics.[18] Community organizations, such as COPS in San Antonio and UNO in Los Angeles, linked local parishes to the politics of their communities. In 1972, 1977, and 1985 Latinos organized three national *encuentros* as a way to bring U.S. Latino Catholics together to discuss their visions, struggles, and proposed changes for the Catholic Church. Christian base communities (CEBs) reached the United States in 1973. Under the leadership of the National Secretariat for the Spanish Speaking in Washington, D.C., over ten thousand individuals participated in CEB workshops in the mid-1970s. CEBs emerged in both rural and urban settings, providing a model of active participation in religious fellowship by the laity.

4. Latino Religious Leaders and Theologians. By the late 1960s, Latino clergy and sisters had begun to organize themselves at the national level. They questioned their insignificant numbers and treatment by the church hierarchy. PADRES (Priests Associated for Religious, Educational, and Social Rights) was formed as a collective response from Latino clergy. Latina sisters developed their own national organization, Las Hermanas (The Sisters), which was cofounded by Sisters Gregoria Ortega and Gloria Gallardo. The small but growing number of Latina and Latino theologians

---

17. Allan Figueroa Deck, *The Second Wave: Hispanic Ministry and the Evangelization of Cultures* (New York: Paulist Press, 1989).
18. Albert L. Pulido, "Are You an Emissary of Jesus Christ? Justice, the Catholic Church, and the Chicano Movement," *American Mosaic* (ed. Y. I. Song and E. C. Kim; Englewood Cliffs, N.J.: Prentice-Hall, 1993) 147–63.

founded the Academy of Catholic Hispanic Theologians in the United States (ACHTUS) in 1988. From its inception, ACHTUS has concerned itself with the inclusion of women, respecting the diversity of U.S. Latinos, recognizing the differences between Latin American theology and U.S. Latino theology, and promoting ecumenism.[19]

5. Latino Institutionalization of Pastoral Centers. In the late 1960s and early 1970s, Latino pastoral concerns were institutionalized: By 1982, every diocese in the state of California had a center for Hispanic pastoral ministry or an office of Hispanic affairs. Organizations such as the Regional Council for the Spanish Speaking (RECOSS) were founded by the bishops to serve the community and provide a vehicle of communication between the diocese, the bishops, and the national office in Washington, D.C. In 1974 the National Office for the Spanish Speaking was elevated and thus became the Secretariat for the Spanish Speaking, a change that occurred under the direction of Paul Sedillo.[20] Eventually, regional offices of Hispanic affairs opened in the Southwest (1974), the Northeast (1974), the Southeast (1978), the Far West (1979), and the Northwest (1981). Regional and national pastoral centers promoted the training of religious leaders, conducted research on Latinos and religion, and published religious materials. The Mexican American Cultural Center, founded in 1972 in San Antonio, played a significant role in the dialogue between Latin American theologians and U.S. clergy and lay leaders. Other centers founded in Florida and New York represented regional concerns.

6. Latinization of the Catholic Church. The last three decades have witnessed considerable demographic shifts in the Catholic Church in the United States. For example, in 1970 Latinos comprised about 20 percent of the U.S. Catholic Church; by 1980 this had increased to about 28 percent; and in 1990 the figure had increased to 35 percent. If current birth and immigration rates continue, by the year 2000 Latinos will represent approximately 45 percent of the U.S. Catholic Church. By the year 2010 Latinos will constitute over one-half of the church. In over a dozen dioceses—including Los Angeles, Brooklyn, Miami, San Antonio, and Santa Fe—Latinos already make up the majority. In addition, twenty-seven other dioceses have a Latino population ranging between 25 percent and 50 percent.[21] As in Latin America, these internal factors coincided with a number of important external factors.

---

19. Allan Figueroa Deck, "Introduction," *Frontiers of Hispanic Theology in the United States* (ed. Allan Figueroa Deck; Maryknoll, N.Y.: Orbis Books, 1992) ix–xxvi.

20. The office was later renamed the Secretariat for Hispanic Affairs.

21. NCCB/USCC Secretariat for Hispanic Affairs, *National Survey on Hispanic Ministry* (Washington, D.C.: National Conference of Catholic Bishops, 1990).

External Social Factors

1. U.S. Discriminatory Social Structures. Latinos share historical ethnic, racial, class, and gender discrimination with many African Americans, Native Americans, and Asian Americans. For example, many Latinos experience residential segregation and poor education and work at low-paying jobs. Latinos have the lowest levels of educational attainment in the United States: lower than Euro-Americans, African Americans, and Asian Americans. About one-half of Latino adults finish high school compared to two-thirds of African Americans and four-fifths of Euro-Americans. Less than 10 percent graduate from college. While employment rates are high among Latinos, they are more likely to be among the working poor. About 11 percent of Latinos and 16 percent of Latinas work in managerial or professional jobs compared to 28 percent of non-Latino men and women. About one-third of Latinos work as operators, fabricators, or laborers compared to one-fifth of non-Latinos. About one-quarter of Latinas work in service jobs compared to less than one-fifth of Euro-American women. The number of Latinos in the professional and managerial class is increasing, but about one-quarter of Latino families live in poverty.[22] Over the last two decades the income gap has widened between Latinos and Euro-Americans.[23]

2. The Strength of Latino Political Movements. As Latino secular and political movements increase their power, their impact is felt in more and more social arenas. For example, the Chicano and Puerto Rican movements in the 1960s and 1970s saw the proliferation of organizations challenging the status quo. Groups such as La Raza Unida Party, Crusade for Justice, Brown Berets, Young Lords, the Puerto Rican Socialist Party, the Puerto Rican Student Union, MECHA, MALDEF, CISPES, and CRE-CEN brought attention to the many issues affecting Latinos. Movements centering around self-determination, the Vietnam War, education, labor, immigration, and sanctuary for Central American refugees contributed to the growing strength of Latinos in civil society. An increase of public elected officials in the 1980s and 1990s brought new opportunities in reform politics to many states and cities.

3. Vatican II and Medellín Conference. Hierarchical shifts at both Vatican II and Medellín influenced the international Catholic community. The

---

22. Latino poverty differs by subgroup. For example, 38 percent of Puerto Ricans, 25 percent of Chicanos, 22 percent of Central Americans, and 14 percent of Cuban Americans live below the poverty level.

23. In 1973 Latino families made 69 percent of what Euro-American families made; in 1980 this figure was 67 percent; by 1989 it had decreased to 65 percent. See *State of Hispanic America 1991: An Overview* (Washington, D.C.: National Council of La Raza, 1992).

opening up of the church in Europe and Latin America set the foundation for new developments in the United States. The debates, politics, and documents from both gatherings profoundly influenced the first critical generation of Latino priests and sisters in seminary formation in the 1960s. While no U.S. Latino attended Vatican II, Father Virgilio Elizondo attended the Medellín Conference in Colombia. His presence initiated an exchange between the early founders of liberation theology and Latino religious leadership in the late 1960s and early 1970s. Vatican II's message of spreading the gospel in the language of the people was interpreted by Latino religious leaders as a basis for linking the Spanish language with music, art, dance, and cultural traditions associated with the church. From Medellín, the "preferential option for the poor" offered a new way of examining the status of Latinos within the church and society. Overall, both events were viewed as institutional breakthroughs encouraging a stronger commitment to social justice.

4. *Influence of Liberationist Theologies and Theologians.* Latino theology was influenced not only by liberation theology from Latin America but also by the contributions of U.S. black and feminist theologies. While black theologians raised the issue of racism, feminist theologians examined patriarchy in light of religious traditions and U.S. social structures. In the first book on Latinas and religion, Ada María Isasi-Díaz and Yolanda Tarango discussed the influence of cultural theology, feminist theology, and liberation theology on their work.[24] Many of the first generation of Latin American liberationists gave their initial U.S. public presentations on liberation theology at the Mexican American Cultural Center in the early 1970s. A liberationist dialogue developed between South American and North American religious leaders through the Theology of the Americas network of conferences and reflection groups. Two major conferences were held in 1975 and 1980 bringing together black, feminist, Chicano, Native American, Euro-American, and Latin American religious leaders.

5. *Competition with Non-Catholic Denominations.* Up until the 1960s, it was assumed that 95 percent of Latinos were Catholic. By the 1970s a shift had begun to take place, with a small but consistent exodus into evangelical denominations. Most studies now show that a variety of evangelical groups heavily recruit Latinos into their churches.[25] Protestant affiliation ranges from about 20 percent to almost 40 percent of

---

24. Isasi-Díaz and Tarango, *Hispanic Women.*
25. See *A Study of Religious and Social Attitudes of Hispanic Americans* (Princeton, N.J.: Gallup Organization, 1978); *Hispanics in New York: Religion, Culture and Social Experiences,* vol. 1 (New York: Office of Pastoral Research, Archdiocese of New York, 1982).

U.S. Latinos.[26] Puerto Ricans exhibit the highest rates, followed by Cubans and Chicanos. Second-generation Latinos have higher rates of Protestant affiliation than first-generation immigrants.[27] Among mainline Protestant churches, Methodists, Presbyterians, and Baptists have the largest amount of Latino members. However, the fastest growing sector is the evangelical, nondenominational churches, accounting for the majority of Latino Protestants.

6. *Increase of the U.S. Latino Population and Urbanization.* The "official" Latino population in the United States in 1990 totaled 22,400,000. The Latino population grew by 53 percent from 1980 to 1990. In comparison, Euro-Americans increased by 6 percent and African Americans by 13 percent. The U.S. Bureau of the Census estimates that in the year 2000 the Latino and African American population will each be about 34,000,000. Many states (for example, Texas, California, New Mexico, Illinois, Colorado, New Jersey) have significant Latino populations. For example, in California there are 7,560,000 Latinos, or 25 percent of the total population, and in Los Angeles County they constitute about 40 percent. Urbanization in the 1980s and 1990s has changed major metropolitan areas such as New York, Los Angeles, Chicago, and Miami. These cities, which previously consisted of one or two major Latino groups, now have many Latino subgroups living within the same communities. The result is a relationship emerging at the regional and national level that is giving rise to a pan-Latino consciousness.[28]

Links between Latin American and U.S. Latino Theology

The link between Latin American and U.S. Latino theology is strong. Religious and social conditions helped engender liberation theology in Latin America, and in turn liberation theology influenced changes in social conditions. Latino theologians in the United States soon recognized their own need for a theology concerned with changing the lives of the exploited. As they reflected on the social conditions of Latinos in the United States and developed organizations to address their concerns, a U.S. version of liberation theology eventually emerged. This theology is uniting sectors of the Chicano, Puerto Rican, Cuban, and other Latino communities. In addition, the influence between the United States and Latin America has become bidirectional. Latino theology in the United States, with its emphasis on

26. Rodolfo de la Garza et al., *Latino Voices: Mexican, Puerto Rican, and Cuban Perspectives on American Politics* (Boulder, Colo.: Westview Press, 1992).

27. Robert O. Gonzáles and Michael LaVelle, *The Hispanic Catholic Church in the United States: A Socio-cultural and Religious Profile* (New York: Northeast Catholic Pastoral Center for Hispanics, 1985).

28. Padilla, *Latino Ethnic Consciousness.*

ethnicity, race, gender, and popular religiosity, is having an impact on Latin American liberation theology. (See fig. 3 as an example of this relationship.)

FIGURE 3

**Influences and Relationship
between Latin American and U.S. Latino theologies**

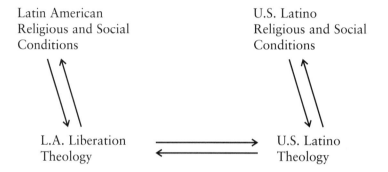

Latin American
Religious and Social
Conditions

U.S. Latino
Religious and Social
Conditions

L.A. Liberation
Theology

U.S. Latino
Theology

Over the last three decades, a bridge between Latin American and U.S. Latino theologians and religious leaders has formed through an exchange of theological ideas, methods of analysis, religious training, and new church models. For example, Virgilio Elizondo, from the United States, and Leonardo Boff, from Brazil, have collaborated on several issues of *Concilium,* an international religious journal. Venezuelan social scientist Otto Maduro influenced a generation of Latin American theologians and social scientists in the 1980s and now resides and teaches in the United States. The first woman president of ACHTUS is a Mexican theologian, María Pilar Aquino. Her work identifies the struggles of Latinas across borders.[29] Other U.S. theologians and religious leaders born in Cuba, Mexico, Puerto Rico, the Dominican Republic, and other Latin American countries have established themselves in the United States. Liberation theology for Latin Americans and U.S. Latinos is fostering a pan-ethnic theology that is uniting believers from all the Latin American countries. In the United States, for example, ACHTUS is a national association that brings together Catholic religious scholars from nine Latino subgroups to develop a *teología de conjunto,* a collective national Latino theology.

The social contexts discussed in this essay have some similarities and many differences. Each theology responds to its particular social location within the social structure. In the United States, theologians from each Latino subgroup focus on the issues reflective of their group experiences, such as immigration, refugee status, statehood, self-determination, exile,

---

29. Aquino, *Our Cry.*

syncretism, and machismo. However, these issues are also linked to broader themes such as praxis, the preferential option for the poor, biblical exegesis, patriarchy, hermeneutics, modernity, and popular religion.

Shared demographic changes augment the crisis within the Catholic Church and its hierarchy. The Latin American Catholic Church is now the largest church in the Catholic world, but this is not reflected in the over-all power structure of the church, which is still concentrated in Europe. In the United States, the dramatic increase of Latinos and the decrease of Euro-Americans in the church is significantly changing the face of that body. Yet this increase of Latino laity has not affected their numbers in decision-making positions. Population shifts have not changed the structure of the hierarchy. More conflict rather than less characterizes the relations at the leadership level and suggests a deepening crisis in both contexts. The decreasing clerical pool remains a fundamental problem for the church's hierarchy. The papacy and conservative national bishops react to progres-sive church sectors by transferring priests to nonactive parishes, restricting priests and sisters from performing their religious obligations, and pres-suring priests and sisters to leave their vocations. Brazilian theologian Leonardo Boff was "silenced" and ordered to stop publishing and mak-ing public presentations. A systematic effort to appoint conservative and ultraconservative bishops by Pope John Paul II is an attempt to control and reverse gains made by liberationists.

In Latin America, as social and political power shifts in civil society, new alignments form between church and state. The traditional alliances be-tween the oligarchy and the Catholic hierarchy are losing their hegemonic control. Civil wars, popular movements, democratic elections, the demise of military dictatorships, and the growing strength of liberation theology have changed the religious and political map of the Southern Hemisphere. In the United States, as organizations develop links between laity, clergy, theologians, and social scientists, the church is challenged to develop spe-cific strategies to address the levels of discrimination and create viable solutions. Laywomen and laymen provide the leadership for many of the organizations intent on creating a model of church that rejects the tra-ditional structure of authority. The Roman Catholic monopoly is finally breaking among people of Latin American origin. If the Roman Catholic Church continues to ignore the poor in Latin America and marginalize Lati-nos at both the leadership and the parish level, its sphere of influence will continue to decrease, as many opt for Protestant denominations to express their faith.

In Latin America, liberation theology emerged as a major prophetic social movement, with recognized leaders, institutional resources, and inter-national legitimacy. In the United States, Latino theology reflects primarily an intellectual prophetic movement among religious leaders with a small but growing number of advocates at the base level. However, in both contexts these theologies of liberation provide examples where religion emerges as a potent force for religious and social change. These theologies are not isolated or spontaneous phenomena, but a consequence of religious, political, and economic forces. The internal and external factors discussed here highlight the interplay of these social forces. Internal contradictions within the Catholic Church and the relationship between the church and other institutions in society contribute to a contextual theology. In both situations, Latin Americans and U.S. Latinos challenge the hegemony of traditional Christian theology, create their own models of church, and develop a theology that reflects their social location in society.

10

The Barrio as the Locus of a New Church

Harold J. Recinos

Latinos in the barrio experience life between suffering and death in a society that negates their right to exist with human dignity. Violence defines the urban streets. Human disfigurement takes the form of a loud cry for liberation. Each day death's silent weeping is heard in the report of gunfire that extinguishes the lives of young Latino men, women, and children. Barrio reality demands a church that notices how life is being crushed daily for persons existing in conditions of oppression and misery. Want is torment and demise in the barrio. Only God's justice will alter the social structures of the barrio and steer them toward life. Thus, Latinos seek God's justice as the defining reality of their lives and the power that converts society.

Blood endlessly pours out of the lacerated bodies in Latino neighborhoods. The news recounts how young Latino men who are judged worthless by the larger society have devised ways to claim social status. Killing a couple of "mushrooms" (small children) in a shootout on the street makes them "bad." The values of capitalist society defined by its sociology of violence best explain this grotesque reflection of personhood. Status rituals of this kind that are performed daily on barrio streets image a deep structure of social alienation. Jesus is repeatedly crucified by these ordeals of outrage. The broken bodies in the barrio point to a Jesus who criticizes any society that fosters death by creating human wretchedness.

Nevertheless, the God who defends life is present in the barrio. Latinos coming from Central America are confronting the false gods of an inculturated Christianity that assure the stability of the status quo and structural violence for the poor. Influenced by Central Americans, barrio Latinos are discovering how the one who was crucified by ruling authorities and human villainy condemns their history of suffering and paucity. Latinos are reshaping the meaning of the words, "I will take you as my own people, and you shall have me as your God" (Exod 6:7; Jer 7:23). In the barrio, the God opposed to all manner of human tyranny is raising disciples who reproduce in daily practice the action of Jesus defined as the way of solidarity and conflict with power.

Mainstream society concludes that the barrio is inferior and worthless; however, Jesus is inseparably identified with its history of struggle. The scriptural witness reports that in Jesus the time of fulfillment appears in the existential setting of marginality. From such a place the poor carpenter from Nazareth of Galilee instructs followers to seek "the kingdom of God and God's righteousness" (Matt 6:33). Latinos in the barrio know this means liberation is to be enacted from a point of departure in their concrete social experience. Below I will begin by examining the christological shifts taking place in the barrio. Afterward, I will discuss the contributions made especially by Salvadoran refugees to church renewal in the barrio.

The Margin Proclaims Good News

The biblical narratives direct attention to the insignificant places of established society as the proper context of divine disclosure. God acted in the particular history of a people who knew the meaning of oppression and suffering as slaves in Egypt. God took the form of rejected and poor humanity in the flesh of Jesus from Nazareth of Galilee. God's liberative purposes for humanity drew near from the margin of organized society. The Word became flesh in the region of Galilee, which was known for its cultural backwardness and unimportance for the status quo in Jerusalem.[1] In Galilee, God took the human figure of a poor and unemployed laborer wanting in formal education.

The barrio church must reexamine its common view of Jesus. For the most part, it has held two images of Christ. First, Jesus is depicted as the suffering Christ who is accessible to those whose own suffering requires comforting (Matt 11:28–30). This Christ who comforts those who suffer does not move persons to examine the brutalizing social order. Because this Christology drives faith inward, it confirms the position that the world cannot be radically transformed. In the barrio experience a suffering Christ provides a strong point of identification for Latinos. However, following Christ requires individuals to develop a more critical understanding of the basis for their personal and social pain in society.

An ahistorical image of the suffering Jesus negates the gospel's unapologetic defiance of all forms of social life that cause human affliction. A Jesus who only provides consolation for persons crushed by a historical reality capable and deserving of change merits no following from the people of the barrio. Jesus' suffering provides Latinos with a reason to question the meaning of their oppressive history. Christians who find solace in this al-

---

1. See esp. Virgilio Elizondo, *Galilean Journey: The Mexican-American Promise* (Maryknoll, N.Y.: Orbis Books, 1983).

ternative image of Jesus are summoned to discover the political meaning of Christ's solidarity with the poor. Christ suffers and dies to give life to outcast humanity. Today, to be an adherent of Christ means enabling organized society to see the results of its own system of oppression in the barrio.

A second image of Jesus depicts him as the glorified Christ who overcomes death and the sins of the world (John 17:4–5). This exalted Christ enchants persons who hope to rise above barrio disorder. A glorified Christ appeals to individuals who want to understand life in the context of ultimate salvation beyond history. In Jesus, they find the one who is "able for all time to save those who draw near to God . . . since he always lives to make intercession for them" (Heb 7:25). This Christology interprets the gospel as a promise of personal salvation apart from social, economic, political, and institutional renewal. Proponents of this viewpoint are least likely to relate God's Word to liberative action in the barrio.

Neither an ahistorical reading of the experience of suffering nor the single focus on personal salvation as flight from the world bears the good news promised by Jesus of Nazareth. The reality of the barrio requires a liberative theological reading of Jesus' ministry. Latinos, who are often less involved in the labor market and more isolated from the wider society than other groups, need to hear good news.[2] The good news is that Jesus calls Latinos to accept their place in a salvific history that refuses to accept that a new way of life will not come to the barrio. Indeed, Jesus instructs Latinos that the barrio poor are favored by God to build a church that is an organizational structure for impacting unjust economic systems and patterns of fellowship (Acts 2:42–47, 4:32–5:11; 1 Cor 1:27–28).

Christ the Liberator in the Barrio

The liberator Christ who preaches and teaches the gospel on the edges of society directs attention to the crisis of agonized Latino existence. In the barrio Christians are listening more closely to the Jesus who questions the presumed correctness of the structures and institutions of society.[3] An encounter with the liberator Christ inspires a fresh reading of the historical experience of the barrio that discloses Latino cries for freedom. Latinos whose faith is awakened by the liberator Christ admit that he provokes human division between members of society (see Matt 10:34–37; Mark 10:29–31; Luke 12:52–53). Nevertheless, Latinos genuinely wish to follow this Jesus and actuate his vision of humanity in the context of the world.

---

2. Marta Tienda, "Puerto Ricans and the Underclass Debate," *The Annals of the American Academy of Political and Social Science* (ed. William Julius Wilson; Newbury Park, Calif.: Sage Publications, 1989) 105–19.

3. See Harold Recinos, *Hear the Cry! A Latino Pastor Challenges the Church* (Louisville: Westminster/John Knox Press, 1989).

The liberator Christ bids followers to vacate the established world that displays so little humanity and enter a new historical community defined as a communion of equals. Jesus' community evolves an ethic of historical action that discerns God's will for creation as the struggle for life in the context of justice, friendship, and equality. Latinos now speak of Christ walking the barrio streets: opposed to forms of spirituality that view faith groups as only societies of the human heart (*societas in cordibus*). The gospel of Jesus is offering another vision of social relationships: a vision of a unique and visible community of just struggle.

This Jesus stands with the poor, denounces the accumulation of wealth, praises individuals who give up their love of money, rejects oppressive behavior, demands that service and humility define community, and makes opposition to injustice essential. In the scriptural witness, he tells the people of the barrio that their poverty implicates the rich (Luke 6:24; 12:13–21), religious authorities (Mark 11:15–39; Luke 11:39–44, 46–52), and powerful officials (Mark 10:42). Barrio existence evidences the negation of life by these privileged classes who propagate oppressive practices.[4] Faith in the liberator Christ means bearing witness to the gospel from within deep concerns for a conflictual reality (Mark 13:9; Luke 21:12–13; 22:36).

Jesus hears the cry of Latinos who know the meaning of oppression and poverty as dominant aspects of their existential reality. The liberator Christ present in the barrio lives in every endeavor to assert life and human values against the real conditions of human violation that bring ill news to the poor. Today, following Jesus means Christians change their lives and willingly choose to live by behavioral standards that empower the barrio community to alter its necrophilic history.[5] Latino Christians are feeling called to form a church that alters the unjust order of life in light of a new vision of human freedom for the barrio.

Jesus understood the oppressive mechanisms of the rich in light of the hope of the poor for a society of justice and communion (Matt 6:24; Luke 6:24). Jesus radically affirmed the poor in the ultimate soil of human life: the God who is father and mother of all creation. Barrio Christians in the process of discovering the liberator Christ clearly discern how the Lord makes them "rich out of his poverty" (2 Cor 8:9). This Jesus organizes the poor into a collective force to demand better health care, housing, education, economic equality, and political voice. The reality of Jesus as emancipator is grasped as a reference to the poor's advancing liberation from situations of oppression, suffering, injustice, and class inequality (Luke 1:46–55).

---

4. Phillip Berryman, *The Religious Roots of Rebellion: Christians in Central American Revolutions* (Maryknoll, N.Y.: Orbis Books, 1986) 378.

5. See Leonardo Boff, "Jesus Christ the Liberator, Center of Faith on the Edge of the World," *Faith on the Edge: Religion and Marginalized Existence* (Maryknoll, N.Y.: Orbis Books, 1991) 119–45.

Jesus spoke the truth of the poor to the powerful, who were untroubled by their sin of oppression. He also warned religious leaders not to lose their lives by seeking social privileges (Luke 11:43; 20:46–47). Jesus taught on the streets that the God who acts by altering power in history seeks to renew the economic, racial, political, social, cultural, and spiritual structures of society (Luke 13:26). This newfound hope in Jesus gives rise to action that seeks to install equity and a new vision of human purpose in the barrio (Gal 5:1). From the standpoint of this liberation Christology, discipleship implies serving the good news of God's lordship in history by caring for mistreated human beings at every level of society (Luke 10:25–37).

A parable that cogently reflects the teaching of the liberator Christ is that of the Rich Man and Lazarus (Luke 16:19–31). This story tells of the rich who control the material conditions of life to the disadvantage of the poor. The parable focuses attention on the reversal of fortune in the afterlife. The social reality described is analogous to the relations that obtain between the barrio and established society. The parable describes the reality of the poor imaged by Lazarus, who is a cripple suffering from a skin disease. Lazarus does not have fine linen or feast sumptuously every day; instead, Lazarus's condition of oppression and suffering causes him to wait for crumbs to fall from the table of a socially indifferent rich man.

God takes the side of the poor in the story. This is made plain by the fact that in the story the rich man is nameless.[6] We do not have to look far to see Lazarus on the streets of the barrio. Salvadoran refugees are a new and growing population in North American Latino communities. Lazarus speaks to the wealthy and morally indifferent North America in the voice of a Salvadoran refugee doctor living in Washington, D.C.—the third largest Salvadoran city in the world. Salvadoran refugees in the barrio interpret their trust in God in terms of the hopes and struggles of the wretched Latinos. Like Lazarus, "Tomás" knows what it means to exist despised by those who control wealth and power in society. He declares:

Repression reached me one day. I was in church. Two army trucks came to the clinic. They opened fire on the clinic. I was wounded along with many others. They put us in the trucks and took us to jail in San Salvador. I was stripped, blindfolded, and placed in a cell. They interrogated and tortured me. My crime was working with the campesinos and the poor. They wanted me to know that torture and death awaited me. They said, "What are you doing working with those people? You are a doctor; you could be driving a late model car and have a great office." You see, the poor are the dangerous ones. I saw why the church needs to be on the side of the poor. All prisoners are tortured in El Salvador. I was given electric shock on my tongue, genitals, and beneath my fingernails. They shot my left arm—accusing me of being a leftist—a sign of helping the poor. I could no longer help the people [Tomás was a surgeon]. I was convinced of not getting

---

6. See Joachim Jeremias, *The Parables of Jesus* (New York: Scribner's, 1954) 183.

out alive, but the *compadrazgo* system saved me. There are colonels in my family. Compadres owe favors; as a result I was freed.

The death squads looked for me and my family. I was urged to flee. I was still wounded from the attack on the clinic, but abandoned my family, leaving behind my pregnant wife. I fled like a criminal, hiding in an onion truck, to Guatemala....I made it to Mexico and spent two years there healing. I never thought of coming to the States, but one day I decided to accompany a group of people crossing over the border. I was part of a caravan of women and children hiding by day and walking at night. I reached Los Angeles. I slept in parks and abandoned buildings. I was afraid, but I wanted to release what was inside me and talk about what was happening in my country.

There is much development here in the United States, but too much disinformation. The poor suffer, die, have pain, scars...people must know. I started to talk. We Salvadoran refugees are here, but we dream of our country, family, and home. Letters from home say death is still there. It is hard to receive these letters....My wife is dead. El Salvador is dying, the church is martyred, most people do not know.

The barrio is that place in society that separates the rich from loathed humanity. The God who favors Lazarus passes judgment on human behavior that permits the torment of the poor to go unnoticed. God takes the side of impoverished humanity who make their home in the barrio street, are utterly forgotten by the powerful of established society, and are sinfully sacrificed to death. Jesus makes plain that Lazarus enjoys the place of honor in God's reign. In contrast, the unnamed rich man who failed to do justice by enacting the social relational pact revealed by Moses and the prophets is harshly judged. He is delivered to a state of permanent suffering in the flames of Hades for not doing God's justice.[7]

Clearly, Jesus was not expounding a teaching on the life beyond death, and he was not recommending that the poor learn to be resigned to their life conditions. Jesus explicitly alludes to a male subdivision of society that shuts out God's Word while enjoying personal security in concentrated wealth. In short, the parable addresses current life by issuing a singular word of warning to *men* who enjoy selfish wealth at the expense of the life of the poor.[8] Jesus was warning those who enjoyed status and rank in a society that promoted behavior opposed to the God incarnate in the poor. If the five brothers of the rich man elect to act with a similar social indifference toward the poor, they too will know the meaning of God's eternal absence.

In the parable, Jesus reminds those who serve the interests of wealth that the existential situation of Lazarus presupposes the reality of God. No amount of wealth will give human beings access to God; instead, serving God in the concrete situations of the oppressed poor renders one capable

---

7. See Gustavo Gutiérrez, *The God of Life* (Maryknoll, N.Y.: Orbis Books, 1991) 57–58.
8. See Jeremias, *Parables of Jesus,* 186.

of receiving the gift of divine union. The parable of the Rich Man and Lazarus makes plain that God conquers human suffering by way of the activity of persons who do not choose lovelessness. For Jesus, God is revealed by Lazarus. In other words, the power of God is present in the weakness and hope of those who exist in life-denying conditions.

The parable of the Rich Man and Lazarus specifically speaks to the wealthy classes of that society. Jesus indicates that their wealth is linked to the actuality of the afflicted poor. The nameless rich man's sin consisted of a neglectful behavior that sanctioned and perpetuated Lazarus's wretched conditions. Most often, the privileged classes in society are agents of a similar destructive pattern that defines their relationship to the barrio. To be sure, in the parable Jesus relates that wealth is not to be concentrated and self-indulgently used by ruling and male-dominated families; instead, wealth is to be distributed across society in the function of serving the needs of the barrio and the global poor—the Lazaruses of our time.

The Church Reborn in the Barrio

For Jesus the term "poor" refers to (1) those whose structured identity attracts social intolerance, and (2) persons who are subhumanized by their material conditions. First, the Scriptures identify the people who endure discrimination as sinners, publicans, prostitutes, and members of the despised professions (Matt 11:19; 21:31–32; Mark 2:6; Luke 15:1; 18:11).[9] People considered the least members of society are typically scorned (Matt 11:25; 25:40–45). Second, the term "poor" decidedly refers to the experience of concrete wretchedness due to material privation (Luke 4:18–19). Thus, poverty brings hunger, thirst, sickness, nakedness, social estrangement, imprisonment, and subhumanization (Isa 58:5–7; 60:1–2).[10]

God's identification with the poor is becoming clearer to the church as it looks to the barrio. The church is discovering that the oppressed and poor are laying Christianity's foundation for the next millennium. The humiliated of the world are now speaking from the context of the barrio in ways that reflect the drama of the Holy Spirit at work renewing hope, theology, and ecclesial praxis. In this new reformation underway in the barrio, the poor teach the universal church that following Jesus in the setting of oppression and suffering means expressing a love that is sacrificially attentive to others (John 15:13). The poor raise ultimate questions for faith and remind the church that Christian love necessitates social transformation.

In the barrio, the privatized Christianity that caused believers to accept a Christology of suffering and glorification is being transformed from the

---

9. See Victorio Araya, "Toward a Church in Solidarity with the Poor," *Faith Born of the Struggle for Life* (ed. Dow Kirkpatrick; Grand Rapids: Eerdmans, 1988) 266.

10. See Jon Sobrino, *Jesus in Latin America* (Maryknoll, N.Y.: Orbis Books, 1987) 90.

perspective of prophetic faithfulness. Salvadoran refugees who take up residence in the barrio are helping Latinos native to North America reflect theologically upon their wretched situation. Salvadoran refugees are having an evangelizing impact on barrio life. Latinos native to the barrio are understanding anew how God's all-embracing reality is a radical counterforce to social injustice. Salvadoran refugees are reinventing the barrio church by making sure faith acquires the liberating historical consciousness it lacked.

Who are the people in the barrio from El Salvador? El Salvador is the smallest republic in Central America, with a population of about five million. Political repression and violence internally displaced or forced 25 percent of the people into refugee status between 1980 and 1992.[11] An estimated one million Salvadorans are living in major urban barrios across the United States. Los Angeles is the second largest Salvadoran city in the world, and Washington, D.C., ranks third.[12] A twelve-year civil war produced a death-toll of an estimated seventy-five thousand persons. Those killed in the civil conflict are remembered as "social martyrs" by Christians committed to the transformation of the authoritarian political regime.

Salvadoran refugees live under conditions of extreme poverty, with jobless rates between 75 and 90 percent. In the States, they fear apprehension and deportation.[13] By the late 1970s, political friction had deepened in El Salvador, and Salvadorans began to migrate to the States for reasons other than economic ones. In the 1980s, open civil war and subsequent economic deterioration were the basic reasons Salvadorans left their country. The U.S. government provided economic, political, and military support to El Salvador's repressive regime. About three-fourths of the current Salvadoran population in the United States came after 1979, when political repression sharpened the crisis in Salvadoran society.[14]

In the 1980s, Archbishop Oscar Romero, Jesuit priests, church leaders, and persons associated with base Christian communities in El Salvador were murdered or disappeared at the hands of right-wing groups and security forces trained by the United States.[15] Even shortly after Archbishop Romero's murder, Congress approved a $5.7 million aid package to the

---

11. See Elizabeth Ferris, *The Central American Refugees* (New York: Praeger, 1987). See also Patricia Weiss Fagen, "Central American Refugees and U.S. Policy," *Regional Dynamics and U.S. Policy in the 1980s* (ed. Nora Hamilton et al.; Boulder, Colo.: Westview Press, 1988).

12. See Segundo Montes and Juan José García Vásques, *Salvadoran Migration to the United States* (Washington, D.C.: Center for Immigration Policy and Refugee Assistance, 1988). See also Patricia Ruggles, Michael Fix, and Kathleen M. Thomas, *Profile of the Central American Population in the United States* (Washington, D.C.: Urban Institute, 1985).

13. See Harold J. Recinos, "The Politics of Salvadoran Refugee Popular Religion" (Ph.D. diss., American University, 1993).

14. Montes and Vásques, *Salvadoran Migration*, 9.

15. See Tom Barry, *El Salvador: A Country Guide* (Albuquerque: Inter-Hemispheric Education Resource Center, 1990) 111. See also Recinos, "Politics."

government of El Salvador. Since the early 1970s, eighteen Catholic priests, a Lutheran pastor, three American nuns, and a lay American church worker have been killed or disappeared.[16] Death and political persecution at the hands of death squads and security forces became a part of daily life for Salvadoran Christians. For Salvadorans, these deaths reproduced the martyrdom of Jesus, who was killed for promoting justice and contesting state power.[17]

Salvadoran refugees with a deep commitment to the liberator Christ have been steadily taking up residence in the barrio. They communicate a faith rooted in the consciousness of the social martyrs that views the church as a Christ-centered vehicle that unmasks sinful structures and demands social change. Essentially, belief in the social martyrs refers to the God who sides with the poor. For Salvadoran refugees, the memory of the social martyrs symbolizes the protest and struggle of the poor who seek to create unprecedented economic, political, and social structures in light of the radical vision of God's reign of justice and love. Thus, new social and political values are gaining a hearing in the barrio and challenging white society's culture of exclusion.

By walking with Salvadoran refugees, Latino Christians in the barrio discover the God of the exodus experience. Thus, the received Christian tradition as represented by the Bible, standard symbols like the cross, or specific texts about Jesus are given subversive power in relation to barrio experience. Salvadoran refugees extend the meaning of the term "poor" in the barrio. This theological category is not exclusive; instead, it alludes to the formation of a global political movement that includes both a multiclass and a class-specific community.[18] This politico-liberation movement embodies the alternative society that Jesus sought to establish to overcome historical oppression. Jesus created an alternative community comprised of persons who once conspired (Matt 10:3) with established society and those who radically opposed it (Luke 6:15).[19] Establishing a new community means serving the interest of the kingdom by assuming the cause of the poor. Generally, the suffering of God revealed by Salvadoran refugees shatters the conservative interpretations of faith and politics held by U.S. Latinos and their North American counterparts. From U.S. barrios, Salvadoran refugees conduct ritual events guided and illumined by the memory of the social martyrs to unite opposed social forces into a new community of solidarity and struggle.

---

16. See Americas Watch, *El Salvador's Decade of Terror: Human Rights since the Assassination of Archbishop Romero* (New Haven: Yale University Press, 1991) 33.

17. See Jon Sobrino, *The True Church and the Poor* (Maryknoll, N.Y.: Orbis Books, 1984) 179–80.

18. William Roseberry, *Anthropologies and Histories: Essays in Culture, History, and Political Economy* (New Brunswick, N.J.: Rutgers University Press, 1989) 231.

19. See Gerhard Lohfink, *Jesus and Community* (Philadelphia: Fortress Press, 1984) 10.

Salvadoran refugee ritual events represent a complex of behavior set in the standardized and repetitive symbolization of the social martyrs. They mold political beliefs and communicate knowledge about social relations. The religion of martyrology of Salvadoran refugees denies theological legitimation to the politics of inequality and the social forces that benefit from it; meanwhile, this belief system demands that individuals sustain a constant bond with the oppressed and exploited classes. Ritual events reveal the memory of the social martyrs as the organized form of the experience of social suffering made into a vehicle that builds a movement to change unjust societal systems.

Ritualized symbols like Archbishop Romero, the Jesuit priests, and the seventy-five thousand killed during the twelve years of Salvadoran civil war both interpret human experience and render social categories for understanding complex political reality.[20] In one base Christian community located in Washington, D.C., Salvadoran refugees fixed their self-identity by way of ritual events in a culture of protest and resistance informed by the gospel and rooted in the poor's local and global historical struggle. Thus, Salvadoran refugees in the barrio reveal Christian self-identity in the form of a personality that acts as a resource for judging and criticizing larger social realities.

For instance, a liturgy consisting of the Salvadoran Campesino Mass defined self-identity in the context of the barrio. Developed in the context of political resistance, the Liberation Mass images the poor as an organized society in which self-identity is molded to contest the oppressive class interests of dominant social forces. As ritual, the Liberation Mass structures knowledge and social experience that promote the conscious embrace of alternative values in the barrio, rooted in social action responsive to the needs in the villages of El Salvador and the local streets of the barrio. Christian self-identity and purpose are expressed in the Liberation Mass as the struggle to build a propertyless world of equality.[21]

Latinos native to North America and exposed to the Liberation Mass are growing with a new faith identity. In the barrio the new experience of church motivates Christians to denounce oppression, distinguish false prophets, and affix belief in the Jesus who clarifies the project of the poor. Private Christianity counsels the church against political activism and focuses on an ahistorical spirituality; however, Salvadoran refugees renewing the barrio church with the Liberation Mass remind all Latinos that, when the poor organize their liberation from oppressed existence, God's reign is historically embodied as anticipatory hope. Worship in the barrio is steadily molding agents of historical change who take up Jesus' conflictive cross and follow (Matt 10:38).

---

20. Recinos, "Politics," 248.
21. Ibid., 253–58.

The Liberation Mass expresses a value system opposed to capitalism. Capitalism generates an inhuman and selfish value system that is incompatible with God's imperative to establish a community of brothers and sisters. For instance, a line from the entrance song of the Salvadoran Liberation Mass relates, "God sends us to make of this world a table of equality, where all work and struggle together, sharing property." With their Salvadoran brothers and sisters, Latino Christians in the barrio now unapologetically proclaim that the God of life sides with the poor and those who give their life for them. The God of life defends the rights of the poor and judges politico-economic systems in light of their contribution to the well-being of the marginal.

One Salvadoran friend told me that the social martyrs live as God's strength in the people. In the context of the barrio, native Latinos are learning that they are called to follow Jesus and the social martyrs who represent the collective purpose of the poor and their allies. Surely, the most valued lesson to be absorbed from the good news delivered to the barrio by Salvadoran refugees is that Jesus and the social martyrs define the future practices of the church. In other words, barrio Christianity is redefining itself in terms of a communitarian culture and an economics of justice in the setting of a conflictive reality that God seeks to change radically.[22]

The New Barrio Church

Storefront churches surfaced on the edges of barrio society in the free space left by mainline denominations most commonly fleeing to white suburbs. For the most part, these churches have not provided the organizational strength for collective action. The traditional barrio pulpit too often characterizes Jesus as a friend of the dominant political and economic order and recoils at the idea of organizing society in light of the alternative vision of the gospel. Outside social forces such as realtors, the dominant class, welfare agencies, and corporate interests have hardly been contested by the outmoded barrio church.[23] The new barrio church will change these conditions of life.

Salvadoran refugees remind all believers to "fill up what is lacking in the suffering of Christ" (Col 1:24) with their own flesh. The new barrio church is inextricably linked to the agony of the barrio and the crucified people of global history. In the new barrio church, Salvadoran refugees are nurturing a Christianity that is historically conscious of the ultimate reality of a creation that groans for liberation and life in God (Rom 8:22). The

---

22. See Walter Brueggemann, *The Prophetic Imagination* (Philadelphia: Fortress Press, 1983).

23. See J. D. Loic Wacquant and William Julius Wilson, "The Cost of Racial and Class Exclusion in the Inner City," *Annals of the American Academy of Political and Social Science* (1989) 8–25.

faith renewal underway in the barrio suggests that there is no turning away from the God revealed by Jesus on the cross, a God who calls humanity to overcome human sin and injustice.[24] The new barrio church does not "grow weary of well-doing, for in due season" it shall harvest a new social reality (Gal 6:9).

Salvadoran refugees offering their testimony in the new experience of church invite Christians to engage in a loving praxis defined as listening, inclusion, and servanthood.[25] First, the praxis of love involves unmasking social structures that deny life to the poor by instrumental use of the social sciences. Second, the theological act that flows from the church's critical grasp of social reality involves becoming a voice of the Latino community, a community now invisible to established society. Finally, the praxis of love consists of the celebration of God's negation of all crucified history in the death and resurrection of Jesus. Jesus' death on the cross and current cry in the barrio are nothing less than the path of a servanthood that renews history and life.

One Salvadoran refugee associated with a base Christian community in the nation's capital observed that "God knows what takes away our basic rights to life. Churches remaining indifferent to injustice, repression, human abuse, exploitation, discrimination, and racism are uncommitted to God's project of life." The barrio reflects the meaning of Jesus' life and liberative mission. Through the new barrio church, Jesus addresses actuality by creating a new people in history that confronts social reality from a vision of humanity rooted in the gospel. The new barrio church coming to life is committed to a liberator Christ who leads Christian action to end dehumanizing poverty and oppression. God's reign is truly near.

---

24. See Jon Sobrino, *Christology at the Crossroads* (Maryknoll, N.Y.: Orbis Books, 1978) 232.

25. See Araya, "Toward a Church," 272.

II

In the World but Not of It

Exile as Locus for a Theology of the Diaspora

Fernando F. Segovia

U.S. Hispanic American theology is a rich matrix within which can be found a wide spectrum of distinctive expressions and a complex theological voice encompassing a broad variety of characteristic inflections.[1] Such theological diversity within the same locus or discourse reflects the enormous diversity that characterizes the U.S. Hispanic American reality and experience.[2] Like the latter, therefore, U.S. Hispanic American theology should be seen as both overarching and disparate, concordant and cacophonous, with an emphasis on both matrix and traditions, voice and accents.

To begin with, many similarities bind together the different components of this reality, make us a voice or a matrix, and bring us all under the same social group and appellation, regardless of the specific nomenclature employed.[3] Such similarities allow, in effect, for a readily identifiable demarcation of social location in terms of ethnic (cultural/linguistic) provenance and sociopolitical status—U.S. Hispanic Americans. Such similarities also account for the many common threads and currents of our emerging theology, well emphasized and developed in the literature.[4] At the same

---

1. See Fernando F. Segovia, "Two Places and No Place on Which to Stand: Mixture and Otherness in Hispanic American Theology," *Hispanic Americans in Theology and the Church* (ed. Fernando F. Segovia; special issue of *Listening: Journal of Religion and Culture* 27 [winter 1992] 26–40).

2. See in this regard Edna Acosta-Belén and Barbara R. Sjostrom, eds., *The Hispanic Experience in the United States: Contemporary Issues and Perspectives* (New York: Praeger, 1988), and Gerardo Marín and Barbara VanOss Marín, *Research with Hispanic Populations* (Applied Social Research Methods Series, no. 23; Newbury Park, Calif.: Sage Publications, 1991).

3. My own preference at this point, as evidenced by the present study, is for the label "U.S. Hispanic American" and the substantive "U.S. Hispanic Americans." For a detailed overview of the discussion regarding nomenclature and the reasons for this particular use on my part, see the introduction to this volume.

4. For a systematic and sustained effort in this regard, see the ongoing work of Roberto Goizueta: "United States Hispanic Theology and the Challenge of Pluralism," *Frontiers of Hispanic Theology in the United States* (ed. Allan Figueroa Deck; Maryknoll, N.Y.: Orbis Books, 1992) 1–22; "*Nosotros:* Toward a U.S. Hispanic Anthropology," *Hispanic Ameri-*

time, many profound differences distinguish the various components of this reality from one another. Such differences account for the various divisions and subdivisions, groups and subgroups, within the category as a whole. Such differences constitute the traditions and accents, the hues and tones, the shades and colors of our emerging theology and must not be overlooked or submerged. Consequently, U.S. Hispanic American theology can be undertaken and analyzed either from the point of view of its overall locus or discourse or from the point of view of its manifold expressions and inflections.

The latter can be readily identified in terms of the various constitutive factors of social location.[5] For the purposes of this study, the following three are paramount.

First, sociocultural identity—the distinctive history, culture, and racial mixture of each geographical area and country within each area. We are all U.S. Hispanic Americans, to be sure, but we also trace our roots to the Caribbean Basin, Central America, North America, and South America. Within such regional variations of Hispanic America, furthermore, we may hail from the Dominican Republic or Puerto Rico (the Caribbean Basin), Nicaragua or El Salvador (Central America), Mexico (North America), or Colombia or Peru (South America). Likewise, we may reflect a primary tradition, physical and/or cultural, of *mestizaje* or *mulatez*.[6]

Second, sociopolitical status—the nature of and rationale for our present status in the United States. Thus, from a legal point of view, we may be born or naturalized citizens, legal or illegal residents, while, from a historical point of view, we may be first-generation immigrants, children—immediate or removed—of immigrants, or descendants of acquired subjects of the country.

Third, socioreligious tradition and affiliation—while we are all in one way or another ultimately related to the Roman Catholic tradition, given the colonial history of our countries of origin or descent, our present socioreligious affiliations are not only quite varied but also increasingly so. As a result, we may be Catholic, practicing or cultural; Protestant, ranging from the mainline churches to the evangelical and Pentecostal churches; or members of other religious traditions, such as Santería for example.

---

cans in Theology and the Church, 55–69; "Rediscovering Praxis: The Significance of U.S. Hispanic Experience for Theological Method," *We Are a People! Initiatives in Hispanic American Theology* (ed. Roberto S. Goizueta; Minneapolis: Fortress Press, 1992) 51–77.

5. By constitutive factors of social location I mean such fundamental dimensions of human identity as, for example, socioeconomic class, gender and sexual orientation, age, sociocultural identity, sociopolitical status, socioreligious tradition and affiliation, socioeducational level, and ideological stance.

6. While the term *mestizaje* has traditionally indicated the miscegenation of the European and the native American, the term *mulatez* has signified in turn the mixture of European and African. However, it is not uncommon to find the first term used metaphorically of all miscegenation. I prefer, however, to use the two terms to point to the different fusions of "races" that have taken place in the whole of Latin America.

Thus, although we share the same home in the United States at present, our country of adoption, as well as similar roots in our past, in our countries of origin—again, by no means uniform, but with certain definite and pronounced similarities that make it possible to speak of a Latin American civilization—the fact is that we do so with many faces, many stories, and many visions of God and the world.[7] As such, it becomes imperative for each component within the group as a whole to give an account of its own visage, its own narrative, its own conception of God and the world. Such is, one might say, the centrifugal dimension of our theological task, as fundamental to our work as its centripetal forces. Such a call for self-definition and self-expression within the whole represents, in effect, a defense against the dehumanizing universalism of any "melting pot" agenda, external or internal, in favor of a "mosaic" or "rainbow" agenda, where differences are neither denied nor looked down upon and where similarities are also acknowledged and valued.[8]

Indeed, it seems to me that the last thing U.S. Hispanic Americans would want to do is to create their own parallel version of a hegemonic "melting pot," that is to say, a reading of the other components of the U.S. Hispanic American reality and experience in the image and likeness of any one specific group or subgroup—a sort of internal ethnocentrism. Quite ironically, to be sure, it may very well be that in the end our close proximity to and interchange with one another within the United States will give rise to a situation of cultural exchange and change far beyond any to be found or contemplated within Latin America itself.[9] For the foreseeable future, however, U.S. Hispanic American theology must continue to negotiate a middle way between a focus on the voice or matrix of the group as a whole and a corresponding focus on the different expressions or inflections of its many and complex components.

In this study I shall begin formulating one such variation of U.S. Hispanic American theology: a theological tradition or accent that grows out of, reflects, and engages my social location within the U.S. Hispanic Amer-

---

7. For a sharp delineation of contemporary civilizations after the collapse of the ideological division between East and West, see the recent discussion involving Kishore Mabhubane, "The West and the Rest," *National Interest* (summer 1992) 3–13; Samuel P. Huntington, "The Clash of Civilizations," *Foreign Affairs* 72 (summer 1993) 22–49; Kishore Mabhubane, "The Dangers of Decadence: What the Rest Can Teach the West," *Foreign Affairs* (September–October 1993) 10–14; and Samuel P. Huntington, "If Not Civilizations, What? Paradigms of the Post–Cold War World," *Foreign Affairs* 72 (November–December 1993) 186–94. See also, more recently, Matthew Connelly and Paul Kennedy, "Must It Be the Rest against the West?" *Atlantic Monthly* 274:6 (December 1994) 61–84.

8. For a recent exposé of the "melting pot" agenda, see Benjamin Schwarz, "The Diversity Myth: America's Leading Export," *Atlantic Monthly* 275:5 (May 1995) 57–67.

9. Indeed, this is a phenomenon that Justo L. González sees as already taking place in the country at large; see "Hispanics in the United States," *Hispanic Americans in Theology,* 7–16, esp. 11–13.

ican reality and experience. I shall call such a variation a theology of the diaspora, a theology born and forged in exile: a variation of U.S. Hispanic American theology with a primary focus on the sociopolitical dimensions of U.S. Hispanic American life, on those who arrive and establish permanent residence in the country as first-generation immigrants. In this its first articulation I shall proceed as follows: (1) an exposition of certain theoretical presuppositions guiding and informing the project as a whole; (2) an analysis of exile as a category in U.S. Hispanic American theology; (3) a recounting of my own myth or narrative of origins, my own journey of exile; and (4) theological reflections from exile and the diaspora.

Diaspora Theology: Theoretical Contexts

The proposed theology of the diaspora is deeply rooted in such contemporary theoretical movements and discourses as postmodernism, postcolonialism, and liberation theology.

Diaspora Theology as Postmodernist Theology

At this point in my life, I would describe my critical, hermeneutical, and theological/ideological agenda as profoundly postmodernist.[10] At the very heart of postmodernism, as I understand and employ the term, lies the fundamental myth or narrative of radical diversity and pluralism, quite different from that of modernism, with its emphasis on universality and objectivity. From the point of view of postmodernism, therefore, there is no *reality* as such but rather a multitude of "realities"; in other words, "reality" is always seen in terms of perspective. As such, there is no universal or objective perspective, no impartial observer or detached narrator; rather, the question of perspective is always seen as radically situated and contextualized from both a sociocultural and a sociohistorical point of view. "Reality" is thus regarded as fluid, polyvalent, polyglot: ultimately and inextricably related, implicitly or explicitly, to the various constitutive factors of social location and human identity. As such, "reality" ceases to be a set of data or facts to be apprehended and described by a detached and independent self and becomes instead a construction involving interaction between "facts" and "self."

---

10. I see all three fronts as interdependent and interrelated. Thus, taking my own field of study, biblical criticism, as point of departure, I would argue that to engage in the study and interpretation of early Christianity is to engage in hermeneutical discussion as well as theological construction. Implicitly or explicitly, therefore, the critic is both a hermeneutician, subscribing to certain theories of meaning and interpretation, and a theologian, espousing certain worldviews with their respective consequences vis-à-vis the world at large. I would describe my own agenda in this regard as follows: an interpretive approach of intercultural criticism; a hermeneutics of otherness and engagement; and a theology of otherness and mixture.

For postmodernism, therefore, all that is, including itself, is a construct, involving a perspective—and hence a poetics, a rhetoric, and an agenda. As such, it calls for profound awareness, especially in light of late modernism, to the effect that all constructs can be deconstructed. At the same time, however, it also calls for a similar realization that there is no choice (outside of nihilism, and that itself is a construct) but to engage in construction, but a construction that demands critical awareness regarding what underlies all construction—its poetics, its rhetoric, and its agenda. In other words, such awareness would encompass, to continue the metaphor, all the manifold elements involved in construction, such as: architectural context; blueprints; ground or terrain; building materials; scaffolding, skeleton, and carapace; finishing touches and decorations; final product; impact on the context, both physical and architectural.

By foregrounding the voice of U.S. Hispanic American theology, approaching that voice as in itself multidimensional and multilingual, and focusing on one particular expression or inflection within such a voice, that of the diaspora, my proposed theological task constitutes an exercise in postmodern discourse, an exercise in the application of its fundamental myth of diversity and pluralism.

Diaspora Theology as Postcolonial Theology

From the theoretical standpoint of postmodernism, all criticism, all hermeneutics, and all theology are likewise regarded as exercises in construction. Consequently, at this point in my life, I do not see the theological task as deductive, systematic, or universal; rather, I look upon it as inductive, contextual, and pluralistic. In other words, all socioreligious discourse about the world, the otherworld, and the relationship between such worlds is seen as tied to perspective, as born out of and forged in praxis—a construct grounded in reality and experience, contextual to the core—with a view of reality and experience as culturally and historically differentiated and in constant flux; and pluralist at heart—with an acceptance of a multitude of constructs reflecting and engaging a variety of realities and experiences across history and culture.

Such a view of the theological task is, I would further argue, postcolonial in nature. First, the logic and discourse of colonialism demand, at their most fundamental level, a binomial opposition between the "we" and the "they": empire and possessions; colonizers and colonized; center and margins. Second, such logic and discourse also involve an inherent evaluation of the oppositions in question: the superiority of the "we"/center vis-à-vis the inferiority of the "they"/margins. Third, such logic and discourse call for tight control as well as a sense of mission on the part of the center with regard to the margins: a necessary submission of the "they" to the "we" as well as a necessary raising of the "they" to the level of the "we," a process usually couched in terms of progress and civilization and calling for the abnegation and dehumanization of the "they" by way of reinvestiture and rehumanization as the "we." Finally, postcolonialism represents the breakdown and demise of such logic and discourse, whether by way of praxis or theory or both: a process and program of decolonization involving a fundamental questioning of and attack on the center by the margins. Its own logic and discourse involve not only an exposé of the perspective behind the "we"/center (its poetics, rhetoric, and agenda) but also a retrieval and revalorization of the perspectives of the "they"/margins (an exercise in poetics, rhetoric, and agenda).

Needless to say, modern Christian theology has been, by and large, a theology of colonization and its discourse a colonial discourse: a theology of the "we"/center, grounded in Western civilization; a theology of enlightenment and privilege, looked upon as far superior to anything that the "they"/ margins could ever produce or aspire to produce; and a theology of hegemony and mission, whereby the margins could be brought under effective control and raised to the civilized standards of the West by way of either its North American or Western European variants. In this regard theological discourse has been no different than any other discourse of the modern world. In recent times, however, this theology of colonization has been called into question and challenged by the children of the colonized, both at the margins and at the center of the empire. Such questioning and attack, representing in effect a process and program of decolonization within theology itself, have foregrounded the central issues of perspective—the issues of poetics, rhetoric, and agenda; the issues that postmodernism places at the heart of the discussion within its basic narrative of radical pluralism and diversity.

By focusing on U.S. Hispanic American theology in general and diaspora theology in particular—theologies that emerge from the margins present within the center itself—and by retrieving and revalorizing such theological matrices and voices, the proposed theological task also represents an exercise in postcolonial discourse, an exercise in its fundamental process and program of decolonization.

Diaspora Theology as Liberation Theology

For nearly a quarter of a century now, the theology of liberation has been making significant inroads in the theological world at large, not only outside the West but also within the West itself. From its beginnings in Latin America, it rapidly expanded to Africa and Asia, while developing roots as well at the very heart of the West, especially among ethnic and racial minorities of non-Western origin. In the course of this global expansion, the theology of liberation has also gone beyond the overriding socioeconomic focus it originally received in Latin America to include a wide variety of socioreligious and sociocultural emphases. Its fundamental relationship to postmodernism and postcolonialism is clear.

First, in contrast to traditional Western theology, with its systematic and universalizing claims, the theology of liberation not only has foregrounded its own social location and perspective but has also exposed the perspective and social location of that dominant theology that pretended to universality and objectivity. It has argued, in effect, for a multitude of matrices and voices, contexts and perspectives. Similarly, in contrast to the theology of the center, with its claims to superiority and hegemony, the theology of liberation has emphasized the margins and declared its independence from the center. As such, it has argued for the validity and dignity of the many loci and discourses of the "they"—the children of the colonized. In many and profound ways, therefore, the theology of liberation has shared in both the postmodernist myth or narrative of radical pluralism and the postcolonial process and project of decolonization.

By focusing on the reality and experience of Hispanic Americans within the United States, seeing that experience and reality as a valid and worthy locus for theological reflection, and pursuing a sustained analysis of one tradition or accent within such a theological voice, the proposed theology of the diaspora further constitutes an exercise in liberation theology, an exercise in its agenda of liberation.

Concluding Comments

The diaspora theology that I envision may be described as a postmodernist theology—a theology that argues for a multitude of matrices and voices, not only outside itself but also within itself, and regards itself as a construct, with thorough commitment to self-analysis and self-criticism as a construct; a postcolonial theology—a theology that is grounded in the margins, speaks from the margins, and engages in decolonization both within and from the center; and a liberation theology—a theology that seeks to re-view, re-claim, and re-phrase its own matrix and voice in the midst of a dominant culture and theology. It is also a theology with exile, flesh-and-blood exile, at its heart and core.

Diaspora Theology: Exile as Locus

U.S. Hispanic Americans have found their way into the United States along a myriad of paths. Three general patterns can be readily identified, each encompassing, to be sure, an enormous number of variations: (1) birth—the path of those actually born in the country as children of immigrants, regardless of sociopolitical status; (2) acquisition—the path of those whose ancestors and lands were taken over by the country as a result of territorial expansion; and (3) immigration—the path of those who have come into the country as first-generation immigrants. Such different paths ultimately account, I believe, for different experiences with and within the country itself: (1) for those born in the country as children of immigrants, minority status vis-à-vis the dominant culture is likely to prevail as the predominant reality; (2) for the descendants of those acquired as political subjects by the country, the status of colonization may displace minority status as the fundamental optic; (3) finally, for those who entered the country as immigrants, the status of exile is likely to prove the primordial reality.

I myself belong within this last category, that of the first-generation immigrant, although with a twist, insofar as my family and I entered the country as political refugees on what was then called a "waiver" visa, never intending to remain in the United States for as long as we have. Despite such original intentions, however, the fact is that I have established permanent residence in the country as a citizen and thus qualify as a first-generation immigrant. At the time of immigration, I was already well on the way toward full socialization in my own language and culture in the Republic of Cuba—a part of Latin American civilization and its particular variation in the Caribbean Basin. With immigration, therefore, I came face-to-face, at a still early age, with a very different culture, a very different language, and a very different process of socialization in the United States—a part of Western civilization by way of its North American variety. All of a sudden and in a matter of hours, I had become the "other." It is this experience of exile and otherness, the experience of the first-generation immigrant and a Janus-like perspective if ever there was one, that grounds my theology of the diaspora.

The Path of Exile

Diasporas are highly complex and multidimensional realities, and thus the term itself admits of various levels of meaning.[11] With regard to U.S. Hispanic Americans in particular, the use of the term can range from the metaphorical to the literal. From a metaphorical point of view, the term can be taken to apply to those born in the country or those whose lands and ancestors were acquired by the country—a reference to those who live as if "in exile" within their own land and country. From a literal point of view, the term naturally applies to first-generation immigrants, those who remember the past, the country of birth, and live in the present, the country of adoption—a reference to those whose exile transpires in somebody else's land and country. The diaspora theology I have in mind emerges out of the latter situation—it is grounded and forged in exile, flesh-and-blood exile.[12]

---

11. See in this regard my "Toward a Hermeneutics of the Diaspora: A Hermeneutics of Otherness and Engagement," *Reading from This Place* vol. 1, *Social Location and Biblical Interpretation in the United States* (ed. Fernando F. Segovia and Mary Ann Tolbert; Minneapolis: Fortress Press, 1994) 57–73.

12. Even then distinctions have to be made in terms of age: (*a*) infants or young children have no memory of their country of birth, but have to live within such memories as conveyed by their parents and/or extended family; (*b*) adolescents and young adults do have such memories, which tend to be constantly reinforced by the presence of the family, and thus ultimately live in both worlds for the rest of their lives; and (*c*) mature adults and

Integral to such a theology of the diaspora is the myth or narrative of origins: the re-collection, re-construction, and re-telling of the passage or transition from the one world to the other, from the world of birth to the world of adoption. Central to diaspora theology, therefore, is the theme of the journey, whereby that which is known and to which one belongs is left behind for an encounter with that which is unknown and within which one dwells as the "other." This journey can take different forms, with varying implications and consequences for the individuals in question; it can range, in effect, from temporary exile, to sustained exile, to permanent exile or immigration.

Thus, if the journey happens to be brief and exile a temporary condition, that which is known retains its freshness and remains largely unaffected by that which is unknown—the experience of "otherness" is short-lived, finds no time for proper incubation, and is quickly displaced by a renewed and restored sense of "belonging." In such a case the exile lives in the world of adoption as if still in the world of birth; the experience of "otherness" is never forgotten, to be sure, but its final imprint is light. However, should the journey prove longer than expected and exile turn into a way of life, that which is known gradually becomes more distant and less familiar, while that which is unknown becomes in turn more familiar and less distant—the experience of "otherness" slowly displaces the sense of "belonging." For the exile the world of adoption demands more and more of his or her attention, while the world of birth turns more and more into a world of memories and dreams. Finally, if the journey proves too long and exile settles into a permanent condition, that which is known and that which is unknown become quite porous—the experience of "otherness" and the sense of "belonging" gradually turn into one and the same reality, with the exile at home every-where but no-where. The exile ends up living in two worlds and no world at the same time, with a twofold voice from no-where. Such happens to be the reality and experience of a large number of U.S. Hispanic Americans—including myself, my family, and my own subgroup.

Our journey and our exile have lasted a long time indeed; our worlds—our constitutive realities and experiences, our optics in and of life, our perspectives in and of the world—have become thoroughly intertwined; our sense of "otherness" and our sense of "belonging" permeate and inform one another at will. We are in the world, indeed in two worlds, but we are not of the world, indeed of no world. Such is the point of departure for my theology of the diaspora.

---

the elderly often have nothing but such memories and live in the country of adoption as if nothing had changed, despite all the evidence and rude reminders to the contrary.

Exile as Theological Category: Reading Justo González

Exile has not been at all a common theme in U.S. Hispanic American theology thus far. At the same time, however, I am not the first to propose it as a fundamental category for approaching and analyzing the U.S. Hispanic American reality and experience. My friend and compatriot Justo L. González has already done so in his own formulation of *mañana* theology, and I should like to enter into critical dialogue with him on this issue.[13] Actually, González has recourse in all to four different categories when addressing the question of U.S. Hispanic American identity: (1) a *mañana* people, with long-standing roots as well as long-ranging aspirations in the country; (2) a people in search of a new life; (3) a people beyond innocence; and (4) a people in exile. In the end, however, this last category of exile emerges as primary. On the one hand, it not only encompasses the other three but also is circumscribed and informed by them; on the other hand, it is given a highly biblical and theological reading. In effect, U.S. Hispanic Americans are described, like the chosen people of Yahweh and the chosen followers of Jesus, as a people in exile, in search of an eschatological *mañana*.

First, González points out that the roots of U.S. Hispanic Americans in this country are by no means recent, as generally believed, but rather quite old and quite deep, deeper and older in fact than those of the dominant culture. In effect, many U.S. Hispanic Americans became part of the United States during the period of national expansion that lasted through most of the nineteenth century and as a result of the expansionist ideology that came to be known as "manifest destiny." Indeed, the country proceeded to acquire—by purchase, military conquest, or outright annexation—the territories of what is now Florida, Texas, New Mexico, Arizona, California, Nevada, and Utah as well as sizeable parts of Colorado, Kansas, Oklahoma, and Wyoming: more than half the territory of what used to be Mexico and more than double the territory of the United States at the time.[14] As such, U.S. Hispanic Americans as a group are not at all the product of recent migrations to the country but rather the product of the migration of the country to their lands.

Among many U.S. Hispanic Americans, therefore, feelings of bitterness run deep, not only because their origins as a group are forgotten but also because of the highly questionable nature and untoward consequences of the expansionist movement and ideology. At the same time, their sense of identity as U.S. Hispanic Americans was never lost, even during the heyday

---

13. Justo L. González, *Mañana: Christian Theology from a Hispanic Perspective* (Nashville: Abingdon Press, 1990) esp. 31–42.

14. The process comes to a climax at the turn of the century with the Spanish-American War of 1898, resulting in the temporary occupation of Cuba (1898–1902), the acquisition of Puerto Rico (1898–), and a view of the Caribbean Sea as a sort of imperial *mare nostrum*. See, for example, Lester D. Langley, *The United States and the Caribbean in the Twentieth Century* (4th ed.; Athens: University of Georgia Press, 1989) esp. 3–14.

of the assimilationist "melting pot" approach to American society. Consequently, González refers to U.S. Hispanic Americans as a *mañana* people—a people who have been around for a long time and will continue to be around for a long time to come.

Second, González sees a growing solidarity emerging among the various U.S. Hispanic American subgroups in the face of similar social and cultural developments. From a social point of view, on the one hand, he finds increased awareness that U.S. Hispanic Americans do not have much of a say in the decisions that shape their lives, regardless of who they are and where they come from. On the other hand, from a cultural point of view, he points to increased interest in Hispanic culture in the face of the highly disparaging view of the culture in the country at large. As a result, González sees U.S. Hispanic Americans as beginning to form and to function as a united front in the sociopolitical arena—a people in search of new life. In so doing, the people who have been around for a long time are attempting to make sure that their *mañana* is very different from their past and their present.

Third, González further argues that U.S. Hispanic Americans, in direct contrast to the dominant culture, are profoundly aware of the non-innocence of history. In other words, U.S. Hispanic Americans look upon their history not as a righteous and blessed enterprise, with a few unfortunate exceptions here and there, but rather as an unmistakable trail of systematic and sustained injustice, marked *inter alia* by such developments as the large-scale dispossession of the native peoples from their lands, the massive importation of slave labor from Africa, and radical violence in the sociopolitical realm. Because of this, González sees U.S. Hispanic Americans as a people whose task is to deconstruct myths of innocence wherever found by raising questions of justice at all times and in all places. Thus, the people who are beginning to work in unison with a different *mañana* in mind place the question of justice at the very core of their agenda.

Finally, González describes U.S. Hispanic Americans as a people "in exile." Such exile may be actual exile, involving those who come to the country for political, economic, or ideological reasons, or any combination thereof. When such exiles make their permanent abode in the country, they become U.S. Hispanic Americans but do not cease to be exiles. Such exile also comprehends those born in the country, insofar as they live in a land that is not theirs and within which they are never regarded as full citizens. For González both groups live in profound ambiguity: while actual exiles oscillate between gratitude and anger toward their host country, given the history of the relationship between the United States and their countries of birth, born exiles have no choice but to dwell in a land that is both theirs and not theirs. In sum, the people who are striving together for a very different *mañana* with justice in mind know that they are exiles and shall always remain in exile.

González brings his discussion of U.S. Hispanic American identity to a close by drawing upon biblical imagery to describe the fate of Hispanic Americans in the United States and casting this fate in highly theological and eschatological terms. On the one hand, he approaches Psalm 137, the exilic lament over the destruction of Jerusalem, in allegorical fashion, with a view of U.S. Hispanic Americans as a contemporary equivalent or anti-type of the exiled Jews in Babylon: a people singing the songs of Zion by the waters of Babylon. On the other hand, he sees this "Zion" of theirs as referring not to their lands of origin or their land of adoption (a physical Jerusalem, as it were) but rather to the coming order of God (a spiritual Jerusalem where justice, phrased in the eschatological terms of Micah 4, shall prevail). As a people in exile, therefore, U.S. Hispanic Americans are said to possess special (socioreligious) insights into what it means to be a pilgrim people of God and followers of Jesus as the one who had no place to lay his head. Clearly underlying and informing such a conception of "exile," therefore, are the other factors of U.S. Hispanic American identity: being a *mañana* people with long-standing roots and long-ranging expectations; being socially and culturally dispossessed as well as noninnocent; having no home and no hope of a home; being in search of a very different kind of home altogether—a life of justice not only for this *mañana* people but for all.

The Path of Exile: Real Exile

I quite agree with González that U.S. Hispanic Americans may be regarded as a people "in exile"—given their long-standing roots in the country, their social and cultural marginalization within the dominant culture, and their own sense of history as anything but innocent. Indeed, it is by no means accidental that he and I should both settle on "exile" as a fundamental category, given our similar sociopolitical origins and background in this regard. At the same time, I see my own approach to this category of exile as taking me along a different path of reflection.

First, as González himself acknowledges in principle given his distinction between actual and born exiles, I regard the category of exile not as a unidimensional and monolingual reality but rather as a polyglot and polyvalent experience. As such, I would argue that the experience of literal exile, in itself quite varied and complex, is quite different from the reality of metaphorical exile, similarly complex and varied in character. I would further argue that by and large such different realities and experiences give rise to different theological expressions within the overall U.S. Hispanic American matrix: different ways of constructing the world, the otherworld, and the relationship between the two. For me it is imperative that such a cacophony of voices come to the fore.

Further, while I also believe that the experience of exile provides unique insights into the relationship between God and the world as conveyed by both the Hebrew and the Christian Scriptures and traditions, I must confess that I do not regard such insights as in any way theologically privileged and would dispense with any view of the group as an allegorical antitype or equivalent of the pilgrim people of God or the wandering followers of Jesus. From a theological and hermeneutical perspective, exile represents a perspective with special insights, to be sure, but it is no different in this regard than any other perspective, as analogies between present and past are sought in any task of theological construction.

Finally, while I agree that exiles do sing incessantly of "Zion" in whatever "Babylon" they happen to find themselves, I see the longings, hopes, and dreams conveyed by such singing as quite complex, quite fluid, and even quite conflicting, with the coming order of God as perhaps one such variant within an incredible and ever-changing *mezcolanza* (jumbled mixture) of past, present, and future. In other words, exile brings about such a Janus-like condition that "Zion" itself is endlessly deconstructed and constructed, as exiles are drawn in various directions at any one time and at all times.

Concluding Comments

In this study the voice that I raise within U.S. Hispanic American theology is that of real, actual or literal, flesh-and-blood exile. It is a voice for which "otherness" and "belonging" have become indistinct, a voice from two worlds and no world, a voice for which the myth or narrative of origins is central. At this point, therefore, I should like to turn to a re-collection, re-construction, and re-telling of my own journey into exile, from the world of birth to the world of adoption.

The Narrative of Origins: The Journey of Exile

The journey in question took place on Monday, July 10, 1961. It was a memorable and historic day, not so much perhaps from the point of view of world affairs but certainly from the point of view of my world and my affairs. Besides, from a postmodernist point of view, what is historic and memorable is directly dependent on the perspective of the observer or narrator in question. Thus, what to many was no doubt a rather uneventful day was to me the most decisive day of my life. The contrast between these two perspectives, the global and the personal, proves illuminating.

Context for the Journey

From the point of view of world affairs, a look at the headlines and major news stories of the day—as reported, for example, in that morning's edition of the *New York Times*—reveals a rather typical, perhaps even quintessential, day at the height of the Cold War between East and West. This was, after all, a period of time that can now be demarcated, with the benefit of hindsight, in terms of two major confrontations between the Soviet Union and the United States, the respective leaders of the two contending ideological blocks: on the one hand, the U.S.-sponsored invasion of Cuba at the Bay of Pigs had taken place but a few months earlier, in April; on the other hand, the Soviet-provoked crisis over Berlin would come to a climax in the following month, in August, with the erection of the Berlin Wall, as symbolic a barrier between the two blocks as the Florida Straits—the sea passage separating the Florida Keys from Cuba and connecting the Atlantic Ocean and the Gulf of Mexico—had already become.

With regard to the United States, where I lay down to sleep that night for the first time in my life, a number of news items focused on the growing severity of the communist threat. There was a report from Moscow to the effect that, during the course of a military parade on Aviation Day, held for the first time in five years, the Soviets had displayed a variety of new large bombers and jet fighters, while Premier Nikita Kruschev had announced a 30 percent rise in the defense budget for the following year. The report interpreted such developments as a clear warning to the West, meant to counter Western moves in the face of impending crisis over Berlin.[15] Another report out of Hong Kong spoke of growing doubts in Asia about the U.S. resolve to defend the region against communism, especially in the light of the communist breakthrough in Laos.[16] Pakistanis, Filipinos, and Taiwanese were wondering out loud whether the United States was willing to fight or just talk as the "Reds" continued to advance in the area. A further report from Tokyo quoted the Chinese foreign minister, Chen Yi, while on a visit to Mongolia of several high-level communist delegations to celebrate the fortieth anniversary of Mongolia's independence from China, to the effect that China would abide by both the 1957 Moscow Declaration and the 1960 Moscow Statement, thus upholding official communist solidarity at the global level. Such declarations were read as a direct response to rumors regarding the existence of a Soviet-Chinese rift.[17] On that day,

---

15. Seymour Topping, "Russians Display New Big Bombers and Jet Fighters," *New York Times,* 10 July 1961, A1. On the day of the journey itself, the secretary of defense, Robert S. McNamara, made it known in Washington that the president had ordered an urgent review to determine whether the United States should increase its military strength to meet the Soviet threat in Berlin, especially given the announcement by Nikita Kruschev regarding the rise in the defense budget. See John W. Finney, "Kennedy Orders Defense Review in Berlin Crisis," *New York Times* 11 July 1961, A1.

16. Robert Trumbull, "Doubts about U.S. Increasing in Asia," *New York Times,* 10 July 1961, A1.

17. "Peiping Endorses World Red Policy," *New York Times,* 10 July 1961, A4. The 1957 Moscow Declaration was a peace manifesto signed by communist parties of sixty-four nations endorsing Soviet global policies. The 1960 Moscow Statement was an agreement to end the ideological quarrel over whether communism would win the world without war (the Soviet position) or through the forcible export of communism to capitalist countries and inevitable war (the Chinese position). On the day of the journey and in the course of the same celebrations at Ulan Bator, Wladyslaw Gomulka, the communist leader of Poland, called for unity in communism while attacking Western reports of disunity. See "Gomulka Hails 'Unity' of Reds; Assails Western Reports of Rift," *New York Times,* 11 July 1961, A1.

therefore, the dangers posed to the country by the Cold War were reported as present everywhere and made to feel quite palpable indeed: from the heart of Europe, to the whole of Asia, to the mainland of China.[18]

With regard to Latin America and the Caribbean, where I awoke early that morning for the last time in my life, the news was, as is still very much the case today in U.S. media at large, minimal and relegated to the inside pages. Even here, however, the East-West framework of events was evident. A report from Washington spoke of the intention of the United States to announce, at a forthcoming hemispheric ministerial conference in Uruguay, a significant increase in its foreign aid package to Latin America within the framework of the "Alliance for Progress" initiative, a move clearly meant to strengthen its influence in the region and thus curtail the spread of revolutionary fervor in light of developments in Cuba.[19] With regard to Cuba itself, a brief report out of Havana announced the forthcoming visit of Yuri Gagarin to the island on July 24 along with the official plans for a hero's welcome.[20] In effect, the dangers of the Cold War were also reported that day as present within the hemisphere itself, indeed as close as ninety miles away, across the Florida Straits.

From a personal point of view, however, this rather typical day of the Cold War era proved to be, with the benefit of over thirty years of hindsight, the most important day of my life. For it was on that day that I embarked on my journey of exile, a journey of mythic proportions across the Florida Straits—that great divide between worlds that so many have dreamed of crossing, where so many have lost their lives while doing so, and through which so many others have had their lives transformed beyond recognition. In effect, this divide signified a cosmic journey involving a variety of highly complex and imbricated worlds: (1) from the world of Latin American civilization, by way of its Caribbean version, to the world of Western civilization, in terms of its North American variant; (2) from

---

18. Indeed, on the very day of the journey, in a speech to the National Press Club in Washington, the secretary of state, Dean Rusk, brought the point home by calling for a common denominator of self-interest among all nations that did not want communism imposed on them. In light of the conflict between the "Sino-Soviet Empire" and the rest of the world, the secretary of state emphasized the need to revive the United Nations as a center of decent world order, to strengthen NATO and the West, and to recapture the Western leadership of revolution in terms of political freedom. See Wallace Carroll, "Rusk Urges West to Lead Crusade on Red 'Coercion,'" *New York Times,* 11 July 1961, A1.

19. Tad Szulc, "U.S. Set to Offer Strong Latin Aid," *New York Times,* 10 July 1961, A10. The article goes on to point out how such policies contradicted traditional U.S. attitudes toward Latin America. It is interesting to note in this regard that in his speech of July 10 to the National Press Club (see n. 18 above), Dean Rusk put forward the "Alliance for Progress" program as an example of the kind of Western efforts needed to recapture the revolutionary tradition of political freedom, as an attempt by the United States to stimulate national growth and social development in the Western Hemisphere.

20. "Cuba to Hail Gagarin," *New York Times,* 10 July 1961, A2. Yuri Alekseyevich Gagarin (1934–68) was the first man to orbit the earth, twice, in space, a feat accomplished by the Soviet Union in January of that same year.

East to West, from the world of state-controlled communism to the world of capitalist liberal democracy; (3) from South to North, from the traditional world of the colonized, with honor and shame as dominant cultural values, to the industrialized world of the colonizers, with the dollar as its core value; (4) from a world that was mine, which I knew and to which I belonged without question, to a world where I represented the "other"— the alien and the foreigner. While the actual journey as such was over rather quickly (waking up early in La Habana, so that my mother and I could make the late morning flight on KLM to Miami; a flight of approximately an hour; and going to sleep that night in Miami at the house of friends of friends of the family), the journey of exile has never ended; indeed, exile has become my permanent land and home—the diaspora.

The Journey Proper

I still recall that journey as if it had taken place but yesterday or last week, although I was only thirteen at the time. Indeed, it is only now, with the advantage and disadvantage of time, that I can see the symbolic and highly ritualistic dimensions of the entire proceedings, properly marking such a transcending occasion and transition in my life in a quasi-sacramental way—a re-birth of water and the spirit, the waters of the Gulf Stream and the spirit of "otherness."

Preparations for the Journey. I recall the preparations for the journey itself. The efforts to get me out of the country, for fear that I would be sent to Eastern Europe for study—standard procedure in the colonies of the Soviet Empire and not at all surprising, given the logic of empires and the weight attached to the center vis-à-vis the margins. The frantic search for a missing passport—sent through mysterious channels for the procurement of the waiver visa necessary to enter the United States, lost in the hectic diplomatic world of the capital, and finally found quite by chance at the embassy of the Dominican Republic. The surprise call on a Friday to the effect that I would be leaving on the following Monday, alone—as so many others did, though in the end a seat came open for my mother as well. The final weekend of visits to family, friends, places—the exchange of goodbyes, *sotto voce* in case somebody might wish to do us harm; the preparation of the one piece of baggage per-person allowed, a sack that came to be known affectionately as *el chorizo* (the sausage) and that was stuffed with clothing for an unspecified period of time in the unknown *el norte*. (I often wonder nowadays what we must have looked like as we donned our distinctive tropical attire in the streets of New York.) And throughout, quite ironically, my own gleeful anticipation of the voyage.

That anticipation of flying for the first time and visiting the United States remained uppermost in my mind. Little did I understand what was going on around me—about what was in the mind of my parents, who were separating for my own sake; about my family, some of whom would never cross the divide; and about our friends, many of whom we never saw or heard from again. I must confess that exile for me had, on the whole, a rather joyous beginning. It was a terrific adventure and, besides, nobody expected it to last very long. Soon we would all be back...next year in La Habana!

Crossing the Divide. I distinctly recall the flight over the divide. The final glance at the house where we lived, as we set off for the airport—faces staring out of the windows, one hand waving goodbye while the other held a wet handkerchief. The long wait at the airport itself in what came to be known as *la pecera* (the fishbowl), where those about to depart were kept together, separated from their families by a thick glass partition from ground to ceiling—sitting there for hours, subject to repeated interrogations, baggage searches, body and even strip searches. The long walk to the plane itself, the taking of seats, the takeoff—and throughout hardly a word on the part of anyone, for fear that next to you or behind you or in front of you someone might be listening, indeed for fear that the plane itself might be called back. Then, all of a sudden, the announcement from the cockpit to the effect that we were now out of Cuban waters and in international waters—pandemonium! I remember the explosion: the clapping, the embracing, and the conversation à la Latin style—emotional, boisterous, heartfelt. The people who had not dared to exchange a word before now proceeded to tell their life story, their apprehensions for the immediate future, their dreams of freedom, and their hopes for a quick return. Finally, the sign from the window that read "Welcome to Miami" and a long walk along endless and curved corridors, leading to the immigration office—more questions, more papers, more information.

Arrival in the Promised Land. I recall our arrival in the United States, our exit into the waiting area, and our first days in Miami. We had no money whatsoever, for those who left were allowed to take nothing out but the one *chorizo*—exiles were completely dependent on the goodwill of family and friends who had already made the journey and who would be waiting for the new arrivals at the airport. Actually, two other items were allowed, a bottle of rum and a box of cigars, which we, like everybody else, dutifully carried—such items would fetch our first earnings at the airport itself. It was our introduction to American culture and capitalism. The opened doors and the avalanche of two different groups of people: those who were there to receive us, speaking in our tongue and giving us as warm a greeting as the goodbyes we had received hours earlier; and those who were there to buy goods, speaking in another tongue and angling for the best deal—we sold it all for ten dollars, the sum total of our wealth, aside from the offer of a room for the next few nights.[21] The room at the inn—I had never experienced such surroundings: carpeting, air-conditioning, color television, a large and well-groomed patio.

Indeed, my earliest memories of the United States have to do with its wealth, a wealth I had never encountered before in my life, a wealth conveyed to me at that time by way of vivid and concrete images: air-conditioned churches with cushioned reclinatories; enormous supermarkets with an endless variety of products, stacked to the hilt, row upon row; suburbia, with enormous distances between houses, immaculate lawns and streets, and nobody to be seen anywhere.

Concluding Comments

In one day, indeed in the space of a few hours, my whole life had changed—my life in Cuba (= Latin American civilization; the East; the colonized; my world) had come to an end, and my life in the United States (= Western civilization; the West; the colonizer; somebody else's world) had begun. The consequences of that journey continue to unfold and multiply, year by year, day by day. In what follows I offer—merely by way of introduction, a first step as it were in this process of theological construction—but a few reflections regarding its theological repercussions and aftereffects.

Diaspora Theology: In the World but Not of It

Thirty-some years later, this cosmic journey of mine into exile and this long experience of exile continue to ground, inform, and shape my theological reflection about the world, the otherworld, and the relationship between the two. It is a reflection with "otherness" at its very core, as if suspended in the air somewhere over the great divide, over the waters of the Florida Straits, looking—like Janus—in various directions at the same time: a part of both worlds and yet of none; at home in two cultures and in neither one; speaking in two tongues with none to call my own; in the world but not of it. Such is the locus and voice of my theology of the diaspora.

From this perspective of exile and "otherness," both worlds and all worlds readily emerge as social constructions: what one world sees and

---

21. Actually, it was twenty dollars. The individual who was sitting next to my mother on the plane and who was also carrying a bottle of rum and a box of cigars, seeing me, had turned to her and offered her the sum total of his possessions, because, he said, we would need it far more than he. What he did—and his name was Manuel García—I hereby tell in memory of him. We never saw him again, but we never forgot his name because he proceeded to identify himself by the eponym *el rey de los campos de Cuba* (the king of the Cuban countryside), with reference to a legendary figure from the time of Spanish colonization who operated in the countryside and stole from the rich to give to the poor. The last time we saw him was at the immigration office. It turned out that he had been a member of the underground resistance in Cuba, had left the country under a false visa, and was waiting for proper contact to be made with the individual(s) responsible for his escape, who resided in New York City and could not be located at the time of arrival.

posits as reality is not the reality that the other world posits and sees. From such a perspective, moreover, it does not matter whether the world in question is the world of the center or the world of the margins, the world of the colonizer or the world of the colonized: the world of hegemony is as much a construction as the world of subordination. Indeed, in the end exile and "otherness" proceed to construct yet another reality—a reality that not only encompasses the world of birth as well as the world of adoption but also goes beyond them into a sort of nonworld. As a result, the exile "belongs" or is "at home" in both worlds, going back and forth repeatedly between them; functions as the other in both worlds, not only in his or her own eyes but also in the eyes of each world; and ends up constructing a "home" of his or her own, a world of otherness, in the process.

From my own home of exile and otherness, construction has inevitably taken place regarding the human world, the divine otherworld, and the interchange between these two worlds. It is a construction with profound ambiguity at its very core.

Constructing the World

From my perspective of exile and otherness, the world of everyday life emerges as deeply divided: overridingly hostile, but calling forth struggle and resistance; fateful and inescapable, yet constantly arousing hopes of and strategies for change and reformation; ultimately resigned and yet endlessly defiant.

To begin with, there is no illusion whatsoever that the world is or can ever be a pleasant or righteous place. It is very difficult for anyone who has had to live through the experience of colonialism and dictatorship, domination and repression, exploitation and civil strife, to put aside the brutal reality of the world: its insecurity; its ill-will and persecution; its suffering and destruction. It is very difficult as well for anyone who has undergone the experience of emigration and exile, loss and dislocation, separation from one's home and resettlement in somebody else's land, to forget the bitter reality of bifurcation and disorientation, rejection and discrimination, longing and anxiety. For anyone who has found himself or herself thrown into both sorts of experiences and discourses, it is extremely hard, if not altogether impossible, to think of the world in terms of well-being and justice. Indeed, one comes very close at times to a view of the world not unlike that which I find in the Johannine literature: the world must be in the hands of the evil one, and all one can do is abide. Without actually positing a corresponding demonic rule of the world—as severely as one is tempted to do so from time to time—such a perspective sees the world as fundamentally and irretrievably unjust, beyond any significant possibility of change or reformation.

At the same time, this rather stark view of the world is counterbalanced throughout by a strong and irrepressible thirst for well-being and justice, a desire to make the world a more pleasant and righteous place in which to dwell. Such passion springs, first of all, from the realization that, bitter and brutal as the world may be, there is no escape from it and hence one must make do, regardless of the context or discourse into which one is thrown. Such passion springs as well from the conviction—likewise forged in the crucible of colonialism and repression, dislocation and rejection—that the world could be and should be a more pleasant and righteous place. Out of this combined belief in both inescapability and alterity comes the resolve to fight back and survive, to engage the world at its own game, with a sense of fairness and a certain *joie de vivre* in mind. The stance adopted thereby is quite unlike that of the Johannine literature: the world may be fundamentally and irretrievably evil, but one sees one's fate and call not in terms of abiding, with eyes fixed on the house of the Father and its many rooms, but rather in terms of resistance and struggle.

To be sure, such struggle for survival always contains within itself a dream of utopia, for significant if not drastic reformation, as one yearns for and may actually come to enjoy a measure of justice and well-being in the world. In the end, however, all such hopes and achievements are re-garded as fragile and fleeting: worth striving for and worth possessing, but also unlikely to get very far or last very long, given the fundamental nature of the world. Such a program of resistance always bears within itself, there-fore, a suspicion that nothing good or just is lasting, that every achievement in this regard can be dismantled in a very short time by the most unex-pected of events and circumstances, that life itself is to be lived by the moment or the day. Consequently, while the struggle for resistance and sur-vival is always seen as very much active and in order, it is also haunted at all times by a corresponding fear regarding how long any advance against evil will last and where its next attack or counterattack will spring from. For such a perspective the world may and does admit of change and ref-ormation here and there, now and again, but not of significant alteration and reform—although the dream always keeps on hoping against hope and experience.

The human world thus forged in exile is both a world of pessimism, where evil is seen as reigning largely undisturbed, and a world of opti-mism, where deliberate measures to disturb evil are nonetheless constantly planned and undertaken—despite the known odds, the meager hopes for victory, and the ever-present conviction that any victory or disturbance is in the end but apparent and short-lived. Such a world is beyond reformation and crying for reformation, beyond justice and well-being and in dire need of them, fatefully resigned and yet outrightly defiant. Such is the world that emerges out of my diaspora: a world of profound ambiguity, with a theo-logical discourse that goes back and forth endlessly—Why bother? Bother we must!

Constructing the Otherworld

From my standpoint of exile and "otherness," the otherworld of God comes across deeply divided as well: transcendent, yet clearly immanent; removed, but unquestionably active; controlled by a God both seemingly uncaring and evidently solicitous.

On the one hand, in keeping with the dominant vision of the world as fundamentally unjust and beyond significant reformation, constant and profound doubts occur and reoccur regarding the nature and role of God. From the experience of colonialism and dictatorship, exile and discrimination, such questions as the following are inevitable and not at all unusual: How can such oppression and suffering, at such levels and of such duration, go on, largely undisturbed and unchecked? How can the forces of evil endure, rule, and prosper as they seem to do? How can one speak of God in such a situation? The God thus constructed is one who is found wanting—a God inexplicably removed and unconcerned, a silent and hiding God.

On the other hand, following upon the resisting vision of the world as crying for reformation and change and in dire need of well-being and justice, there is also overriding confidence in God as well as constant appeals to God. Despite all questions and doubts regarding God, the conviction exists that God does act and will act—sometime, somewhere. Consequently, God is never left alone in silence and withdrawal; rather, God is constantly besieged and disturbed: Act here! Speak now! Be God! The God constructed thereby is, above all, one believed to have supreme authority over the world and absolute power over evil itself and thus called upon incessantly to deploy such power and exercise such authority, to take charge in the face of what seems like a cosmic moral vacuum or even a cosmic immoral force. Such a God is a God to be awakened and roused into action, and for this purpose all the spirits of the earth and over the earth are called upon to be of aid, with pacts and bargains struck over and over again: Do something! Say something! Wake up! In the face of God's seeming silence and hiding, therefore, there is always the hope that one of these earthly or heavenly hosts will cause God to hear, take notice, and move to action; indeed, there is the conviction that so it will happen.

The God thus forged in exile is a God both slow to act and sure to act. While construed as transcendent and remote, unaware of what is taking place in the world, such a God is ultimately regarded as providential and accessible, and hence called upon, even badgered, to assume that role. Such a God is beyond comprehension or explanation: trustworthy, but hard to find; providential, but so slow to act; helpful, but variable. This God is a God in charge of creation but forgetful of it; a God who may know the exact number of hairs on our head but often proceeds as if "it" could care less; a God who has to be persuaded, probed, bargained into action. Such is the God that emerges out of my diaspora: a profoundly ambiguous God, a God that calls forth perpetual doubt and unremitting faith—a God that seems not to bother and a God who must be bothered and does bother.

Constructing the Relationship

Finally, from my perspective of exile and "otherness," the relationship between such an everyday world and such a divine world further appears as divided to the core: uncertain, yet indispensable; limited, but effective; frustratingly questionable, yet eminently trustworthy.

First, in line with the overriding view of the world as unjust and a corresponding view of God as passive and unmoved in the face of evil, the relationship with such a God in the world is seen as both uncertain and limited. It is uncertain insofar as there is no guarantee of assistance or intervention at any one time or in any one place; it is limited insofar as such intervention and assistance, when in evidence, are not seen as dislodging evil but merely as disturbing it in passing fashion. Second, in keeping with the resisting view of the world as crying for justice and well-being and the overriding view of God as ultimately providential and in charge, the relationship with such a God in the world is also seen as indispensable and effective. It is indispensable insofar as the struggle for resistance and survival, limited as it may be, is regarded as impossible without the intervention and assistance of God; it is effective insofar as such assistance and intervention are taken for granted and the struggle is seen as yielding results, ad hoc and insignificant perhaps, but results nonetheless—actual disturbances of evil and victories of justice and well-being. Besides, there is always that persistent dream that perhaps one day significant if not overwhelming reformation will take place.

The relationship between world and otherworld, humans and God, thus forged in exile is a relationship of absence and presence, uncertainty and certainty, limitation and power. It is a relationship built on sustained unreliability yet absolute confidence, lack of response but undeniable dialogue, lack of action yet proven commitment. Such is the human-divine relationship that emerges out of my diaspora: a profoundly ambiguous relationship vis-à-vis God in the world—a relationship that often despairs of bothering with the otherworld and yet looks upon such bother as both essential and dependable.

Concluding Comments

This first articulation of a theology of the diaspora on my part makes it very clear that it is a theology engaged in a constant process of construction and deconstruction: while deconstructed by the brutal and bitter reality and experience of the world, it immediately proceeds to construct an alternative world and vision out of that same reality and experience. The result is a theology with a rather bleak view of the world, yet driven by a constant determination not only to reform and change the world but also to enjoy it; a theology with a solid belief in God, yet in constant despair about God and God's ways and means; a theology with a firm trust in God's power and work, yet always frustrated by the unreliability and limits of such work and power. Like exile itself, out of which it proceeds, it is multilayered and multilingual—a theology of mixture and otherness.

Conclusion

I have sought in this study to provide a beginning formulation for a theology of the diaspora within the wider matrix and voice of U.S. Hispanic American theology, a theology forged from the locus and perspective of real exile. As with exile itself, the result is a theology that cannot help but look in various different and even conflicting directions at all times, gathering together within itself the affirmations and contradictions, the joys and frustrations, the challenges and obstacles of a life of "otherness." It is a theology that sees itself in terms of diversity and pluralism, perspective and construction, and sets out to expose and examine the social location of such a perspective and the foundations of its constructions—a postmodernist theology; a theology that seeks its matrix and voice in the margins and sees such discourse and locus as valid and imperative—a postcolonial theology; and a theology that is committed to critical self-retrieval and self-expression—a theology of liberation. Above all, it is a theology of "otherness": in the world but not of it.

12

Theologizing from a Puerto Rican Context

Yamina Apolinaris and

Sandra Mangual-Rodríguez

This study must be read from the perspective of Latin America, the Caribbean, and Puerto Rico. While the authors claim a Caribbean Hispanic American matrix of cultural identity, the geographical and vital space in which they find themselves inscribed is that of Puerto Rico. One of us was born in New York, to which her family had immigrated on a temporary basis during the 1950s,[1] looking for the land of milk and honey.[2] The social imagery constructed around such a fascinating promise led one of us to believe as a child that people in the United States did not die. Both of us pursued graduate studies in the United States, working among Hispanic American communities and suffering with them the pain and tragedy of different forms of exile. While there we experienced on a voluntary and short-lived basis a form of exile; at the same time, however, ever since we have been able to reason, we have known what it is to be aliens in our own land.

One of us left the Catholic Church as an adolescent, converting to Protestantism, while the other grew up in a Protestant family. We are both Protestant women in a country where Catholics constitute a majority. Both

---

This is a translation by Fernando F. Segovia of the original article in Spanish, "Teología desde el contexto puertorriqueño."

1. Puerto Rican migration has been studied extensively. This migratory movement to the United States was started and backed by the Puerto Rican government in the 1940s. For a good analysis, see Luis Nieves Falcón, *El emigrante puertorriqueño* (Río Piedras, P.R.: Editorial Edil, 1975).

2. Metaphors associated with "honey" are among the most ancient metaphors in religious thinking associated with the kitchen. The bees produce the honey, but nature makes it available to human beings without much effort. The history of the struggle and work of Puerto Ricans in the United States destroys this myth. For a structuralist linguistic analysis, see Claude Lévi-Strauss, *Mitológicas: De la miel a las cenizas,* vol. 2 (Mexico City: Fondo de Cultura Económica, 1971).

of us are also pastors in different mainline churches of the United States in Puerto Rico, with a history of pastoral work in the island as well as in the United States. At the present time we are engaged in various other forms of ministry as well. One has served for five years now as executive minister of the Baptist Churches of Puerto Rico;[3] the other is Presbyterian and has been a professor of ministry at the Seminario Evangélico de Puerto Rico for the last six years.[4] We think, speak, and dream in Spanish, although one of us is completely bicultural and bilingual, while the other struggles with English and manages to survive. Given our present and past experiences as well as those of our families, we neither confess nor believe that *el norte* (the North) is the promised land. The life of struggle and contradictions at the heart of our own country, the rest of the Latin American continent, and the Caribbean Basin in particular has left a profound mark upon us. Its individual and collective characteristics, some of which we share with the Hispanic American communities in the United States, account in part for the visions, discourses, and practices that inform the theological task in Latin America and the Caribbean. We espouse a liberationist consciousness and praxis, and we support nontraditional forms of ministry, although we continue to function within institutional structures.

This study has two goals: first, to acquaint the reader with the Latin American and Caribbean contexts so that the theological reflection of our continent can be more readily understood; second, to make known the various paths of theological reflection to be found within Puerto Rico itself.

The Latin American Reality

Latin America forms part of the American continent of the New World, recognized as such by European explorers and conquistadores since the end of the fifteenth century. Latin America is also a continent with original and culturally indigenous peoples whose history goes back far beyond five hundred years. It is a continent that extends over seven million square miles and thus is as large as the territories of Canada and the United States combined. It is a Western continent of approximately five hundred million

---

3. The feminization of the Protestant hierarchy in Puerto Rico deserves close study. Such a study has been suggested since 1991 by Sandra Mangual-Rodríguez, given the fact that a number of mainline Protestant churches have, since 1985, elected both ordained and lay women as leaders: Ana Inés Braulio by the Presbyterian synod; Miriam Visot by the Methodist church; and Yamina Apolinaris by the Baptist churches.

4. The Seminario Evangélico de Puerto Rico is a graduate, interdenominational divinity school, which in 1994 will celebrate its diamond anniversary. It is known as a "school of prophets." By the end of the 1970s, women formed a significant part of its student body; at present, they constitute 48 percent of the student body. Ninety percent of the Protestant pastoral leadership (in the mainline churches) are graduates of the school. A large number of Puerto Rican pastors and evangelical leaders presently residing in the United States are also graduates of the school.

inhabitants,[5] with a sad tradition of European and North American colonization and plunder, thus making it part of the Third World alongside the continents of Africa and Asia.[6] The Spanish conquest of America in the sixteenth century has been an object of dispute since its very beginnings; however, in this last decade of the twentieth century, the dispute has become much sharper as a result of the quincentenary of the "evangelization and conquest" (1492–1992).

As in the past, so now in the present the native communities of the continent have forcefully pointed to the brutal character of such nomenclature, taking up once again thereby the struggle for national liberation so well known throughout the world. One of the genres of the new ethnography giving voice to this struggle is that of the community witness. In the person of Rigoberta Menchú of Guatemala, the winner of the Nobel Peace Prize for 1992, the genre has gained luster and strength.[7] Her denunciation has been joined by hundreds of voices, past and present, who condemn the results of the conquest from the point of view of Christian faith. To be sure, there are also voices that condone it. Such a diversity of responses and positions regarding historical facts has always existed, though not openly, in the Christian church of Latin America. Justo González calls attention to this twofold reality: "Few North Americans are aware of the degree to which the Catholic Church in Latin America was an arm of the powers of conquest, colonialism and oppression. Even fewer are aware of the other reality: the underside of the Church, which repeatedly de-cried and opposed these powers."[8]

Also to be heard are the voices of Latin American women who denounce the costs of the conquest from the point of view of all the women who became the property of the conquerors.[9] Nancy Cardoso Pereira, a Brazilian theologian, formulates her indictment of such a development as follows:

5. It is estimated that by the end of the twentieth century there will be more than three hundred million Latin Americans living in conditions of extreme poverty.

6. In the light of the new social and political conditions in the world, the term "Third World" has acquired new geographical and ideological connotations; for example, it is possible to speak of the presence of a "Third World" in the "First World."

7. See *Mi nombre es Rigoberta Menchú y así me nació la conciencia* (ed. Elizabeth Burgos; 8th ed.; Mexico City: Siglo XXI, 1992). The English translation of this work (*I, Rigoberta Menchú: An Indian Woman in Guatemala* [New York: Routledge, 1985]) has become an object of discussion in a number of universities in the United States, where it has been assigned as required reading; see in this regard John Beverly, "Post-literatura? Sujeto subalterno e impase en las humanidades," *Postdata* 2:5 (1992) n.pp., and Mary Louise Pratt, "Humanities for the Future: Reflections on the Western Culture Debate at Stanford," *The Politics of Liberal Education* (ed. Darryl J. Gless and Barbara Herrnstein Smith; Durham, N.C.: Duke University Press, 1992) 13–31. Another such testimony is that of Domitila Barrios, *Si me permiten hablar: Testimonio de Domitila: Una mujer de las minas de Bolivia* (ed. N. Viezzer; 4th ed.; Mexico City: Siglo XXI, 1979).

8. Justo González, "The Two Faces of Christianity," *Judson Bulletin* 6:1 (1987) 19.

9. Julia Esquivel, "Conquered and Violated Women," *1492–1992: The Voice of the Victims* (ed. Leonardo Boff and Virgilio Elizondo; *Concilium* 232; London: SCM Press; Philadelphia: Trinity Press International, 1990) 68–77.

"The condition regarding the oppression and submission of women in the Latin American continent precedes the coming of the colonizer. However, it is with the conquest—characterized by acts of violence and violations against the native peoples, especially the women—that an authoritarian, sexist, and repressive society begins to take shape."[10]

Other Latin American women add their voices of protest against the effects of the cultural clash brought about by the Iberian conquest of Latin America on the sexuality and bodies of the indigenous women.[11] Broader sectors of the Protestant church in Puerto Rico have also engaged in a critical analysis of the entire process of conquest and evangelization.[12] However, the history of Latin American domination does not implicate Europe alone, from which almost all the countries of Latin America gained their independence in the course of the nineteenth century. The constant interventions of the United States throughout the twentieth century, particularly in the countries of Central America, created a framework of neocolonialism that in turn has kept alive the project of emancipation, given the structures of poverty, dependence, and alienation operative in these countries.

A number of other world powers, such as Great Britain, have contributed to this tradition of interventionism in Central America, a region marked by devastation, given the effects of industrial progress, wars, foreign debt, military regimes, foreign policy, and anticommunist discourse. All of these factors have brought about a destabilization of the economies and internal political processes of the countries in question.[13] One need only recall the recent history of Guatemala, Honduras, El Salvador, Nicaragua, Panama, and Belize.

South America has fared no better. The recent military governments of Chile, Brazil, and Argentina have left behind a sad history of repression, war, death, hopelessness, and tragedy. The social, political, economic, and cultural cost of these interventions on the part of the military has been

---

10. N. Cardoso Pereira, "Liberación y paz desde la perspectiva de la mujer," *Liberación y paz: Reflexiones teológicas desde América* (ed. Moisés Rosa Ramos; Guaynabo, P.R.: Editorial Sonador, 1988) 39–48, esp. 39.

11. See, for example, Sylvia Marcos, "Curas, diosas y erotismo: El catolicismo frente a los Indios," and Cristina Grela, "La principal dominación," *Mujeres e iglesia: Sexualidad y aborto en América Latina* (ed. Ana María Portugal; Washington, D.C.: Catholics for a Free Choice; Mexico City: Distribuciones Fontamara, 1989) 11–34 and 51–60, respectively.

12. See Luis N. Rivera Pagán, *Evangelización y conquista de América* (San Juan: Editorial Cemí, 1990); English trans.: *A Violent Evangelism: The Political and Religious Conquest of the Americas* (Louisville: Westminster/John Knox Press, 1992). See also Luis N. Rivera Pagán, Raúl Vidales, and Diego Irarrazaval, *La esperanza de los vencidos: Hacia una visión crítica del quinto centenario* (Guaynabo, P.R.: Editorial Sonador, 1989).

13. For a detailed history of the Latin American reality, see Mortimer and Esther Arias, *The Cry of My People: Out of Captivity in Latin America* (New York: Friendship Press, 1989); see also Eugenio Rivera Urrutia, Ana Sojo, and José Roberto López, *Centroamérica: Política económica y crisis* (San José: Editorial DEI, 1986).

quite high, as the theological reflection coming out of such contexts readily shows. When already in the 1960s this Latin American reality began to reach truly scandalous proportions, faith responded with a theological reflection grounded in this very same context of poverty and in solidarity with an impoverished continent, though also with hope in the Christ of history.[14]

It should not be forgotten that Latin America is a continent with a long and profound history of religious faith. Its spirituality is more than five hundred years old, but European evangelization as well as the later reevangelization on the part of U.S. Protestantism ultimately forged a continent that is primarily Christian in character. Out of this faith have emerged a variety of religious discourses, ranging from those that legitimate and support military dictatorships and poverty to those that call for resistance and the overthrow of such conditions to those that discourage and alienate the people from their social responsibilities.

As an example of the first type of discourse, in 1974 the Evangelical Church of Chile expressed its support for the government of General Augusto Pinochet, out of fear for the danger posed by communism to the country. Such a position was explained as follows by a church official:

Today we halt on our way to give testimony of our gratitude to God for having delivered us from Marxism through the uprising of the Armed Forces, which we recognize as the rampart raised by God against atheistic impiety.... We are here to support our government in the courageous and determined struggle against Marxism.... The evangelical church is present, and aligns itself with its governors, so demonstrating the unity which in the diversity of institutions we marvelously keep.[15]

Recent studies of Protestantism in Latin America confirm the growing fundamentalist evangelical movement in churches and free religious organizations, autonomous as well as missionary, all of which have the following theological traits in common: (1) conservatism as regards doctrine; (2) emphasis of a literal interpretation of the Scriptures; (3) opposition to what they characterize as antibiblical and demonic forces such as communism and secular humanism; (4) little or no tradition of social teaching; and (5) a futurist eschatology that puts distance between the people and their social context.[16]

At the same time, other churches have rediscovered in the biblical message the witness of God's continuous commitment to the pursuit of justice among peoples and nations. This rediscovery has, for example, led the

---

14. Leonardo Boff, Y la iglesia se hizo pueblo: Eclesiogénesis—la iglesia nace del pueblo (Santander: Editorial Sal Terrae, 1986); English trans.: Ecclesiogenesis: The Base Communities Reinvent the Church (Maryknoll, N.Y.: Orbis Books, 1986).

15. Pablo A. Deiros, "Protestant Fundamentalism in Latin America," Fundamentalisms Observed (ed. Martin E. Marty and R. Scott Appleby; Chicago: University of Chicago Press, 1991) 142–96, esp. 142–43.

16. Ibid, 169–78.

Presbyterian Church (USA) to inquire into the state of human rights, democratic development, and the progress of economic justice in countries such as El Salvador, Guatemala, Honduras, and Nicaragua. The Presbyterian task force was surprised by the strong Christian identity present in Central America and the widespread use of faith language to define and debate the dynamics of the present crisis in the region. They concluded as follows:

Theological questions are difficult to avoid in an environment where the very terms for understanding reality are so often expressed in the language of faith. This is true whether the speaker is Nicaraguan Foreign Minister Miguel d'Escoto retelling the story of the Good Samaritan or Cardinal Obando y Bravo preaching from the Managua pulpit.... From presidents to guerrillas, from elected representatives to refugees, the common language of expression is the language of Christian faith. It is a language we share—and thus confronting Central America is a special challenge to our own theological understanding of who we are as a church and what we understand God's purposes to be for us as well as for the people of Central America.[17]

The report ends with a radical denunciation of a social situation marked by poverty, war, ecological destruction, and the violation of human rights. The report further argues that war lessens the chances for democracy, respect for human rights, as well as social and economic justice; that respect for human rights in the region is minimal; and that the abject poverty suffered by a majority of the population is rooted in a history of economic exploitation.

Pentecostalism represents another movement that has emerged with great force in Latin America. Theories abound that this movement above all others places the faithful in contact with their Latin American "soul," furnishing thereby an alternative to the social and economic dislocation suffered by the multitudes.

In the end, however, there is no doubt that liberation theology has proved to be, from the point of view of governments and religious institutions alike, the most controversial religious movement of Latin America.[18] In liberation theology both life itself and the crucified peoples[19] become a theological locus from which social reality as well as traditional theological discourses are challenged. With liberation theology new subjects in the

---

17. See "Report and Recommendations of the Task Force on Central America," adopted by the General Assembly of the Presbyterian Church (USA) in 1987, in *Presbyterian Church (USA): Minutes of the 199th General Assembly, 1987*, pt. 1: *Journal* (New York: Office of the General Assembly, 1987) 344–402, esp. 346.

18. Gustavo Gutiérrez is widely recognized as one of the pioneers of this movement; see his *Teología de liberación—perspectivas* (4th ed.; Lima: Centro de Estudios y Publicaciones, 1984); English trans.: *A Theology of Liberation* (rev. ed.; Maryknoll, N.Y.: Orbis Books, 1988).

19. Jon Sobrino has recourse to this metaphor when speaking of the poverty and victimization of the Latin American peoples. See his "The Crucified Peoples: Yahweh's Suffering Today," *1492–1992: The Voice of the Victims*, 120–29.

theological task, new models of ecclesiology, new texts and hermeneutical keys, and above all new eschatological and soteriological projects have come to life in Latin America. This mode of doing theology has been neither understood nor accepted in a number of theological schools of the United States. Indeed, one of us harbors a sad experience of ridicule and humiliation upon the submission for a theology class of a study written from the point of view of Latin American social reality. At present, the theologies of liberation and their bibliographies are clearly on the rise, with the result that Latin American theology—with its objects of reflection, its theological subjects, its locus, and its overall discourse—has found legitimacy. Such legitimacy has taken on even greater importance in those circles where the discussion has recently turned to the concomitant phenomenon involving the global breakdown of socialism and the still vibrant and ongoing theology of liberation. We believe that Justo González, Catherine González, and José David Rodríguez are correct in affirming the integrity of Latin American liberation theology in its own right.[20]

The Caribbean Reality

The Caribbean is an archipelago extending from the entrance to the Gulf of Mexico and adjacent areas on the eastern coast of North America to the proximities of the northern coast of South America. It includes as well the so-called Caribbean countries located on the continent, from French Guyana to Mexico.[21] It is a region consisting of approximately forty countries, with a population in excess of one hundred million people. It is also a region that is ethnically rich, where almost all of humanity is represented. As such, it is a multicultural and multilingual region, where Spanish and English join such other languages as Dutch, French, Creole, Papiamento, Hindu, Chinese, Javanese, as well as a number of local creations derived from the various autonomous linguistic roots. Afro-Caribbean culture is very much alive in this region and represents, together with the extensive black population of the area, one of the most interesting challenges to theology and the theological task.[22] Indeed, Caribbean men and women have begun to recover and reaffirm this black culture, so undervalued not only in the region itself but also in the rest of Latin America, as well as advance quite innovative proposals in the development of such a theology. In her

20. Justo and Catherine G. González, *The Liberating Pulpit* (Nashville: Abingdon Press, 1994). See also José David Rodríguez, *Introducción a la teología* (San José: Editorial DEI, 1993).

21. Luis A. Passalacqua, "Puerto Rico y el Caribe: Cinco etapas," *Problemas del Caribe Puertorriqueño—contemporary Caribbean Issues* (ed. Angel Calderón Cruz; Río Piedras, P.R.: Instituto de Estudios del Caribe, 1971) 61–81.

22. Catherine A. Sunshine, *The Caribbean: Survival, Struggle and Sovereignty* (Boston: Epica Publications, 1985).

study of the black women of Central America, Luceta A. Christian speaks eloquently in this regard:

Whenever reference is made to the contribution of black culture to Central American society, it is solely in terms of the achievements of black men. As a result, we find it necessary to raise our voices of discontent and suffering, voices filled as well, however, with a heartfelt hope in a new dawn, when we shall be able to realize ourselves as subjects, without denying anybody's rights.... The situation of Central American women leads us not to lamentation but to a struggle for life.... The death and resurrection of Christ take on added significance in this struggle on the part of black women.[23]

Noel Leo Erskine is a Jamaican Baptist who has studied the Caribbean religious movement known as Rastafarianism. In its beginnings in the 1930s, this movement looked upon the emperor of Ethiopia as the eternal and trinitarian God and urged all Jamaicans to reject Jamaica in favor of Ethiopia. Around the 1960s, the movement began to teach that Africa is in Jamaica, and this in turn became a call to Africanize Jamaica. For Erskine, however, the strength of the movement lies in its conception of the immanent presence of God in the context of human life. Such a concept he explains as follows:

Traditional Christianity seldom depicted God as involved in the blackness of black lives. God was often transcendent without being immanent. The Rastafarians have served to remind the Christian church that the God who would liberate the oppressed from a distorted estimate of themselves cannot be an alien or a foreigner. He cannot be a stranger to blackness.[24]

Although the colonial model operative in the rest of Latin America, a model involving the extermination of large segments of the indigenous population, is also reproduced in the Caribbean, a rich Afro-Caribbean culture, with a very distinctive form of religious syncretism, does come to life in the region. Such distinctiveness has been associated with the belief that human beings are surrounded by spirits, be it the Holy Spirit or other spiritual powers, so that it becomes imperative for human beings to maintain good relationships with the spirits if they wish to benefit from their assistance and avoid their wrath.[25] Both Cuban Santería and Haitian Voodoo share such a belief in spirits.

---

23. L. A. Christian, "La mujer negra centroamericana," *Teología desde la mujer en Centroamérica* (ed. Irene Foulkes; San José: Sebila, 1989) 22–30, esp. 22, 29.

24. Noel Leo Erskine, *Decolonizing Theology: A Caribbean Perspective* (Maryknoll, N.Y.: Orbis Books, 1981) 113. Erskine argues that the Rastafarian movement calls into question the social structure of a white colonial society that keeps black people in captivity. The movement took the name of King Ras Tafari of Ethiopia, who, in the course of his coronation as emperor in 1930, was proclaimed by his Jamaican followers as God's messiah for the liberation of Africans from colonialism.

25. Harold Turner, "New Religious Movements in the Caribbean," *Afro-Caribbean Religions* (ed. B. Gates; London: Ward Lock Educational, 1980) 49–57.

Within the Caribbean Basin one finds a broad political and economic spectrum, ranging from a classic colony (Puerto Rico) to a socialist republic (Cuba). Almost all Caribbean countries gained their independence in the twentieth century. However, a number of these independent countries were the object of military interventions on the part of the United States during the 1980s; such, for example, was the case of Grenada. Leslie Lett, an Anglican priest from Antigua, denounces the U.S. messianism at work in this military operation, while elaborating a theology of "parachute incarnation": "From the colonial perspective, the story of the Incarnation was and continues to be distorted to mean that the 'inherent inferiority' of black people always requires a miraculous Rescuer, Invader and Big Brother, to parachute down in our midst, to sort things out and save us from ourselves."[26] Dion E. Phillips and Alma H. Young have argued that this military intervention in Grenada represents a demystification of the concept of the English Caribbean as a bastion of order and democracy, exposing it instead as a region quite susceptible to military government, like the rest of Latin America.[27]

Despite the struggles for political sovereignty, those Caribbean nations that have gained political independence have not attained economic independence. A number of experts have argued that the limits for acceptable sovereign actions in the region have been severely circumscribed by both the economy and the national security interests of the United States.[28] One should not forget, however, that other world powers—such as the Soviet Union, Great Britain, and France—have also had their say in the Caribbean. Consequently, any hope for economic self-determination is frustrated to the extent that all decision making is determined by economic forces from outside the region and rapid changes in the global relationships of power and the economy. In the Caribbean as well as in the rest of Latin America, the strategies for a common market as well as unity and solidarity decrease as the economic power and interests of the powers represented in the region increase. At the same time that outside support for the integration of these countries into the international economic order intensifies, in the Caribbean itself a suspicion regarding the political agency behind this new "postcolonial" condition in all of Latin America but especially in the Caribbean also grows. Indeed, the Fourth Conference of Latin American Bishops, held in October 1992 in the Dominican Republic, expressed pastoral concern regarding this new economic order being forged in Latin America, questioning the limits of the proposed freedom of the marketplace and addressing the characteristics it must have in order to be of service

---

26. Cited in Sunshine, *Caribbean,* 208.
27. Dion E. Phillips and Alma H. Young, "Toward an Understanding of Militarization in the Third World and the Caribbean," *Militarization in the Non-Hispanic Caribbean* (ed. Dion E. Phillips and Alma H. Young; Boulder, Colo.: Lynne Rienner Publishers, 1986) 1–16.
28. Ibid, 2.

to the multitudes. Some of these concerns come to light in the pastoral proposals advanced by the conference:

We must strengthen the knowledge, diffusion, and practice of the social doctrine of the church; foster at all levels and in all sectors a social pastoral agenda that takes as its point of departure the preferential option of the gospel for the poor, promoting initiatives of cooperation within a market economy; lay the grounds for a real and efficient economy of solidarity, without bypassing the corresponding creation of socioeconomic models at both a local and national level; back the search for and implementation of socioeconomic models that bring into play freedom, personal and collective creativity, as well as the regulatory function of the state, without forgetting the neediest sectors of society; promote international economic relations that facilitate the transfer of technology in an atmosphere of social reciprocity; and denounce any market economy whose negative effects fall mainly on the poor.[29]

The Puerto Rican Reality

Puerto Rico is an island encompassing thirty-five hundred square miles of territory. It may be variously described as (1) an Afro-Caribbean nation; (2) a land expropriated by the Spanish Crown; (3) a walled city; (4) a minority with dreams of freedom; and (5) a people acquired and militarized by the United States. In what follows we shall use these metaphors to provide an overview of the history of Puerto Rico.

Puerto Rico as an Afro-Caribbean Nation

In a highly suggestive essay, the Puerto Rican writer José Luis González has described Puerto Rico as a four-storied country.[30] His main thesis is twofold: first, that four different layers characterize the people of Puerto Rico; second, that of its three historical roots (the Amerindian *taína,* the Spanish, and the African) the third, that of Africa, is the most fundamental. In fact, González goes on to argue that the first Puerto Ricans were actually the black *criollos* (individuals born on the island). He is further in agreement with many other researchers who have claimed that the Puerto Rican mulatto has been largely ignored both as a sector of the population and as a historical subject, indeed far more so than any other group.[31] This black Puerto Rican culture, a culture characterized by resistance, has never been

---

29. *Desde el Caribe* 1:1 (December 1992) 1–11, esp. 5–8; this is a journal published three times a year by the organization Proyecto de Justicia y Paz en Puerto Rico under the auspices of the National Council of Churches of the United States.

30. Justo L. González, *El país de cuatro pisos y otros ensayos* (Río Piedras, P.R.: Ediciones Huracán, 1989).

31. See, for example, Luis Nieves Falcón, "La ruta del legado colonial," *La tercera raíz: Presencia africana en Puerto Rico* (Río Piedras, P.R.: Centro de Estudios de la Realidad Puertorriqueña [CEREP] and Instituto de Cultura Puertorriqueña [ICP], 1992) 15–25.

acknowledged, analyzed, or fostered by the national culture, that is to say, the official or dominant culture of the landowning elite.

With respect to popular religiosity, it is widely recognized that the blacks imported from Africa brought with them a well-defined and established system of religious practices, which was opposed by the European segments of society. A brief but suggestive study in this regard is that of William Loperena, a Puerto Rican Episcopal priest.[32] Loperena comments on these African theological systems and applies to Afro-Caribbean theology the findings of the English ethnologist Mary Kingsley regarding the fundamental goals of such systems. Four such goals are identified: (1) the preservation of human life; (2) providing a happy transition for the human soul at the time of death; (3) the attainment of material prosperity; and (4) controlling the forces of nature. By way of conclusion, Loperena points out that, under the pretext of failing to understand its magic and syncretism, the religious authorities of Puerto Rico always rejected Afro-Caribbean theology. In response, the religious authorities claimed to preach a European or North American theology that was pure, orthodox, and true. In the end, colonial power proved so overwhelming that it managed to delegitimize the black experience and hence the ancient spirituality of both Amerindia and Africa, with its sense of musical freedom and its carnavalesque character. At the same time, racism became institutionalized, and *mulatez* (the racial mixture of black and white) became such a shameful legacy that it was completely passed over. It should not be at all surprising, therefore, that González's thesis has acquired so much relevance today, given its argument that Puerto Rican society was "whitened" during the beginning and middle of the nineteenth century (the country's second story) by way of extensive immigration from England, France, Holland, Ireland, Corsica, Majorca, and Catalonia.

Puerto Rico as a Land Expropriated by the Spanish Crown

In Puerto Rico as in the rest of Latin America, the European conquest brought about a total humiliation of the native population, putting down the many forms of resistance offered by the indigenous communities. Perhaps the greatest indignity was the illegitimate expropriation of the land, the main means of production on the island during the fifteenth and sixteenth centuries.[33] Through force and deception, a concept of property and economic production foreign to the natural social environment was imposed on the native populations, for whom land was a common good that existed for the benefit of all. At the same time, the broader indigenous vision of a natural equilibrium in the social environment was altered. With the expropriation of the land, the new economic principles, and the system of exchange and production on the part of the colonizers, values and

---

32. William Loperena, "Teología Afrocaribeña," *Claridad;* this is a weekly newspaper published by the Partido Socialista Puertorriqueño (Socialist Party of Puerto Rico).
33. Nieves Falcón, "Ruta," 16.

actions were adopted that were meant to advance the individual material welfare of the new privileged classes. For Puerto Rico the net result was a subservient, poor, and working society, whose land became a commodity and a means for profit on the part of the conquerors. As in the case of ancient Israel, Puerto Rican society survived in "tents" built by the conquerors, who restricted the natives' access to the land that had once been theirs. Such actions anticipated the later Puerto Rican migrations, as a result of which Puerto Ricans would travel in circles, contemplating from afar the land that remains so close to them.

Puerto Rico as a Walled City

In Puerto Rico as in a number of other countries of the Caribbean, the impressive fortifications built around cities can still be seen. San Juan is one of those walled cities from the colonial era. The Fort of El Morro and the Fort of San Cristóbal are but two of these gigantic structures built by the hands of black slaves in the service of the conquerors. The cruelest paradox at the heart of such fortifications is the fact that, as better ramparts and a greater line of defense were secured by the Spaniards, the Puerto Rican people became ever more defenseless and fragile. Its enemies were now to be found within their own homes, with total control over them and robbing them of all their riches and possessions. The other great paradox, as many Puerto Rican theologians and historians have observed, is the fact that the conquest was supported and driven by Christian doctrine.[34] In effect, the liberating memory of Christ as well as the faith that calls for a peace built on justice were relegated to the periphery, to the margins, as a result of the central role played by glory, material wealth, and human power in the conquest.

Indeed, even today there is a dearth of voices from Spain willing to come forward and acknowledge this historical holocaust of human, cultural, material, economic, and political proportions. Recently, we had the opportunity to listen to one such voice on the occasion of an ecumenical gathering of women. The organizer of the event was a Spanish woman who ended her presentation by asking for forgiveness on the part of the Puerto Rican public present for the atrocities committed during the conquest. With tears in her eyes, that lone woman, in solidarity with just and peaceful causes, condemned with indignation and profound sadness the whole enterprise of her compatriots; in so doing, through her prophetic action, she provided a powerful model of ministry for women, a model that must be multiplied among men as well.

---

34. Rivera Pagán, Vidales, and Irarrazaval, *Esperanza*, 33–35; see also Joaquín Mortiz, ed., *1492–1992 La interminable conquista: Emancipación e identidad de América Latina* (Mexico City: Grupo Editorial Planeta, 1990).

Puerto Rico as a Minority with Dreams of Freedom

From the beginning of the nineteenth century, proindependence conspiracies and acts of resistance arose in Puerto Rico, to the great concern of the Spanish authorities. A large part of this activity in favor of liberation took place within the larger framework of insurrectionary tendencies in other territories of Spain as well as internal conflicts within Spain itself.[35] In Puerto Rico such a silent class war and ongoing political revolution came to a head on 23 September 1868 with the Grito de Lares (Cry of Lares), the proclamation of Puerto Rican independence. On that day a provisional government, of very brief duration, was formed. The following declaration of the newly formed republic was affixed all over San Juan:

Manifesto of the *borinqueño*[36] patriots in charge of the revolutionary movement. Being in agreement to the effect that the time has come to take up arms in order to make holy the cause of our rights, we declare ourselves ready to die rather than continue living under Spanish domination. In order to avoid being characterized as an unruly mob or a mutinous rebellion and [to be] regarded instead as a patriotic movement with the aim in mind of shaking off the onerous yoke and creating a free country, we hereby make it public as evidence to the whole world.[37]

The colonial government responded with military aggression—pursuing, capturing, and putting to death both the male and female protagonists of this patriotic revolution—as well as a temporary restriction on the civil liberties of all citizens. A number of government officials acknowledged that the social and economic situation of the Puerto Rican people was one of misery, but they refused to grant legitimacy to such claims, for fear of even greater separatist movements against Spain. At the same time, government officials were reassured by the fact that the number of individuals taking part in such proindependence activities remained minimal. Such is the sentiment expressed by Governor Pavía in his letter of 1868 to the new government of Spain:

They have sought to petition the provisional government of the country on behalf of civil liberties, rights, and other such benefits; however, when I realized that such petitions had begun to take on a completely unacceptable language and form, due to the activities of a number of individuals in certain locations, I banned all such representations, which naturally, as a result, came to nothing. In this way calm has been restored, and it is my hope that the agitators will be ultimately controlled by the good sense of the population at large.[38]

---

35. Juan Bosch, *De Cristóbal Colón a Fidel Castro: El Caribe, frontera imperial* (La Habana: Editorial de las Ciencias Sociales, 1983) 593–619.

36. This is a term meaning "Puerto Rican," derived from the indigenous name for the island, *Boriken,* and hence emphasizing the nationalist character of the movement. TRANS.

37. Cited in Germán Delgado Pasapera, *Puerto Rico: Sus luchas emancipadoras (1850–1898)* (Río Piedras, P.R.: Editorial Cultural, 1984) 202.

38. Cited in ibid., 221.

The reference to the population at large as not taking part in the insurrectionary movements dating from the beginning of the century can be readily explained in terms of the power and domination of foreign colonization. Such a historically contextual interpretation comes to expression in the following citation:

Visible support for independence in Puerto Rico society is presently small. That is, no more than 6–7 percent of the electorate votes for the Puerto Rican Independence Party or the Puerto Rican Socialist Party in current elections. This fact must be placed in historical perspective, however, since support for independence has always ebbed and flowed according to certain short-term conditions, including economic fluctuation and the level of political repression.[39]

The minority that dreams of independence for the country has paid a high social price indeed. Its dream has turned into a nightmare, insofar as both the ideal of independence and its representatives have been criminalized. At the present time and completely against the grain, only a small minority continues to keep alive the dream of national liberation. One of the most faithful and constant exponents of this ideal in the Catholic sector was the Jesuit monsignor Antulio Parrilla Bonilla. His homily on the occasion of the 101st anniversary of the Grito de Lares presupposes a liberating Christology:

Jesus felt the pains and sufferings of his country. He cried for his country and lamented what was going to happen to it within a few years: its total destruction by the Romans.... A society that fails to provide a full and happy life here on earth for all of its members has no right to exist. It must open itself to radical social changes that will make possible such a reality.... In other words, the work of liberation must be carried on.... The case of Puerto Rico forms part of a larger process being fought by all the oppressed of the world.... One must see Christ behind all such movements of liberation.[40]

Since the 1960s, a Puerto Rican theological and pastoral agenda of decolonization has also come to the fore in a variety of Protestant sectors as well as in a number of progressive ecumenical movements; however, such groups shall always remain a minority in the country.

Puerto Rico as a People Acquired and Militarized by the United States

In July 1898 the armed forces of the United States invaded Puerto Rico. This represents, according to the metaphor of José Luis González, the third story of Puerto Rican reality. As part of the treaty that brought the Spanish-American War to an end, Puerto Rico was taken away from Spain and became a colony of the United States. In the eyes of the United States,

---

39. Sunshine, *Caribbean*, 171.

40. Antulio Parrilla Bonilla, "Homilía de la misa de la CI conmemoración del Grito de Lares," *Puerto Rico: Supervivencia y liberación* (Río Piedras, P.R.: Ediciones Librería Internacional, 1971) 144–47.

Puerto Ricans were seen as an unfortunate people from the very beginning of their history, insofar as they were the recipients of Western culture at the hands of Spain. In Puerto Rico, therefore, the United States saw the need to extend its agenda of civilization.[41]

The United States has viewed the Puerto Rican people as sickly, weak in spirit, and submissive, a view that favors a military apparatus of vigilance and control over the citizenry. With the Foraker Act of 1900, the militarization and political control of Puerto Rico by the United States became institutionalized. Moreover, if one takes into account the strategic location of the island, situated as it is at the very entrance to the Caribbean Sea, this project of militarization begun by the United States on Puerto Rican soil becomes readily understandable. Such militarization involves as well the primacy of military priorities and goals at the expense of all local and civil institutions. With this military government Puerto Rico remains trapped under the military and economic sphere of influence and control of the United States.[42]

Within the context of World War I (1914–18), the United States turned the citizens of Puerto Rico into American citizens (1917). Since that time Puerto Rico has taken part in every military conflict in which the United States has become involved. Such a swift process of occupation and militarization had important cultural repercussions. Indeed, in less than two decades, Puerto Rico found itself partaking of and living in two great worlds: the Hispanic world and the world of the United States. The language and flag of the United States became part of Puerto Rican culture, while an accelerated model of industrialization set out to combat the social poverty and misery of the country.

This new Puerto Rican identity, integrated into and assimilated to that of the United States, has distanced the country from the rest of Latin America. The U.S. passport and the project of industrialization have become symbols of a higher "cultural" status. However, after four decades of this political experiment, such symbols still reflect their arbitrariness. Thus, the possession of U.S. citizenship means that Puerto Rican sovereignty resides in the Congress of the United States; similarly, the Foraker Act serves as a reminder that militarization forms part of our everyday reality, reaching even into our public housing projects, as recent events have shown. The police and the military reserve invade the public projects, relying for their justification on a criminalist perspective of positivist character, backed by the communications media as a whole. Further, social statistics as well as new federal policies force us to deconstruct myths and knock down the idols of progress, developed by and large by the multinational corporations, which

---

41. See Bosch, *Colón,* 621–47.

42. John Enders, *La presencia militar de Estados Unidos en Puerto Rico* (Río Piedras, P.R.: Proyecto de Justicia y Paz, 1981).

up to now have enjoyed tax-free status and now threaten with leaving the island, exposing thereby the underlying reality of a precarious and artificial economy.

Consequently, a fundamental question has come to the fore in Puerto Rican society: What will be the final price of technology and globalization? There are those who anticipate, perhaps prophetically, a very high price indeed. Thus, for example, one Puerto Rican intellectual believes that the country will experience an even greater displacement of workers and a new subjectivity brought about by the new conditions operative in the world of labor:

Puerto Rico is in the process of becoming a post-work society, which has already engendered post-work sensibilities, entitlement "attitudes" and the conditions that qualify it as perhaps an unexpected but nearly inevitable location for the paradoxical outcomes of contemporary restructurations of global capitalism and colonial/post-colonial ensembles.[43]

The Puerto Rican church must continue to accompany the Puerto Rican people on its path toward the future; however, that world built upon false hopes and promises has to be left behind in order to give way to the life and shalom of God. In the tradition of the Christian faith, there is a powerful seed of life and well-being.

Theology from the Puerto Rican Context

We should now like to take a look at the second evangelization of Puerto Rico (the Protestant evangelization), which began at the beginning of this century. The Protestant faith arrived in Puerto Rico as a result of the U.S. invasion. The tradition of an individualist, intimate, and personal experience has taken root in Puerto Rican soil, despite the Catholic religious and cultural sense of community present in the hearts of the Puerto Rican people. This new evangelization on Puerto Rican soil has been driven by the active participation of Anglo-Saxon missions, which together with their Puerto Rican counterparts have played a leading role in educational, social, and pastoral affairs. In this regard, however, the pastoral and organizational role of laywomen at the beginning of the century has never been officially recognized. By and large, the ordained ministry has received all the credit for such work, no doubt, as one can readily surmise, as a result of sexism. At present, however, given the new historical juncture, a number of Puerto Rican Protestant women have begun to study the role of women in the church throughout its entire history.[44]

---

43. María Milagros López, "Post-work Selves and Entitlement 'Attitudes' in Peripherical Post-industrial Puerto Rico" (unpublished paper, 1993).

44. Sandra Mangual Rodríguez, "La mujer y la iglesia protestante en Puerto Rico" (unpublished paper, February 1991); Carmen Margarita Sánchez, an alumna of the Seminario Evangélico de Puerto Rico, is also pursuing such studies.

Puerto Rican male Protestant thought has recently become the object of rigorous study. This is due in large part to the work of two young Puerto Rican theologians, Luis Rivera Pagán and Luis Rivera Rodríguez. On the one hand, Rivera Pagán has analyzed four theological paths taken by four different Puerto Rican academics in the second half of the twentieth century.[45] On the other hand, Rivera Rodríguez has examined the methodological presuppositions and ideological commitments of two other Puerto Rican theologians, coming to the following conclusions in the process: (1) the link between faith and theology is present in both; (2) the primary subject of Puerto Rican theology will have to have at the very least a Puerto Rican identity; and (3) the optimal locus for such a theology is none other than Puerto Rico itself.[46] For Rivera Rodríguez the major difference between these two theologians lies in their respective understandings of the immediate object for theological reflection and the ideological commitment of the theological subject. Such methodological and ideological differences lead him in turn to distinguish between two different types of theology in Puerto Rico: Puerto Rican theology (*teología puertorriqueña*) and theology with an option for Puerto Rico (*teología puertorriqueñista*). These two types of theologizing are summarized as follows:

Puerto Rican theology has to do with critical reflection on God and the fundamental issues of human existence and human destiny in history from the point of view, directly or indirectly, of Puerto Rican experience, carried out from a Christian perspective and praxis and undertaken mainly by those who reside in the island. Theology with an option for Puerto Rico has to do with critical reflection, from the point of view of Christian faith and praxis, on God, the human condition, and human destiny within the Puerto Rican experience and context, undertaken by Puerto Ricans residing in the island, Puerto Ricans of the diaspora, and non–Puerto Ricans residing in the island who make an option for Puerto Ricanness (*puertorriqueñidad*).[47]

For Rivera Rodríguez such an option for Puerto Ricanness involves the affirmation, promotion, and defense of cultural identity, political and economic sovereignty, the integrity of the Puerto Rican patrimony, as well as love for and service to the Puerto Rican people.

In the light of these definitions, the thesis of Rivera Pagán regarding the theological pluralism at work in Puerto Rican Protestantism can be more readily understood. For him, Domingo Marrero and Ángel Mergal emerge as the fathers of Puerto Rican theology. Although neither of them is directly engaged in the discussion regarding the poverty, misery, and exploitation of Caribbean Latin America, both are indirectly concerned

---

45. L. N. Rivera Pagán, *Senderos teológicos: El pensamiento evangélico puertorriqueño* (Río Piedras, P.R.: Editorial La Reforma, 1990).

46. L. Rivera Rodríguez, "Teología puertorriqueña: El problema metodológico," *Casabe: Revista Puertorriqueña de teología* 2 (February 1990) 5–7, esp. 7.

47. Ibid., 6.

with the question of human destiny. While Marrero develops such concerns from a philosophical perspective, Mergal is more interested in the psychological constitution of the human being and its ability to respond to the will of God. Although Rivera Pagán acknowledges the validity of both of these theological paths, he does point to the complete absence of the social context. He seems to suggest thereby that lacking in such theologies are the elements of ideological suspicion, fundamental questioning, and political analysis of events fundamental to the Latin American context, such as the processes of colonization and conquest. Such perspectives, completely bypassed by both Marrero and Mergal, become an object of reflection for Samuel Silva Gotay, the third theologian dealt with by Rivera Pagán. Silva Gotay is a Puerto Rican who adopts the optic of Latin America by subscribing to the Third World emphasis present in the Latin American theological reflection on liberation. He summarizes the process involved in such theologizing as follows:

Once the theologian, in conjunction with other intellectuals of a society, admits that the political realm is not a reflection of principles grounded in ahistorical essences, the political ethic of the social order loses its validity as an absolute ethic and the new praxis makes fun of the old theology. From this point on, a relative political ethic is in order, an ethic that is historically grounded in the well-being of the real human being and that is determined at any given moment by political protest against the conditions of life as well as a project for a new world as its point of departure. The ethic of the social order becomes an ethic of liberation. The political realm ceases to be a politics of order and becomes a politics of the liberation of the social order, while the theology of the social order becomes a theology of liberation.[48]

Although the synthesis advanced by Rivera Pagán regarding Puerto Rican Protestant thought is tight and quite attractive, it does have its limitations. Thus, it is in the end a systematization of a number of Protestant lines of thinking, all of which not only emerge from the academy but are also the product of men. In Puerto Rico, however, there are other frames of reference from which to analyze the course of Protestant thinking.

Thus, for example, since 1919 the Seminario Evangélico de Puerto Rico—an institution of theological education in the Protestant Reformed tradition—has prepared men and women for Christian ministry and discipleship in a complex and changing society. Through the years the "theological locus" of the school has been the local church, whose membership reflects the whole of Puerto Rican society with all of its tragedies, forms of resistance, and hopes. One of the immediate challenges facing the school at this point is that of classifying and analyzing the different models of pastoral leadership it has offered in the last seventy-five years, in order to

---

48. Samuel Silva Gotay, *El pensamiento cristiano revolucionario en América Latina y el Caribe* (3d ed.; Río Piedras, P.R.: Ediciones Huracán, 1989) 185.

face with wisdom and confidence the new contextual and global challenges of the twenty-first century.[49]

Another expression of Puerto Rican theology since the 1970s has been the emergence of ecumenical groups with an agenda of political activism. Such groups have provided a space outside the academy for Puerto Rican theological reflection and ministry—an example of what Samuel Pagán has characterized as contextual theology or José David Rodríguez has called pastoral theology.[50] The Puerto Rican National Ecumenical Movement (MEMPRI) is one of these groups. The group has developed a socioreligious discourse oriented toward national liberation within the context of Puerto Rican colonization; its aims include both a pastoral agenda of decolonization and a pastoral ministry with a preferential option for the poor. Eunice Santana, a Protestant pastor and leader of the World Council of Churches for Latin America and the Caribbean, served as its coordinator until recently.[51] The Puerto Rican church owes a debt of gratitude to the men and women of this movement, who initiated a new mode of critical reflection on the Christian faith as well as a new mode of suffering, given the consequences of such reflection in a country and a church where patriotism is seen as offensive.[52]

The Caribbean Project for Peace and Justice (Proyecto Caribeño de Paz y Justicia) is another ecumenical group engaged in theological reflection in Puerto Rico.[53] Alongside Margarita Pérez, a committed Catholic woman, Protestant Christians work with young people and all of society in actively opposing the recruitment and participation of Puerto Rican youth in the military conflicts of the United States. Its most recent effort in this regard took place within the context of the Gulf War, an educational crusade joined by the Baptist churches of Puerto Rico at the time. The work of the project for the children represents yet another program that calls into question the agenda of war and militarization at work in Puerto Rican society. The goal of this programmatic project for the children is to raise consciousness with regard to the high levels of violence present in children's games and toys. Along the same lines though from a more global perspective, the theological reflection of Rivera Pagán regarding a theology

---

49. See the suggestive study by Jorge Bardeguez, former professor at the Seminario Evangélico, regarding models of pastoral leadership in Puerto Rico: "Modelos de pastoral en Puerto Rico," *Casabe: Revista Puertorriqueña de teología* 3 (October 1991) 6–8.

50. For Pagán, see *Púlpito, teología y esperanza* (Miami: Editorial Caribe, 1988); for Rodríguez, see *Introducción*, 21–22.

51. MEMPRI, formerly known as PRISA, now has a new leadership and is working on a new focus.

52. One of the most interesting debates now going on in Puerto Rico has to do with the use on the part of political parties with assimilationist platforms of symbols traditionally associated with proindependence movements, such as the language and flag of Puerto Rico.

53. This group has just celebrated twenty years of witnessing in Puerto Rico and is presently engaged in a process of internal reorganization and the development of a new public image.

of peace should be highlighted.[54] Indeed, Rivera Pagán identifies himself as the fourth Puerto Rican theologian in question.

The Pentecostal movement is another form of religious expression in Puerto Rico worth mentioning here. At present, the Protestant community of Puerto Rico constitutes 30 percent of the population, and the majority of those Protestants are Pentecostals. This is, therefore, a religious movement that is experiencing rapid growth in the island. In general, its approach to the Bible may be classified as literalist; its hermeneutical keys as apocalyptic and otherworldly; and its church organization as dependent on certain charisms of the Spirit and/or the charisma of the pastor. Despite such theological orientations, there is something admirable, though somewhat paradoxical, at the heart of the Puerto Rican Pentecostal world: not only is its commitment to social work quite strong, but also its participation in the public sphere is quite high. Thus, as part of its ministry, the movement has reached out to the most despised segments of society, such as those afflicted with AIDS and drug addicts of any kind; as a result, Pentecostalism has earned an important place in Puerto Rican society. In addition, the Pentecostal churches have had the wisdom of adapting their liturgy to the musical and popular ethos of large sectors of Puerto Rican society. Such developments have led a number of intellectuals (such as, for example, Samuel Silva Gotay) to suspect that we find ourselves before a phenomenon worthy of the most rigorous investigation.

Two new themes have recently emerged within Puerto Rican Protestant circles: material prosperity and mental health. These themes have been pursued above all in new churches, free and autonomous churches proliferating at present throughout all of Puerto Rico and growing at a rapid pace among individuals from the upper-middle class. This particular development, as yet not analyzed at all within Puerto Rico itself, does merit a passing mention in this study. Quite recently, one finds as well the emergence of ecological reflection from the point of view of Christian faith. This is a discussion that will continue to grow in the years to come, given the high levels of environmental pollution on the island as well as the lack of regulation concerning all such polluting activities.

Finally, the emergence of Puerto Rican women as new theological subjects must be mentioned. Both sexist culture and patriarchal ideology are being denounced by women committed to the faith and life of the church. However, it must be sadly admitted that, despite the fragmentation observed in Puerto Rican Protestant thought since the 1960s, Puerto Rican theology has failed to mount a proper critique of that set of relationships that proceeds to construct gender on the basis of sex, places excessive value on the contribution of men, and passes over the history of women in society

---

54. L. N. Rivera Pagán, *A la sombra del Armagedón: Reflexiones críticas sobre el desafío nuclear y la militarización de la ciencia* (Río Piedras, P.R.: Editorial Edil, 1989).

and the church, spheres where they have always been present as active subjects. In their development of a theology from the point of view of women, Puerto Rican women have been inspired by women from all over the world. Indeed, we have engaged in dialogue with Hispanic American women in the United States, celebrating our areas of agreement while making concrete our own struggle in the Puerto Rican context.[55]

In 1991 COMMADRES, a community of women gathered together for ecumenical dialogue and reactions, came into being. This is a reflection group involving Christian women in dialogue with society and the church; its role is twofold: to give birth to ideas, analyses, proposals, and concrete actions regarding the problems that confront both women and society at large; to contribute to the formation of a different society. Its name is derived from a socioreligious tradition of Latin America, whereby women become related to one another as sisters (*comadres*) for the purpose of baptizing children and assuming responsibility for their upbringing and education. The group represents an alliance among women with the purpose of assuming responsibility as a group for the growth of faith, justice, and hope for a different society, a society where peace with justice and dignity function as its dominant values. Thus, COMMADRES involves proclamation, denunciation, celebration, action, and embracing—a life that affirms union among women, where one can find the voice of resistance, power, tradition, and liberating faith.

This new theological task on the part of Puerto Rican women is paradigmatic insofar as it takes seriously into account the discussion of patriarchy and sexism without bypassing the other social dilemmas that confront Puerto Rican society, such as militarism, the criminalization of nationalism, and colonization. Puerto Rico must continue to develop a theological discourse with a greater and more deliberate discussion of gender violence, while at the same time continuing to pass judgment on issues of peace, poverty, dependency, mental crisis, and racism. Quite ironically, women have become aliens within a promised land as well as within walls: kept behind doors and absent from the decision-making process even in those circles that preach liberation.

Conclusion

The authors of this work are, above all, preachers of the gospel and the word of God, and we believe that faith and the Bible are important traveling companions in the task that lies before us. We look forward to a day in which we will be able to speak of our own *mulatez* without feeling as aliens

---

55. See Ada María Isasi-Díaz and Sandra Mangual-Rodríguez, "Roundtable Discussion: *Mujeristas:* Who We Are and What We Are About," *Journal of Feminist Studies in Religion* 8 (1992) 105–25, esp. 105–9 and 113–16.

in our own bodies. We dream of a day in which the Puerto Rican people will be able to leave behind their mentality of colonization and look forward to a liberated country, where we can all live without feeling as aliens in our own land. Our hope is for a city without walls, without a false sense of security, where neither dignity nor self-esteem nor natural resources are imprisoned or plundered. We visualize a society where the shalom of God can break out, where neither terror nor fear represents our daily bread. We pray with confidence that the Lamb that appears on our national seal will be identified with a continent that has suffered violence, ill-treatment, and humiliation. We believe that Christ has risen and has embarked on the way. We join the millions of pilgrims from all of Latin America who, despite their closeness to one another, do not recognize the face of their neighbors. We join the pilgrims from the rest of America, the Hispanic Americans, with whom we share many a cause and many a hope. Our hearts burn and tremble in our hope for a new dawn.

13

The Collective "Dis-covery" of Our Own Power

Latina American Feminist Theology

María Pilar Aquino

The purpose of this reflection is twofold. First, I seek to examine briefly the sociocultural context of Latina American feminist theology, from whose perspective I speak. Second, I wish to explore some characteristics of this theology. I will concentrate more on the methodological aspects of this theology than on its central themes, since I want to identify the elements that place Latina American thought within the wider context of feminist theologies. To be sure, the growing incorporation of women into the theological task converges with the increasing incorporation of other women into the social and ecclesial realms. For Latina American women, the exercise of imagination—inventing new ways to struggle, resist, and survive—and the possibility of choosing a different future have finally been liberated from their long captivity by a combination of hope, joy, and suffering within our daily struggles.

What we see today in the mainland of Latin America and in the Caribbean is a widespread movement of women who are increasingly aware of the multiplicity of our shared, oppressive situation. Women are taking responsibility for reality and the steps necessary to direct our present history toward a different future, more congruent with our own interests and based on our own consciousness and condition as women.

The purpose of my reflection implies by necessity a critical reference to the sociohistorical context from which Latina American feminist theology emerges and develops. For us indigenous women, mestizas, or Afro-Caribbean women, it is radically impossible to disregard the fact that we sprang from a conquered and colonized continent. Our ways of looking at life, understanding our own existence, and interpreting our faith-experience are all indelibly marked by this fact, regardless of whether it results in the perpetuation of an oppressive reality or brings forth emancipating experiences. Even today the consequences of this historical fact are very much present in our daily life and affect not only how we understand ourselves but also how we do theology—what criteria we select for our theologizing, what theological themes we emphasize, and what the ultimate purpose of our theology is. This is what I intend to address here.

I use the term "Latina American" to refer to women of the Latin American continent and the Caribbean who, for one reason or another, understand ourselves as belonging to the Latin American sociocultural universe. There are several reasons for my use of this term: (1) because of my own background, having been born and raised on the southern side of the artificial borders imposed by Euro-American expansion; (2) because the term correlates with others used by different women in reference to their own cultural identities, such as "African American," "Native American," "Asian American," or "Euro-Americans"; and (3) because both technically and formally the term "Hispanic" belongs to the Spaniard women of yesterday and today. At present, after more than five hundred years of forced cultural displacement, the Latina communities find themselves in a clear process of self-identification with their native cultures. Spain, in contrast, finds itself, today as in yesteryear, in an obvious process of self-identification with the European, Western world. Therefore, from all viewpoints, I find it inadequate to call ourselves "Hispanic."

The *Covering* of Women's Subjectivity

From the standpoint of many Latina American women, the five hundred years of European presence in Latin America have served not so much as an occasion for imagining what our history actually was or could have been but rather as an occasion for a continuing *dis-covery*. This is so because the Iberian powers in Latin America—as well as the powers that succeeded them—really *covered*, concealed, and hid dramatically two realities, falsifying their truth in the process. First, these powers' own reality was covered with the veil of the Christian faith, hiding their true intentions and motives. Second, they violently covered up most of what existed in Latin America before their successive arrivals. They accomplished this concealment either through the force of arms or, often enough, through the power of theological reasoning.

The great European invasions did not *discover* but rather *covered* whole peoples, religions, and cultures and explicitly tried to take away from the natives the sources of their own historical memory and their own power. Patriarchal Christendom, expressed both as state and as church, also hid the vision and interests first of native women and then later of black slaves and mestizas. In the face of this cover-up, given the obscurity to which we were condemned by patriarchal Christianity, Latina American women today propose to transform that which covers the sources of our own strength. That is, we seek to *un-cover* the truth and bring to light our collective will to choose a different path.

The patriarchal tradition of the churches has ably demonstrated its inability to respond creatively to the challenges coming from changing historical realities. When facing new situations, the institutional church (with few exceptions) arrives late, does so at a snail's pace, or simply does not arrive at all. In the case of the colonial church, its arrival resulted not in an *unveiling* of the good news contained in the "great mysteries" of our ancestral cultures but rather in a *covering up* of not only the great injustice and violence committed against the native peoples but also their own knowledge and achievements.

Just as in the past, it is today difficult to accept or support the notion that the church of the sixteenth century systematically and frequently defended the conquered peoples of Latin America. It is true that, after the great theological controversies, the church did recognize the human status of the indigenous peoples. But when it did so, it was too late. The massacres committed by the conquerors had made entire peoples disappear from the face of the earth. Very slowly, the church is recognizing the human status and dignity of the black peoples, but even today it has yet to recognize effectively the full human stature of women. From a theological standpoint, the behavior of the institutional church can only indicate a systemic resistance to the re-creating activity of the Spirit of God in the world. Indeed, it seems that the re-creating power of the Spirit finds its major opposition in the power of the patriarchal church.

The consequences of the transposition of European Christendom to Latin America can be seen in their brutal realism when viewed from the perspective of the conquered and colonized peoples. As has been widely pointed out, in the context of colonial history one cannot separate the power of the church from the power of the crown. Both converge on common values and ends; therefore, the economic and political conquest seems to be as necessary as the process of Christianization, according to the Roman model of the times. This relationship of "mutual intrinsic need" between ecclesiastic and royal powers, accepted as self-evident for a very long time, makes it impossible to eliminate or even diminish the responsibility of the church and of Spain in what really happened to our peoples.

To illustrate this point, let me mention the following events.[1] The process of conquest and colonization brought with it the destruction of ancestral

---

1. See Laurette Séjourné, *América Latina: Antiguas culturas precolombinas* (Mexico City: Siglo XXI, 1987); idem, *Pensamiento y religión en el México antiguo* (Mexico City: Fondo de Cultura Económica, 1988); Carmen Ramos Escandón, "Mujer y sociedad novohispana," *ISIS Internacional* 10 (December 1988) 21–31; José Oscar Beozzo, "A mulher indígena e a igreja na situação escravista do Brasil colonial," *A mulher pobre na história da igreja Latino-Americana* (ed. María Luiza Marcílio; São Paulo: Paulinas, 1984) 70–93.

productive systems on which the indigenous economy was based. This destruction not only deprived the communities of their goods and lands but also excluded women from playing an integral role as actors in the indigenous economic processes. The European invasion uprooted the community organizational units and placed in their stead new ecclesiastical and secular structures, taking from the peoples their own power of self-determination and self-sustenance. In some cultures political life had not reached the level of patriarchal rigidity that existed in the great native empires, and women participated in the decision-making processes. With the imposed European stratification, women's fate was decided by patriarchal authority in both its religious and social expressions. With the massive arrival of "white men," the models of ethnic interaction were undone; the indigenous, black, and mestizo men were regarded as belonging to an inferior racial category; and the indigenous and mestiza women—and, to an even greater extent, the black slave women—had to add to their now imposed sense of racial inferiority a version of social subjugation based on the principle of the superiority of men over women.

In the religious sphere the church acted as a mechanism creating social consensus, thereby contributing to the preservation of the colonial system. The church implanted beliefs, practices, and symbols that were alien to the worldview of the native peoples. In this way the church reproduced the ethical codes of European patriarchal Christianity, whose effects on women included submission and self-devaluation. For European Christianity the role of women was focused on human reproduction, although it also used their human energy as forced labor in both the private and public spheres. Perhaps the area that affected the conquered peoples—and women in particular—most deeply was that related to their self-identity. The racist, ethnocentric principle of white, European superiority suppressed the human integrity of the native peoples and did so with even graver results for women, given the suppression of their own subjectivity.

This is why it is necessary to oppose the myth put out by the Iberian world to the effect that the conquest took place in order to evangelize and Christianize the peoples of Latin America. As Ignacio Ellacuría has pointed out, such an affirmation is not only a myth but a total lie: "The truth is very different: Spain went to America to dominate, to conquer, and to expand her power and sources of wealth. Spain came accompanied by the ideological or ideologized baggage represented, particularly at that time, by the Roman church."[2] Thus, the European invasion, along with the reproduction of Iberian Christendom, was, rather than a discovery by the conqueror, a historically violent and violating cover-up of the conquered peoples.

---

2. Ignacio Ellacuría, "¿Descubrimiento o encubrimiento? Quinto centenario América Latina," *SPES* 68–69 (1990) 54.

The magnitude of the subjugation of entire peoples, cultures, and religions carried out by the colonial enterprise merely demonstrates (in other words, *dis-covers*) the real interests and values that accompanied it. From the perspective of Latina American peoples, Western culture and church are the ones that are dis-covered by laying bare their praxis and behavior, thereby showing their true identity. Furthermore, Western church and culture, in order to believe that their identity and presence in this continent were truthful and good, had to declare the physical and cultural nonexistence of the colonized; otherwise, they would have been faced with the need to declare their own illegitimacy.

The natives' diverse cultures, linguistic variety, religions, symbols, words, and ways of relating to the earth were all declared illegitimate in favor of the European hierarchical, patriarchal model and were then thoroughly *covered* over. With this in view, Ellacuría states: "In reality, it is the Third World that *dis-covers* the First in its negative and more realistic aspects."[3] Thus, what must be done today is, on the one hand, to continue reminding the geopolitical North that its behavior has not changed much in the last five hundred years and, on the other hand, to bring to light that which the conquerors tried to cover, that which makes up our own source of power to transform the present order and rebuild our hope.

We do not start at ground zero when faced with the task of transforming and rebuilding our realities and cultures. On the contrary, many popular movements have preceded us. With their struggles and resistance they have refused to pay the tribute imposed by the imperialistic powers. In the case of women, opposition to the hierarchical and colonizing powers has occurred in several ways. The activities of women often crossed the lines of the private and public spheres, whether through collective participation in movements of rebellion against the colonial situation or through painful protest in the religious arena, whether in the building of underground networks to nourish solidarity or through keeping and transmitting subversive memory. Their activities and their participation, often a display of social power, correct the androcentric version of history that regards Latina American women as peripheral to the preservation of the liberating traditions of our cultures. Despite the magnitude of the *cover-up* of the struggles and accomplishments of women, their common resistance and struggles throughout five hundred long years of vassalage demonstrate that it is possible to break the imposing and domineering matrix of patriarchal power in its social and religious expressions. Five centuries of colonial history force us to publicly and collectively un-cover the power that the "coverers" tried to suppress.

---

3. Ibid., 54.

The Affirmation of Women's Own Alterity

Despite the efforts of many individuals and social movements that sought a thorough renovation of the Roman church during the fifteenth and sixteenth centuries, it seems that nothing of substance occurred that would indicate a massive move by the church away from its tradition of hierarchical power to the egalitarian traditions of Christianity. From an objective, factual perspective, Luther's affirmation (in his writings after 1520) that neither the Roman church nor the pope wanted to allow reformation despite the critical need for it seems to have been and continues to be undoubtedly accurate.[4] The church of today still identifies itself as a pyramidal hierarchy ruled by men, provided by God with all earthly and heavenly power, or so it is believed. Needless to say, such an ecclesiology lacks, at the very least, an adequate pneumatology.

This male-centered vision of the church finds its legitimacy in the sacralization of ecclesiastical power that it claims to have derived from Jesus Christ. Pope Alexander VI, head of the Borgia family, expressed this vision quite clearly, as pointed out by Luis Rivera Pagán: "Papal authority, inherited from Christ, is full and absolute. 'Since Christ was given the entire earth,...his vicar therefore has the right, based on the faith of St. Peter, to dominate over all the earth.' "[5] By its own logic, this sacralized hierarchical-patriarchal power was extended over the structures of political power to such a degree that it was able to conceive and implement a multilayered, varied, and combined system of absolute domination of peoples and cultures.

Although this notion of hierarchical-patriarchal power began centuries before, it lasted throughout the medieval period and had become quite explicit by the end of the fifteenth century, as the merging of the interests of Rome and the Iberian crowns shows. In the sixteenth century, however, it reached its high point at Trent, later undergoing further expansion during the seventeenth century. The church understood itself as the "perfect society" whose direction is determined by Rome. To preserve itself, it emphasized the principles of submission and obedience to the monarchy, the ecclesiastical hierarchy, and the social and familial authority of men.

The church we have known since 1492 is a church in conflict, polarized by diverse and even opposed ecclesial traditions in which, nonetheless, the patriarchal dimension has been dominant. One cannot but agree with those who have argued that the history of contact between the European conquerors and the Latin American peoples has been one of conflict and

---

4. Evangelista Vilanova, *Historia de la teología cristiana* (Barcelona: Herder, 1989) 2:207.

5. Luis N. Rivera Pagán, *Evangelización y violencia: La conquista de América* (San Juan: CEMI, 1991) 59.

crisis rather than one of creative building.[6] The Nicaraguan poet Gioconda Belli points out that for Latin America, "The present is not a loving result that can balance positively the deficit of the years of submission.... We continue to be different types of 'colonies' yearning for the times in which we bloomed among our own authentic native cultures."[7] The European invasion of the Americas introduced a powerful coercive structure based on physical violence and on rigid systems of political and ideological control, among which the hierarchical structure of Christianity played a fundamental role.

The asymmetrical social order imposed during a colonial period of over three hundred years was later adjusted by the national states beginning in the nineteenth century. However, these changes did not result in a transformation favoring more justice, as expected by the popular sectors of Latina American societies. On the contrary, this adjustment gave way to a social process, now based on the principles of modernity, that came to rob the already colonized peoples of their own ability for self-determination, their vision, and their lifestyles, besides leading them into an attitude of alienation and self-devaluation. The structures of power, as well as the religious and political principles that legitimize these asymmetrical, "modern" social relationships, were imported from Europe and so were the implied categories upon which the privilege of men over women was based. The European patriarchal structure found reason to flourish in the social relationships that existed in patriarchal indigenous societies, such as the Aztec and Inca empires. In this way, although the indigenous men were condemned to justify their own humanity vis-à-vis the European, not even this possibility was open to indigenous or mestiza women, and much less to the black slave women. The gravity of this phenomenon can be better appreciated when we consider that it was not until the mid–twentieth century that some countries recognized women's right to vote.

Nonetheless, the fifteenth and sixteenth centuries offered some support to the emancipating experiences of women, but only in a fragmentary way, due to the androcentric character of history. In many instances, the humanistic tradition of the Christian faith gave women the arguments necessary to struggle and to resist. Peruvian sociologist Carmen Lora notes that, even

---

6. See, for example, Orlando O. Espín, "Tradition and Popular Religion: An Understanding of the Sensus Fidelium," *Frontiers of Hispanic Theology in the United States* (ed. Allan Figueroa Deck; Maryknoll, N.Y.: Orbis Books, 1992) 67–68: "As peoples of their times, the Spaniards who came to the Americas believed themselves to be superior to all other peoples, and their religion the only one worth professing. The same intransigent attitude that led to devastating wars of religion in Europe became the common attitude of Europeans confronted with Amerindian or African populations and their cultures and religions. The European invasion and conquest of the Americas did not take place for purely humanitarian or Christian reasons. The conquerors came in search of material rewards."

7. Gioconda Belli, "Porque aún Lloramos," *1492–1992. La interminable conquista* (ed. Rubén Dri, Pablo Richard, and Enrique Dussel; San José: DEI, 1990) 64.

with the complexity of the Christianizing enterprise in the continent, the history *dis-covered* from below, from its reversal, indicates that

religion played a much more complex role, [that] the Indo-American women had the capacity to discern the [Christian] message from the cultural clothing that wrapped it. They created mechanisms of cultural resistance that kept many of the ancestral values alive while incorporating elements of the gospel message.[8]

During the colonial era, the privileged mechanism of control over women was the patriarchal family, since this mechanism was the basic unit on which the pyramidal social system was based. The hierarchy of gender, with the assumed supremacy of men, was explicitly paralleled in the hierarchies of social class and race. The submission of women to the authority of men was a basic requirement to guarantee social cohesion.[9] Women, in this context, were subjected to patriarchal power through the state and the church, both controlled and directed by men. The rights of women surfaced only so long as they were not in conflict with the patriarchal religious and political power.

However, this situation was not the same for all women. During the colonial era, white and *criolla*[10] women could have a more active role in the public sphere (since, for example, they could be recruited by the church for charitable work), but black or native women and mestizas did not even have this possibility. Further, the convents exercised considerable influence on women, given the fact that cloisters were often spaces of relative independence vis-à-vis submission to father or husband. Although the clergy had influence in the internal life of the convents and these were organized as a replica of patriarchal power, women had access to some decision making in the missions, schools, or hospitals, and even in education, as Sor Juana Inés de la Cruz's writings indicate. For women from the popular sectors of society and the subaltern races, the sphere of popular Catholicism became the means through which they could exercise considerable symbolic power. This was so because, while the official world of the Roman Catholic religion was controlled by the hierarchy, women had influence among their own people through their transmission of and sharing in the community's vision of the faith.

Although women had some effect in the social relations of the public sphere, since these emphasized family and group cohesiveness, the subordination of women to the patriarchal power was maintained in the private

---

8. Carmen Lora, "Mujer latinoamericana: Historia de una rebeldía: América del Sur," *Aportes para una teología desde la mujer* (ed. María Pilar Aquino; Madrid: Biblia y Fe, 1988) 42.

9. Silvia Marina Arrom, *Las mujeres de la Ciudad de México 1790–1857* (Mexico City: Siglo XXI, 1988) 98.

10. *Criolla* women are the descendants of Spaniards or Portuguese born in Latin America.

sphere, especially when it came to sexuality and human reproduction. Despite the restrictions imposed by the hierarchical order during the colonial period, women were able to expand their collective sociopolitical participation using religion as a platform. In many instances, for example, the activities of women in the strictly political field were legitimized when they appealed to religious ethical values.[11] In this way, women politicized the religious principles available in their day in order to affirm their emancipating possibilities.

Seen from the perspective of contemporary feminism, generally speaking, the organizing experiences of women did not constitute a collective front against patriarchal oppression.[12] In many instances the more prevalent identification of women was with the interests of the social class or race to which they belonged. More telling is the fact that the struggles of women were not activated by an awareness of the systemic, multiple, and articulated character of the oppression affecting them as women.

Although women attempted to alleviate their sufferings and achieve greater space for sociopolitical participation, they did not gain the social power necessary to transform the structures of colonial society.[13] The same occurred among the pioneering groups of Latin American feminism and in the women's movements dating from the end of the last century and the beginning of the current one.[14] However, I want to stress that these women could not face patriarchal oppression in the same terms as we do today, nor could they struggle for autonomy and self-determination based on a feminist consciousness as we understand it today, and yet their struggles were not "feminist-less" or "nonfeminist." The simple fact is that the category of sex/gender as an analytical and political tool, and as an articulating principle of thought, represents an achievement of this century. In my view, it is anachronistic to judge as nonfeminist the past struggles of women, when they did not have and could not have had the theoretical framework present in today's feminism. Nevertheless, in a continent conquered by men, colonized by European powers, and brought to submission by the white race, the organizing capacity of women and their impact in the socioreligious milieu have helped to obtain at least minimum recognition that we exist and that we are a part of society. This is indeed a great achievement for Latina American women.

---

11. María José Rosado Nuñez, "La situación de la mujer en la Iglesia Católica" (unpublished article) 4.

12. María Pilar Aquino, "Feminismo," *Conceptos fundamentales del Cristianismo* (ed. Casiano Floristán and Juan José Tamayo; Madrid: Trotta, 1993) 512.

13. Karen Offen, "Defining Feminism: A Comparative Historical Approach," *Signs* 14 (1988) 119–57.

14. Lora, "Mujer," 25–34.

The Right to Choose a Different Future

Under the influence of European philosophical and political currents of the so-called Enlightenment, the struggles of Latina American women toward the end of the nineteenth century and the beginning of the twentieth centered on social and political rights.[15] The principles activating these struggles were those of human dignity, human integrity, and equality and justice for women. Therefore, although not called "feminist," these struggles could be rightfully claimed by today's Latina American critical feminism as a necessary moment in our feminist tradition.

Both in Europe and in Euro-America women's movements were mainly concerned with overcoming the legal and epistemological restrictions that placed women in a subordinate status. In the face of a modern world that everywhere recognized the right of full political participation for all adults, women demanded laws that would grant them equal legal rights with men.[16] Thus, as pointed out by Concepción Torres and Patricia Reséndiz, the struggles for voting rights, improved access to education, and equity in working conditions were the determining factors of these movements.[17] In this context, especially in Brazil and the Caribbean, the movements for the emancipation of black people from slavery became quite relevant. Indeed, although these women's movements were activated by the principle of ontological equality between men and women, historically such equality was not transferred in an equivalent manner to black, mestiza, or indigenous women or applied in an equivalent way to the relationships between the hegemonic centers of power, such as Europe and the United States, and the peoples of the geopolitical South.

Movements for the emancipation of women, both in form and agenda, demanded larger quotas of participation for middle- and upper-class women, but these rarely affected the real life conditions of women from the popular sectors of society, who were also discriminated against because of their race. For example, in education, legal rights, or worker demands, white women from the middle and upper classes certainly obtained better opportunities. Black, mestiza, and indigenous women, however, did not make such gains, even after most of the Latin American countries gained their independence from the colonial powers in the nineteenth century. As Carmen Lora points out:

The advent of independence, if it marks the beginning of another era on our continent, did not mean the rupture of the economic and cultural dependence on other

---

15. Concepción Torres and Patricia Reséndiz, "La lucha de las mujeres en América Latina y el Caribe, I–II," *EMAS: Pensamiento y Luchas* 3 and 4 (1990 and 1991).

16. Nonetheless, as in other latitudes, such "equality of rights" was based on the model of the adult white male as the norm. See Offen, "Defining Feminism," 123.

17. See Torres and Reséndiz, "La lucha."

centers such as France, England, or the United States. It did not mean any change of condition for the indigenous peoples or women.[18]

On the contrary, the incorporation of the continent and the Caribbean into the geopolitical, military, and financial domain of North American capitalism, now interlaced with the strong patriarchal structure imposed on the continent by the Iberian colonial domination, gave rise to new social mechanisms that operate, even today, to the detriment of women.[19] This new situation, instead of benefiting women, only served to *diversify* their oppressive situation.

Therefore, the context of our theology is a social milieu that has produced a systemic, articulated, and multifaceted oppression of women. It seems that this context can be transformed only by a self-conscious, interrelated, multifaceted, sustained, and collective effort. Dominant asymmetrical power, including patriarchy, is polycentric and involves multiple power relationships. Asymmetrical power carries within it a relational character that expresses itself in multiple forms. Consequently, movements for justice and social change are required to recognize and accept the inevitable diversity of the struggles that oppose asymmetrical power. Therefore, taking into account the heterogeneity and diversity of current social movements, contemporary Latina American feminist experience is making a real contribution. Women from our sociocultural world, and from within our condition as women, want to exercise the right to be actors in the social and ecclesial processes within which we live and demand that such a right be recognized collectively and publicly.

Today, the unifying element of Latina American feminist movements is their common rejection of the established asymmetrical order rooted in patriarchy, colonization, and present-day capitalism. The central thread that binds all the Latina American women's liberation movements is the search for true autonomy as well as social and political recognition of women's human integrity.[20] Nonetheless, it is necessary to note that not every women's movement is informed by the political principles of critical feminist vision. It is interesting to see, for example, that many Latin American women believe certain principles work in their own interest when they actually work in the service of the values ordained for them by patriarchal society. Hence, both in Mexico and in South America, many of these movements will not call themselves "feminist" but rather "feminine."[21] From my

---

18. Lora, "Mujer," 25.

19. These aspects are not dealt with in the studies undertaken by Western and geopolitical northern feminism.

20. See María Candelaria Navas Turcios, ed., *Jornadas feministas: Feminismo y sectores populares en América Latina* (Mexico City: EMAS, CIDHAL, GEM, 1987); Teresita de Barbieri and Orlandina De Oliveira, "La presencia política de las mujeres: Nuevos sujetos sociales y nuevas formas de hacer política," *ISIS Internacional* 11 (1989) 67–78.

21. Aquino, "Feminismo," 513.

point of view, the use of this concept presents enormous ethical, political, and epistemological difficulties due to the significance that the term "feminine" has in the androcentric world and how it serves to reproduce the patriarchal order. In addition, the term "feminine" is the one endorsed by the conservative sectors of the church and society, for whom it functions as a weapon against the feminist movement. In many cases, resistance to the feminist vision and strategy comes not only from men and the androcentric culture but also from women themselves.

In the context of Latina American communities, the process of becoming aware of women's own interests takes on different characteristics in each movement, due to the variety of contextual locations.[22] Although every feminist movement recognizes the personal and collective experiences of struggle against oppression as the starting point for analysis and an identification of common problems and strategies, such experiences are also varied. Among Latina American women it is understood that there can be no "unique experience" as single criterion for the development of consciousness (for example, social class, race, or gender), since the experience is different in the hegemonic countries of the North and the dominated countries of the South. Different experiences will also be found among white women vis-à-vis black, indigenous, and mestiza women. Those who belong to the dominant cultures do not share the context of those who are the subalterns. The experience of oppression and marginalization that women have had is shaped in different ways, as are our needs and interests, in accordance with the concrete contexts in which we find ourselves.

This observation means that the development of critical feminist awareness takes place at different levels and is not exempt from contradictions. Such awareness cannot be appreciated unidimensionally but only in relation to real social practices and in correlation with the forces that interact in the different historical contexts. Such an assertion emphasizes the fact that feminist awareness, as intellectual and experiential process, starts with the events lived by women *without creating an abstraction out of these*. Women acquire critical awareness of and by themselves starting from their own reality. The Peruvian feminist Virginia Vargas states:

Women build themselves from the concrete daily life situations. . . . Individually and collectively, [they build themselves] from the history of life that contains other oppressions and discriminations, anchored in marginalized life because of class, age, or region. These [other experiences of oppression and discrimination] begin to acquire their true meaning when understood through the unique experience of women's gender-based oppression.[23]

---

22. Ibid., 516–17.
23. Virginia Vargas, "Aportes teóricos: Educación popular y construcción de la identidad de género," *Tejiendo Nuestra Red* 2 (1989) 16.

Finally, the current experiences of women seem organized around a number of common principles, which in turn trigger further struggles. The following are a number of these fundamental principles and goals that we struggle for:

- a social order where human relationships can be symmetrical and equal

- access to and exercise of real egalitarian and liberating political power

- the implementation of a vision in which biological differences do not create hierarchical relationships but rather affirm the diversity of humans in a political equality

- the elimination of the current hierarchical structures of gender while rebuilding the mechanisms for personal and collective participation

- egalitarian redistribution of public and private social labor

- mutual self-determination in the exercise of sexuality and the implementation of mechanisms that would ensure the physical and spiritual integrity of men and women

- the attainment of basic rights necessary for the existence and survival of humans and other creatures of the earth, together with the reconstruction of mechanisms that will rehabilitate the earth and assure the universal, austere, and sustainable use of its resources

- recovery of and equal access to those conditions of human renewal for well-being, relaxation, and creativity

- shared responsibility in all aspects of human existence and its development, especially in childhood and old age

Needless to say, these expressions, and others not mentioned here, reclaim for men and women the basic human freedom to choose a different route.

Today, this vision activates in women that original freedom to make decisions—a freedom so often suppressed by the church, by the suppressive logic inherent to modernity, and by patriarchal society. The exercise of true freedom helps to translate this vision into the language of each culture, thereby nourishing the vision of a new creation. As Latina American feminist women well recognize, "En nuestra diversidad está nuestra riqueza, en nuestro proyecto común está nuestra fuerza" (In our diversity lies our richness, in our common project our power).[24]

---

24. Materials from the third Encuentro Continental de Mujeres, held in 1988 in La Habana, Cuba, in *Frente continental de mujeres contra la intervención* (La Habana: n.p., 1988) 2.

Reappropriating Our Right to Think and Dissent:
Latina American Women in Theology

It must be recognized that, in general, Latin American liberation theology done by men has been insensitive to the experience of women and has not given any relevance to their transformative practice as motivated by faith. This theology, including the works of some women theologians, has also *covered* the existence of women as a formal theological subject. Consequently, Latin American liberation theology has also appropriated the unfortunate patriarchal expression from Matthew's Gospel, "besides women and children" (Matt 14:21), and incorporated it into its own interpretative categories of reality and faith.

I want to make clear, however, that without liberation theology the incorporation of Latina American women in the theological task simply could not have been possible. Liberation theology has been, to a great extent, the theology that opened up to women the possibility of participating in the elaboration of a theological discourse based on our own experience.[25] Feminist theology refers, in my view, to a personal and collective effort of critical reflection on the experience of God's activity in the lives of poor and oppressed women as we struggle for justice and life. Today women are giving new directions to the finality of theology: theological knowledge has as its goal the realization, extension, and fulfillment of the liberating purpose of God in our own historical circumstance.

Theological reflection carried out by Latina American women is in a process of maturation. In the United States,[26] in the Latin American continent, and in the Caribbean,[27] one can see the emergence of feminist theological thought. This theology has the ability to respond to our questions and desires in the very search for and selection of new concepts that allow for the coherent expression of our experience of faith in tune with our sociocultural universe and within the framework of our own liberating traditions. The feminist theological thought being developed by a new generation of Latina American feminist theologians understands itself within the framework of liberation theologies that accompany critically the pro-

---

25. In another place I have presented the reasons for this phenomenon; see María Pilar Aquino, *Our Cry for Life: Feminist Theology from Latin America* (Maryknoll, N.Y.: Orbis Books, 1993) 62–77.

26. Although the number of Latina feminist theologians is on the rise (for example, Jeanette Rodríguez and other women members of the Academy of Catholic Hispanic Theologians of the United States [ACHTUS]), Ada María Isasi-Díaz is the one who has had a truly important role by opening new ways of thinking our own faith-experience through *mujerista* theology.

27. The works of Ivone Gebara, Elsa Tamez, María Clara Bingemer, Ana María Tepedino, Raquel Rodríguez, Tereza Cavalcanti, and Nelly Ritchie are already well known. Some of these theologians, however, do not characterize themselves as "feminist" (Tamez, Bingemer) and take no part in the elaboration of a feminist theology; at the same time, a new generation of excellent Latin American feminist theologians is on the rise.

cesses of oppressed peoples in the transformation of their sufferings. It also understands itself, however, as in critical distance from any theological discourse that hides the struggles of women, such as androcentric liberation theologies. It seeks to contribute to the creation of an alternative order built on the principle of fullness of life for all creation.[28] This new current of thought understands itself as part of that great flow of vital intelligence that runs through the world of the poor, wishing to collect especially the cries, struggles, and hopes of poor and oppressed women qua women.

The preceding affirmations assume that we are interested in the eradication not only of the causes that impoverish women along with our people but also of those that oppress us because of our condition as women, given the polymorphous character of oppressive structures in today's society and church. In our context, both society and church continue to be strongly patriarchal, perpetuating the colonizing behavior that *covers up* the very existence of women. At this juncture, feminist theological discourse becomes a constitutive element of the strategies for liberation. Three main features of this theology should be highlighted.

1. The first feature of this theology is the very fact that women are creatively participating in the elaboration of theological knowledge. Latina women are not surprised that theology has been considered traditionally a discipline of, for, and by men. Iberian patriarchal colonization made this fact very clear. Latina American women, however, bring a new element to theological discourse. This new element can be expressed only by dealing with and overcoming serious obstacles and problems. Among these are the following: (*a*) While in many countries in Europe theology is recognized and accepted as a legitimate field of learning, in Latin America theology is not a profession recognized by either governments or society. (*b*) While in North America lay or religious women can attend state or church universities to obtain degrees in theology or religious studies and then use their education as a means to support themselves, in Latin America laywomen have not had this chance and cannot consider theology as a way to make a living.

A number of factors account for such a situation in Latin America. First, laywomen theologians would never be able to teach theology in state universities because such posts do not exist. Second, women who come from the poor classes can have access to academic theology only if supported by a few, sensitive institutions. Third, universities affiliated with Catholic or Protestant churches give preference to male clerics (with a few exceptions in Brazil and Costa Rica). Fourth, Catholic universities, by and large, would not easily tolerate a "liberation theologian," and much less a "feminist." Fifth, while in Europe and North America there are many universities

---

28. Ivone Gebara, *Poder e nao-poder das mulheres* (São Paulo: Ediçoes Paulinas, 1991) 33–41.

with religious studies departments and significant money for funding schol-
arships, this is simply not the case in Latin America, and these resources
are nonexistent in the Caribbean. I know of no Latin American bishop
who would grant a scholarship to a woman for the purpose of studying
theology.

The consequences for women can be readily discerned. Let me mention,
for example, the fact that in five hundred years of the presence of Christianity in Latin America, we can count with the fingers of one hand the number
of women who have obtained doctoral degrees in theology. There are not
even ten of us in the vast expanse of the continent, and not all of us have
incorporated the category of sex/gender as a constitutive matrix for our
theology. In the case of Latina American women theologians in the United
States, we often see ourselves at an academic disadvantage vis-à-vis Euro-
American women, who limit our access to the academic posts they hold
and in many instances even fight us, while continuing to call themselves
"feminists."

2. The second feature of Latina American feminist theology is its
understanding of women as being simultaneously subjects and objects of
theology. This understanding has had a significant impact on the epistemological framework of liberation theology. Until very recently, questions
coming from the physical and spiritual experience of women had been covered up, taken for granted, or passed over by the theologies created by men
(most of whom are white and members of the clergy). In their theology the
voice and expectations of women are often subsumed under the generic category of "the poor." Such emphasis and reflection on the concept of "the
poor"—informed strictly by the significance it has in dialectical theory and
concentrated until recently on class conflicts—have resulted in the concealment of the multiple power relations faced by women and the creation of
an androcentric discourse. With this procedure, an *abstraction* was made
as to who makes up the "poor and oppressed." In this way it was forgotten
(covered up) that impoverished indigenous, black, and mestiza women are
the ones who bear the heaviest burden of oppression. The struggles of these
women, even their very existence, were not incorporated by Latin American liberation theology as a crucial "reading key" of religious and social
processes.

In contrast, feminist theological thinking understands that reflection on
the experience of God, within liberating practice, has to account for the
struggles of women. Moreover, Latin American feminist theology must
construct itself self-consciously, selecting feminist movements and women's
movements as its privileged interlocutors. This implies that feminist theology must confront and assist the transformation of the structures that
cause the daily erosion of women's lives, their dependents, and the earth.
That is to say, theological reflection must confront historical reality *as it is
and as it presents itself*. We cannot pass over the convergence and mutual

reinforcement of three structures that act together in today's society and church, creating a triadic system: (*a*) totalitarian capitalism in its neoliberal version; (*b*) the patriarchal structure pervading all aspects of existence; and (*c*) contemporary colonialism, which continues to legitimize the supremacy of modern Western culture and white male paradigms to the detriment of other cultures, races, and, especially, women.

3. A third feature of Latina American feminist theology is the relevance and importance given *to daily life*.[29] This theology understands that active paradigms, traditions, and categories supporting the social construction of reality reside and operate in the daily life of people. They are all actualized in personal and collective living, thereby enabling the reproduction or transformation of the present order. In the daily life of people reside the values and categories on which social consensus is based.

Theology done by men has created an abstraction of daily life, and here I point particularly to Latin American male liberation theologians. Such an abstraction can be readily perceived in the following two ways: (*a*) the exclusive emphasis given to conflict in the public sphere, resulting in a *covering up* of the violence done to women in the private sphere; and (*b*) the self-interested lack of awareness of the political character of the biological, the sexual, and the domestic, thereby maintaining the subaltern status of women.

The abstraction made of daily life also appears in the priority given to the transformation of the global socioeconomic structures, while overlooking the changes that ought to take place in daily life. This in turn has caused a deviation in the understanding of reality, underestimating the transforming potential found in the personal and private arena. When daily asymmetrical relationships between men and women in the private or public spheres are not perceived, existence is dissociated and alienation occurs in daily life. In other words, due as much to the division established by patriarchal culture between the public and private arenas as to the lack of awareness of its "daily" character, the theological outlook of men has obscured the oppressive relationships that are lived out in the private arena and has hidden the relationships of dominance and violence carried out in both arenas.

Daily life, in the androcentric perspective, does not contain any epistemological value, nor does it form part of its comprehension of reality. Consequently, daily life does not affect the theological task. Latina American feminist theology, in contrast, understands that in daily life the real existence of people is carried out. Daily life is where real transformations take place. Daily life has to do with the totality of life. It produces, reproduces, and multiplies the totality of social relationships. In it anyone can clearly discover the concrete exercise of male power. Asymmetrical re-

---

29. See Aquino, *Cry for Life*, 33–37.

lationships occur in a repetitive and continuous form in both the public and private arenas, because this is how they acquire a daily character. In this sense, life has a fundamental political and religious role in the theological task of women. Its importance is even greater from the standpoint of the Christian faith, since theological reflection seeks to contribute to the creation of new models of social relationships. In other words, because the liberating traditions of Christianity demand human relationships based on solidarity and egalitarian discipleship, theological discourse must contribute to the end of inertia in oppressive daily relationships. Women emphasize that the processes of liberation in the public sphere cannot happen separately or at the margin of the liberating experiences occurring in the private realm. Both spheres must interrelate in their shared struggle for the fullness of life, justice, and common solidarity. Only through this interrelation can there be a new way of experiencing daily life. Furthermore, we have no other place to actualize the egalitarian ethical values of Christianity outside of daily life.

The transformation of the current social system, rooted as it is in an oppressive daily life, is a task equally for women and men. What women propose in theological reflection is a joint effort to eliminate the ancestral divisions affecting humanity. In the same way, both men and women must commit ourselves and learn to relate to the earth in nondomineering ways. As Tereza Cavalcanti points out, "Only on a socialized earth, with all its products and wealth fairly redistributed, can women give birth to new, communitarian women and men, a free and solidarious generation."[30] This vision empowers the social construction of justice and human integrity according to the liberating traditions of our native cultures, biblical Israel, and the early church.

Concluding Comments

For many Latinas it is clear that neither the church nor society has granted women, willfully, the right to imagination and theological creativity. We have appropriated that right as a means of expressing our commitment to a different future for ourselves and for those who depend on us. We are convinced that things should and can change. This leads us to dissent from the current asymmetrical order. Latina American feminist theology seeks to maintain the dialogical tension between present reality and God's activity in history, which is always unpredictable and always beyond manipulation.

---

30. Tereza Cavalcanti, "Produzindo teología no femenino plural: A propósito do III Encontro Nacional de Teologia na Perspectiva da Mulher," *Perspectiva Teológica* 20 (1988) 363. See Catharina Halkes, "The Rape of Mother Earth: Ecology and Patriarchy," *Concilium* 206 (1989) 91–100; and idem, *New Creation: Christian Feminism and the Renewal of the Earth* (Louisville: Westminster/John Knox Press, 1991).

It is from here that feminist theological creativity derives, since in the effort to formulate new questions and in the search for new answers, the theological task of women remains ever open to God's wisdom. Theological contents are elaborated at the convergence of the liberating traditions of the Christian faith and our own sociocultural universe. Latina American women cannot forget that fullness of life, integrity, and self-determination cannot happen at the expense of our daily wasting away. Similarly, we must remember that human integrity is not possible if we are systematically condemned to haggle for our own integrity. Liberation cannot be achieved at the price of hiding the violence women suffer in daily life, a violence sometimes caused by women themselves. On the contrary, instead of losing ourselves by fighting against each other, in a manner similar to that of patriarchal power, our great challenge is the collective *un-covery* of our own power to raise ourselves up and the *dis-covery* of our own strength to bring about a different future.

Part Three _____

Expressions of Hispanic/Latino Theology

14

U.S. Hispanic Popular Catholicism as Theopoetics

Roberto S. Goizueta

> *Before the message there must be the vision, before the sermon the hymn, before the prose the poem.*
>
> *Before any new theologies however secular and radical there must be a contemporary theopoetic....*
>
> *It is not enough for the church to be on guard against the Philistine in the world. Philistinism invades Christianity from within wherever the creative and mythopoetic dimension of faith is forfeited. When this happens doctrine becomes a caricature of itself. Then that which once gave life begins to lull and finally to suffocate us.*
>
> —Amos Niven Wilder, *Theopoetic*

One of the most devastating consequences of Western rationalism on Christian theology has been the divorce between theological form and content. This reduction of the theological enterprise—no longer rooted in a way of life—to the development and communication of ideas has been accompanied by the depreciation of preconceptual knowledge, now universally suspect because of its diffuse and hence "contentless" character. In turn, the traditional forms for communicating such knowledge—symbol, ritual, narrative, metaphor, poetry, music, the arts—are necessarily marginalized as unacademic and unscholarly, that is, as pure (aesthetic) form without (conceptual) content. The effects for theology have been little short of catastrophic as the ruminations of professional theologians in the West have become increasingly irrelevant not only to the churches and the everyday lives of Christians but also to the very academy with which modern Western theology has cast its lot.

The research for and writing of this essay were supported by a Summer Research Stipend in the History of U.S. Hispanic Catholics from the Cushwa Center for the Study of American Catholicism at the University of Notre Dame.

Having spent so many decades attempting to prove ourselves true scholars by demonstrating the "scientific" status of our discipline to a skeptical
academy, we have been left in the lurch by the very scientists upon whom
we had sycophantically modeled ourselves—they themselves, it seems, are
no longer interested in the quest for scientific objectivity, having moved on
to quantum physics, relativity, energy fields, quarks, and the like. Similarly,
we have become increasingly irrelevant to the faith communities that we
claim to represent and, therefore, increasingly desperate in our attempts to
say *something* that actually *matters* to people—not least of all to ourselves.
Theology has indeed become academic.

In his plea for a theopoetic as a response to the marginalization of theology in contemporary society, Amos Niven Wilder calls for a renewed
recognition of the fact that "the structures of faith and confession have
always rested on hierophanies and images" and that "human nature and
human societies are more deeply motivated by images and fabulations than
by ideas."[1] A theology that fails to thus move and motivate cannot claim
to be speaking of the liberating God of the exodus or the crucified God
of Calvary: "We speak about a theopoetic because the theme of divinity
requires a dynamic and dramatic speech."[2] "How could Christianity have
become such a universal power," asks Hans Urs von Balthasar, "if it had
always been as sullen as today's humourless and anguished Protestantism,
or as grumpy as the super-organized Catholicism about us?"[3] Unmoved by
their own sullen and grumpy religious traditions, Western Christians have
learned—out of frustration—to look elsewhere for inspiration and enthusiasm: Eastern religions, pagan mythologies, New Age mysticism, and so
on. Even the phenomenal growth of evangelical, fundamentalist, and Pentecostal forms of Christianity can be partially attributed to the failure of
modern mainline Protestantism and modern European Catholicism to tap
the theopoetic or aesthetic roots of Christian theology.

To emphasize the theopoetic is not to suggest, however, that reason is
an insignificant element of theological reflection or that aesthetic form is
separable from theological content. On the contrary, we must recover the
fundamental unity of what modern epistemologies and anthropologies have
divided: namely, human praxis itself. In so doing, we would recover a fuller
sense of God's revelation and, therefore, of the theological task. We must
seek an increased "attention to the modes and vehicles of the Word."[4] To
insist on the theopoetic basis of theology is simply to aver, as Heidegger

---

1. Amos Niven Wilder, *Theopoetic: Theology and the Religious Imagination* (Philadelphia: Fortress Press, 1976) 1–2.

2. Ibid., 12.

3. Hans Urs von Balthasar, *The Glory of the Lord: A Theological Aesthetics*, vol. 1,
Seeing the Form (San Francisco: Ignatius Press, 1982) 494.

4. Wilder, *Theopoetic*, 6.

does, that all original ideas are of their essence poetical.[5] Sixto García contends

that theological language is, in one certain and specific sense, poetic language, even the most dense and difficult to decode. The theologian, hence, is not only the interpreter of the faith experience of a community of which he or she is an active member, but also its poet, who has before him or her unlimited possibilities of liberationist and redemptive creativity.[6]

The origin of reason is in-spiration or en-thusiasm, that is, the indwelling of the Spirit or God.[7] Theology, therefore, must be attuned to "the deeper vocabulary and idiom of the Spirit."[8] "One does not persuade," writes Gaston Bachelard, "except by suggesting the fundamental dreams, except by restoring to thought its avenues of dreaming."[9] This does not suggest a disparagement but only a contextualization, more precisely a re-form-ation, of reason and rational analysis.[10] Only when the link between theopoetic imagination, understood as a divine indwelling, and reason is severed does the latter degenerate into a dry, "grumpy" rationalism, deprived of enthusiasm, spirit—and, therefore, deprived of truth.

Likewise, ethics is born of imagination:

Creative imagination is the supreme faculty of moral humanity. Through it persons perceive the possible that is latent in the actual but that would be unseen by any less exalted consciousness. Because the process of moral decision-making is not just a process of passing judgment on the goodness and badness of persons or on the rightness and wrongness of actions, moral thinking at its best must perceive values that do not yet exist and must bring them into being through productive acts.[11]

Rubem Alves warns against separating the ethical imperative from the aesthetic imagination: "The goal of all heroic struggles for the creation of a just and free world is the opening of spaces for the blossoming of the gar-

---

5. See Sixto García, "A Hispanic Approach to Trinitarian Theology: The Dynamics of Celebration, Reflection, and Praxis," *We Are a People! Initiatives in Hispanic American Theology* (ed. Roberto S. Goizueta; Minneapolis: Fortress Press, 1992) 116. In this article García examines the role of the U.S. Hispanic theologian as a poet within the community. See also his "United States Hispanic and Mainstream Trinitarian Theologies," *Frontiers of Hispanic Theology in the United States* (ed. Allan Figueroa Deck; Maryknoll, N.Y.: Orbis Books, 1992) 92–93.

6. García, "Hispanic Approach," 116.

7. Von Balthasar, *Seeing the Form,* 35.

8. Wilder, *Theopoetic,* 6.

9. Cited in Rubem Alves, *The Poet, the Warrior, the Prophet* (London: SCM Press, 1990) 103.

10. For a discussion of the proper and necessary role of critical rational analysis vis-à-vis preconceptual forms of knowledge, see Orlando Espín, "Tradition and Popular Religion: An Understanding of the *Sensus Fidelium,*" *Frontiers of Hispanic Theology,* 62–87, esp. 65–67, 77–80.

11. Stephen Happel and James Walter, *Conversion and Discipleship: A Christian Foundation for Ethics and Doctrine* (Philadelphia: Fortress Press, 1986) 168.

den [of paradise]."[12] When this link is severed, ethics degenerates into mere legalism.

And all three—imagination, reason, and ethics—have a single common and unifying ground: human praxis. More precisely, the affective, aesthetic imagination, the rational intellect, and ethical-political commitment are all intrinsic dimensions of human praxis.[13] As intersubjective action that reveals the intrinsic beauty, goodness, and truth of human community as an end in itself, human praxis calls forth imagination as we confront an-other, which itself calls forth both empathic action vis-à-vis the other, or authentic intersubjectivity, and rational understanding and communication with the other. (Too often, praxis has been simply reduced to ethics, with the inevitable consequence that praxis has been divorced from both theory, or critical reflection, and aesthetics, or affective, imaginative cognition. I am suggesting that praxis *grounds* aesthetics, theory, *and* ethics.)[14]

As I use the term, then, "praxis" is by definition communal or intersubjective action that has no external end or goal other than the action or relationship itself. Therefore, praxis is inherently aesthetic, involving an affective engagement with an-other, and ethical-political action, oriented toward the liberation of the other qua other, without which there can be no genuine relationship or community. Praxis is nothing other than human intersubjective action—that is, the relationships among whole human persons in community—as an end in itself. As such, it implies an ethical-political commitment to the promotion of those relationships insofar as they foster the full humanity (including the affective life) of the subjects, or persons, and therefore actually constitute authentic relationships between subjects.[15]

Thus, while a theopoetic gives rise to theological theory and ethics, theopoesis is itself rooted in communal, intersubjective praxis. Without a theopoetic mediation, any ethical or theoretical understanding of human praxis will reduce praxis (that is, the human person) to, respectively, a mere

---

12. Alves, *The Poet,* 127.

13. This fundamental unity and rootedness in praxis preclude the possibility of a theopoetics immune to theological and ethical critique. There can be no apolitical or a-theological affect any more than there can be an apolitical or affectless theology; the most sterile logic cannot be completely devoid of affect any more than a mind can exist without a body. A theopoetics that sets itself over against theology and ethics distorts human praxis and, thus, expresses a distorted view of the God revealed in that praxis.

14. A full, systematic development of the theoretical warrants for this assertion is beyond the scope of this essay, which focuses on U.S. Hispanic popular religiosity. For fuller discussions, see my articles: "Theology as Intellectually Vital Inquiry: The Challenge of/to U.S. Hispanic Theologians," *Proceedings of the Catholic Theological Society of America* 46 (1991) 58–69; "Rediscovering Praxis: The Significance of U.S. Hispanic Experience for Theological Method," *We Are a People!* 51–77. See also Happel and Walter, *Conversion and Discipleship,* esp. 107–11, 167–77, 216–22.

15. See Goizueta, "Rediscovering Praxis," and Joseph Dunne, *Back to the Rough Ground: "Phronesis" and "Techne" in Modern Philosophy and in Aristotle* (Notre Dame, Ind.: University of Notre Dame Press, 1993) 9–10.

instrument of ethical-political transformation or an abstract, ahistorical, conceptual "existence." In other words, when the focus of the theologian is exclusively either theological content or ethical-political means and ends, the crucial importance of form (that is, aesthetics, affect) is ignored. Can we truly speak *about* God if we cannot speak *as* God speaks in our world, that is, if we are blind to the *form* of God's revelation—in, for instance, the affective, preconceptual dimension of human relationships? And, if God is revealed through and is made present in the affect that "accompanies" human action, can we ultimately love other persons, or God, without being moved or affected by those relationships? Can any theology that calls it-self Christian ever be *un*enthusiastic or *un*inspired while still claiming to be speaking of God? If we are speaking about a God who, we claim, is loving, empowering, and liberating, a God for whom we are willing to lay down our very lives, will our theology be credible if its very form (for example, "sullen," "humorless," and "grumpy") denies that central claim? If God is also revealed through our affect, can we speak about a living God, a God of life, if our words and manner of speaking do not convey precisely that life and spirit? Can our theologies *de*note the "truth" while nevertheless *con*noting a lie?

As R. G. Collingwood observes with respect to written words, "If you don't know what tone to say them in, you can't say them at all: they are not words."[16] The tone of our words and the way we speak them must be consonant with their content, the reality about which we speak; our theological words then must be able to convey, or connote, the fact that the reality about whom we speak—that is, God—transcends all words and concepts. A theology that reduces aesthetic form to conceptual content is not—to paraphrase Collingwood—theology at all. "God needs prophets in order to make himself known, and all prophets are necessarily artists. What a prophet has to say can never be said in prose."[17] Prose is nec-essary for communicating the experiential knowledge of God, but prose always remains beholden to its poetic heritage: as Wilder avers, the vision *makes possible*—that is, does not obviate—the message, the hymn the ser-mon, and the poem the prose. The tone of our prose either will reflect the origins of our theologies in poetry or will obscure those origins. A Christian theopoetics would thus insist that our sermons be preached in the right tone and our theologies be con-formed to the praxis of the faith community.

At the same time, however, unless a Christian theopoetics is itself grounded in historical praxis, or communal intersubjective action as an end in itself, the imagination, the affect, and their evocative, symbolic, or poetic expressions will not promote such intersubjectivity but will, instead, serve

---

16. R. G. Collingwood, *The Principles of Art* (Oxford: Clarendon Press, 1938) 266.
17. F. Medicus, as cited in von Balthasar, *Seeing the Form*, 43.

the equally ahistorical ends of an instrumentalist ethics and a conceptualist theology, which will remain uninformed by a now disembodied theopoetics. When—rather than historical praxis—aesthetic ambiguity, otherness, and "feelings" become ends in themselves, praxis becomes paralyzed. The danger of such a historical paralysis is acknowledged in the following words that the Nicaraguan poet Juan Gonzalo Rose writes in a letter to his sister: "I ask myself now / why I do not limit my love / to the sudden roses, / the tides of June, / the moons over the sea? / Why have I had to love / the rose *and* justice, / the sea *and* justice, / justice *and* the light?"[18] A dehistoricized theopoetics is no less dangerous than a dehistoricized ethics or theology; such a theopoetics would be mere, narcissistic aestheticism. Theopoetics can never be an end in itself.[19]

---

18. Cited in Gustavo Gutiérrez, *We Drink from Our Own Wells: The Spiritual Journey of a People* (Maryknoll, N.Y.: Orbis Books, 1984) 163–64.

19. For more extended discussions, see Goizueta, "Theology as Intellectually Vital Inquiry," and "Rediscovering Praxis." As a form of revelation, theopoetics always points beyond itself; by definition, *theo*poetics points beyond mere aesthetics to a God who is made manifest in life itself, that is, in human praxis. Aestheticism is the consequence of a theopoetics that ceases to point beyond itself. One of the most imposing figures in modern Western aesthetics, the German composer Richard Wagner, was perhaps the most influential exponent of this aestheticism in late nineteenth-century Europe, with his influence extending far beyond the artistic world. Explicitly setting out to make of art a religion with its temple at Bayreuth, Wagner reduced all knowledge and ethics to aesthetics, or "feeling." In what amounts to a fine definition of aestheticism, he writes: "Only through *itself*...does...feeling become intelligible to itself: it understands no language other than its own....Now, an action which is to justify itself before and through the feeling, busies itself with no *moral;* its whole moral consists precisely in its justification by the instinctive human feeling. It is a goal to itself, in so far as it has to be vindicated only and precisely by the feeling out of which it springs" (cited in Albert Goldman and Evert Sprinchorn, eds., *Wagner on Music and Drama: A Compendium of Richard Wagner's Prose Works* [New York: Da Capo Press, 1964] 189–90). The goal of art, as represented by the romantic theater, thus became that of "reducing the audience to an unthinking, highly suggestible mass in which the individual was transported out of himself and made to drift with the tides of the universe" (Goldman and Sprinchorn, "Introduction," *Wagner on Music and Drama,* 29). Is it any wonder that Wagner's operas and philosophy were idolized by Hitler and fueled his drive for absolute power? To absolutize the preconceptual is to absolutize ambiguity, and absolute ambiguity is the handmaiden of totalitarian domination; both are ultimately nihilistic. Although it seems that Wagner himself perceived this danger at a later point, it was already too late. The damage had been done. Intoxicated by his vision of the state-as-aesthetic, which would be supported by an "unthinking, highly suggestible mass," Hitler was deaf to Wagner's later warning: "In youth we turn to Art, we know not why; and only when we have gone through with Art and come out on the other side, we learn to our cost that we have missed Life itself" (cited in George Bernard Shaw, *The Perfect Wagnerite: A Commentary on the Niblung's Ring* [New York: Dover, 1923] 99). Aestheticism, or absolute ambiguity, is seductive for the same reason that mass movements are seductive: they hold out to us the possibility of a flight from the demands of human consciousness and historicity. Hitler and Wagner were cohorts in the late romantic/postmodern project of deconstructing the self; in the name of that project, more than six million selves were "deconstructed" in the ovens of Nazi Germany. The dangers of an aesthetics oblivious to its intrinsic connection to rational thought and ethical action, insofar as all three are grounded in life-as-an-end-in-itself, can hardly be overstated and are evident in the corpses of the concentration camp victims.

U.S. Hispanic Popular Catholicism

As a principal mediator of the historical praxis of our communities, U.S. Hispanic popular religiosity mediates the relationship between aesthetics, ethics, and reason intrinsic to that praxis. Consequently, as we will see, popular religiosity can be an expression of a liberating, U.S. Hispanic theopoetics, which would in turn in-form U.S. Hispanic theology, not simply by providing theological content for the latter, but by actually shaping the form of our theological discourse.

In this essay, then, I will explore the relationship between praxis, *theopoesis,* theology, and ethics as it manifests itself in U.S. Hispanic popular religiosity and, specifically, popular Catholicism.[20] In its retrieval of popular religiosity as a *locus theologicus,* U.S. Hispanic theology can contribute to a renewed appreciation for the importance of a Christian theopoetic or aesthetics.[21] Properly understood as itself grounded in the historical praxis of an oppressed community, such a theopoetic would in-form the theological reflection of U.S. Hispanics in general and U.S. Hispanic theologians in particular. It is manifested especially in the popular religiosity of our communities. In retrieving popular religiosity as a *locus theologicus,* U.S. Hispanic theologians emphasize the importance of theopoetics for the identity and self-understanding of U.S. Hispanics, while at the same time pointing to one of the most significant differences—and sources of alienation—between U.S. Hispanic Christians and Anglo Christians.

Latinos and Latinas live in a world where God is revealed primarily in flesh and blood, in symbols and images; in Anglo society and its form of Christianity, we are faced with a God who is revealed primarily in clear and distinct ideas. Thus, for U.S. Hispanics, the greatest theologians are those members of our communities who most fully *embody* their faith: the saints, whether those publicly acknowledged by the church or the "hidden" saints in our families and communities. Truth, insists Justo González,

is concrete, historical truth. It does not exist in a world of pure ideas but rather is closely bound with bread and wine, with justice and peace, with a coming Reign of God—a Reign not over pure ideas or over disembodied souls but over a new society and a renewed history.... Our understanding of the nature [that is, form]

---

20. While I would suggest that the various expressions of U.S. Hispanic Protestantism also reveal the praxeological and theopoetic foundations of theology and ethics, the development of such a thesis is beyond the scope of my essay and my competence. I would, instead, refer the reader to the groundbreaking work of Samuel Solivan, especially his development of the notion of "orthopathos."

21. Hans Urs von Balthasar has written voluminously on a Christian theological aesthetics (*Glory of the Lord;* see, for example, n. 3 above and n. 43 below). In retrieving this critical dimension of the Christian faith and tradition, he has performed an important service. A serious drawback of his project, however, is that because it is not grounded in the historical praxis of oppressed communities, that is, in the preferential option for the poor or "ugly" as these are concretely present in our world, it yields an aesthetics that, by virtue of its abstraction, comes dangerously close to the very aestheticism he ostensibly rejects.

of truth must be such that the particular man Jesus, at a particular time and place, can say, "I am the truth."[22]

Such a view of the nature of Christian truth implies that, for the U.S. Hispanic theologian, "just as important as the written texts of tradition (or, in fact, more important) . . . is the *living witness and faith* of the Christian people."[23]

Popular religiosity is one important aspect of that embodiment in our Latino communities.[24] Orlando Espín and Sixto García define popular religiosity as "the set of experiences, beliefs and rituals which ecclesially and socially peripheral groups create and develop in their search for an access to God and salvation."[25] Thus, U.S. Hispanic popular religiosity is, by definition, a theopoetic mediation of the historical praxis of an *oppressed, marginalized* community. Because of its sociohistorical origins and locus on the "periphery," U.S. Hispanic popular religiosity "is probably the least 'invaded' area of any of the Hispanic cultures, one of the most 'popular' of our peoples' creations, and the more deeply 'ours.' "[26] In a world that denies "our" existence as persons with our own histories, "our" popular religiosity is thus a radical affirmation of the fact that, against all odds, we have been, are, and will continue to be full human persons with our own histories and identities. These have been acknowledged and affirmed by God. For a people victimized through conquest, "the conquered's fundamental core religious symbols provide the ultimate root of the group's identity, because they mediate the absolute."[27]

Hispanic popular Catholicism, then, is that version of the Catholic faith "born of popular religiosity and handed down through generations by the laity more than by the teachers and ordained ministers of the Church."[28] In the face of a Catholicism experienced as alien and foreboding, "it was the deep faith and simple home practices of our *abuelitas* and *abuelitos* (grandparents) that sustained us in the faith and maintained us loyal to the Catholic tradition."[29] Ours is a popular wisdom that

creatively combines the divine and the human, Christ and Mary, spirit and body, communion and institution, person and community, faith and homeland, intelli-

---

22. Justo González, *Mañana: Christian Theology from a Hispanic Perspective* (Nashville: Abingdon Press, 1990) 50. To Hispanics, it sometimes seems as though Anglos do not really believe that "the Word was made flesh."

23. Espín, "Tradition and Popular Religion," 64.

24. For a fascinating analysis of popular religiosity as an "embodiment" of dogmatic truth, see Espín, "Tradition and Popular Religion."

25. Orlando Espín and Sixto García, "'Lilies of the Field': A Hispanic Theology of Providence and Human Responsibility," *Proceedings of the Catholic Theological Society of America* 44 (1989) 73.

26. Ibid.

27. Virgilio Elizondo, "*Mestizaje* as a Locus of Theological Reflection," *Frontiers of Hispanic Theology*, 107.

28. Espín and García, "Lilies of the Field," 75.

29. Elizondo, "*Mestizaje*," 105.

gence and emotion. This wisdom is a Christian humanism that radically affirms the dignity of every person as a child of God, establishes a basic fraternity, teaches people how to encounter nature and understand work, and provides reasons for joy and humor even in the midst of a very hard life.[30]

This popular wisdom is expressed primarily, though not exclusively, through symbol and ritual. Gilbert Romero has examined the role of symbol and ritual in U.S. Hispanic popular religiosity:

Every devotional practice in religiosidad popular has a certain amount of symbolism: significant event, gesture, object, place, and the like. And it is these symbols that have a revelatory dimension.... Symbolism gives participatory knowledge that is self-involving. That is to say, the symbol speaks to us only insofar as it draws us into its world of meaning.... Symbol, insofar as it involves the knower as a person, has a transforming effect.... Symbolism has a powerful influence on commitments and behavior, stirring the imagination and releasing heretofore untapped resources of energy.[31]

These symbols—and the attendant narratives and rituals—serve the theologian as reminders that, in the words of Sixto García, "the Hispanic mind, especially the religious-theological mind, performs in deep contact with myths, stories, traditions, and nature, and this contact, this dialogue, requires a poetic framework in its theological formulations."[32] A theology that truly reflects and expresses "the Hispanic mind" will do so not only in content but also in form; a U.S. Hispanic theology cannot help but be, at bottom, a theopoetic discourse nourished by the symbols, rituals, and stories in which are embodied our profound faith in the living God. Insofar as these are *lived* or participatory symbols, rituals, and stories, they reflect not only the U.S. Hispanic mind but also the historical praxis of U.S. Hispanic communities; they reveal not only *what* we believe but also *how* we live and *how* we believe. ("How" here refers not to technique or method but to form, that is, the form that our lives and beliefs take.)[33]

Precisely because the formal or aesthetic dimension of that praxis is as properly "U.S. Hispanic" as its ethical-political intent or its theological content, a theopoetics will be a necessary propaedeutic to any U.S. Hispanic theology. If our task is to articulate the theological significance of the praxis of our communities, and if a principal expression of that praxis is our popular religiosity, then the theological significance of our popular religiosity derives as much from the form, or aesthetics, that characterizes our symbols, rituals, and practices as from the beliefs or worldviews

---

30. Juan Carlos Scannone, cited in Allan Figueroa Deck, *The Second Wave: Hispanic Ministry and the Evangelization of Cultures* (New York: Paulist Press, 1989) 116.

31. C. Gilbert Romero, *Hispanic Devotional Piety: Tracing the Biblical Roots* (Maryknoll, N.Y.: Orbis Books, 1991) 51. For an analysis of the affective power of symbol, see also Bernard Lonergan, *Method in Theology* (New York: Seabury Press, 1979) 64–69.

32. García, "A Hispanic Approach," 116; see also García, "Trinitarian Theologies," 93.

33. See Espín, "Tradition and Popular Religion," 64–65.

expressed therein. Consequently, a theology that takes popular religiosity seriously, not simply as an object of theology but as a *way* of expressing the community's living encounter with God, cannot degenerate into conceptualism without thereby implicitly denying that which it explicitly proclaims. If popular religiosity is the *"form* of faith's self-understanding" in the U.S. Hispanic community, this way of being religious ought to be reflected not only in the content of our theologies (as when popular religiosity is an object of or source for theological reflection) but also in the very form of our theologies (what they evoke and connote).[34]

If the epistemological privilege of the poor implies that the poor have a privileged access to the content of revelation ("what" is revealed in the historical praxis of marginalized communities), so too does it imply that the poor have a privileged access to the form of revelation ("how" it is revealed, expressed, embodied, and lived out).[35] If the Hispanic theologian is to understand and articulate the meaning or content of our community's faith, that understanding and articulation must be in-formed by the very manner in which our faith is lived out in the community, a manner that is essentially theopoetic. It is a manner whose passion and fervor bespeak a profound communal experience of and relationship with the living, liberating God.[36] Thus, the U.S. Hispanic theologian not only "talks about" and analyzes that profound communal experience of God but seeks to incarnate it in his or her theology, so that the theologian's words will not merely provide information *about* this God but will actually facilitate the community's relationship *with* God, a relationship already mediated through popular religion. If not in-formed by that relationship, our theology denies its own roots.

It is the form of our popular religiosity, the manner in which it is lived out (that is, the "way" we are religious) that, grounded in the historical praxis of the U.S. Hispanic community as a marginalized community,

34. Douglas John Hall, *Thinking the Faith: Christian Theology in a North American Context* (Minneapolis: Augsburg, 1989) 84. Hall defines theological contextuality as taking seriously the form in which the content of the faith is understood and expressed in a particular community.

35. This is in no way to suggest that popular religious expressions ought to be immune to theological critique or critique from the larger ecclesial body in its magisterial function. Indeed, insofar as those expressions continue to bear the marks of centuries of conquest—political, cultural, economic, and ideological—such critique is essential: "If the Christian people's reality is mainly a wounded and invaded context, the truth that the Spirit stirs within them will then express itself in a wounded and invaded manner" (Espín, "Tradition and Popular Religion," 77). See ibid., 77–80, for a more extended discussion of the limitations of popular religiosity. See also n. 80 below for an example, in Marian symbolism, of the limitations of popular religiosity.

36. See Espín, "Tradition and Popular Religion." In this article, Espín explores the relationship between aesthetic or theopoetic form and theological content by interpreting popular religion as a *way* of life and prayer that, rooted in an intuitive, preconceptual "sense" of the Christian truth, reflects the *sensus fidelium* (as distinct but inseparable from the dogmatic content of the faith).

reveals the intrinsically liberating character of U.S. Hispanic popular religiosity. While the theological content of that popular religiosity may, to the modern Western mind, appear to suggest a spiritualized, dualistic eschatology that would promote a this-worldly passivity and resignation, the theopoetic form of popular religiosity—again, grounded in the historical praxis of a marginalized community—reveals its true liberating power. To examine the importance of this theopoetic for U.S. Hispanic theology, I will focus on two symbols, the crucifix and Mary, that play key roles in U.S. Hispanic popular Catholicism. As Espín and García point out, the crucified Christ and Mary are the two great symbols "that appear to be central and organizing symbols in Hispanic popular Catholicism," and these symbols are inextricably related in our spirituality.[37]

The Crucifix

The centrality of the crucifix in Hispanic popular Catholicism is hard to miss, even for the most casual outside observer:

It would be difficult to find a Catholic Church in Latin America, or even in a U.S. Hispanic barrio, without an image of the suffering Christ. The craftsmen and artificers spare no sensibilities in conveying, in wood and paint, the agony and suffering of their blood-covered Christs....Hispanic popular participation in the Paschal triduum traditionally emphasizes the celebration of Good Friday....The Paschal Vigil and Easter celebration, in some instances, are quite anticlimactic to the celebration of Good Friday.[38]

Espín and García explain that the symbols and popular Catholic devotions surrounding Jesus' passion "represent the co-suffering of Jesus the Christ with the poor, the hungry and the oppressed of the celebrating Hispanic communities."[39] Virgilio Elizondo writes in a similar vein:

It should not be surprising that devotion to the crucified Lord—scourged, bleeding, agonizing—is one of the deepest traits of the Mexican American faith. *Cruz* ("cross") is a not uncommon name given to [Mexican American] children. *El Viernes Santo* (Good Friday) is the Mexican American celebration *par excellence.* ...The drama of Good Friday is not just celebrated ritually in the churches but lived out by the Mexican American people. Beginning on Holy Thursday with the agony in the garden, on Good Friday the way of the cross is reenacted by the people, then the crucifixion, and the seven last words from Jesus on the cross. Fi-

---

37. Ibid., 70.

38. Orlando Espín and Sixto García, "Hispanic-American Theology," *Proceedings of the Catholic Theological Society of America* 44 (1989) 85.

39. Orlando Espín and Sixto García, "Sources of Hispanic Theology," 10 (unpublished paper delivered at the annual meeting of the Catholic Theological Society of America, Toronto, 1988).

nally, in the evening, there is the *pésame a la Virgen* ("visit to the Virgin")....The final Good Friday reenactment is the burial service.[40]

In the context of modern rationalism, these images and practices may appear as morbid glorifications of death and suffering; in the context of modern instrumentalist rationality, they may appear as useless aberrations inasmuch as, by focusing on suffering, they cannot serve as instruments of liberation. In the context of postmodern aestheticism or a romantic, dehistoricized aestheticism, these images and practices may be idealized as aesthetic representations of otherness, difference, and nonidentity—precisely vis-à-vis the modern rationalist emphasis on conceptual uniformity and identity.

Yet these interpretations abstract the U.S. Hispanic spirituality of the cross from its historical context. The crucified Christ of Latino popular religiosity is a symbol whose theopoetic, evocative otherness is derived not only from its substantive value as a work of art but also from its ongoing history within that community and the form or manner in which the community "participates in" the symbol. It is this historical context itself and, thus, the manner of participation that are "other" and that, thus, lend the symbol its transformative power: "Though many of these images or paintings [of the crucified Christ] may have true artistic value in themselves, the religious value is usually conveyed not by beauty itself but by the work's ability to elicit feelings of solidarity and compassion."[41]

This solidarity and compassion become, in turn, the basis of the community's identity and, thus, of its ability to withstand and resist the imposition of identity from without. What makes such solidarity and compassion possible is the community's own experience of crucifixion, the community's own historical participation in Jesus' crucifixion: "His [that is, the crucified Christ's] passion and death express his solidarity with all men and women throughout history who have also innocently suffered at the hands of evildoers."[42] The crucifixion is the definitive verification of our belief, as Christians, that "the God of the Bible is neither a *tremendum* nor a *fascinosum,* but first of all an *adorandum.*"[43] Only when viewed within the context of his own historical praxis does the cross of Jesus attain ethical-political significance as a theopoetic symbol of empowerment and liberation; only when viewed within the context of our historical praxis as a community does the crucified Jesus attain ethical-political significance as

---

40. Virgilio Elizondo, *Galilean Journey: The Mexican-American Promise* (Maryknoll, N.Y.: Orbis Books, 1983) 41–42. See also Espín, "Tradition and Popular Religion," 70–71, for descriptions of the symbols and religious practices associated with the crucified Jesus and Good Friday.

41. Espín, "Tradition and Popular Religion," 70.

42. Ibid., 71.

43. Hans Urs von Balthasar, *The Glory of the Lord: A Theological Aesthetics,* vol. 7, *Theology: The New Covenant* (Edinburgh: T. and T. Clark, 1989) 268.

a theopoetic symbol of hope—a hope born of the crucified Jesus' identification with us in our own crucifixion: "The broken humanity of Jesus stands as a sacrament of the brokenness of the body of the Hispanic communities. Jesus the Christ is our brother in sorrow and oppression, and we can touch him, mourn with him, die with him, and yes, also hope with him."[44] For this reason, the symbol is almost always a crucifix, rarely an empty cross.

Yet this liberative power of our identification with the crucified Jesus becomes evident only if we shed an instrumentalist view of liberation, wherein only two options are available: (1) as a symbol, the crucified Christ can be "used" by the people as an instrument of their liberation; or (2) it can be rejected as "useless" for the liberation struggle. The presupposition that the value of a symbol is dependent upon its usefulness, however, turns the symbol into a manipulable concept or instrument, effectively divesting it of its theopoetic liberative power, which belongs to it precisely qua symbol. When theopoetics is reduced to ethical-political praxis, the value of the cross is predicated upon its "usefulness" in bringing about the resurrection: Jesus had to die in order to be resurrected, but, in and of itself, his death had no significance. It would then follow, of course, that an identification with the crucified Christ, rather than with the resurrected Christ, would hinder the movement toward resurrection and, hence, liberation.

For Foucaultian, poststructuralist, postmodernist aestheticism, on the other hand, the very notion of liberation is nonsensical: "The concept of liberty is an 'invention of the ruling classes' and not fundamental to man's nature or at the root of his attachment to being and truth."[45] Hence,

Foucault's style is scrupulously non-judgmental, his commentaries purged of the least hint of normativity.... This stylistic mode is not far at times from a certain perverse eroticism, as the most sensational materials—the torture of a human body, for example—are mediated through a distanced, dispassionate tone, a measured, mandarin French serenely unruffled by its own shocking contents.[46]

Form remains divorced from content; if modernity absolutized content, postmodernity will now absolutize form.

The struggle for liberation is incompatible, furthermore, with the postmodernist deconstruction of the subject: *Who* struggles? *Who* becomes "free"? As Russell Berman observes, "Because there is no original identity of the individual, it makes no sense to thematize the individual's freedom."[47] The human face is but a mask—and an infinitely interchangeable

---

44. García, "A Hispanic Approach," 118–19.
45. Michel Foucault, cited in Russell A. Berman, *Modern Culture and Critical Theory: Art, Politics, and the Legacy of the Frankfurt School* (Madison: University of Wisconsin Press, 1989) 21–22.
46. Terry Eagleton, *The Ideology of the Aesthetic* (Oxford: Basil Blackwell, 1990) 384.
47. Berman, *Modern Culture*, 21.

one at that.[48] This is a dehistoricized theopoetics, a disembodied aesthetics, form without content.

In the context of such a dehistoricized aesthetics, the countenance of the crucified Jesus can have no history; it is

merely another particular mask constructed by discursive constellations and derived from epistemic structures prior to any experience. The mask consequently lacks any expressive character; indeed the question of expression becomes moot after the tidal liquidation of the subject. Given its thorough contingency, the mask is linked to an imagery of perpetual change; the sea can erase one face in order to make room for another, another drawing in the sand, equally arbitrary and equally ephemeral. What is lost is the ... construction of the face as a palimpsest, bearing the marks of its own history, never fully erased and therefore the foundation of a complex autonomy. What is lost is the plausibility of an emancipatory project; one may or may not concede such a plausibility, but one cannot convincingly argue that genealogy and emancipation are compatible.[49]

The postmodern aesthete thus joins the modern ethicist in rejecting the liberative power of the bloodied Crucified One so central to Latino popular Catholicism: the latter by denying its emancipatory usefulness, and the former by denying the usefulness of emancipation. In so doing, both views dehistoricize the image of the crucified Christ, uprooting it from its place in the life of Jesus and in the life of the crucified community identified with him. There is little difference between the faceless masses of modernity and the interchangeable masks of postmodernity.

It is precisely its particular form within the historical praxis of the Latino community—wherein that praxis finds theopoetic expression in the participants' identification with the Crucified One—that makes the image more than an aesthetic representation of otherness or an instrument for or against liberation. The fundamental and indispensable ground of human freedom is the *historical* expression of otherness, difference, or particularity in confrontation with the totalitarian structures of identity; the tortured visage of the crucified Jesus, bearing the marks of violence and yet capable of rending the heavens with the cry, "My God, my God, why have you forsaken me?" is such an expression.

At the moment when Jesus asserts that, despite all attempts to destroy him (even, so it seems, by God), he remains a person, a human subject—at that moment, he has already conquered death. His otherness resides, above all, in his capacity to *resist* the violent attempts to deny that otherness. The crucified Jesus does not give in but remains a person, a subject to the end, some*one* who, despite all attempts to reduce him to mere inanimate matter, continues to suffer, to feel, and thus to live.

---

48. Ibid., 22.
49. Ibid.

As Karl Rahner insists, then, "The resurrection of Christ is not another event *after* his passion and death....The resurrection is the manifestation of what happened in the death of Christ."[50] Hans Urs von Balthasar reminds us of the biblical grounds for such a view:

For John (as already for Paul), the Resurrection of Jesus is indeed a new act of God the Father, but one demanded by the inner logic of the act of judgment on the Cross and to this extent contained within it: so much is this so, that in John the raising up upon the Cross and the raising up into glory are one single event, just as for Paul no one is raised up apart from the one who was crucified.[51]

The crucified corpus, though hardly in itself an "instrument" of liberation, remains nevertheless a force for liberation. As Russell Berman observes,

Extraordinarily diverse human activities, from the work of art to the grimace of pain, record the experience of violence and suffering, and by recording it point it out and thereby point to its end. Appearance is the vessel of this expression and therefore the agency of criticism: "In the death struggle of the creature, at the opposite pole from freedom, freedom...shines out irresistibly as the thwarted destiny of matter...." The suffering creature, its mask distorted by pain, gives expression, now as a subject, to the suffering and calls the pain into question. It is not at all the ruling classes who invent liberty but the victim who is able to thwart or at least to articulate the wish to thwart the destiny of matter....The sign, the record of violent power—the writing in the face, the scar, the tattoo, the castration—marks it, remembers it, and, the labor of enlightenment, thwarts the brute force of a destiny blind in the excessive glow of power.[52]

By identifying our own history with the history of violence and suffering made visible in Jesus' grimace of pain on the cross, U.S. Hispanics record our own experience of violence and suffering, "and by recording it point it out and thereby point to its end." The blood and the wounds are the visible memories of his and our suffering. To erase them is to erase those memories and, with them, our very identity as persons, without which there can be no liberation that arises out of our own history as subjects.[53] "Every rebellion against suffering," contends Johann Baptist Metz, "is fed by the subversive power of remembered suffering....The Christian *memoria* insists that the history of human suffering is not merely part of the pre-history of freedom but remains an inner aspect of *the* history of freedom."[54] The epitaph is a radical slogan; it is what stands between the person-as-subject and the

---

50. Karl Rahner, *Theological Investigations* (London: Darton, Longman and Todd, 1966) 4:128.
51. Von Balthasar, *Theology: The New Covenant*, 228.
52. Berman, *Modern Culture,* 20, 26.
53. Ibid., 24.
54. Johann Baptist Metz, *Faith in History and Society: Toward a Practical Fundamental Theology* (New York: Seabury Press, 1980) 110, 112.

person-as-object.[55] The ability to suffer, to shed tears, and to remember the suffering of the past—thereby resisting the temptation to give in to a numbing despair in the face of those forces that would reduce the person to mere inanimate and unfeeling matter—is the beginning of any authentic liberation. The lamentation is a cry of protest and, therefore, a cry of freedom: for the oppressed, "day comes like a lamentation arising from the depths of the heart."[56] Dietrich Bonhoeffer writes:

Not only action but also suffering is a way to freedom. The liberation lies in the suffering, in that one is allowed to give one's cause out of one's own hands and lay it in the hands of God.... Whether the human act is a matter of faith or not, depends on whether or not man understands his suffering as a continuation of his action, as a perfection of freedom.[57]

Only a free subject can suffer—and that suffering is itself a protest against the denial of his or her freedom. As the Latino sociologist David Abalos avers, "People forbidden to feel their own deep discontent cannot generate the conflict and the energy necessary to break the old and transform their lives."[58]

The Latino community's persistent cry, "My God, my God, why have you abandoned me?" echoes Jesus' cry on the cross and, in so doing, represents the oppressed community's refusal to accept death as the final word. As surely as Jesus' cry, with its implicit refusal to stop believing in "my God, my God," revealed the utter powerlessness of the principalities and powers in their attempt to crush him, so too does our people's cry on the cross reveal the impotence of the dominant society in its attempt to effect a monolithic totalitarian identity through coercion and co-optation—or to dehistoricize our suffering by turning it into a disembodied example of "otherness" that can make no ethical-political claims. "*I am a person*"— no statement is more revolutionary or liberating than this. It was implicit in Jesus' cry on the cross and is at the very heart of our community's identification with the crucified Christ.

It is not the vivid depiction of Jesus' suffering that induces passivity and resignation. Precisely the opposite is the case: what induces passivity and resignation is the premature dehistoricization of the crucifix, whereby it is divorced from its own history. I would suggest that the sense of hope, joy, and empowerment is much more palpable, for example, in barrio churches, with their bleeding, contorted images of the Crucified One, than in Anglo, suburban churches with their empty crosses or their ostensibly more

---

55. Ibid., 126.

56. From "Santa María de Iquique," a cantata by Claudio Sapian, cited in Gustavo Gutiérrez, *On Job: God-Talk and the Suffering of the Innocent* (Maryknoll, N.Y.: Orbis Books, 1987) 102.

57. Cited in von Balthasar, *Theology: The New Covenant*, 538.

58. David Abalos, *Latinos in the United States: The Sacred and the Political* (Notre Dame, Ind.: University of Notre Dame Press, 1988) 67.

"hopeful," more "liberating," and more "aesthetically pleasing" images of the resurrected Christ, with arms gloriously outstretched, superimposed on an all-but-invisible cross. His face is no longer bloodied. Gone are the wounds "which render the victims identifiable."[59] Gone is the grimace, the "reservoir of potential protest."[60] In its place we encounter an "unmoving and unmoved countenance," the " 'baby face' of practical men, politicians, priests, managing directors, and racketeers."[61] This Christ is not a person but a type, a paradigm, an idea: the theopoetic image has been displaced by the theological idea.[62] The hymn has been displaced by the sermon. The hope of a liberation born of the history of suffering has been displaced by the indifference of the ahistorical, amnestic concept, whether in the form of the faceless subject of modernity or the interchangeable mask of postmodernity. The incarnation has been displaced by a gnostic, spiritualized Christ.[63] And this bloodless Christ has given us bloodless theologies. Modernity and postmodernity have objectified the crucified Jesus and, in so doing, have forgotten who he was—and who we are: "All objectification is a forgetting."[64]

No—insist U.S. Hispanics, in their daily identification with the crucified Jesus—his blood-stained countenance is no mere mask; on the contrary, "with his death, the final mask has been removed, and reality is seen for what it really is."[65] An *anti*mask, the crucified Jesus' countenance is a liberative theopoetic symbol precisely because "in his death, Jesus, who had died as a reject, a blasphemer, and political rabble-rouser, now appears for what he really is: the innocent just one who is the victim of the sin of the world."[66] If the crucified Jesus' countenance reveals who he really is ("Truly, this man was God's son!"), then our own scarred countenances also reveal who we really are: human beings, children of God, persons. If his tortured visage subverts our commonplace aesthetic, revealing the beauty of him whom the world considered ugly, so too do our faces reveal the beauty of those whom the dominant culture has rejected: "Isaiah's phrase, 'He had neither form nor beauty,' determines the precise locus from which God's unique beauty radiates."[67] If the crucified Jesus' wounds revealed his innocence, ours reveal our own innocence: "When I suffer much," says a Hispanic woman, María, "I think, 'But he suffered so much and through no fault of his own.' At times I say, 'My God, why do

59. Ibid., 24.
60. Ibid.
61. Ibid., 20.
62. Ibid., 23.
63. See von Balthasar, *Theology: The New Covenant*, 482.
64. Max Horkheimer and Theodor Adorno, *Dialectic of Enlightenment* (New York: Herder and Herder, 1972) 230.
65. Elizondo, *Galilean Journey*, 78.
66. Ibid.
67. Von Balthasar, *Seeing the Form*, 55.

I have to suffer so much? Do I merit such suffering? I am not that bad of a person.' "[68] "I am not that bad of a person..." the beginning of liberation. My God, my God, why have you abandoned me? I am not that bad of a person.

No—insist U.S. Hispanics—Jesus' resurrection does not resolve or justify his experience of abandonment and his death any more than the future liberation of our people resolves or justifies our past and present suffering. That is precisely the argument of the dominant culture: "The suffering of their fathers finds consolation in the happiness of the descendants, in past sufferings rendered worthwhile in a future harmony."[69] We, on the other hand, reject any "freedom" that pretends to overcome the suffering of the present and past—as courageously as Ivan Karamazov rejected the prospect of an eternal harmony purchased by the tears of children. So the blood and the scars will remain on the corpus. Without them, the Crucified One would no longer be a theopoetic symbol that affirms our cries, thereby affirming our human dignity and empowering us for resistance. Instead, the crucified Jesus would be reduced to a mere concept that, like all concepts, resolves the disjunctions of concrete history into an abstract harmony, purchased by the tears of the children:

On the contrary, Christianity in its message of redemption, does not offer definitive meaning for the unexpiated sufferings of the past. It narrates rather a distinct history of freedom: freedom on the basis of a redeeming liberation through God in the cross of Jesus. It is not by chance that this history narrates the descent into hell. This affirmation is by no means a mythological category which should be quickly deleted or relativized as a subsequent interpolation into the Christian memory of redemption under the pretext that it does not belong to the genuine concern of Jesus. In this way, the apocalyptical sting has been drawn from Christian soteriology and, in this way too, its decisive sense of freedom has been obscured. This descent, this being together with the dead on the part of the crucified Christ, points to the original liberating movement of the history of redemption.[70]

In a society that defines liberation as victory over suffering, as the possibility of a life without suffering, the ability to shed tears, to weep, is the most profound and fundamental form of resistance. The Hispanic devotion to the crucified Jesus is born of the courageous refusal to be denied our human right to weep, without which there can be no liberation. The surest way to destroy us is to deny us the ability to weep by insisting that our tears stand in the way of our future liberation. We will then learn to distrust our own instincts, our own experience, and, therefore, ourselves.

Just as the theopoetic significance of the crucifix derives from the symbol's grounding in the praxis of our communities, so too do the tears we

---

68. Cited in Ada María Isasi-Díaz and Yolanda Tarango, *Hispanic Women: Prophetic Voice in the Church* (San Francisco: Harper and Row, 1988) 36.

69. Metz, *Faith in History and Society*, 129.

70. Ibid.

shed before the crucifix derive their significance from our communal life: "What is most holy about a temple is that it is where we go to weep together. A *Miserere,* sung in common by a multitude scourged by destiny, is as valuable as a philosophy. It is not enough to cure the plague, one must know how to weep it."[71] Ethics impels us to cure the plague; theopoetics empowers us to weep it.

Ours are tears of suffering, not tears of sadness.[72] Sadness is passive; suffering is active. Sadness is a personal, private feeling; suffering is an intrinsic aspect of human intersubjective praxis, that is, of life in community.[73] The active and communal dimensions of suffering are what make it capable of engendering solidarity and hope. For the U.S. Hispanic community, the theopoetic and hence ethical and theological significance of the crucifix derives from the community's participation in the symbol as an expression of its intersubjective, historical praxis, in which we are implicitly affirmed as subjects or persons, precisely in and through our *common* history of suffering (which includes, is borne by, and is centered on the crucified Jesus), a history that is the source of our solidarity with each other and with Jesus Christ—and, therefore, the source of our empowerment. Then—only then—can the ethical-political "struggle for liberation" begin . . . when we suffer *together* while, together, continuing to cry out, "I am not that bad of a person."

To suffer with others is to resist objectification (whether through instrumentalism or conceptualism); it is to resist the objectification of Jesus and of the person. To suffer with others is thus to affirm the intrinsic inviolability of the person, the intrinsic and absolute value of intersubjective, historical praxis, of life itself—even in the face of all "projects" of liberation. Indeed, compassion (literally, "suffering with") is the very heart of a truly liberating praxis, for compassion is what distinguishes common suffering, which is always subversive, from mere personal sadness, which fosters resignation and passivity. "If it is experienced as a personal disgrace," contends Francisco Moreno Rejón, "an illness is exhausting and engenders self-centeredness and alienation. Seen as part of the pain of all the poor, it allows for rebellion in the face of pain."[74] And then—only then—is true joy born: "The joy of the poor is not 'logical,' thus it is often

---

71. Miguel de Unamuno, *Del sentimiento trágico de la vida: En los hombres y en los pueblos* (Madrid: Espasa-Calpe, 1971) 21; my trans.

72. Francisco Moreno Rejón, *Salvar la vida de los pobres: Aportes a la teología moral* (Lima: CEP, 1986) 156.

73. See Metz, *Faith in History and Society,* 57.

74. Moreno Rejón, *Salvar la vida,* 156; my trans. Justo González describes the empowering effects of *common* suffering in his recounting of the Lope de Vega play *Fuenteovejuna.* In that story, the inhabitants of a town, Fuenteovejuna, rebel and murder the tyrannical commander who ruled over them. When a judge seeking to find the "culprits" asks the identity of the murderers, the townspeople respond, "Fuenteovejuna, my lord." González observes (*Mañana,* 28–29) that, in their answer, "they are not simply trying to cover up for one another. What has happened is that through their suffering and final uprising, such

incomprehensible and bothersome. Theirs is a subversive joy."[75] The hope of liberation, or resurrection, can never erase or expiate the sufferings of the past and the present but must instead be given birth by the living memories and symbols of those sufferings: the tears, the blood, the scars, the crucified Jesus.

Our Lady Of Guadalupe

And thus, the second major symbol in U.S. Hispanic popular Catholicism is explicitly a symbol of celebration, a symbol of the hope that persists in the very midst of our suffering, the symbol of Mary: "People celebrate the passion events with processions, where parish or community leaders bear the bleeding image of the suffering Christ, followed by the icon or statue of *la Madre Dolorosa* (the Sorrowful Mother)."[76] In the community's religious rituals these images are mutually implicit and often appear together in popular religious celebrations and devotions, for Mary is the mother of the crucified Jesus—and, therefore, the mother of her crucified children. Yet, as is the case with the crucifix itself, the theopoetic significance of the U.S. Hispanic identification of Mary with the symbol of the crucified Jesus cannot be fully understood in abstraction from the history of Marian symbolism in Latino communities. While that history reveals Mary's identification with the crucified Jesus and her crucified children, it likewise reveals crucifixion as the locus of resurrection—and, precisely because the crucifixion of Jesus is identified with the crucifixion of her children, his resurrection becomes identified with our resurrection as a people. *Because* Jesus' death was not only his, but also ours, so too is his resurrection ours. Because the crucifixion was not a once-for-all historical event but is an ongoing reality in our lives, so too is the resurrection an ongoing reality—not only in our personal lives but, more specifically, in our solidary unity as, indeed, "a people." Insofar as the particular Marian symbols embodied in the popular Catholicism of different Latino communities are linked historically to the emergence of the mestizo and mulatto peoples of the "New World," these symbols identify Jesus' resurrection in a very concrete way with the birth, or resurrection, of a new people, what José Vasconcelos called *la raza cósmica* (the cosmic race).

This is nowhere more evident than in the symbol of and devotion to Our Lady of Guadalupe.[77] In the story of Guadalupe, the Virgin appears

---

solidarity has arisen that they do believe that it was the town, and not any individuals in it, that killed the commander."

75. Moreno Rejón, *Salvar la vida,* 156; my trans.

76. Espín and García, "Hispanic-American Theology," 85; see also Espín, "Tradition and Popular Religion," 70–71.

77. Aware of the great diversity in Marian popular religiosity among Latinos, I am taking Guadalupe as but one example, although I believe that, given the influence of Guadalupe,

on Mt. Tepeyac to a poor indigenous man, Juan Diego, who is asked to take a message to the local bishop. The bishop, of course, refuses to believe the illiterate man's testimony and insists that Juan Diego prove its credibility by furnishing a sign to the effect that he has indeed seen the Virgin. After hearing of the bishop's response, the Virgin tells Juan Diego to gather the flowers that he will find growing on top of a hill and to take them to the bishop, who will know that, in that place and at that time of the year, no flowers could possibly grow naturally. Gathering these in his *tilma* (cloak), Juan Diego takes them to the bishop. As he unfolds the *tilma*, the flowers "dropped to the floor and as they did the precious image of the always holy virgin Mary, Mother of God, appeared on the tilma."[78]

The encounter between Our Lady and the poor, indigenous man, Juan Diego, takes place in 1531, at the darkest moment in the history of a conquered people and, at that moment, signals and makes possible the emergence of a new people. Virgilio Elizondo notes this historical relationship:

I do not know of any other event in the history of Christianity that stands at the very source of the birth of a people like the appearance of Our Lady of Guadalupe....Guadalupe is not just an apparition, but a major intervention of God's liberating power in history. It is an Exodus and Resurrection event of an enslaved and dying people.... Guadalupe is truly an epiphany of God's love at the precise moment when abandonment by God had been experienced by the people at large.... It is in this climate of the stench and the cries of death that the new and unsuspected beginning would take place. Like the resurrection itself, it came at the moment when everything appeared to be finished.... The natives who previously had wanted only to die now wanted to live; dances, songs, pilgrimages, and festivities resumed![79]

Guadalupe's history within the oppressed community, as the symbol of that community's birth, makes the resurrection a transformative reality in the present, in the lives of the community. The resurrection is now an empowering, theopoetic symbol because it is rooted in the specific history of a particular community and, thus, affirms that community's identity as a

this is arguably the predominant Marian symbol among U.S. Hispanics and, in some cases, has been "adopted" by non-Mexican Hispanics. For a similar analysis of the Cuban patroness, Nuestra Señora de la Caridad del Cobre, see José Juan Arrom, *Certidumbre de América: Estudios de letras, folklore y cultura* (Madrid: Editorial Gredos, 1971) 184–214. For a study of the diversity of Marian popular religiosity, see Stephen Holler, "Hispanic Marian Popular Religion in the United States" (unpublished paper presented to the annual meeting of the Association for the Sociology of Religion, 18–20 August 1992).

78. Virgilio Elizondo, *La Morenita: Evangelizer of the Americas* (San Antonio: Mexican American Cultural Center, 1980) 80.

79. Virgilio Elizondo, *The Future Is Mestizo* (Bloomington, Ind.: Meyer-Stone, 1988) 59–64.

people in the face of its ongoing crucifixion. In the face of the dominant culture's ongoing depreciation and rejection of our history, our culture, our community, and our very humanity, Guadalupe affirms and accepts us and, in so doing, empowers us: "Her presence is not a pacifier but an energizer which gives meaning, dignity and hope to the marginated and suffering of today's society. Her presence is the new power of the powerless to triumph over the violence of the powerful."[80]

As with the crucifix, the power of Guadalupe derives not only from the symbol itself but also, and more specifically, from the history of the symbol in the life of an oppressed community. Like that of the crucifix, Guadalupe's theopoetic power is, in that context, a subversive power: that which the world condemns is chosen and embraced by God. The divine is here revealed in—of all things!—a mestizo Virgin, a woman of mixed blood, La Morenita. Not only is the Virgin's image itself that of a mestizo, but also the story and symbolism are themselves examples of theopoetic *mestizaje*, embodying—like so much popular religiosity—the creative confluence of indigenous symbolism and Christian symbolism: "It was not only an apparition, but the perfect synthesis of the religious iconography of the Iberian peoples with that of native Mexicans into one coherent image."[81] Thus, in the Virgin's identification with Juan Diego, the mestizo community finds its own identity valued: we are indeed created in the image of God, who is revealed through and in the mestizo. Just as the "ugliness" of the

---

80. Elizondo, *La Morenita,* 120. The function of Guadalupe, and popular religiosity, as a source of communal identity and, therefore, empowerment (beyond any explicitly theological content) is illustrated by the following humorous story recounted by the Methodist theologian Justo González: "When I was growing up, I was taught to think of such things as the Virgin of Guadalupe as pure superstition. Therefore, I remember how surprised I was at the reaction of a Mexican professor in seminary when one of my classmates made some disparaging remarks about Guadalupe. The professor, who was as Protestant as they come and who often stooped because he was then elderly, drew himself up, looked my friend in the eye, and said: 'Young man, in this class you are free to say anything you please. You may say anything about me. You certainly are welcome to say anything you wish about the pope and the priests. But don't you touch my little Virgin!'" (*Mañana*, 61). At the same time, however, we must bear in mind that a very real aspect of the history of Marian symbolism in U.S. Hispanic communities is the often oppressive effect of that symbolism on U.S. Hispanic women. Like all symbols, Mary remains ambiguous and, when "used" by men to legitimate patriarchy, can be a force for oppression rather than liberation. I am aware that this ambiguity merits much more than a footnote and must be integrated into our interpretation of the Guadalupe event in a systematic way. U.S. Hispanic male theologians have only begun to do that. I know that, in dialogue with Latinas, our understanding of Guadalupe is sure to develop in the coming months and years. Latinas remind us that we must resist a dehistoricizing, and therefore oppressive, romanticization of popular religiosity; see Isasi-Díaz and Tarango, *Hispanic Women.*

81. Elizondo, "*Mestizaje,*" 109. For Elizondo's fascinating examination of the *mestizaje* manifested in the story and symbolism, see especially his *La Morenita* and *The Third Creation: A Woman Clothed with the Son* (Maryknoll, N.Y.: Orbis Books, forthcoming). See also Espín, "Tradition and Popular Religion," 72–73, for a description of Guadalupan symbols as reflecting such a synthesis.

Crucified One subverts any merely human aesthetic, so too does the beauty of La Morenita, for it is the beauty of the mestizo, of the poor, a beauty rejected by the conquerors. It is a beauty recognizable only to those whom the world has deemed ugly and de-formed.

In the person of La Morenita and in the flowers and the music that accompany her, the beauty of the Lord is revealed to Juan Diego, who, in turn, is asked to convey it to the unbelieving bishop. The revelation that takes place is not a theological revelation, nor is it merely a revelation of divine beauty; it is the revelation of divine beauty *within the oppressed community's history of suffering.* The very fact that the divine is revealed to Juan Diego, not first in the form of words, but in *flor y canto* (flowers and song), is itself an affirmation of his identity and, thus, a challenge to the Spanish colonial empire:

The first striking thing upon reading the legend is that Juan Diego heard *beautiful music,* so beautiful that he thought he was in paradise. Music alone was capable of communicating truth. It was the medium of divine communication. In some way, he was in the presence of the gods. The Lady did not have to explain to him that she was of heavenly origins, he could easily comprehend this by the mere fact that she was appearing and speaking in the midst of the most beautiful music he had ever heard. The music itself was sufficient to establish the veracity and importance of the Lady.[82]

Again, it is important to note that the form of the revelation is as significant as its content. That the divine could be revealed in the form of music was both an affirmation of Juan Diego's own community and heritage and an affirmation of the priority of theopoetics over theology: the beautiful music, the sound of birds singing, is evidence enough to Juan Diego of a divine revelation. He later receives further evidence in the form of the flowers the Virgin asks him to take to the bishop as a sign of the truth of his story:

The beautiful flowers which appeared in the cold December morning in the desert hill-top of Tepeyac were the sign chosen by the Lady. This will complete the divine revelation begun with the sign of music. In the midst of *flor y canto,* God is manifested for the Nahuatl world. For the native world, this was the final touch that assured the people that what happened at Tepeyac was of God. . . . Guadalupe is the truth of beauty and the beauty of truth.[83]

The actual theology of Guadalupe, as articulated by the Virgin in her words to Juan Diego, is literally parenthetical; the theological explanation is enclosed within music, which begins the revelation, and flowers, which end it. The information conveyed is secondary to the relationship between

---

82. Elizondo, *La Morenita,* 87.
83. Elizondo, *Third Creation,* chap. 4.

La Morenita and Juan Diego (and, through him, the entire oppressed community), a relationship mediated by the theopoetic symbols of song and flowers:

Many of our modern day programs give a lot of information, but little or no experience of the divine. We speak a lot about God but do not lead people into a mystical experience of God as Juan Diego had at Tepeyac, and millions continue to have today when they are in her presence. . . . We have an overabundance of doctrinal truths and we have had many arguments and fights over them, but we have been poor and lacking in beautiful truth, that is, the absolute and eternal truth which shines through and is experienced in beauty. We in the West have been strong on the rational and logical but very weak and suspicious on the mystical and poetic. We are afraid of dreams and apparitions, even though the Bible is full of them, because they are beyond our control.[84]

Indeed, we *ought* to be suspicious of the mystical and poetic when these emerge from within the history of conquest and domination, for then these lead to "artificial and unnatural ideas about beauty which are dehumanizing and destructive."[85] But such aestheticism is alien to a theopoetics that, born from within the history of the victims, affirms the victims' own beauty and dignity. The theopoetics of the victims—insofar as it is truly theirs—is always empowering and liberating, simply by virtue of the fact that it is, indeed, *theirs*.

This implicitly political dimension of all truly popular theopoetics is evident in the symbol and legend of Guadalupe. One should note, for example, that "we speak about Guadalupe as an apparition, but it is really much more of an encuentro, a coming together of two friends. It is very similar to the encounter-appearances of the Risen Lord with his Apostles."[86] This understanding of the form of the Guadalupe event, arrived at through an analysis of the dialogue between the Lady and Juan Diego as recounted in the story, is important for what it (again, as distinct from the content of the revelation) conveys about not only who the Lady is but also who Juan Diego is. An apparition always has an active subject, the one who appears, and a passive object, the one to whom he or she appears; an encounter always involves two active subjects, two "others," who encounter each other. To understand the Guadalupe event as an encounter is thus to recognize that, in that event, Juan Diego and the community he represents are no longer the passive objects of someone else's history but are now human subjects themselves, with all the rights and dignity such an assertion entails. And that is precisely what is suggested in the Virgin's form of address to Juan Diego: "My most abandoned child, my

---

84. Ibid., chaps. 4 and 6.
85. Ibid., chap. 6.
86. Ibid., chap. 4.

most dignified Juan."[87] As one capable of perceiving the truth in the song and flowers, *and* responding to that revelation, Juan Diego is revealed as a human person, even in his abandonment. What "appears" is not simply the Virgin but Juan Diego himself—as a dignified human person confident enough to insist on the veracity of his experience before the skeptical bishop who, like the dominant European culture as a whole, wanted to deny his truth-claims:

Juan Diego is converted from non-being to becoming a full, confident and joyful person. He is transformed from his debasement and shame to a new confident self-image. He is a man! He is free, trusted and self-assured.... On his way to the Bishop's palace with the requested sign, Juan Diego is a totally different person than the broken-down man we had met earlier. "*He was in a hurry and happy, with a confident heart.... he was enjoying the perfume of the beautiful flowers.*" (v 89)... She reveals to Juan Diego the ultimate truth about himself: he is most dignified and to be trusted fully with the Word of the Mother of God.... Juan Diego is converted from seeing himself and thinking of himself as the oppressors saw him and coming to appreciate himself as God knows and appreciates him. This is the new life-giving power of God irrupting in the poor who through God's call begin to believe in themselves.[88]

Through the many popular religious devotions and practices surrounding Guadalupe, the oppressed community participates in this encounter through the community's own identification with Juan Diego and the Virgin. The community, like Juan Diego, is affirmed and dignified by its active participation in the encounter.

We are no longer merely passive recipients of theological "truths"; we are now active participants in salvation history. Insofar as they demand such participation, then, the symbols and rituals of popular religiosity affirm our dignity as persons: only persons can act and participate, only objects are passive recipients "acted upon" by others. If, in the popular spirituality of the crucifix, the marginalized community is empowered by its common experience of crucifixion, in the popular spirituality of Guadalupe, the community is empowered by its common experience of resurrection, "the new life-giving power of God."

Thus, Our Lady of Guadalupe affirms the liberating power of the cross as the place where we experience the resurrection. By participating in the Guadalupe story, we affirm our dignity as persons in the face of crucifixion and dehumanization. We experience the resurrection in God's unbounded love for us. In the story and symbol of Guadalupe, we know that God embraces what others have dismissed. That which has been defiled and deformed will itself become the symbol of a new birth, as Jesus himself did on

---

87. Ibid., chap. 5.
88. Ibid.

the cross and as Mary did on Tepeyac. If the mestizo Virgin of Guadalupe symbolized the future of the new Mexican people, so too must our *mestizaje* today symbolize the future of a new Pan-American people, and a new humanity: "Races and nations had been opposed to each other, but as the mother of all the inhabitants of these lands, she would provide the basis for a new unity."[89] And she will continue to do so. The racial and cultural conflict that has destroyed so many of our ancestors, and continues to oppress us today, now provides the basis and impetus for the forging of a new universality, one that will not extinguish the particularity of our history but will, instead, be mediated by our historical particularity— for the good of all humanity. As racial and cultural mestizos, we are the symbols and harbingers of this new, liberating universality. The racial and cultural "impurity" that had been rejected as inhuman now becomes the symbol of a new, inclusive humanity that does not dissolve but welcomes difference.

Concluding Comments

Indeed, the theopoetics embodied in the symbols of our popular religiosity gives expression to the historical praxis of our mestizo community. The very nature of the *mestizaje* portrayed in the symbol and story of Guadalupe precludes an immediately theological interpretation since no logical, "rational" explanation—theological or otherwise—is capable of expressing the tension of biculturality without dissolving it; the experience of *mestizaje* thus had to be expressed first in a popular religious symbol, story, and ritual—Guadalupe—before its theological significance could be explained rationally. Conceptual, logical reason is at home only in the rarefied world of either/or and is stultified by the mestizo world of both/and. It must dissolve the tension into one of the polarities: either white or black, either European or Native American, either Latin American or "American." Consequently, only in our theopoetic appropriation of symbol, story, and ritual has the U.S. Hispanic community been able to preserve its identity as mestizo, not as either/or but as both/and. Conversely, in a dominant Anglo culture obsessed with racial and cultural purity (either/or), theology has virtually suffocated theopoetics: all symbols wither in a land where everyone must wear either a white hat or a black hat. Symbols cannot be pure or they cease being symbols. Only concepts are pure.

As mestizos, we know that our history and identity are tinged with the blood of rape and conquest, that the mixture of European, Native American, and African cultures did not take place without much violence, perpetrated by some of our ancestors against other ancestors: we are the

---

89. Ibid., 64.

children of both rapist and *la chingada* (the raped woman). In the face of Western rationalism, where black cannot coexist with white, good with bad, "I" with "you," or affect with intellect, no rationale could possibly justify our conviction that the *mestizaje* or impurity resulting from this unspeakable violence will not, from now on, be experienced as a disgrace but as a sign of divine favor:

> As Hispanics, our is a noninnocent history. We do have our heroes, from whose deeds and inspiration we draw strength. But our heroes do not wear white hats, like the Anglo heroes of the West.... Sometimes some of us long for the self-assured innocence of Anglo history—To be able to claim that aside from some minor mistakes, we and our ancestors have been right! But such innocence has not been granted to us, and for that we must be thankful, for it would be a guilty innocence.[90]

This experience can best be conveyed through the multivalence of symbols. "The symbol," writes Bernard Lonergan, "has the power of recognizing and expressing what logical discourse abhors: conflicts, struggles, destructions."[91] In the Latino community's theopoetic expressions, our mestizo identity—marked as it is by so many "conflicts, struggles, destructions"—can be fully recognized, affirmed, and valued in all its dimensions and colors. To stifle that theopoetic power by trying to "make sense" of it theologically, or trying to "make use" of it ethically, *before* one has actually *participated in it* would be to stifle the voice of God, who speaks through popular religious symbols, which affirm the value of our identity as mestizos.

The liberating power of theopoetic symbols in Hispanic life is poignantly expressed in a story recounted by Arturo Bañuelas. The story also illustrates the dangers of subordinating theopoetics to the demands of a "liberating" theology. Bañuelas tells of a priest who visited a very poor Mexican woman and, in her home, saw a picture of the *divino rostro*, a graphic depiction of the bloodied and tortured face of the crucified Jesus. Thinking that such a picture could only exacerbate this woman's everyday suffering, the next time he visited he brought her a cross on which was superimposed a risen Jesus, with arms raised heavenward. The woman thanked him and placed it in a corner of the room, leaving the *divino rostro* in its place of honor. Expecting her to replace the more somber, depressing picture with the more hopeful, risen Christ he had just brought her, the priest asked the woman why she did not take down the *divino rostro*. "You see, father," she began to explain, "things in my family are pretty

90. González, *Mañana*, 40.
91. Lonergan, *Method*, 66; see also Stephen Happel, "Sacrament: Symbol of Conversion," *Creativity and Method: Essays in Honor of Bernard Lonergan, S.J.* (ed. Matthew Lamb; Milwaukee: Marquette University Press, 1981) 283.

rough. My husband and I don't get along too well, and I think my daughter is on drugs or something. She spends a lot of time away from home and
never talks to me about what's going on or how she is. Sometimes I just
feel like running away from it all, and then I sit down and cry, and I look
at that picture of the *divino rostro,* and I know that he understands what
I'm going through, that he's been through it too, and I know that he loves
me and that somehow he's going to take care of my family. That's what
gives me the strength to go on and to keep trying to love my family and
make things better."[92] Before the message, the vision...before the sermon,
the hymn...before the prose, the poem.

92. This story was told to me in a personal conversation with Arturo Bañuelas and was
also recounted in a lecture he presented at Loyola University of Chicago in March 1993. I
am grateful to my student Steve Corder, who attended that lecture, for his account of the
story.

15

A Theological-Ethical Analysis of Hispanic Struggles for Community Building in the United States

Ismael García

North American Hispanics embody all major racial groups—African, Asian, Caucasian, and Indian. This has led some to argue that Hispanics represent the emergence of a new person whose identity has been shaped through a history of interracial mixtures. Such cross-racial fertilization enhances the wondrous variety of what is at the heart of God's intention in creation and in a special way makes God rejoice. Hispanics are also ethnically diverse, representing more than twenty-three different nationalities, each with its unique cultural integrity. Hispanics are members of all the major religious faiths, although Christianity represents by far the dominant religious ethos of the people. Moreover, while there has been a growing secularization within the Hispanic community, a strong religious sense still dominates Hispanics' view of the meaning and purpose of life. Their religiosity is for the most part a synthesis of many religions and sects, a creative mixture of beliefs that represents their conviction that ultimately all religion is good.

Hispanics narrate a plurality of stories retelling the why, when, and how of their arrival and settlement in a particular region of the United States. While some are descendants of original residents in territories that later became part of the United States, others are newcomers. Hispanic citizens with a strong sense of belonging and identity exist side by side with first- and second-generation Hispanics who struggle with the issue of who they are and whether or not they will ever become first-class citizens. Among the more recent immigrants, some came and still come escaping the political turmoil caused by rightist dictatorships or leftist revolutionary movements back home. Others came and continue to come in order to escape poverty and strife, to become better educated, and to improve their economic lot and enjoy a better standard of living. A few well-educated persons, most of them educated here in the United States, came to forward their technical expertise and enjoy the rewards of meaningful work that only a highly technological society could afford them.

Given this cultural, racial, economic, and political diversity, it should come as no surprise that one finds within the Hispanic worldview diverse value commitments and conceptions of the good life. Value commitments and notions of the good life are neither arbitrary nor abstract creations; on the contrary, they are rooted in and emerge out of the life journey of a people. They emerge from those core experiences—shaping events, achievements, accidents, and crises—that shape a people's character. Thus, diversity of journeys or core experiences always entails some diversity of value options and commitments.

In this study I will examine the moral values of Hispanics' struggle to empower and emancipate their communities. These are the values that Hispanics proclaim as essential to what it means to be human, to live a good life and sustain a humane community. These values define the directions of the various journeys Hispanics travel as they redefine their identity and purpose as residents and citizens of the United States.

The aforementioned diversity of values has had positive as well as negative consequences. On the positive side, it has allowed segments of the Hispanic population to constitute themselves as communities of support and action, with a strong sense of identity, direction, and meaning. On the negative side, it has tended to keep the larger Hispanic community fragmented and in conflict with itself. This state of affairs has, directly or indirectly, supported the condition of poverty and powerlessness under which most Hispanics are forced to live. I would argue that the Christian religious heritage contains resources for overcoming some of the negative consequences of the pluralism of values existing within the Hispanic community. Our theological traditions allow us to reinterpret and transfigure our understanding of our value commitments in ways that can facilitate the process of Hispanics working in solidarity toward the creation of a more inclusive and compassionate community. As Hispanics create new coalitions without surrendering their diverse moral visions, they will not only advance the well-being of their own community but also provide a witness and a vision whereby the United States can become a more inclusive and compassionate society.

Pluralism of Values and Visions
of the Good Society

In order to examine how Hispanics have come to formulate the different value configurations and notions of the good society that inform their sense of what makes life human, I propose to look at the different spheres within which they have chosen to struggle for emancipation.[1] Three spheres have been dominant in the framing of this Hispanic commitment to emancipation: the political sphere, the social sphere, and the cultural sphere. Within each of these, a particular hierarchy of values has emerged as normative; and a particular substantive interpretation of such values has been developed.

The Political Sphere

Hispanics who have chosen the political sphere as the main context in which to struggle for the emancipation of their people give power a primary place in their configuration of values.[2] In their view, politics has to do primarily with the production, distribution, and accumulation of power: the manner in which power is presently accumulated and distributed keeps Hispanics and other ethnic minorities in a permanent position of disadvantage. In this perspective the present social, economic, and political institutions are seen as essentially oppressive. Thus, as long as these institutions endure, it will be impossible for most Hispanics to enjoy a good life. It is imperative, therefore, that Hispanics organize themselves politically, in solidarity with other people of goodwill, with the intention of transforming major social institutions.[3] Nothing less than direct political intervention and the conscious exertion of countervailing power will create possibilities for disadvantaged groups to open society to new possibilities that can be more life-affirming for all.

This perspective assumes a conflictual model of society. It sees the dominant value system as neither universal nor the result of rational persuasion or social consensus. Dominant values are the product of that uneasy truce and compromise that emerged from the struggle of different social groups attempting to defend and assert their interest on the whole. Political, social, and moral discourses are in themselves ineffective means to bring about the necessary institutional changes. Structural changes will come only

---

1. My use of the term "sphere" is a revised version of Michael Walzer's use of the term in his book *Spheres of Justice: A Defense of Pluralism and Equality* (New York: Basic Books, 1983). See also Hannah Arendt, *The Human Condition* (Chicago: University of Chicago Press, 1958).

2. Typologies are ideal constructions that overemphasize the main traits of a given position. Thus, they always distort the uniqueness and integrity of every particular movement. The purpose of the typology I present here is not to encourage pigeonholing one movement or idea into any one type. Rather, typologies work best when used to identify how a movement or idea both fits into and is different from a given type. Most actual movements will either fit somewhere between two of the types or will have elements of all the types. Liberation movements, socially radical groups, and progressive community-organizing groups would be representative of this ideal type.

3. It has never been the habit of Hispanics to vote in blocks. Although they have tended to support candidates of the Democratic Party, there are cases in which they have favored Republican candidates. Today the voting habits of the community are mixed. Hispanic candidates, particularly in the Southwest, who have had successful political careers have based those careers on coalition politics.

when Hispanics are able to accumulate and assert enough power to make others understand that it is in their best interest to respond to the needs of Hispanics.

Politics, as power conflicts, is perceived as a zero-sum game: the more others have, the weaker our position. Since this perspective assumes the position of the powerless, the question of accumulating power takes a tactical precedence over concern with the distribution of power. Concerns about the distribution of power are important, given the long history of the corruptive nature of absolute and unchecked power. However, from the perspective of the powerless, among whom Hispanics are inordinately represented, it is imperative to pay close attention to the ways in which Hispanics can accumulate power in order to transform the present configuration of power within society. The present configuration of power significantly restricts Hispanics from affirming their legitimate interests, while allowing others to assert an undue amount of influence over society as a whole.

The question of the accumulation of power is imperative because how the social structure restricts and empowers one's action is central to the question of what it means to be human and what it means to live a good life in a just society. If absolute power corrupts absolutely, it is equally true that absolute lack of power corrupts absolutely. A powerless group is left with no way to affirm and defend the goodness of its being. Both our humanity and the possibilities of a good life are dependent on our capacity to have enough power to see that we have the resources and services needed to pursue them. Even more important, to be empowered means to be able to participate in and exercise the rights of membership as well as to bear responsibilities and duties within the community to which one belongs. These are essential elements for any community or individual to experience self-worth and fulfillment.

The ideology of the division of power and the systems of checks and balances, however, have more value and substance than mere rhetorical attractiveness. To keep power accountable, it must be distributed. It is indispensable that people remain actively engaged in the social process of mass mobilization through which the major social decisions of society are made and change is brought about. This process itself entails a wide distribution of social, economic, and political power.

However important power is, those who struggle within the political sphere recognize that power is not an end in itself. In their view, power is at the service of justice, and justice is understood primordially in political terms. It has to do with the creation of a community of citizens actively engaged in determining the destiny they want to pursue in common and the sacrifices they are willing to undertake in order to obtain their goals. Justice consists of the creation of social institutions that sustain a participatory community actively involved in the pursuit of humane ends. It has to do with those experiences of solidarity that come from sharing in one another's burdens and celebrating one another's joys.

The political definition of justice is given priority over its economic implications because it is assumed that politically empowered and active citizens will have a greater capacity to assure for themselves the material and human resources they need to enjoy the good life. Democratic control and ownership as well as the experience of community are what make and keep life human. Participating meaningfully in the creation of an inclusive and compassionate community is seen as more imperative to being human than merely having more. Hispanics overall suffer not so much from lack of means, although there are depressed areas in urgent and critical need of basic material goods and services, but rather from nonintegration and lack of participation in the process by which the nation determines its destiny.

Those who assume the perspective of the political sphere assume that community is a more basic reality than individuality. Who we are is significantly determined by the communities to which we belong. The greatest injustice Hispanics have had to endure is the fragmentation within their own community and the fragmentation this sustains within the larger society. This division fuels dehumanizing forms of economic and political inequality. A just community creates a context for the emergence of other central moral values: freedom, equality, order. Freedom in this perspective entails more than what is normally understood by the term "human rights." It entails not just being safe from undue intervention (freedom from) but also accountability to others. To be free is to serve the other, in particular the poor and powerless within society. It is to serve community, to be inclined to sacrifice one's own interest for the well-being of the whole. Equality is defined in comparative terms: it seeks the relative well-being of all members of society and a commitment to overcome those forms of socioeconomic inequalities that make it impossible for people to relate on an equal basis. As a minimum, equality is defined as the social quest to prevent economic inequalities from exceeding a reasonable limit. When power is at the service of justice, and justice sustains freedom and equality, it is reasonable to expect the emergence of a form of order that will provide the needed regularity that enables us to depend on one another.

The Social Sphere

Other Hispanics strive for the emancipation of their communities within the social sphere.[4] From their point of view, the main cause of the powerlessness and exploitation most Hispanics experience is the lack of strong social institutions to serve and protect their interest. What Hispanics need more than anything else is to continue to sustain and create their own insti-

---

4. Most churches, mainline or free, conservative or liberal, are overall representative of this ideal type.

tutional structures. Social institutions provide centers of authority by which the community can organize its own internal life in light of its self-given values and traditions. Institutions also provide those effective social mechanisms needed to influence the larger society. Institutions are also significant insofar as they play a prominent role in determining the practices that shape our behavior and mold our character. They are bearers of the beloved traditions and help us fashion new ways of expressing ourselves. This makes them worthy of our support and respect.

Those who work within this sphere resent the accusation from those who work within the political sphere that all institutions are oppressive and cannot be counted on to help the community achieve its emancipation. From their point of view, those who work within the political sphere are naive in their belief that Hispanics can affect social change only through the political process. To make their case, they point out that Hispanics are too few in numbers, too diverse ethnically and nationally, and too dispersed geographically to build the kind of coalitions needed to make a political difference. Furthermore, Hispanics have demonstrated a traditional preference for engagement in local issues and politics rather than in national agendas and politics.[5] Thus, they conclude that direct political intervention will prove to be a less effective vehicle of change than the institutional approach. Hispanics, then, need to create a plethora of economic and social services to assist and direct the community in its journey to create a better state of affairs. Many identify the local church as a key institution in this regard. The church enjoys a privileged position of trust within significant sectors of the Hispanic community and is perceived as the institution that can best contribute to a strengthening of the family, which is seen as the basic social institution for advancing the well-being of the community.

Social sphere activists view society as a harmonious order open to change and improvement. This is the foundation of their reformist attitudes. Nonetheless, they encourage local constituencies to remain vigilant regarding their institutions. Local constituencies must push for reforms when institutions do not follow their internal procedures, when they fail to represent their constituency, or when they betray their goals. Those persons' reformist and gradualist attitudes reveal their conviction that prevailing social institutions within the Hispanic community are by and large faithful servants of the community. Overall, Hispanic institutions are seen as embodying the values and goals that fit the Hispanic way of living and as a positive presence for the well-being of the community. This makes them legitimate centers of authority and acceptable to all members of society, including the poor.

---

5. Many political analysts have argued that one reason the Democratic Party appointed Henry Cisneros as Secretary of Housing and Urban Development was to regain the loyalty of its Hispanic constituency and to motivate Hispanics to be more active in national issues as opposed to their traditional concerns for local issues.

Political activists argue that one of the imminent dangers of the social sphere position is its tendency to be overly nostalgic about the folklore and values of the homeland, missing thereby the uniqueness and significantly different social conditions that Hispanics confront in the United States. From the perspective of the social sphere, the danger of the political alternative is that it underestimates the centrality of order in social life. Furthermore, its conflictual understanding of society and its focus on society as a whole rather than on local issues enhance the danger of anarchy and chaos, which already afflict and undermine the well-being of the community. In the view of the social sphere activists, it is a tactical mistake to assume that the community can risk a greater level of conflict and chaos in order to pursue the promise of some future greater harmony, reconciliation, and solidarity. These disagreements between the political and social sphere alternatives are neither arbitrary nor a matter of temperament. They are based on different convictions regarding how the world works and how values are related to one another. Such disagreements are a matter of political wisdom, of beliefs about how fast and how much the social world can be changed. From the perspective of the social sphere activists, people change slowly and need institutions to assist them in making those gradual changes.

Regarding the issue of power, those who work within the social sphere agree that power is necessary for the community to be able to defend and assert its interests. However, power must be institutionally channeled. They also believe that power should be widely distributed so that more institutions can realize their goals. Whenever one sector of society is able to accumulate too much power, weaker institutions and the interests they represent will be threatened. Thus, at present, it is preferable for Hispanics, who have only weak institutions, to advocate a wide distribution of power. The emphasis on the accumulation of power will be ideologically manipulated by the powerful to justify and expand the inordinate power they already control.

Furthermore, given their assumption of overall harmony and consensus within society, they believe that power does not have to be a zero-sum game and that social values are not necessarily the outcome of the fragile consensus of unstable and temporary power plays. Institutions provide the necessary power base to assure procedures that enable us to persuade others by means of words and deeds rather than by sheer coercion. Power remains necessary, but it is exercised best through socially accepted procedures and institutional channels that allow citizens to express and pursue their interest in an orderly and civil manner.

From the perspective of the social sphere activists, order as a moral value is neither derivative nor secondary; rather, it is foundational for the good life and for other moral values to emerge and sustain themselves. Institutional order frees us from chaos and the uncertainty and insecurity chaos entails. Order enables us to enjoy the constructive exercise of our freedom and the pursuit of life's new possibilities. Religiously speaking, institutional order is an expression of that ontological ordering through which God sustains communal life and keeps it human. As such, institutions are seen as essential elements in the historical process of humanization.

In this perspective, order rather than power becomes the first principle of social well-being. However, order, like power, is not an end in itself. It is foundational for the emergence of other moral values, in particular the value of freedom. A well-ordered society enhances freedom. Negatively speaking, order frees us from the instability, uncertainty, and ambiguity of chaos or anarchy. Positively speaking, order enables us to know our rights and entitlements. It enables us to experience freedom as an act of self-initiation. In short, a well-ordered society forwards our autonomy, curtailing undue interference from other individuals and institutions and allowing us the liberty to do as we please.

Freedom, therefore, is understood in a significantly different way than that advocated by those who struggle within the political sphere. The focus shifts from freedom as service to others and sacrifice for the well-being of the whole to a narrower sense of freedom as liberty or the right for uncoerced self-initiation. This view of freedom has a more individualistic bent. Politically, it expresses a commitment to democracy or representative government and, economically, to the free market—all of which maximize the freedom of the individual to live according to her or his choices. This is another reason why this position advocates a wide social division of power and limits the capacity of the state to intervene in one's life.

On the basis of the commitment to order and freedom as liberty, justice is given a procedural definition. Justice no longer consists of the creation of a participatory community pursuing a common good and seeking the relatively equal provision of basic needs for all members of society. Rather, justice consists of the creation of social procedures that guarantee people an equal opportunity to compete for the social positions, goods, and services available within society. Equality of opportunity could or could not entail the provision of basic goods and services; that is, it could be fair or formal equality of opportunity. The social sphere perspective recognizes that freedom as liberty feeds social inequality. However, according to this view, as long as the institutional procedures are fair, people abide by them, and no one has been coerced or cheated, the resulting inequalities brought by our free and voluntary transactions are fair and just, no matter how unequal the result might be. Justice does not concern itself with end results. It consists of the establishment of social procedures that sustain and maximize the freedom of all members of society. This marks one of the greatest discords between the social sphere and the political sphere alternatives. The latter claims that the existence of significant economic and social discrepancies between social groups is itself a sign that there is no equality of opportunity. From the perspective of the political sphere, end results are a legitimate concern of justice.

Finally, the social sphere perspective upholds a contractual as opposed to an organic notion of community. Communities, like institutions, are the result of our voluntary transactions. We create and support them because we will derive at least as much benefit from them as the investment we place in them. Communal life is not intrinsic to what it means to be human; it is rather an instrumental good, providing those goods and services we need to enjoy the good life. Community exists for the sake of individual freedom. According to this view, there is nothing more dangerous and detrimental to social life within the United States than to abandon our commitment to individual rights and freedom for the sake of group life. The option for the group leads to victimization of the individual, to not being able to forward his or her well-being.

The Cultural Sphere

Hispanics also struggle for the emancipation of their people within the sphere of culture. They agree with those who struggle within the political and social spheres that power and order are significant elements in the creation of any just community. However, they have a different understanding regarding the causes and dynamics of the oppression of Hispanics in the United States. More fundamental than questions of political powerlessness and institutional bankruptcy are those related to our personal and communal identity as well as to our sense of self-respect and worthiness. The following questions lie at the forefront of this struggle: Who are we as a people? What is our unique contribution to our common life? What gives meaning and value to our being?[6]

The oppression Hispanics have been forced to endure has had more devastating consequences for the community than poverty, powerlessness, and institutional chaos. The oppression of Hispanics is defined as the social process through which society, institutionally and systematically, disregards, stereotypes, and denigrates the racial makeup, language, potentiality, capacities, heritage, customs, and traditional habits of the Hispanic community. This negative projection of who Hispanics are and what they are capable of has had the consequence of devaluing and undermining the community's sense of self-worth and self-confidence as well as the moral and aesthetic value of its culture.

The ideology of the melting pot is particularly singled out and denounced as a contributing factor to this oppressive process. This ideology is based on the assumption that immigrants from all over the world gather

---

6. The La Raza movement, Chicano community-organizing groups, and similar groups within the Puerto Rican community are examples of this type. Paulo Freire has provided an ideological basis for some of the goals of recent Latin American and Central American groups.

in the United States to create a new people. In order to become a new person—defined as a U.S. citizen committed to a new sense of the value of the individual, individual rights, and the democratic creed—each individual has to abandon or give secondary importance to his or her traditional loyalties. Thus, individuals' ethnic, racial, and national loyalties and even cultural and religious traditions must be relativized or abandoned altogether if they are to become new persons within the new nation. While this process of assimilation seemed to have worked fairly well for most Europeans, particularly the dominant Anglo-Saxon group, it has proven to be quite detrimental to people of African, Asian, and Latin American descent. Many original inhabitants, people of color, were overrun and massacred by the Anglo-Saxon newcomers, who eventually became the dominant group and established the norms of the culture. Black Africans, who were brought against their will to work the land and build cities, and the Chinese, who created a system of rail transport that interconnected different regions of the new nation, never received full rights of membership. They were and remain victims of that racism that constitutes the main sickness and most obvious contradiction and failure of the founding ideals of North America. Even today, if they are fortunate enough to have achieved economic success, they remain second- and third-class citizens. The proponents of the ideology of the melting pot simply did not have them in mind when they concocted this vision.

Those who struggle within the field of culture argue that, while forced to exist as outsiders, ethnic and racial minorities are still expected to take responsibility for integrating themselves into the dominant society. For the dominant group this means that racial and ethnic minorities have to assimilate themselves to the standards of Anglo-Saxon culture. Hispanics argue that even today the dominant Anglo-Saxon groups do not understand that they themselves must change in order for integration to take place. Hispanics do not perceive the commitment from anglophiles to work toward integration, so they remain suspicious of all talk of assimilation and integration presented within the framework of melting-pot imagery.

The ideology of the melting pot not only has contributed to keeping Hispanics at the margins of social existence, the eternal outsiders, but also threatens to leave Hispanics bereft of any alternative community that can provide structures and symbols from which to derive a positive meaning and direction for their lives. To surrender loyalty to their ethnic heritage in order to become a component in the melting pot is tantamount to risking being left without a context for identity and meaning. The abandonment of ethnic loyalties, the traditional source of Hispanic being and belonging, is most likely to keep them marginal, invisible social beings who must endure the threatening experience of being nonpersons. Many Hispanics today know what this means. The loss of community is so drastic that many see fit to call life within the ghetto—where violence and fear rule, the clear signals of absence of community—"communal life."[7]

Those who struggle within the cultural sphere denounce and disavow the ideology and policies of the melting pot and in its place advocate some form of cultural pluralism in which the natural givens of race and ethnicity become the defining unit of communal life and the ethnic group becomes the basic unit of society. Their liberating social vision involves the creation and structuring of a society composed of diverse and well-integrated racial and ethnic communities. These communities will be better able to provide each individual member with a well-defined sense of self. The new social order will allow the different ethnic groups that constitute it to have equal standing and enjoy the rights, responsibilities, and duties that come with being full members of society.

The first objective of this cultural revolution is to raise the community's consciousness of the values of its heritage. It puts the community back in touch with its roots and traditions. Among other things, it entails the retrieval of ancestral history, those indigenous beginnings that embody the wisdom of the people. It stresses the importance of preserving their language; celebrating their religious and cultural heritage, folklore, and culinary styles; and, most importantly, retrieving their history of political and social struggles. This history embodies the memory of resistance and survival that is central to understanding the character and unique way of being of the people. This process is indispensable if the people are going to have a future as a people. Through it heroes are rediscovered; the crises that shape the character of the people are retold; and major events and achievements are brought to light once again in order to enhance the people's pride. When this history is well done, it even includes the story of those abuses and shortcomings of the community that have also played a prominent role in shaping its identity. The arts, music, graphics, paintings, poetry, novels, and stories are also part of this process of cultural emancipation and affirmation. They provide a unique symbolic structure of meaning and magic that evokes a sense of awe and oneness among the people.

It is not enough, however, to rediscover the history of how and why Hispanics came to be in America and to reaffirm their traditional cultural heritage. It is equally important that Hispanics, particularly the latter generations, find the space and support they need to give expression to their new identity as Hispanics in the United States. It is interesting to notice how

---

7. Many economically depressed Hispanic communities reveal a deterioration of personal, familial, and communal relationships. When people are deprived of these islands of human stability, it becomes almost impossible to develop within them a critical consciousness of, a moral commitment to, and a daring engagement with the cause of social transformation. In fact, public and communal life is almost completely disregarded, and only individual personal accomplishment remains. The main problem confronted by successful individuals is how to use their resources and talents for things other than consumption and personal gratification.

first- and second-generation ethnic churches within the Hispanic and other ethnic communities struggle with these issues. Many of these churches, usually dominated by the older generation, expend great effort preserving the culture and ways of the homeland for the young. Usually they worship in their own language and celebrate traditional festivities and folkloric events. This is definitely a contribution to the process of preserving the culture of the ethnic group. Still, by and large, churches do not do an adequate job of enabling the young to express their own identity as Hispanics who live in the United States. This has led to fragmentation and the enhancing of internal conflicts within many church communities.

Those who struggle within the cultural sphere pay particular attention to educational or school politics.[8] They understand better than those who work from within the other spheres how the debate about school curriculum is a significant political matter. Schools, in particular public schools, provide the main forum for future citizens to learn about the contributions and achievements of one another's racial and ethnic groups. They play a prominent role in shaping the identity of future citizens and molding their perceptions and attitudes. For this process of citizen formation to fit our democratic tradition, it is important that schools be well integrated, that is, that there be within their walls members of various racial and ethnic groups. Within the schools teachers are not the only ones who teach— students also learn from one another. They learn the art of living together in a context of respect and support. Consequently, our schools are centers where students come to learn not just how to read and write but also how to become citizens capable of living together within a democratic society.

The value of equality of worth and self-respect becomes the central moral value within the sphere of culture. Most Hispanics argue that equality entails more than mere formal equality of opportunity. The dominant view is that, as a minimum, a society must offer fair equality of opportunity. Fair equality of opportunity requires an adequate investment of social resources to redress the history of injustice under which most Hispanics have been forced to live. The aim of this social investment is to enable racial and ethnic minorities to compete on a level playing field with their fellow citizens. Job programs and quality education are seen as key factors in overcoming the social barriers that have been placed in the way of racial and ethnic minorities. Job training programs and adequate employment are particularly important factors in generating the kind of social and economic stability that enables the community to sustain itself and prosper.[9] This notion of equal well-being for racial and ethnic groups entails

8. One area in which various Hispanic groups have been able to work together is in the political struggles to keep bilingual education and the teaching of Spanish. This is once again a forefront political issue that brings Hispanics together.

9. Affirmative action programs have fallen into great disrepute. This is one of the key achievements of the conservative forces that have dominated the political scene in recent

a notion of social justice that is focused on the group rather than on the individual. The interest of the ethnic group becomes the standard by which relative well-being is measured and compared. The goal of egalitarian social policies should be to keep the necessary inequalities that are part of social life within reasonable and acceptable limits.

Within the cultural sphere, freedom is more than liberty or the right to do as one pleases. Freedom has to do primordially with the capacity to establish meaningful relationships with others. Freedom and equality are intrinsically related. People recognize each other as equal and worthy of respect only when there is relative equality. One can properly claim to be free only when one has the resources to make meaningful choices. Equality is perceived as being foundational for power and for the ethnic group to order its internal life and relate to others from a position of relatively equal strength.

In this perspective group interest becomes so dominant that it is not clear how one relates to society as a whole. Thus, the perspective cannot avoid giving the appearance of fueling social division and social conflict.[10] Its fragmented vision of society makes it very much at home with social-contract theories. Community might be seen as organic within the racial ethnic group, but between itself and other racial groups community is instrumental. The larger social whole is viewed in contractual terms where different groups agree regarding the conditions under which they will work together. The aim of the larger community becomes fairness and efficiency for the sake of the overall well-being of the racial and ethnic groups that constitute it.

From Conflict to Solidarity

It is important to note that the three positions examined above affirm similar value commitments. They all uphold the values of freedom, equality, power, community, justice, and order as essential to what it means to be human and to live in community. This consensus should not surprise us since it merely expresses the fact that these are the foundational, culturally

years. We must recall that there have always been affirmative action programs. Some were created as incentives to attract particular immigrants; others have supported farmers; others, soldiers. It is clear that such programs will not solve the extreme condition of poverty within the Hispanic community. They will not overcome the extreme inequality that exists between the social classes at present in our society. But they are still important programs insofar as, without them, the economic and social condition of all communities will become worse than it already is.

10. One of the dangers of this position is to emphasize ethnic pride by merely reacting against the racism that is prevalent in society. This negative, defensive posture is an important element in the quest for self-identity. However, one must avoid falling into forms of Hispanic tribalism. We must recall that democratic politics works by numbers. If a more just economic redistribution of resources and a redistribution of power are to take place, there must exist a well-organized, multiethnic, and multiracial political force.

ingrained moral values of our shared political and religious tradition. They also agree that we find guidance for our actions not in one value but in a configuration of values.[11] Thus, since values at time conflict with one another, it is to be expected that the moral life is lived in various levels of creative tension. Finally, they all agree that our basic moral principles are intrinsically related and interdependent in such a way that if any one value is consistently disregarded or denied, all values are placed in jeopardy.

Each position, however, argues for a different ordering of the values they all uphold. The political sphere gives priority to power; then moves to community, equality, and freedom; and ends up with order. The social sphere gives priority to order; then moves to freedom; then, to justice and equality; and ends with community. The cultural alternative starts with equality; then moves to power and community; and concludes with justice, freedom, and order. This different ordering is a matter of political prudence, the way each position understands how the world works and how values relate to, follow, and depend on each other.

While all the positions agree that the values of freedom, equality, and community are essential for being fully human and for the possibility of creating and sustaining community, they each give a substantially different meaning to each of these terms, which in turn accounts for the differences in their vision of the good society. At times, their understanding of each value is so narrowly defined that it seems they are advocating different values and antagonistic social interests. As long as freedom is reduced to liberty or wanting to do as one pleases and being left alone to do so (the social sphere), equality is defined as sameness (the cultural sphere), and community loyalty is seen as implying a high level of self-sacrifice from its individual members (the political sphere), then the principles will, in fact, be antagonistic to one another, and each Hispanic group will, at best, be working parallel to the others. The differences between them are real and threaten to become a practical obstacle for the possibility of Hispanics coming to work together in the struggle to emancipate their people.

The Christian tradition might provide a way out of this impasse. It can provide us with a theological point of view that transfigures our interpretation of the values of freedom, equality, and community and makes manifest their indispensable and essential role in keeping life human and sustaining community. Such a transfiguration of the core human values has practical implications: socially, it enhances the possibility for Hispanics to establish coalitions and to work in solidarity for the well-being of their communi-

---

11. The notion of a configuration of moral values is a revision of Richard McCormick's views presented in "A Commentary on the Commentaries," *Doing Evil to Achieve Good: Moral Choices in Conflict Situations* (ed. Richard McCormick and P. Ramsey; Chicago: Loyola University Press, 1978) 71–72.

ties; politically, it creates conditions for society at large to become more inclusive and compassionate.[12]

First, from a theological point of view, we value freedom or liberty because it enables us to be creative agents. Creative agency, part of being in the image of God the Creator, is at the core of what it means to be human. It entails the capacity to conceive and bring about that which is new not only within the artistic realm but also within all realms of life. It is what keeps us dissatisfied with the powers that be and motivates and enables us to pursue the vision or historical project of creating a more inclusive and compassionate community. Second, from a theological point of view, we are of equal value and worth, owe others equal respect and recognition, only because God loves us equally. This essential equality enables us to and demands from us that we create structures of mutual support. We are not only equal; we are also essentially relational beings, beings who can flourish only within the context of relational dialogue, mutual care, and fidelity. To be fully human is to recognize and undertake obligations toward others beyond what is due to them as a matter of right. We were created as men and women to live in faithful relationships. Faithfulness and mutual commitment alone can keep life human. Our sin and inhumanity to one another had their beginning and still sustain themselves through the breaking of ties of fidelity. All acts of domination reveal our sinfulness and represent the continued threat to our humanity.

Finally, from a theological point of view, we value community because we know that we are not just individuals, nor merely relational beings, but members of wholes, for example, nations and complex cultures. The drive toward community is a basic component of our humanity. Today, most economic and political forces drive us toward more inclusive communities, even in spite of ourselves. Nationalism, which denies the drive toward inclusiveness, brings forth some of the worst cruelty humans commit against one another. We have more things in common with one another than things that separate or distinguish us. This is what enables us to continue to struggle for the practical possibility of living in solidarity with one another. It seems to be a basic lesson of our sacred Scriptures that God calls us as a people and calls us for peoplehood, or for the creation of the beloved community through which we serve one another or become a blessing to one another.

In short, from a theological point of view, we are able to transfigure the substantive content of those core values that keep life human and sustain community. Creative agency now becomes the substance of liberty; fidelity in relationship becomes the substance of equality; and participa-

12. I am using the notion of the theological transfiguration of value developed by Warren R. Copeland, *Economic Justice: The Social Ethics of U.S. Economic Policy* (Nashville: Abingdon Press, 1988).

tory community becomes the substance of power. This transfiguration of values has the additional benefit of enabling us to perceive explicitly the essential interrelatedness and interdependence that exist among these core moral values.

The theological transfiguration of freedom, from liberty into creative agency, entails a shift of vision from self-centeredness and self-fulfillment into other-regard and other-service. The relational nature of all creative processes is more clearly perceived as an extension of our relational nature. We can better come to understand how every act of creation and every creative agent needs both the active assistance and passive witness of others. We can even come to see our creations as tied to that unbroken chain of creativity that began long before we were even conceived, the legacy from our ancestors. As we have freely received from them, we should freely give to those who will come after us. Creative agency, therefore, must express what is valuable and meaningful for ourselves as well as what is of value, meaning, and service for others. Creation is no longer imprisoned in individuality and subjectivity; it also has a public presence and reveals accountability and gratitude to the community.

The theological transformation of liberty into creative agency also transforms our understanding of community. As the community is necessary for creative agency to take place, providing the creative agent with resources and a context of meaning within which his or her creation makes sense, it is equally recognized that the community itself depends, for its survival and well-being, on the creative capacity of its members. The community cannot expect from its members only commitment and sacrifice but must itself support the emergence of the creative individuality of its members. The just community creates conditions for its members to express what makes them unique and distinct from fellow citizens. Diversity and pluralism become the mark of a healthy community.

Finally, a community of creative agents entails a commitment to equal respect and regard for all its members. We seek and respect the judgments of our equals in determining the merits of our creations. To be treated as an equal is not to be treated in the same way as everyone else but rather to be supported in our agency. To deny or curtail our creativity is to undermine our humanity. Equality within a pluralistic community forwards the creative freedom that overcomes sameness and homogeneity. Nothing is more unjust and oppressive than demanding that the less talented equal the performance, productivity, and creativity of the more talented or demanding that the exceptional limit themselves to the social medium. A just society encourages diversity and finds ways of sustaining it, while allowing its members to rejoice in their differences.

A theological point of view, therefore, critically affirms the core moral values that sustain the struggle to advance the well-being of the Hispanic community, as this is undertaken within the political, social, and cultural spheres. It is an affirmation of this struggle in the sense that the core values of freedom, equality, and power/community are validated as indeed being foundational for what it means to be human and for the creation of a just community. It is a critical affirmation in that it calls us to adopt a more comprehensive understanding of freedom as creative agency, of equality as a capacity to establish relationships within and outside our ethnic community, and of empowerment as community building where individuals can find self-identity as they seek to forward their vision of the public good. This transfiguration of foundational human values can make the struggle for the emancipation of the Hispanic community more inclusive, synthesizing the values and goals that are presently being fought for within the different spheres.

The practical implications of this process of the transfiguration of values are crucial. To begin with, it entails the courage to see an occasion for both self-criticism and self-affirmation in the struggle within a sphere different from the one to which we are committed. Each group, within its own sphere, must affirm the value of what it struggles for, while recognizing the limits of its individual struggles. The fundamental problems confronted by the Hispanic community involve too much dehumanizing poverty, equally dehumanizing powerlessness, and too little self-respect and self-love, accompanied by a disproportionate sense of self-loathing. This situation is too complex and too urgent to be dealt with in only one of the spheres. Each one of these problems requires particular forms of commitment and solutions. Thus, the struggle for the emancipation of the Hispanic community cannot but take place within different realms at the same time. No one sphere can address all the problems.

It is possible, for example, as witnessed by the Hispanic middle class (although not only by them), to be free from dehumanizing forms of poverty, to have meaningful work and even some significant degree of power, and still be enslaved by a negative image of oneself. One the one hand, the internalization of the negative self-image by which the wider society devalues our capacities, mocks our intelligence, and disregards our sense of the beautiful and the good can lead to hatred for one's Hispanicity. On the other hand, we can possess a positive image of self and still forget that without political power and economic resources our sense of values can become folkloric, remain abstract ideals with no possibility of historical realization. The dynamics by which we solve issues of self-identity are different from those by which we solve problems of powerlessness and poverty. In spite of the fact that they are related, each must be dealt with on its own terms, and all have to be taken care of with the same intensity and intentionality.

Most of the struggles in which Hispanics are engaged take place within their own local communities. Since these communities are widely dispersed within the United States, there exists little or minimum awareness of some of our greatest social and political achievements. It is essential that Hispanics continue to find ways of coming together to inform one another of their achievements and shortcomings. Their different struggles need to be critically evaluated by all. These encounters can serve as a basis for the creation of structures of solidarity among Hispanics in spite of differences in the spheres within which they work. Hispanics can no longer afford to undermine this work through petty divisions and squabbles. Pettiness feeds that cynical attitude that leads to the vision that there is nothing Hispanics can do to change their local and national standing.

Ultimately, what matters is that the Hispanic community be served in ways that allow it to affirm its freedom, power, and cultural identity. The struggle must take place on many fronts. Sometimes, it expresses itself as a great leap forward, with significant achievements taking place; at other times, it is less glamorous, merely resisting losses within the political, cultural, and economic spheres. Nevertheless, all of the struggles are necessary and significant, and we must learn how to be both a critical voice and a motivating voice in one another's struggles. What we need is not a unified movement but a movement in which honest conversation, constructive critique, and mutual support can take place. We have already begun the journey toward the creation of a more compassionate and inclusive society. Our capacity to enhance our particular visions so as to include all those who struggle within the different spheres will get us there faster.

16

Popular Catholicism

Alienation or Hope?

Orlando O. Espín

Popular Catholicism is one of the most distinctive and pervasive elements in all of the Latino cultures in the United States.[1] It is arguably one of their most fundamental matrices and historically seems to have acted as bearer of some crucial dimensions of the Latino worldview. For as long as U.S. Latinos remained a mostly rural or small-town population, popular Catholicism's universe could be plausibly maintained by the people and pastorally ignored by the anglophone church authorities. However, this century—and more particularly the second half of this century—has witnessed a vigorous challenge to the cultural assumptions of reality behind Latino popular Catholicism. Though still very much alive and important in all Latino communities, this religious universe has begun to face the modern, urban world as never before. And yet, given popular Catholicism's role in the past as crucial bearer of identity and values, the current challenge involves and implies more than just the possible transformation of religious forms or styles, or even the demise of a centuries-old type of Christianity.

This essay assumes as correct the view that religion is the socialization of the experience of the divine,[2] thus necessitating a two-sided approach to the

---

1. There are other, non-Christian "popular religions" in several of the U.S. Latino communities (for example, Santería or Regla de Osha, Voodoo, Abakuá, Palo Mayombe or de Angola, Spiritism, etc.). Within Latino Protestantism a number of churches can be described as part of the popular religion universe (for example, the Church of Mita and a number of other small and not too orthodox churches). I have argued elsewhere that some types of Latino Pentecostalism may be classified as popular religion as well (see "Pentecostalism and Popular Catholicism: Preservers of Hispanic Catholic Tradition?" *ACHTUS Newsletter* 4:1 [1993] 8–15). I will not be discussing any of these religions in this chapter, however, limiting myself to popular Catholicism as certainly the most widespread and culturally important of all of them.

2. I have surveyed much of the literature on the diverse definitions of religion (in theology and the social sciences) and given the reasons for my own definition of religion as well as the bibliographical support for it in my *Evangelización y religiones negras* (4 vols.; Rio de Janeiro: PUC, 1984) esp. vol. 2.

study of religion: one that concentrates on the sociohistorical dimensions and another that focuses on the experiences of the divine claimed by the believers and that ultimately explains *why* people believe. A multidisciplinary approach, therefore, where the social sciences and theology take each other seriously, is here assumed as the best course to follow.[3]

Latino popular Catholicism is a religion.[4] More concretely, it is a religion of those treated as subalterns by both society and church in the United States. On the basis of its centuries-old history, Latino popular Catholicism can be characterized as an effort by the subalterns to explain, justify, and somehow control a social reality that appears too dangerous to confront in terms and through means other than the mainly symbolic.[5] However, this popular religion is founded on the claim that the divine (identified by the people as the Christian divine) has been and is encountered by them in and through the symbols (ritual, ethical, and doctrinal) of popular Catholicism.

This essay, working from an interdisciplinary point of view, will modestly attempt to indicate the main roles played by U.S. Latino popular Catholicism as religion. Many other important themes, otherwise needed for a thorough analysis of popular Catholicism, can only be hinted at or indicated in passing. At the end it should become clear that the alternative answers implied in the essay's title are, of themselves, insufficient.

---

3. It will become evident that this essay—as well as most of my work on popular religion—is dependent on the thought of the Italian social philosopher Antonio Gramsci and the Brazilian sociologist of religion Pedro Ribeiro de Oliveira. For Gramsci, see: *Gli intelletuali e l'organizzazione della cultura* (Brazilian trans.: *Os intelectuais e a organização da cultura* [Rio de Janeiro: Civilização Brasileira, 1979]); *Note sul Machiavelli, sulla politica e sullo stato moderno* (Brazilian trans.: *Maquivel, a política e o estado moderno* [Rio de Janeiro: Civilização Brasileira, 1980]); *Lettere dal carcere* (Brazilian trans.: *Cartas do cárcere* [Rio de Janeiro: Civilização Brasileira, 1978]); *Letteratura e vita nazionale* (Brazilian trans.: *Literatura e vida nacional* [Rio de Janeiro: Civilização Brasileira, 1978]); *Il materialismo storico e la filosofia di Benedetto Croce* (Brazilian trans.: *Concepção dialética da história* [Rio de Janeiro: Civilização Brasileira, 1981]); *Quaderni dei carceri* (Turin: Einaudi, 1975). For de Oliveira: *Religião e dominação de classe* (Petrópolis, Brazil: Vozes, 1985); *Evangelização e comportamento religioso popular* (Petrópolis, Brazil: Vozes, 1978); *Éléments pour une étude sociologique de la magie* (Louvain: Institut des Sciences Politiques et Sociales/UCL, 1967); *Catequese e socialização da fé* (Rio de Janeiro: CERIS, 1974); *Catolicismo popular na América Latina* (Rio de Janeiro: FERES-AL, 1971); "Catholicisme populaire et hégémonie bourgeoise au Brésil," *Archives des Sciences Sociales des Religions* 47:1 (1979) 53–79; "Catolicismo popular como base religiosa," *CEI-Suplemento* 12 (1975) 3–11. The influence of these two thinkers is so evident in this essay that I will refrain from referring to them constantly and repetitiously. The titles mentioned in this note are the ones I have used here.

4. The use of the term "popular" does not merely or mainly imply "widespread," although this is also meant. "Popular" is meant to convey the origin and social location of the religion and of those who participate in it. Furthermore, I avoid the use of the term "religiosity," often applied to this symbolic system, because of the implied ideological (and dismissive) judgment on the people's religion.

5. See Orlando Espín, "Religión popular: Un aporte para su definición y hermenéutica," *Estudios Sociales* 58 (1984) 41–57.

The Experience of the Divine

To speak of religious phenomena, experiences, and practices presumes an understanding of "religion." However, the term "religion" has been defined in theology and the social sciences in so many and often contradictory ways that one may wonder if there has been or ever will be a commonly accepted definition. There is no question that many of these efforts at defining religion have indeed contributed to a better understanding of the religious universe. Stripped of the occasional pretensions of being absolutely correct, much of what theology and the social sciences have contributed has withstood the test of history. And yet there is no question that all attempts at defining religion have always demonstrated the ideological interests of the researcher. This essay is no exception.

As I stated earlier, I see religions as the socialization of the experience of the divine. This definition seems to respect the contributions of both theology and the social sciences, without belonging exclusively to one or another discipline. By "experience of the divine" I understand an encounter between a human being (or group) and some One who is strongly felt, who is undoubtedly experienced as near and as good, and who (however briefly) grants complete meaning and fulfillment to that human being's (or group's) life. It seems that this type of experience is available to many and not just to a few especially sensitive people.

Studies of religion uncover frequent testimonies of this kind of experience among religious subjects. The social sciences should observe and study how people live and organize their religions in society and the consequences of those acts. But social scientists should not judge as true or false human participation in the experience of the divine. In other words, the experience of the divine is beyond the observation of the nonparticipant. The effects of the experience are indeed observable, but not the experience itself or its meaning for the believer. Of the experience and its meaning we have only the witness of those who claim to have shared in it.

The experience of the divine always occurs in human culture, as we shall see. But without a prior, explicit acknowledgment that religion is born out of an experience that is perceived by the believers as an encounter with the divine (however the latter is explained), we would not do justice to the faith of the believers nor would we understand that very core that their witness claims as the most fundamental reason for their belief. In no way does this acknowledgment impose on the researcher the need to accept the existence of "the divine" or "God," or anything concerning "God" either. It does, however, respect the most basic starting point: any religion exists *because* those who believe in it claim to have encountered the divine. And it is this claim—whose experiential core is unavailable to nonparticipants—that makes a believer out of a human being.

The Socialization of the Experience of the Divine

Experience and Culture

Even after emphasizing that the experience of the divine lies at the core of all religion and that without this one element there would be no religion, we must also recall the evident: no experience of the divine occurs in a vacuum. The same testimonies that point to the human encounter with "God" signal precisely that it is an *encounter*. One of the two involved is, by definition, contextualized in a concrete culture, in a concrete society, and in a concrete history. From the perspective of the human partner, the experience of the divine is possible only through cultural, social, and historical means.

Thus, when human beings believe themselves to be encountering the divine, they are in fact encountering that which culture allows them to understand precisely as "divine." This fact does not refer primarily to questions about the existence or nonexistence of God. It does refer to the inculturation of all religious experience, if it is human and understandable for humans. All possibility of a pure, a-cultural encounter with the divine is, therefore, excluded. The One met in any religious experience is only the humanly comprehensible One. To pretend to have a pure encounter with God would be, in theological terms, equivalent to possessing God (even if for a fleeting instant). This pretension is idolatrous, theologically speaking. No religion, regardless of its type or history, has ever believed that what it affirms of the divine is all that can be affirmed of or about it.

If the human partner in the experience did not have the means of understanding and interpreting it, he or she would not have had it. The culture within which the experience happens offers the human subject the hermeneutic tools needed: symbols, language, patterns of imagination, and so on. Cultural diversity makes possible the diverse interpretations of the religious experiences of humankind. Therefore, the cultural "idiom" of an individual or group will shape the language, symbols, and so on used by that individual or group in the process of interpreting religious experience, thereby shaping the experience itself as "religious" and the image(s) of the One encountered as "divine."

Society and Conflict

Culture does not exist in a historical vacuum. In a dialectical process, it is born in and of society. Every human society creates culture, and every culture in turn enters the process that creates society. So if the experience of the divine can only happen in culture, this also means that it can only occur in society. And just as culture imposes its epistemological, hermeneutic limits on the religious experience, so does society. The "place" of a religious individual or group in society will also shape the language, symbols, and so on used by that individual or group in the process of interpreting religious experience, thereby also shaping the experience itself as "religious" and the image(s) of the One encountered as "divine." Therefore, not only culture but social place makes possible the diverse interpretations of the religious experiences of humankind.

The above remarks might not seem important until we recall that in today's urban societies the social place of individuals and groups and the cultures and subcultures born in and from those societies bear the mark of conflict. Whether or not we wish to consciously identify or name the conflict, it is not possible to believe in good conscience that millions of Latinos chose to become part of the subaltern social place in contemporary U.S. society. It is simply impossible to argue that there is something genetic or deliberately chosen in the subaltern social place of U.S. Latinos. The fact (and it is unfortunately a fact) that most Latinos are at society's bottom has a great deal to do with ongoing conflict. The experiences of the divine culturally and societally available to them bear this mark.

The hegemonic[6] epistemology in U.S. society has managed to keep Latinos and their popular type of Catholicism "in their place." And it is from this place that they claim to have experienced the divine. So, if our preceding observations are correct, the "God" experienced by U.S. Latinos is necessarily culturally and socially contextualized in ways possible only to them and expressive of the language, symbols, understandings, and image(s) of the divine shaped by *their* culture, by *their* social place, and by the *conflict* underlying much of U.S. society. Thus, their religion cannot be like the religion of other Christians whose social place is different, who might not be at the bottom of society's ladder, and/or who benefit from the current configuration of U.S. society.[7]

Socialization of the Experience of the Divine within a Society in Conflict

Any individual or group may experience the divine.[8] No important differences can be found among people's and groups' fundamental claims to having encountered the divine, but important differences can be found regarding how the divine is imaged, how the experience is undergone and interpreted, and so on. And just as it is impossible to conceive of the existence of an event without some prior understanding that would allow it

---

6. I am using "hegemony" in the Gramscian sense. See L. Gruppi, *O conceito de hegemonia em Gramsci* (2d ed.; Rio de Janeiro: Graal, 1978); also, H. Portelli, *Gramsci et le bloc historique* (Paris: Presses Universitaires de France, 1972).

7. Although I will be referring exclusively to the U.S. Roman Catholic Church in this essay, I believe that, *mutatis mutandis,* my remarks are applicable to mainline American Protestant churches as well.

8. Max Weber seemed inclined to think that religious "virtuosi" were the most apt to experience the divine. It appears that Weber assumed that the creation of religious symbols, and so on (that is, the sphere of the "virtuosi"), was the identifying measure of those capable of the experience. Obviously, this assumption is not self-evident. See Max Weber, *The Sociology of Religion* (London: Methuen, 1966).

to be labeled as "existing," it is equally impossible to speak or conceive of an experience of the divine without the prior understandings provided by culture and social place. Therefore, the most important difference among individuals and groups in reference to experiences of the divine will have to do with which interpretations and images of it are presented to the rest of society and how they are received. In other words, even if it may be true that the divine can be experienced by anyone or any group, the very instant an experience is perceived as "of the divine," the culture and social place of the individual or group utilize hermeneutic tools made available by that person's or group's standing in society, thereby making any subsequent testimony or report of the experience acceptable and "respectable" in society in the same manner and degree as are given to the culture and social place of that individual or group.[9]

The religious subject will interpret and attempt to remember, symbolize, and live by that which he or she experienced in the encounter with the divine. When this interpretation and these attempts are shared by others who also claim to have met "God," there a religion is born. When an individual or group "pours" the experience of the divine into meaningful symbols, images, memories, ethical or doctrinal explanations, and guidelines for living that can be shared by others in society, there the experience becomes socialized. This socialization, obviously, is not the result of detached calculation.

In theological terms, there is religion only where the experience of God has become truly incarnate in the culture, history, and life of the believing people. And, among other consequences, this implies, for example, that the Catholicism of the hegemonic group and their allies in a society will express itself through the symbols, the images, and the lifestyles of hegemony, which are not those of the Catholic subaltern groups in that same society.[10] To the degree that the hegemonic religious symbols, images, and lifestyles have penetrated the subaltern level, and to the degree that the memory of Christianity's subaltern origins have remained among the hegemonic groups, to that degree people on both sides of society can claim to participate in the same Catholic religion.[11]

Society and culture exist prior to religion. And if it is true that Catholicism, of its very nature, must be incarnate in and symbolize the social and historical realities of the believers, then there cannot be only one way of being Catholic.[12] The different ways will reflect the conflicts, the social places,

---

9. On this, see my "A 'Multicultural' Church? Theological Reflections from 'Below,'" *Implications of the Multicultural Church* (ed. W. Cenkner; forthcoming).

10. See H. Portelli, *Gramsci y la cuestión religiosa* (Barcelona: Laia, 1977; Spanish trans. of *Gramsci et la question religieuse* [Paris: Anthropos, 1974]) 141–62.

11. Ibid., 43–94.

12. I found stimulating, on this point of Catholicism's "sacramental ethos" and the "catholicity" it entails, the sequential reading of David Tracy, *The Analogical Imagina-*

the classes, and everything else that are common part and parcel of human societies.[13] If in the United States the Latino communities are by and large discriminated against, the object of racism and bigotry, and the victims of injustice, then their Catholicism cannot possibly be understood without further prejudice unless the conflicts and suffering of these communities are admitted as truly *shaping* their experience of God and their socialization of it. But by the same token, to the degree that other U.S. Catholics (including some Latino Catholics) have benefited by their access to the hegemonic groups and ideologies (whose byproduct has been the marginalization of most Latinos), to that degree their Catholicism is *shaped* in the likeness of society's victors and as religion participates in the hegemonic power and culture that legitimize the marginalization of others.

Roles of American Catholicisms in Society

Any religion may exhibit several roles in any given society, depending on the social place of the believers. Any religion may play, at any one time, more than one role or change it in the course of its history. Catholicism*s* (Latino, Euro-American, African American, and so on) in the United States are no exception.

1. The Legitimizing Role. If hegemony in society is dependent on the ability of a given group to persuade other groups within that society that it is the best qualified to lead, then this persuasion requires the creation and distribution of explanations, symbols, justifications, and a "reading" of reality that legitimize the leading group's pretensions. To the degree that the other groups in society (especially the subaltern groups) accept the validity of the explanations and justifications, and to the degree that they assume the symbols of the leaders, the hegemony of the latter is secured. Given the conflictiveness of modern societies, the creation and dissemination of a leading group's reasons for hegemony do not happen without some form of coercion. And yet no acceptance of the reasons for hegemony is ever complete or without some doubt.

The dominant group will attempt to present its leadership role and its explanations as necessary and, when expressed through religious categories, will affirm that its role is divinely sanctioned and willed and that its explanations are either "revealed" as truth or as close to truth as possible. There is no better argument in favor of a particular group's hegemony (and hence, in favor of a particular social formation) than to spread the

---

tion (New York: Crossroad, 1986); Andrew M. Greeley, *The Catholic Myth* (New York: Scribner's, 1990); and W. G. Jeanrond and J. L. Rike, eds., *Radical Pluralism and Truth: David Tracy and the Hermeneutics of Religion* (New York: Crossroad, 1991).

13. See F. Houtart, "Religion et champ politique: Cadre théorique pour l'étude des sociétés capitalistes périphériques," *Social Compass* 24:2–3 (1977) 265–72; idem, "Weberian Theory and the Ideological Function of Religion," *Social Compass* 23:4 (1976) 345–54.

belief that it is divinely established or sanctioned. Obviously, there can be no possible appeal beyond God's decision. The sad story of Christianity's role in the justification of U.S. slave-holding society and its complicity in legitimizing the doctrine of manifest destiny are clear examples of this. And these are also examples of how the reasons in favor of a group's hegemony are created and disseminated not only in the direction of the subaltern groups but also toward the very interior of the leading group. The rulers eventually become convinced of their "right" to rule and of other groups' "inferiority."[14]

There is no question that religion has played and still plays this legitimizing role in U.S. society. And large segments of Euro-American Catholicism, in their attempt to become acceptable to the hegemonic group, seem to have paid (for their admission into "respectability" and mainstream, middle-class status) the price of joining the latter's legitimizing effort. Euro-American Catholicism has very often lent its religious categories, symbols, and institutions to the hegemonic group's efforts at spreading its reasons for social dominance. One consequence of this price has been the internalization (by those "mainstreamed" Catholic segments) of hegemonic explanations concerning Latino social "inferiority" and lack of leadership capabilities. This in turn has justified the frequent treatment (doctrinal and pastoral) of Latino popular Catholicism as religiously and ecclesially "inferior," defective, or of insufficient quality.[15]

I am in no way implying that all Euro-American Catholics are consciously or culpably aware of the legitimizing function that their religion has in society. However, each of these individual's "reading" of the meaning of the experience of God, the doctrinal and pastoral shape of his or her

---

14. What might be *sincerely* and ultimately perceived as "real" and "true," therefore, becomes socially constructed products at the service of the hegemonic group and a successful result of the arguments of hegemony even within the dominant sectors of society. It should be clear by now that social hegemony and dominance, in my view, are not causally linked to or mainly the consequence of control over the means of production (as in classic Marxist thought). On the contrary, it seems to me that the opposite is more correct, that is, that cultural and symbolic (ideological) hegemony is established before any economic "success" can befall a given group. History seems to point to cases in which those who did not control a society's means of production nevertheless ended up influencing its symbol-making processes and thereby provoked a transformation of the society's social configuration. For the traditional Marxist views on the relationship between culture, religion, dominance, and the control over means of production, see the fine collection of texts edited by H. Assmann and R. Mate, *Sobre la religión* (2 vols.; Salamanca: Sígueme, 1974–75). For the classic study on the "construction" of reality, see Peter L. Berger and Thomas Luckmann, *The Social Construction of Reality: A Treatise on the Sociology of Knowledge* (New York: Doubleday, 1967).

15. The most complete history of Latino Catholicism in the United States is the one edited by J. Dolan, A. F. Deck and J. Vidal, *A History of Hispanic Catholics* (3 vols.; Notre Dame, Ind.: University of Notre Dame Press, 1994). For the particular history of Latino *popular* Catholicism in the United States, see my study, "Popular Catholicism among Latinos," in vol. 3 of that work. To the best of my knowledge, this is the only comprehensive history written on the subject.

religion, and her or his understanding of Catholicism's role in our society is very often in harmony with the legitimizing explanations and symbols of U.S. hegemonic ideology. The private intentions of the individual believer do not cancel, unfortunately, the social consequences of his or her religion's public role.[16]

Latino popular Catholicism, insofar as it too participates in U.S. society, exhibits the several roles of any U.S. religion, and thus it can also favor the legitimizing efforts of the hegemonic group. This Catholicism too has functioned as a channel for the dissemination of explanations and justifications that, through religious categories, are directed at the subalterns in our society. Therefore, to the degree that popular Catholicism has been a successful tool in the internalization of their subaltern status by Latinos, to that degree their religion has played the role of legitimizing contemporary U.S. social formation and dominant ideology. And because of this, popular Catholicism might have become, in many instances, a weapon for the alienation of and the social (and thereby ecclesiastical) control over U.S. Latinos.

2. The Rebellious Role. As I said earlier, the process of creating and disseminating the explanations, justifications, and symbols that legitimize the hegemony of a group in society is never completely successful. Those who benefit from hegemony as well as those who (as subalterns) internalize its reasons are always left with some margin of doubt. In theological terms we might speak of hegemony as incapable of completely erasing a "hermeneutic of suspicion." It also seems that the legitimizing process suggests to both groups that doubt is not desirable and that guilt should be felt in response to it.[17] This doubt is all too frequently sensed and not reflected upon. It is symbolized rather than explained. It can externalize itself through ecclesiastically and socially uncomfortable or unsettling actions and rites, or it can be sensed through the quiet disregard of ecclesiastical or social norms, orthodoxy, and decisions. It is a refusal to yield to legitimation, often without knowing what or why. And it is always the proof that the legitimation of one group's hegemony in society has not fully succeeded.

And yet when the doubt is allowed to become conscious, and when inescapable suspicion results from a confrontation with reality that profoundly and unequivocally calls into question the explanations and justifications of hegemony, then the same religion that acted as accomplice in the

---

16. See Pedro Ribeiro de Oliveira, *Religião e dominação de classe*, 205–346; J. M. Tavares de Andrade, *Religiosité et système symbolique* (Paris: Institut des Hautes Études d'Amérique Latine, 1976).

17. This guilt, as a response to doubt in the process of establishing hegemony, is not the same as the theological concept of sin. Nevertheless, it often occurs that the dominant ideology utilizes the category of sin, torn out of its theological mooring, in order to reinforce its effort to stamp out the margin of doubt I am referring to here. A solid analysis of the Catholic, theological meaning and dynamics of sin might be a way of augmenting this doubt.

legitimating process can become the source and channel of serious, explicit challenge to the hegemonic group and to its explanations, justifications, and symbols. In other words, a popular religion can be either liberating or alienating in U.S. society. It will play these roles to the degree that it is either confronted by truly human, social reality or allowed to escape into a self-created, self-deluding, and therefore false world. The experience of doubt will lead to either role only insofar as the perceived needs and interests of Catholics are served by and through either role. In contemporary U.S. society there does not seem to be room for really credible intermediate options that appeal to some sort of social neutrality.

The rebellious role is possible for both Euro-American and Latino Catholicisms.[18] But this possibility might not be likely among those who have the most to lose in symbolic, ecclesiastical, or social terms by a more prophetic (and in some sense, rebellious) stance on the part of their faith community. The more frequent outcome, at least on the part of Latino popular Catholicism, has been a mixture of roles in the subaltern's attempt to survive within an adverse context while somehow hoping for and promoting a favorable change in that context.

Latino Popular Catholicism: Its Roles in U.S. Society and the U.S. Church

The subalterns in society are so because they do not have the means of creating and, more specifically, disseminating the explanations, justifications, and symbols needed to convince the rest of society that they—and not the current socially dominant group—should be entrusted with the leadership (or partnership in the leadership) of that society. In other words, they do not have the means to vie for hegemony. Hence, the subaltern groups have no decisive control, for example, over education or mass media. They have no important role in creating, disseminating, and sustaining the symbols and myths through which the society understands, organizes, and justifies itself. Their arguments in favor of change are not distributed by them to the rest of society, but only by the means of dissemination controlled by the current hegemonic group. Consequently, the subaltern arguments are very seldom allowed to appear as actually capable of convincing supposedly rea-

---

18. Since most U.S. Latinos share cultural roots with the peoples of Mexico and the Antilles, it might be useful to recall the roles that the Virgin of Guadalupe and the Virgin of la Caridad played in the development of the national conscience and independence of Mexico and Cuba, respectively. See, for example, J. Lafaye, *Quetzalcóatl and Guadalupe: The Formation of Mexican National Consciousness, 1531–1813* (Chicago: University of Chicago Press, 1976); and the very telling "Petición de los veteranos del ejército de liberación cubano al papa Benedicto XV para que declare como 'Patrona de la República de Cuba' a la Virgen de la Caridad del Cobre," *La Virgen de la Caridad, patrona de Cuba* (ed. M. Vizcaíno; Miami: SEPI, 1981) 28–29.

sonable members of the society. Reason, after all, is purveyed by the current socially dominant group as the domain of the hegemonic sectors.[19]

U.S. Latinos, as a consequence of the occupation or purchase of their lands in the nineteenth century, became the recipients of the dissemination of justifications, symbols, and explanations of the dominant, victorious group and their social allies. Education, mass media, local ordinances, execution of justice, and so forth, all communicated to Latinos that their social place in the country they were being forced to join was to be inferior to that of the victors.[20] They were told, through the dissemination vehicles of hegemony (symbolic and coercive), that they were to remain secondary and ancillary and that they were inferior because of either historical inevitability or the will of God.

As we saw earlier, the process of legitimizing hegemony always involves the internalization of the reasons of the victors by the vanquished, although always leaving a margin of doubt. Latinos have not proven to be the exception to this process. The anglophone Catholic Church, probably seeking to escape Protestant prejudice against it, as well as desiring to reap the benefits of joining the U.S. mainstream, became an active participant in the process of legitimation and became an important vehicle for the explanations, symbols, and justifications of the victors to penetrate Latinos and for keeping the latter "in their place."[21] In siding with the hegemonic group, the

---

19. On this point, see two excellent articles by Robert S. Goizueta: "U.S. Hispanic Theology and the Challenge of Pluralism," *Frontiers of Hispanic Theology in the United States* (ed. Allan F. Deck; Maryknoll, N.Y.: Orbis Books, 1992) 1–22; and "Rediscovering Praxis: The Significance of U.S. Hispanic Experience for Theological Method," *We Are a People! Initiatives in Hispanic American Theology* (ed. Roberto S. Goizueta; Minneapolis: Fortress Press, 1992) 51–78.

20. From among the very vast and growing bibliography on this point, see, for example, R. Horsman, *Race and Manifest Destiny: The Origins of American Racial Anglo-Saxonism* (Cambridge, Mass.: Harvard University Press, 1981); R. Acuña, *Occupied America: A History of Chicanos* (2d ed.; New York: Harper and Row, 1981); D. Montejano, *Anglos and Mexicans in the Making of Texas, 1836–1986* (Austin: University of Texas Press, 1987); M. Barrera, *Race and Class in the Southwest: A Theory of Racial Inequality* (Notre Dame, Ind.: University of Notre Dame Press, 1979); and L. Pitt, *The Decline of the Californios: A Social History of the Spanish-Speaking Californians, 1846–1890* (Berkeley: University of California Press, 1966).

21. See A. Chávez, *The Old Faith and Old Glory: The Story of the Church in New Mexico since the American Occupation* (Santa Fe: Santa Fe Press, 1946); J. P. Dolan, *The American Catholic Experience: A History from Colonial Times to the Present* (New York: Doubleday, 1985); D. F. Gómez, *Somos Chicanos: Strangers in Our Own Land* (Boston: Beacon Press, 1973); R. F. Heizer and A. F. Almquist, *The Other Californians* (Berkeley: University of California Press, 1971); J. Hurtado, *Social Distance between the Mexican American and the Church* (San Antonio: Mexican American Cultural Center, 1975); M. J. McNally, *Catholicism in South Florida, 1868–1968* (Gainesville: University Presses of Florida, 1984); L. J. Mosqueda, *Chicanos, Catholicism, and Political Ideology* (New York: University Press of America, 1986); M. Sandoval, *On the Move: A History of the Hispanic Church in the United States* (Maryknoll, N.Y.: Orbis Books, 1990), and idem, *Fronteras: A History of the Latin American Church in the U.S. since 1513* (San Antonio: Mexican American Cultural Center/CEHILA, 1983); T. E. Sheridan, *Los Tucsoneros: The Mexican Community in Tucson, 1854–1942* (Tucson: University of Arizona Press, 1986);

Euro-American Catholic Church chose to marginalize most Latino Catholics while concurrently blaming them for the officially sanctioned pastoral and social neglect.

Legitimation

Latino popular Catholicism has also contributed to this marginalization. As I said at the beginning of this essay, Latino popular Catholicism can be characterized as an effort by the subalterns to explain, justify, and somehow control a social reality that appears too dangerous to confront in terms and through means other than the mainly symbolic. However, this popular religion is founded on the claim that the divine (identified by the people as the Christian divine) has been and is encountered by them in and through the symbols (ritual, ethical, and doctrinal) of popular Catholicism.

Popular religion can and does legitimize the current U.S. social formation by, in the first place, offering Latinos what appear and claim to be plausible symbolic and ritual means of explaining adverse reality and advancing in it. These means, however, seem to have minimally sufficient sociohistorical efficacy. Popular Catholicism's foundational worldview posits as evident certain premises that do not coincide with those of contemporary, technological society's own worldview.[22] It is impossible in this

---

A. M. Stevens-Arroyo, ed., *Prophets Denied Honor: An Anthology of the Hispanic Church in the United States* (Maryknoll, N.Y.: Orbis Books, 1980); D. J. Weber, ed., *Foreigners in Their Native Land: Historical Roots of the Mexican Americans* (Albuquerque: University of New Mexico Press, 1973); and especially the three volumes of *A History of Hispanic Catholics*.

22. I am in no way implying or suggesting that the worldview of modern, technological society is superior to the Latino popular worldview. In fact, I could argue that the latter contains and expresses some fundamental humanizing and liberating elements altogether missing or lost in so-called modern American society. However, the fact remains that U.S. Latinos must live in and adapt to a technologically and symbolically "modern" context, and so must their popular religion. The alternative to adaptation is either nonviable cultural anomie (which cannot be sustained for long without disastrous social and cultural consequences) or a maddening and doomed attempt to keep modernity at bay (as in the case of some Protestant Pentecostal and Catholic charismatic or traditionalist groups, and even in the case of those who—in the name of the people's struggles—want to establish an inverse form of apartheid). Adaptation to modern society does not, however, imply "buying into it" uncritically, nor does it involve an assimilationist tendency. Perhaps the concept and dynamics of *mestizaje*, as suggest by Virgilio Elizondo and others, might illumine the preferred outcome (on the part of U.S. Latinos) to the challenge posed by modernity. See Virgilio Elizondo, *Christianity and Culture* (San Antonio: Mexican American Cultural Center, 1975); idem, *Mestizaje: The Dialectic of Cultural Birth and the Gospel* (3 vols.; San Antonio: Mexican American Cultural Center, 1978); idem, *Galilean Journey: The Mexican-American Promise* (Maryknoll, N.Y.: Orbis Books, 1983); idem, *The Future Is Mestizo: Life Where Cultures Meet* (Bloomington, Ind.: Meyer-Stone, 1988). Suggestive and useful on this point also are N. García Canclini, *Las culturas populares en el capitalismo* (Mexico City: Nueva Imagen, 1982); M. de França Miranda, *Um homen perplexo: O cristão na sociedade* (São Paulo: Loyola, 1989); F. Hinkelammert, *Las armas ideológicas de la muerte* (Salamanca: Sígueme, 1978); A. Mirandé, *The Chicano Experience: An Alternative Experience* (Notre Dame, Ind.: University of Notre Dame Press, 1985); A. Parra, *Dar razón de nuestra esperanza: Teología fundamental de la praxis latinoamericana* (Bogotá: Publicaciones de la

essay to thoroughly discuss the modern clash between worldviews witnessed within U.S. Latino popular religion. Nevertheless, let me indicate some of the premises.

The operative worldview foundational to Latino Catholicism posits that the divine intervenes constantly, daily, in human reality[23] and that God's decisions are the ultimate reason and cause for all that exists. What exists can really change only as the result of God's will or by God's permission. Otherwise change is merely temporary and apparent. Therefore, human efforts at transforming what exists are doomed to failure if they do not correspond to the divine will. This will, unfortunately, is not easily known, and its unveiling is probably the most important (although not the most frequent) role of the church's ministers.[24]

This foundational, operative worldview also assumes that human existence, from its beginnings, has always included the conflict between good and evil, between good persons and evil persons.[25] It is assumed as self-evident that God established humankind as divided between the rich and powerful on one side and the poor and weak on the other. It is also assumed that the latter are very frequently being tested for their patience and humility and, if not lacking, will be rewarded eternal life. The rich and powerful, if they are generous and fair in their use of wealth and power, can also be granted the eternal reward.

Finally, this operative worldview considers as evident that people can leave their divinely appointed state in life only by two means: either by a divine decision that will allow them to change places in society as the prize

---

Universidad Javeriana, 1988); R. Rosaldo, *Culture and Truth: The Remaking of Social Analysis* (2d ed.; Boston: Beacon Press, 1993); J. C. Scannone, ed., *Sabiduría popular, símbolo y filosofía* (Buenos Aires: Guadalupe, 1984); and F. Taborda, *Cristianismo e ideologia* (São Paulo: Loyola, 1984).

23. See my "The Vanquished, Faithful Solidarity and the Marian Symbol: A Hispanic Perspective on Providence," *On Keeping Providence* (ed. B. Doherty and J. Coultas; Terre Haute, Ind.: St. Mary of the Woods College Press, 1991) 84–101; and, idem, with Sixto García, " 'Lilies of the Field': A Hispanic Theology of Providence and Human Responsibility," *Proceedings of the Catholic Theological Society of America* 44 (1989) 70–90.

24. The "daily, ordinary ministers" of Latino popular Catholicism are not those ordained by the church. The ordinary ministers are usually the grandmothers and other older women. Occasionally, older men also exercise leadership roles. The sine qua non conditions for this "daily, ordinary ministry" seem to be wisdom, a compassionate life, and the gift of counsel (thereby allowing for some exceptions on the age requirement). The laity, not the church's ordained ministers, are the real leaders in popular Catholicism. The ordained clergy's sphere seems to be the strictly ritual and "sacramental," as well as socially legitimizing activities. They are perceived, however, as the *probable* final arbiters of the divine will, although only in cases of substantial disagreement or indecision on the part of the "daily ministers." But even here, the role and advice of the ordained are judged in popular Catholicism under the scrutiny of wisdom, compassion, and their proven gift of counsel. See my "Popular Catholicism among Latinos."

25. This is clearly seen (as well as the other premises), for example, in Victor Villaseñor's remarkable cultural and family saga, *Rain of Gold* (Houston: Arte Público Press, 1991). Much of U.S. Latino literature expresses the same fundamental worldview.

320 _____ Orlando O. Espín

for successfully completing a series of tests or challenges, or as the result of another divine decision caused or encouraged by the people's fervent, sincere prayer and penance.

Needless to say, today's U.S. society does not base its operative worldview on these premises. Though it is clear that some non-Latino segments of society share some of these important elements of the Latino worldview, it is also obvious that a more technological, secular set of assumptions is operative in the larger society (even when verbally confessing to believe, perhaps sincerely, in the more traditional premises).[26] Among the "churched" population these traditional assumptions do not appear as operatively self-evident either. The hegemonic ideology is secular indeed, founded on a set of well-known secular worldview-building premises.

Thus, Latino popular Catholicism (which is still the majority religion among U.S. Latinos) is based on a very different set of assumptions about reality and its transformation, their common result being either a symbolic quest (through prayer, rite, and penance) to persuade the divine to act or a self-restraining attitude that leads to social quiescence. As I mentioned earlier, the will of God is considered to be the final justification and explanation of reality. Unveiling this will and making it known are important tasks of the church's ministers (as representatives of God), according to popular Catholicism. It thus seems that the anglophone church, which trains and controls the ordained ministers, has had in its hands (not always successfully, for reasons explained earlier) a powerful means of control and suppression of Latino hopes for justice and change and thereby a powerful means of enforcing compliance with the current hegemonic social formation and ideology in the United States.

Latino popular Catholicism, by its own worldview's assumptions and by the means made possible by these assumptions, has contributed to legitimizing the hegemonic pretensions and claims of society's dominant group. An important traditional channel for any important option for change (that is, the unveiling of the divine will by the clergy), which could have plausibly served as a bridge between cultures and worldviews, has been compromised by the double circumstances of the anglophone church's historical need for acceptability in mainstream U.S. society and the anglophone hierarchy's canonical control over the training and pastoral work of the clergy (often resulting in the "deculturation" of and feelings of shame in Latino seminarians and priests). Thus, popular Catholicism has been left to its traditional worldview and means, thereby impeded from entering a process of adaptation that could lead it to empower the people in U.S. society. This popular religion in the United States has all too frequently been left to serve at best as a compassionate sedative to injustice or as an in-

---

26. See R. Bellah et al., *Habits of the Heart* (Berkeley: University of California Press, 1985).

efficacious palliative to the harsh treatment meted out by the dominant society.[27]

Rebellious Hope

Are U.S. Latinos so naive that they cannot see how their popular religion can be an obstacle to their quest for justice? How does the doubt left by the dissemination of the reasons for hegemony relate to Latino religion in the United States? These and other questions must be asked when seeking to understand the roles of Latino popular Catholicism in the United States. We have already pointed to the legitimizing function it plays. Let us now look at other possibilities.

Latinos are certainly not naive. It takes a great deal of courage and intelligence to survive and preserve significant portions of one's cultural identity in an inimical social context that is founded on very different assumptions about existence. Weakened and sufficiently convinced by the reasons for hegemony disseminated by society's dominant group and its ecclesiastical allies, Latinos have managed to keep alive (and share among themselves) the doubt about the legitimacy and finality of the current U.S. social formation and the hegemonic ideology that sustains it. Popular Catholicism, as weakened and sufficiently convinced as the people themselves, has nevertheless acted as a very important preserver of their dignity and identity and as a guarantor of their hope that the transformation of reality is still possible. Thus, in ways that are far from idyllic and quite expressive of the subaltern condition, popular religion has the role of keeping a rebellious hope alive. How?

Latinos have not usually produced, disseminated, or controlled what is said about them in U.S. society. This is a part and consequence of their subaltern condition. Therefore, the contents of self-definition, of self-identity (and thus of the resulting sense of dignity and self-worth), are received by Latinos, in the "public" realm, as filtered through and shaped by the holders of hegemony. The family and immediate neighborhood's interpersonal network (that is, the "private" realm) are often no match for the hegemonic avalanche of symbols and justifications, in spite of their opposite message. The presence of the mass media within the Latino home has penetrated

---

27. See National Conference of Catholic Bishops, *The Hispanic Presence: Challenge and Commitment* (Washington: United States Catholic Conference, 1983) 26–27. The more recent (1987) *National Pastoral Plan for Hispanic Ministry* of the Roman Catholic Church merely repeats the 1983 official views on popular Catholicism. In Latin America (and this, therefore, is applicable to the U.S. context only after cautious and critical appraisal) there is at least one suggestive and thorough study on the different approaches that church authorities, theologians, social scientists, and even political activists have taken in reference to the people's Catholicism; see C. Johansson Friedemann, *Religiosidad popular entre Medellín y Puebla: Antecedentes y desarrollo* (Santiago de Chile: Publicaciones de la Universidad Católica, 1990). I know of no equivalent published work in reference to U.S. Latino popular religion.

and often broken down the thin barrier between the public symbols of the dominant and the people's private self-definition.

Popular Catholicism stands out as one of the very few social (public and private) spaces that have been able to preserve some high degree of protagonism for Latinos, albeit oftentimes symbolic. The all too frequent pastoral indifference of so many in the anglophone church toward Latinos turned out to be an opportunity for Latino popular Catholicism to reaffirm its historical roots as laity-run and -oriented and as parallel to the institutions and ordained ministries of the church. Though explicitly self-identifying as Catholic, popular religion has had a long tradition of autonomy (and at times defiance) vis-à-vis the institutions and ministers of the church and, occasionally, of prophetic opposition to them.[28]

Contemporary popular Catholicism cannot be misread as a bastardized, insufficient, or superstitious version of so-called normative Catholicism. The observations offered earlier in this essay concerning the socialization of the experience of the divine should make us suspect that much of what passes for religiously "normative" or "orthodox" is so because it was also (or became) hegemonic. But more importantly, Latino popular Catholicism sinks its roots in a specific patristic and postpatristic understanding and practice of Christianity and is thus evidently older than the Tridentine and post-Tridentine "norm" put forth by the anglophone church. Though not in necessary opposition to Trent, it preceded it to the Americas by several generations, becoming the established mode of Catholicism (the one in which native and slave populations were evangelized).[29] It cannot be simply dismissed as a decayed form of Christianity without some implicit (or explicit!) complicity with the current hegemonic ideology and without twisting post-Tridentine Roman Catholicism's claims of continuity with its earlier, patristic, and medieval counterparts.[30]

Today's Latino popular Catholicism still bears the marks of its history, of its Iberian roots, and of the traumatic conquest of Amerindians and African slaves by Christians.[31] It still displays, often through powerful symbols, the

---

28. See my "Popular Catholicism among Latinos."

29. Ibid. See also my "Tradition and Popular Religion: An Understanding of the *Sensus Fidelium*," *Frontiers of Hispanic Theology*, 62–87.

30. Important on this point are the powerful remarks of Gary Macy: "People speak of the history of the Roman Catholic Church, or of the Anglican Church, or of one of the Protestant churches as if somehow that particular group (and only that group) started with the apostles. They forget that none of these groups existed before the reformation. Before the reformation, Christians were simply Christians—eastern and western Christians sometimes, but mostly simply Christians.... The different Christian groups have a single, common past that reaches from the time of the apostles to the time of the reformation. Each of the different groups emerging from that past can find its roots there because the past which Christians have inherited is a pluralistic past. What was lost in the reformation was not just Christian unity, but toleration of pluralism" (*The Banquet's Wisdom* [Mahwah, N.J.: Paulist Press, 1992] 10 and 14).

31. See Luis N. Rivera Pagán, *Evangelización y violencia: La conquista de América* (San Juan: Cemí, 1991).

expressions of the despair of the vanquished and of their hope for justice.[32] This religion's survival, in spite of five hundred years of efforts to suppress, educate, or convert it, reveals it as the enduring language of a subaltern people. Religious in expression, content, and experience, this language has long been the code through which hope and courage have been shared and maintained as plausible by generations of Latinos. Fundamental cultural values have found their place in and their medium of dissemination through popular religion.[33]

Lastly, and perhaps ultimately more importantly, popular Catholicism embodies a *rebellious hope* by its very existence as religion.[34] If, as we saw earlier, religion is the socialization of the experience of the divine, and if in Latino Catholicism the divine is identified with the Christian divine, then this religion of the subalterns claims that the *Christian* God is to be found in and through the culture and experiences of those considered insignificant by U.S. society and church.[35] Even admitting the effects of the explanations, justifications, and symbols of hegemony on subaltern, Latino popular Catholicism (because of its implied claims as socialization of the experience of the divine) may be understood in theological terms as potentially a prophetic sign of rebellion against many attempts to equate the ecclesiastically normative, orthodox, or canonical with the hegemonic. And in social terms, it may still be comprehended as containing a powerful suspicion (vis-à-vis current U.S. social formation) that has in the past and could in the future translate into social protagonism.

Needless to say, Latino Catholicism in the United States, although preserving its "hermeneutic of suspicion," has not very often gone beyond its hope into concrete action. The suspicion or doubt it carries seems to convey that today's social and ecclesiastical realities are not final. This doubt points to the possibility of another future, for it suggests a suspicion that the present (including popular religion's own present) does not express all that can and should be.

---

32. See my "Trinitarian Monotheism and the Birth of Popular Catholicism: The Case of Sixteenth-Century Mexico," *Missiology* 20:2 (1992) 177–204; also idem, "Grace and Humanness," *We Are a People!* 133–64.

33. Without suggesting that Rosa Luxemburg was in fact thinking of popular Catholicism, I think it possible to say that her few writings on the social role of religion seem akin to my point. It is a shame that this European thinker's work (1870–1919) is not well known in the U.S. academic context. See her selected writings on religion in Assmann and Mate, *Sobre la religión*, 2:190–232.

34. This same point, on a broader context, is convincingly argued by Victor Lanternari in his classic work *The Religions of the Oppressed* (London: Macgibbon and Kee, 1963).

35. See my "The God of the Vanquished: Foundations for a U.S. Latino Spirituality," *Hispanic Americans in Theology and the Church* (ed. Fernando F. Segovia; special issue of *Listening: Journal of Religion and Culture* 27:1 [1992] 70–83.

Concluding Comments

Contemporary popular Catholicism among U.S. Latinos can be judged as alienating the people by assisting in the dissemination of the "reasoning" of hegemony that maintains Latino subaltern status in society. But popular Catholicism can also be judged as offering some of the most powerful and culturally authentic arguments and motives for social protagonism. It too can be (and is) the bearer of a rebellious, prophetic hope that the present is not the last word in history. Consequently, on the one hand, the dismissal of the religion of Latinos as only or mainly a shackle vis-à-vis the necessary struggles for a better future might be in itself a disguised contribution to the dominant ideology that indeed purveys the people's Catholicism as ignorant and magical. On the other hand, the attempt to preserve popular religion as if it were a folkloric curiosity, a piece of the Latino past, or a tool for better evangelization, might be as dismissive of the people as all the past attempts to destroy their religion (and indeed may be even more dismissive). This apparent "preservation" can be a powerful ally of the hegemonic ideology.

Ultimately, the better judgment seems to conclude that popular Catholicism has been and is extremely important in Latino life. It is too complex in its genesis and history, contents, and sociocultural roles to be summarily dismissed or superficially examined. It has defied all efforts to destroy it and has shown extraordinary adaptability. No one academic discipline could ever hope to understand and explain it with sufficient adequacy. Is this religion promoting a sedating alienation or a hopeful social protagonism? Both. And much more.

17

Un poquito de justicia— a Little Bit of Justice

A *Mujerista* Account of Justice

Ada María Isasi-Díaz

The president of the *Madres Cristianas*—Christian Mothers—group of the parish where I worship in New York City on weekends called me early in February. She wanted to invite me to plan and lead a *servicio de la amistad*—a friendship service—at her house. After all, she could not let the month of St. Valentine's go by without gathering friends and celebrating something so important as friendship. I was happy to accept the invitation and to be present on a Sunday afternoon with about fifteen others (all but three were women) to celebrate friendship and community. During the service we had an opportunity to share what it is that we expect from friends and what we have to offer to friends. Later, we ate together, talked endlessly about the islands where we were born, and reminisced about customs of our birth-lands that had been very important for us since our youth. We lamented, too, the loss of certain cultural practices instrumental in teaching us about ourselves and about life that have served as resources for our survival as a minority culture within the United States.

As story after story was shared, it became very obvious that these women (the men were mostly silent or talked among themselves) had lived many times the "no greater love" message of Jesus recorded in the Gospel of John and read during the *servicio de la amistad*. The women's theological understanding of this central text of Christianity is revealed not in elaborated discourse but rather in thought-full implementation. For them "no greater love" is *not* a matter of dying for someone else but a matter of not allowing someone else to die. For them "no greater love" is a matter of taking in children who are not necessarily blood relatives but whose parents cannot provide for them. For them "no greater love" is a matter of worrying about their neighborhood instead of worrying about ways of making it out of the neighborhood. For them the "no greater love" has to do with *un poquito de justicia*—a little bit of justice—that they think society owes the

Latino community so "at least our children can have a fighting chance to survive the drug war." For them the "no greater love" is nothing but the justice-demand that is a constitutive element of the gospel message.

Latinas' Cries: Starting Point for Understanding Justice

As is true of all our theological work, the reason for articulating a *mujerista* perspective of justice is to contribute to the struggle for the liberation of Latinas, which cannot happen apart from the liberation of all Hispanics and all oppressed people. Our goal is to do away with injustice, to create spaces for justice to flourish, so that the unfolding of the kin-dom[1] of God can become a reality in our lives, in our society. And where are we to start?

Mujerista theology has consistently insisted on the lived experience of Latinas as not only the *locus theologicus*, the starting place of theological reflection, but the very source of our theology.[2] It is not surprising then that as *mujerista* theology attempts to articulate an understanding of justice, our starting point is the cries against injustice of grassroots Latinas who struggle daily to survive.

We have insisted on the lived experience of Latinas as the source of *mujerista* theology because we believe in the ongoing revelation of God in our lives. Further, we certainly believe that fidelity to the gospel message requires us to have a preferential option for the poor and the oppressed. A third reason has to do with the commitment of *mujerista* theology to provide a platform for the voices of grassroots Latinas. Providing Latinas with opportunities to articulate their understanding of religious beliefs and practices is a consciousness-raising enterprise and, as such, a liberative strategy.

Consciousness raising from a *mujerista* theology perspective has to do with sharing understandings about beliefs and practices that are oppressive for Latinas. The sharing—putting in common—of religious beliefs that oppress us helps Latinas to know that they are not mistaken in rejecting such beliefs, that they are not alone in thinking that "there is really no way God makes that happen, or permits it, or requires that of us." By sharing their beliefs Latinas begin to understand how religion has been used to control them, to silence them, to keep them submissive. Sharing often helps them to see clearly that what they say they believe is not always what they "really

---

1. I do not use "kingdom" because it is obviously a sexist word that presumes that God is male. In addition, the concept of kingdom in our world today is both hierarchical and elitist, which is also why I do not use "reign." The word "kin-dom" makes it clear that when the fullness of God becomes a day-to-day reality in our world, we will all be kin to each other.

2. See Ada María Isasi-Díaz and Yolanda Tarango, *Hispanic Women: Prophetic Voice in the Church* (Minneapolis: Fortress Press, 1993); Ada María Isasi-Díaz, *En la lucha—In the Struggle: A Hispanic Women's Liberation Theology* (Minneapolis: Fortress Press, 1993).

believe." Group theological reflection makes it possible for the real religious beliefs and understandings of Latinas to come to the surface, to be articulated. And those true, nonconscious religious beliefs, although often suppressed, are many times the real source of these women's strength as they struggle for survival *día a día*—day in and day out.

A fourth reason for using the lived experience of Latinas as the source of *mujerista* theology, of listening to the cries of Latinas as the starting point for an elaboration of justice, has to do with the demand that the gospel message makes on all Christians to stand in solidarity with the poor and the oppressed.[3] To stand in solidarity with the poor and the oppressed one has to start by listening to their cries. Solidarity is a response to the cry for justice of those who are victimized. Those who are nonpoor or less poor, nonoppressed or less oppressed, are not capable of deciding on their own to be in solidarity with those who suffer oppression. Because the preferential option for the poor and the oppressed is based on the gospel message found in Matt 25:31–46, we can assert that the "grace of conversion" is given as we listen to what the oppressed have to say and as we discover how we ourselves are involved in and profit from oppressive structures.

Five Modes of Oppression

What is injustice? What is oppression? Elsewhere we have explored the particulars of the oppression suffered by Latinas.[4] Here we will continue to examine the nature of this oppression because it is the starting point in the struggle for justice, which is the goal of our theological practice. We approach justice by examining the structures of oppression that force Latinas to live in the midst of unjust structures. *Mujeristas'* understanding of justice, therefore, is not based on philosophical speculations regarding what criteria to apply in determining what is due to Latinas. Justice for us refers not only to what we receive but also to our active and effective participation in making justice a reality. "A just social order cannot be created for the poor nor can it be created without them. It needs their active participation at all levels of the struggle and our committed solidarity with them."[5]

Injustice causes the poor and oppressed to suffer "inhibition of their ability to develop and exercise their capacities and express their needs,

---

3. I have dealt with the issue of solidarity at length elsewhere. See Ada María Isasi-Díaz, "Solidarity: Love of Neighbor in the 1980s," *Lift Every Voice: Constructing Christian Theologies from the Underside* (ed. Susan B. Thistlethwaite and Mary Potter Engels; San Francisco: Harper and Row, 1990) 31–40.

4. Isasi-Díaz and Tarango, *Hispanic Women*; Isasi-Díaz, *En la lucha*, chaps. 1 and 2.

5. Ismael García, *Justice in Latin American Theology of Liberation* (Atlanta: John Knox Press, 1982) 82.

thoughts, and feelings."[6] Injustice, however, is not only a matter of personal suffering caused by given individuals:

Oppression also refers to systemic constraints.... Its causes are embedded in unquestioned norms, habits, and symbols, in the assumptions underlying institutional rules and the collective consequences of following those rules.... Oppression refers to the vast and deep injustices some groups suffer as a consequence of often unconscious assumptions and reactions of well-meaning people in ordinary interactions, media and cultural stereotypes, and structural features of bureaucratic hierarchies and market mechanisms—in short, the normal processes of everyday life.[7]

There are different reasons, or combinations of reasons, for the oppression Latinas suffer. Therefore, it is not possible to give one definition of our oppression or, indeed, of any oppression. We do well in our analysis of oppression to look at different modes of oppression operative in people's daily lives. Certainly there is no moral primacy among the causes or factors or elements of oppression: there is no one oppression that is worse than another, no one face of oppression that is more oppressive than another. Often we suffer oppression one way while we oppress others in another way. Differentiating the modes of oppression, however, does help us to grasp the dynamics of oppression, and this, we hope, will help in the development of strategies in the work for justice.[8]

Exploitation is one mode of oppression. It has to do with processes that transfer the results of the labor of Latinas to benefit others. When we talk about exploitation we are talking about what work is, who does what for whom, how work is compensated, and how and by whom the result of that work is appropriated. The energy of Latinas is "continuously expended to maintain and augment the power, status, and wealth of the haves."[9]

The fact that, in general, Latinas' wages are below those of Euro-Americans and Latino men is one sign of exploitation. The fact that Latinas in factories around the United States are paid according to what they produce instead of according to the amount of time they work is a matter of exploitation. But exploitation of Latinas has to do not only with their labor in factories, industrial plants, and other economic institutions of society. Latinas also suffer gender exploitation. In their homes Latinas work for their men. Latinas are, most of the time, responsible for keeping house for their husbands or male partners; Latinas often are responsible for "finding" the economic resources needed to keep a roof over their own heads as well as those of their children and male partners, to provide for the food

---

6. Iris Marion Young, *Justice and the Politics of Difference* (Princeton, N.J.: Princeton University Press, 1990) 40.

7. Ibid., 41.

8. The basis for the analysis of oppression that follows is presented and explored by Young in *Justice*, chap. 6.

9. Ibid., 50.

and medical expenses of the family. Latinas also are responsible for providing for the emotional needs not only of the children in the family but also of the husband, father, and brothers.

Moreover, Latinas suffer exploitation in the churches. They do much of the work while the priests or pastors take credit for it. Latinas are the economic backbone of most of the churches, but they are not allowed to participate—never fully, seldom partially—in the decisions of how the monies they work so hard to collect are to be spent. Latinas are the ones in charge of cleaning the churches, making and setting up decorations for Holy Week and Easter, for example; Latinas are, to a large extent, the ones responsible for bringing men and children to church. But their work is not recognized, nor is it compensated. Instead, it is appropriated by the men who control what happens in the churches. For example, in many churches Latinas are not included among the twelve who get their feet washed by the pastor during the Holy Thursday celebration; in many other parishes they are included only after long and bitter arguments with the priests year after year. Considering all that Latinas contribute to make Holy Thursday celebrations meaningful for their communities, their exclusion from leadership roles in the celebration itself is exploitation.

The second face of oppression is that of marginalization. This is perhaps the most dangerous form of oppression: as marginalized people Latinas are part of a category of people who are not seen as contributing to society and, therefore, are subject to severe material deprivation and even extermination. The marginalized are surplus people who not only are considered to be useless by others but come to understand themselves that way as well. Marginalization "involves the deprivation of cultural, practical, and institutionalized conditions for exercising capacities in a context of recognition and interaction."[10] All this leads to lack of self-respect, to a crisis of identity, to lack of self-worth, to *un hastío*—a disgusting boredom—that is totally destructive. It is not surprising, then, that in different areas of the country Latinas are increasingly among those who abuse alcohol and drugs.

Latina women are marginalized by the dominant culture and within it, but patriarchal understandings and structures also marginalize us within our own communities. I have heard so many times in different meetings and gatherings of Latinos and Latinas, "Aquí las mujeres no tienen nada que decir" (Here the women have nothing to say). And even when we are discounted, when we are marginalized, I marvel at the faithfulness of grassroots Latinas to our communities. At those same meetings when some Latinas have tried to disagree with Latinos conducting the meeting and have been ignored, I have seen the Latinas sign up to carry out whatever has been decided.

---

10. Ibid., 55.

Powerlessness is a third face of oppression. As powerless persons, Latinas lack authority. Power is exercised over us: we are to do what we are told; we have little or no autonomy, little or no opportunity to be self-defining, to assert our interests and visions of what we believe is good for our communities. As powerless persons, Latinas lack status, are not considered respectable. Latinas cannot presume, as others in the society do, that they will be trusted and respected unless they do something to forfeit that trust or respect. Latinas know that we have to earn trust, that we have to earn respect, and that we have to keep earning it or we will not have it.

This is true even of those of us who are professionals, who have earned high academic degrees and hold positions of regard. As a Latina professor of theology, I can fill several pages with stories of the demands students make of me, the negative attitude some have toward me, their lack of respect for my authority.[11] I must confess that I have been slow to recognize this. It has been my women colleagues who have pointed out to me that the same students who have disregarded my critiques and evaluations have accepted without questions similar decisions about the quality of their work from other professors. And if this is so for professionals, how much more difficult is it for grassroots Latinas?

Because powerlessness results in lack of autonomy, powerlessness makes it extremely difficult for Latinas to exercise their creativity: "Si yo pudiera" (If only I could)—that is the repeated cry of Latinas who have very few, if any, avenues for developing and expressing their creativity. It seems that only in the role of mothers can Latinas find some space to be creative. But then, whatever creativity Latinas might have in the way they nurture and educate their children is seriously curtailed by the expectations society has of motherhood and also by the imperative need Latinas have to teach their children how to survive. How can we teach our children to be free if we have to keep them inside the house so they will not be shot to death? How can we teach our children to ask questions, to dream dreams and see visions, when we know that to survive one has to comply?

The fourth face of oppression is cultural imperialism, the very basis for ethnic prejudice and racism. To experience cultural imperialism is to experience how the dominant meanings of a society render our particular Latina perspectives invisible. It means to be stereotyped precisely as "other," as "outsider." Cultural imperialism in its concrete form of ethnic

---

11. Of course, I could retaliate against those students by giving them low grades. But, first, I believe that would be unethical. Second, though I try to do what I believe I should do as a professor, the fact that I am a junior professor without tenure and that the evaluation of courses students submit to the dean will play a role in my review for tenure certainly has made me put up with behavior from students that I find objectionable. The point I am making here, however, is that this attitude toward me of some students—enough to be noticed though by no means a great number—creates an atmosphere around me and about me that results in weakening my authority and power not only with the students but also with the institution at large.

and gender-based prejudice against Latinas means that the experience and culture of non-Latinas are the norm in this society. Non-Latinas "project their own experience as representative of humanity as such,"[12] and our own experience is constructed largely as deviant and inferior:

The culturally dominated undergo a paradoxical oppression, in that they are both marked by stereotypes and at the same time rendered invisible. As remarkable, deviant being, the culturally imperialized are stamped with an essence. The stereotypes confine them to a nature which is often attached in some way to their bodies, and which thus cannot easily be denied. These stereotypes so permeate the society that they are not noticed as contestable.[13]

But the most destructive aspect of cultural imperialism—of ethnic prejudice and racism—is not what it does to Latinas but what it makes Latinas do to our own selves. Little by little we internalize the way the dominant culture sees us—when it sees us—for we are always obliged to act according to the image society has of us. Little by little our own culture and our self-understandings become as invisible to ourselves as they are to the dominant culture. And that invisibility finds expression in a rejection of our cultural customs and values, in a rejection of ourselves as Latinas that is all the more insidious because of how imperceptible it is, even—perhaps mainly—to ourselves.[14]

The fifth face of oppression is systemic violence. Latinas live with the fear of random, unprovoked attacks on their persons or property that have no motive but to damage, humiliate, or destroy them. What makes the violence Latinas suffer a face of oppression is not the particular acts—no matter how horrible they are—but the fact that there is a societal context that makes such actions possible and acceptable. This is why the police, for example, feel free to treat grassroots Latinas with violence, something they, in general, are less likely to do to Euro-American women, and much less to middle-class Euro-American men. And what about domestic violence, a pervasive crime Latinas of all economic strata repeatedly suffer? The "No te metas" (Do not interfere) response to domestic violence makes it obvious that this kind of violence is acceptable to society at large and to our own Latino communities.

But what perhaps makes violence such a destructive force of oppression is that the suffering violence inflicts, both physically and psychologically, is so devastating and all-encompassing, that the possibility of such violence becomes an ever-present threat coercing us day in and day out. The possibility of displeasing her male partner who will show his displeasure by beating her, for example, will keep a Latina from going to women's meet-

---

12. Young, *Justice*, 59.
13. Ibid.
14. María C. Lugones, "On the Logic of Pluralist Feminism," *Feminist Ethics* (ed. Claudia Card; Lawrence: University Press of Kansas, 1991) 35–44; Young, *Justice*, 60.

ings—relating to church or community matters—where she is appreciated and needed. The fear of rape, the number one form of violence against Latinas and all women in the United States, is such a threat to us that many Latinas live very restricted lives as a means of self-protection. The insidiousness of violence, then, is that it becomes a threat, and threats are economic means of coercion: they get Latinas to do what they do not choose to do without the oppressor having to actually spend any energy, without the oppressor having to do anything.[15]

A *Mujerista* Account of Justice

The reason for taking time to study oppression is to find effective means of working against it and for justice. The reason for articulating a *mujerista* understanding of justice is to bring about justice. Being a liberative praxis, *mujerista* theology has to be effective, in this case contributing to the elimination of injustice. This means that our understanding of justice has to be precise enough to force an option.[16] Elsewhere I have sought to spell out particulars of a *mujerista* vision of justice by describing Latinas' *proyecto histórico*—our preferred future.[17] Here, starting from the injustice Latinas suffer, and keeping our eyes firmly fixed on what we see as conditions for and of the kin-dom of God—our vision of justice—I try to make explicit some principles of justice that embrace and reveal Latinas' expectations regarding a just world order. The elements of justice presented here are not a theory of justice in the classical sense. That is, they do not constitute a construct that applies "to all or most societies, whatever their concrete configuration and social relations, from a few general premises about the nature of human beings, the nature of societies, and the nature of reason."[18] I refer here to a *mujerista account* of justice instead of to a *mujerista theory* of justice. But the elements of this account, I believe, must be included in all accounts of justice. How the elements are understood, what is their concrete and historic content, may vary, but the following elements should be present.

The first element of a *mujerista* account of justice has to do with its goal: establishing justice rather than building a systematic theory. The liberative praxis of Latinas to establish justice starts by claiming an intrinsic union between practice and reflection. Praxis is not to be understood as action apart from reflection but rather refers to reflective action. However, a *mujerista* account of justice does not avoid rational thinking. Latinas' liber-

---

15. For a comprehensive analysis of force, threat, and coercion as elements of oppression, see Thomas E. Wartenberg, *The Forms of Power* (Philadelphia: Temple University Press, 1990) 91–104.

16. For a fuller treatment of this issue, see Isasi-Díaz, *En la lucha*, 34–45.

17. Ibid.

18. Young, *Justice*, 3.

ative praxis is not a doing without a thinking.[19] The thinking and reflecting, the analysis and arguments, that are part of Latinas' liberative praxis clarify the meaning of ideas and issues, describe the relations among ourselves and between Latinas and society at large, and make clear our vision—our ideals and principles. Because the aim of a *mujerista* account of justice is not correct articulation (though it does not exclude it) but effective justice-seeking praxis, our account of justice is a process that reflects the ever-changing reality of Latinas.[20]

The second element of a *mujerista* account of justice refers to its concreteness, with its contextualization: it has to be concrete, and, therefore, it has to be historical. This is why a *mujerista* account of justice begins with injustice: that is the reality the vast majority of Latinas live today. Our account of justice does not depend on philosophical reasoning but on the stories of oppression Latinas tell.[21] The role those stories play in elaborating a *mujerista* account of justice builds on and supports the contention that we must construct our articulation of justice from within the struggle for justice, from the perspective of injustice. This means that we need good social, political, and economic descriptions and analyses of Latinas' reality, always keeping in mind that our descriptions and explanations have to be critical; they have to evaluate and point to liberation.[22]

The third element of a *mujerista* account of justice is the other side of the previous one: our account of justice points to a discontinuity—some discontinuity, *not* total discontinuity—with our past and present reality. This means that justice "is not dependent on the possibilities inherent in the past."[23] This discontinuity is based on the role that the realization of the kin-dom of God plays in Latinas' *proyecto histórico* (historical project).[24] In *mujerista* theology history is one; there are not two histories, a secular one and a sacred one. The history of salvation—the realization of the kin-dom of God—does not happen apart from the daily struggles of Latinas to survive: "Without liberating historical events, there would be no growth of the Kingdom. But the process of liberation will not have conquered the very roots of human oppression and exploitation without the coming of

---

19. See Isasi-Díaz and Tarango, *Hispanic Women,* chap. 1, for a wider discussion of this point.

20. This does not mean that we embrace relativism, though we do indeed accept a certain amount of relativity as a given. Process and change are here to be seen as parts of development, of growth, but within the definitiveness that liberation as the goal of justice indicates.

21. Karen Lebacqz, *Justice in an Unjust World* (Minneapolis: Augsburg, 1987) 150–51.

22. Young, *Justice,* 5.

23. Lebacqz, *Justice in an Unjust World,* 153.

24. This claim to a discontinuity between what is and what justice will be is also based on the epistemological privilege of the poor and the oppressed that we claim for Latinas and to which we referred above.

the Kingdom, which is above all a gift."[25] But though the kin-dom is a gift of God, it also "requires certain behaviors from those who receive it. It is *already* present in history, *but* it does not reach its complete fulfillment therein. Its presence already produces effects, but these are not *the* coming of the Kingdom [*sic*], not *all* of salvation; they are anticipations of a completion that will be realized only beyond human history."[26]

The fourth element of a *mujerista* account of justice has to do with recognizing and dealing with differences rather than just acknowledging the "problem" of differences.[27] This means that justice has to move beyond acceptance that there are different ways of being to real interaction. Interaction between those who are different is not possible unless one recognizes how cultural imperialism functions in the United States, how those who do not belong to the dominant group are conceptualized as other, as inferior and deviant.[28] Interaction among Latinas and non-Latinas will lead to participation and inclusion in a way that does not require us to renounce who we are. Interaction leads to opportunities for Latinas to make their own contribution to what is normative in society, to have a *papel protagónico* (protagonist role) in society. To recognize and deal with differences, to embrace differences, is to reject assimilation, to reject an essentialist meaning of difference that places groups and persons in categorical opposition, in mutual exclusion.[29] To embrace differences means to understand differences as "ambiguous, relational, shifting, without clear borders that keep people straight—as entailing neither amorphous unity nor pure individuality."[30] To embrace differences means to insist on the specificity of Latinas as relational rather than as a substantive category or unequivocal attributes:

A relational understanding of group difference rejects exclusion. Difference no longer implies that groups lie outside one another. To say that there are differences among groups does not imply that there are not overlapping experiences, or that two groups have nothing in common. The assumption that real differences in affinity, culture, or privilege imply oppositional categorization must be challenged. Different groups are always similar in some respects, and always potentially share some attributes, experiences, and goals.[31]

Because embracing differences requires interaction and because interaction cannot happen without honest dialogue (which in turn requires equalization of power among those dialoguing), the fifth element of a *mujerista* account of justice has to deal with power. A *mujerista* understanding

---

25. Gustavo Gutiérrez, *A Theology of Liberation* (2d ed., Maryknoll, N.Y.: Orbis Books, 1988) 104.
26. Ibid., 227 n. 103.
27. Lugones, "On the Logic," 38.
28. Young, *Justice*, 58–61.
29. Ibid., 168–73.
30. Ibid., 171.
31. Ibid.

of power, like our account of justice, starts from the underside of history, from those who are powerless. Power, therefore, has to be understood both as a personal and as a structural process that can be used for oppression or liberation. Oppressive power uses force, coercion, and/or influence to control, to limit, the self-determination and decision making of individual persons or groups of persons.[32] Liberative power uses power to transform oppressive situations, situations of domination. In a transformative use of power a

dominant agent... exercises power over a subordinate agent for the latter's benefit. ...However, the dominant agent's aim is not simply to act for the benefit of the subordinate agent; rather the dominant agent attempts to exercise his power in such a way that the subordinate agent learns certain skills that undercut the power differential between her and the dominant agent. The transformative use of power is a use of power that seeks to bring about its own obsolescence by means of the empowerment of the subordinate.[33]

Two points need to be clarified here. First, in a transformative use of power, the learning of skills by the subordinate agent is a matter of taking power, of becoming self-defining and self-actualizing. It is precisely because of this that the power of the dominant agent becomes obsolescent, non-operative. Second, the word "empowerment" can indeed be read to mean that power is given, not taken. My contention here is that transformative power is exercised within the context of a relationship, of a give-and-take between dominant and subordinate agent in which not all the giving is done by the dominant and not all the taking by the subordinate but in which both agents give and take. It is my contention that the kind of relationship needed for the development of a relationship—for the presence of transformative power—has to be one of solidarity between those who have power and those who are powerless.

The process of solidarity, like the process of power and of justice, starts with the cry of the oppressed, with the oppressor listening intently to what the oppressed have to say. This listening requires and at the same time results in vulnerability on the part of the powerful, an attitude that will lead them to understand how they benefit from oppressive structures and how they contribute to the oppression of those whose cries are awakening them to their own injustice. This is all part of a process of conversion that results in the oppressor being in solidarity with the oppressed, in using his or her privileges to undo oppressive structures. The oppressor has now become "friend" and has to establish a dialogic relationship—a relationship of mutuality—with the oppressed. It is within this relationship of mutuality that

---

32. I am influenced in my treatment of power by Wartenberg, *Forms of Power.*
33. Ibid., 184.

both the dominant and the subordinate agents empower each other, that transformative power is exercised.[34]

The sixth element of a *mujerista* articulation of justice is the Latinas' belief that justice cannot be achieved at the expense of justice for others.[35] Therefore, we reject theories of justice such as utilitarianism and the liberal understanding of entitlements, which are in many ways responsible for the present meritocratic society of the United States in which the main concern is to be sure everyone has an equality of opportunity to release one's "energies in the pursuit of economic prosperity and political domination."[36] Believing that no one is expendable, our *mujerista* account of justice "requires redistribution from those who are better off to those who are worse off until that point after which further redistribution no longer increases the long-term absolute size of the shares of those who are worse off."[37]

But a *mujerista* account of justice goes beyond redistribution and calls for restitution.[38] It does so not with a spirit of vengeance, to get even. It does so not out of a sense that we have a right to receive back what was taken from our communities and nations of origin, for we demand restitution on behalf of what we need for justice to exist and flourish now and in the future and not in view of what we had in the past.[39] If there is no sense of restitution, redistribution can be seen by the rich and powerful as an injustice and by the poor and oppressed—by Latinas—as a handout. Furthermore, without some restitution Latinas will not be able to capitalize on what they receive through any form of redistribution. This means that Latinas and other poor and oppressed people will always be in the posi-

---

34. For a much more elaborate explanation of the process of solidarity, see my article in *Lift Every Voice*.

35. Of course, to bring justice for the poor and oppressed is at the expense of the inordinate material benefits and privileges of the rich and powerful. But justice looked at from this perspective is not at the expense of justice for the rich and powerful but at the expense of the injustice that benefits the rich and powerful.

36. John Rawls, *A Theory of Justice* (Cambridge, Mass.: Harvard University Press, 1971) 106.

37. This refers to Rawls's "difference principle." Our use of it does not mean that *mujerista* theology appropriates all aspects of Rawls's analysis and elaboration of justice. However, much of the experience of Latinas bears out several of the key elements of Rawls's conception of justice. This quote is to be found in Jeffrey Reiman, *Justice and Modern Moral Philosophy* (New Haven: Yale University Press, 1990) 273. Reiman understands justice to be reason's answer to subjugation and sees this theory of justice as providing a much-needed foundation for Rawls's difference theory, which he embraces but considers to have a weak foundation based on moral intuition rather than on "moral principles required by reason" (20). For Reiman the difference principle provides the "general structure of social justice" (20). Reiman believes that instead of redistributing goods, what needs to be redistributed are the titles to the labor of others (275).

38. I am grateful to Carmen Torres-Reaves, one of the Latinas studying in the graduate program at Drew University, for helping me to see the importance of restitution in our account of justice.

39. Here I am not necessarily denying or affirming that we have such a right. This is an extremely complex issue that must be dealt with at length. Here I am simply asserting that this is not the main reason for considering restitution as an element of justice.

tion of having to demand redistribution, and our lives will continue to be controlled and limited by the rich and powerful. Without some operative sense of restitution we will not have a society where all have access to what they need to be creative, self-defining persons, who participate in setting what is normative for society and who have the opportunity to share in societal goods. Redistribution that includes restitution will result in "mutual benefits" that express "a conception of reciprocity,"[40] which is an intrinsic element of the mutuality we see as central to a *mujerista* account of justice.

The seventh element of a *mujerista* account of justice is the insistence at all times that Latinas' rights are both socioeconomic rights—having to do with restitution and redistribution—as well as civic-political rights. Justice has to do with the right we have to food, adequate housing, health care, access to the fertility of the earth, the productivity of industrialized society, and the benefits provided by social security. For us justice also has to do with freedom of religion, expression, assembly, and due process of the law; participation in the creation of social and political structures; and participation in the leadership and government of such structures in a much more direct way than is at present provided in the "representative form" used in the United States.[41]

At first glance this proposal having to do with rights could be seen as being quite the same as the classical, liberal agenda of justice. However, it seems to me that there are four important considerations to be made before this judgment is passed on our proposal. First, as the first element of this *mujerista* account of justice makes clear, we see this account as a process, a first moment in the process. Keeping this in mind while looking ahead at the eighth element that is required for an effective account of justice, the insistence on these two kinds of rights as a starting place for Latinas' struggle for justice for themselves and their communities is a logical place to start. Second, by itself this element of our account of justice might not seem very radical, but taken together with the other elements of this *mujerista* account I believe makes it a very radical proposal. Indeed, one should think of the radicalness of claiming socioeconomic and civil-political rights when part of the claim would include a new way of understanding and dealing with power as well as a redistribution of wealth and privileges coupled with restitution.

Third, this call for recognition and granting of rights to Latinas is coupled in this account with a radically different understanding about differences than the prevalent one of equality (the third element). This means that the claiming of rights is not so that Latinas can become just like the rest of the people of society but rather so that Latinas and our communities

---

40. Rawls, *Theory*, 102.
41. A more complete delineation of these rights can be found in David Hollenbach, *Justice, Peace, and Human Rights* (New York: Crossroad, 1990) 1–125.

can be an intrinsic element of U.S. society without losing our specificity. For that to happen in this society a radical change as to how this society understands itself has to happen. Finally, in emphasizing both socioeconomic as well as civic-political rights, this *mujerista* account of justice makes it clear that considerations of social justice (what are considered by some to be macro issues) cannot be articulated apart from personal justice (usually classified as micro issues) and, therefore, considered by many liberals as unimportant. As *mujeristas* we hold to the dictum that "the personal is political" and that the separation of the so-called private from the public sector has played a significant role in our oppression as women.

The eighth and final element of a *mujerista* account of justice brings us back to a passing comment made earlier: our account of justice has to be useful; it has to be effective. In order to be so, our account of a *mujerista* account of justice has to help Latinas to understand our world, to locate ourselves concretely in it, and to see the role we play in maintaining such a world. Our account of justice has to denounce injustice, but it also has to indicate modes of resistance instead of encouraging complicity with injustice.[42] A *mujerista* account of justice, we repeat, has to announce our *proyecto histórico* in a precise enough way so as to make choosing necessary, so as to force an option against injustice and for justice.

"No Greater Love": A Matter of Justice

That Sunday afternoon of the *servicio de la amistad* I understood better than ever what I had read years before: "One of the most disastrous errors in the history of Christianity is to have tried—under the influence of Greek definitions—to differentiate between love and justice."[43] This was exactly what we had been saying all afternoon and into the evening as we shared stories about our lives and our *añoranzas* (nostalgic yearnings). By early evening I was once again in awe at the depth of theological understanding of these grassroots Latinas.

I am convinced that these women live Anselm's definition of theology: "faith seeking understanding." Their religious practices (devotional practices such as praying the rosary, praying to the saints, making offerings at their home altars; also the way Latinas daily bring their religious understandings to bear on what we do, on the decisions we make) are not unreflected customs they do automatically. We learned our religious practices mostly from our mothers, our aunts, and our grandmothers. As we

---

42. See María C. Lugones and Elizabeth V. Spelman, "Have We Got a Theory for You! Feminist Theory, Cultural Imperialism and the Demand for 'The Woman's Voice,'" *Women and Values: Readings in Recent Feminist Philosophy* (ed. Marilyn Pearsall; Belmont, Calif.: Wadsworth, 1986) 26–28.

43. José Porfirio Miranda, *Marx and the Bible: A Critique of the Philosophy of Oppression* (Maryknoll, N.Y.: Orbis Books, 1974) 61. For a clear and good explanation of the interrelation between love and justice, see García, *Justice*, 99–102.

watched these older women, Latinas learned not only these religious practices but also their meaning. Together with the manner of performing these practices we learned that these practices were to sustain our lives, were to give us *fuerzas para la lucha* (strength for the struggle). These practices were to be in many instances *los medios para la lucha* (the means for the struggle).

I drove home that Sunday evening reaffirming my conviction that the women with whom I had shared several hours are *mujerista* theologians. They can indeed give us a clearer understanding of who God is, how we touch the divine in our daily lives, how we live the gospel message of justice and peace.

18

Metamodern Aliens
in Postmodern Jerusalem

_____ *Justo L. González* _____

In 1981 a North American theologian, Lonnie Kliever, wrote a book seeking to survey contemporary theology, and he could find no better title than *The Shattered Spectrum*.[1] While acknowledging that there have always been differences of opinion in the church and among theologians, he stated: "In the modern era, theological disagreements have usually occurred along fairly predictable lines. The varieties of theological outlook roughly took the form of a spectrum, ranging from the conservers on the right to the liberalizers on the left."[2] Then he went on to show that this spectrum was no longer intact. A wide divergence of perspectives and concerns had resulted in the emergence of a series of theological perspectives of such variety that the spectrum could no longer hold them: theologies of secularity, of process, of liberation, of hope, of play; narrative theologies, ethnic theologies, feminist theologies, womanist theologies, Third World theologies, and so on. Although Kliever does not use the term in his book, what he is describing is the impact of postmodernity on theology.

Critique of Modernity

Today, through an entire constellation of events, we are coming face-to-face with the limits of modernity. In the political realm, we are faced not only with the end of colonialism but also with the end of an era when it was taken for granted that the cultures of the North Atlantic were superior to the rest. On the socioeconomic front, some years ago we thought that there were two great economic and political systems vying for world supremacy, but we have seen the demise of orthodox state socialism, and we are also witnessing an acute crisis in its capitalistic counterpart. Above all, we are

---

1. Lonnie D. Kliever, *The Shattered Spectrum: A Survey of Contemporary Theology* (Atlanta: John Knox Press, 1981).
2. Ibid., 1.

beginning to understand the degree to which supposedly objective rationality reflects the perspective of the observer, and there is therefore increasing doubt about any claim to universality.

It is within this context that we must understand the current crisis in theology. The traditional place of what the medieval world called "the queen of the sciences" was seriously threatened by modernity. In the field of theology, the modern age began with a debate regarding the authority of Scripture vis-à-vis tradition and eventually led to a situation in which neither Scripture nor tradition had much authority. Scientific objectivity held sway, and theologians strove to develop a theology that was objective and, in its own way, scientific. On the one hand, conservative theologians insisted on the objectivity of Scripture, much as chemists insisted on the objectivity of their experiments. Those, on the other hand, who thought that it was time to move beyond conservatism yielded to the lure of modern objectivity in a different way, by devising a method of reading Scripture that was in fact a capitulation to the spirit of modernity. As one of the leading biblical scholars of our time has said:

The methods in which we have been schooled inevitably operate with hidden criteria (modern rationalism) that decide beforehand what would be included in a text. This method has devised respectable strategies for disposing of what is unacceptable to the modern consciousness, so that issues of artistry that constitute new reality have been handled either by dismissive labels of literary genre or by source divisions that divide and conquer ironies and contradictions in the text. The outcome of historical criticism is most often to provide a text that is palatable to modern rationality, but that in the process has been emptied of much that is most interesting, most poignant, and most "disclosing" in the text.[3]

In more recent times, however, modernity has been discovering its limits. I well remember the day the Russians launched their first, and surprising, sputnik. I was at Yale at the time, and the place was buzzing with what we then called "the conquest of space." Some of the top scientists at the university were giving interviews about the enormous implications of this momentous step. Then, I went to class, and one of this country's great prophets, by the name of H. Richard Niebuhr, opened his lecture with what turned out to be the most profound statement that I heard that day:

There once was in the middle of the Pacific a great freighter tossed by wind and wave, its vast hold carrying a million pounds of potatoes. There was in one of these potatoes, in a sack deep in the hold, an enterprising and hungry worm. It happened that one day this particular worm ate through the skin of its potato and, having looked at the skin of the next potato, came back to its fellow worm, and proclaimed with awe: "We have conquered space!"[4]

---

3. Walter Brueggemann, *Texts under Negotiation* (Minneapolis: Fortress Press, 1993) 58.

4. These are obviously not Dr. Niebuhr's exact words, but rather my recollection of them more than thirty-five years later.

I thought I understood what he meant and laughed at his wit. But I was so caught up in the spirit of modernity that I did not really understand. Space was out there to be conquered, just as the supposedly wild West had been conquered, just as famine and illiteracy would soon be conquered. More than a decade later, when the first astronaut walked on the moon, my heart thrilled at the famous words, "One small step for a man; a giant step for mankind." Today, quite apart from the obvious sexist language of that statement, I have come to realize that what was happening was precisely the opposite of what was thought. That supposedly gigantic step, rather than a new beginning, was the end of the modern dream of the conquest of space. True, we have continued sending probes into space, and even building a space station. But if there is anything we have learned it is that those other potatoes are much farther away than we thought and their skin much thicker than we had imagined.

Ours is a time of limits. We are learning that the earth has ecological limits and that we trespass on those at our own peril. We are learning that there are limits to economic growth. The current generation of American youth will be the first in a long time not to reach higher economic levels than the previous generation. Politicians might still say that this is the result of bad economic policy and that the trend could be reversed with proper management. But the fact is that there is a limit to economic growth and that, even though we might push at the limits here or there, the limits are still there.

We are also learning that there are moral limits. Part of the myth of modernity was that morality could be reduced to rational standards. The problem is that we who think we are so good at reasoning are even better at rationalizing, and very poor at telling the difference. We have increasingly educated entire generations into the modern myth that the best and perhaps the only moral limits are those we set ourselves—and we have reaped a society of greed, violence, and destruction.

Finally, we are learning that reason has its limits. Already half a century ago the Spanish philosopher José Ortega y Gasset was warning us about the limits of rationality. "Reason," said he, "is a narrow band of analytical clarity between two unfathomable strata of irrationality." Then he continued, "In spite of appearing otherwise, rationalism is in fact an attitude characterized, not by observation, but by command. In rationalism, thinking is not mere seeing; it is legislating, commanding."[5] And elsewhere, referring to what we today would call modernity, he says: "Reason was...a belief. For that reason, and only for that reason—certainly not for other attributes and graces peculiar to it—could reason compete with the reli-

---

5. José Ortega y Gasset, "Ni vitalismo ni racionalismo," *Obras completas* (Madrid: Revista de Occidente, 1947) 6:277–79.

gious beliefs that until then had held sway."[6] As a result of these and other statements, Ortega was faulted for being a "perspectivist"—in other words, for placing such emphasis on the perspective of the knower that objective knowledge was no longer possible.

In more recent times, we have learned that the limits of objective reason are greater than any that Ortega even suspected. Ortega's perspectivism was rather limited, having to do mostly with one's beliefs and personal history. Today we realize that every brain is part of a history, a culture, a tradition; that every brain is connected to a stomach; that even the most "objective" rationality has agendas and perspectives that are far from universal and objective.

This recognition of limits marks the passage of modernity. Modernity opened with a vision of boundless horizons, of a universal culture, of unimpeachable objectivity. It closes with the recognition that horizons, culture, and even objectivity are always limited by particular perspectives, by social location, by personal and corporate agendas, and even by material impossibilities. All of this has led to a far-reaching discussion of "postmodernity." Critics and historians of art and literature speak of postmodernism as a style in art and in culture that comes after modernism and that is characterized by joining the conventions and traditions of classical art forms with their popular counterparts. Although this is part of the postmodern phenomenon, postmodernity is much more. It is an entire mind-set, a new period in the history of North Atlantic culture, that recognizes the limits of modernity and of the assumptions on which the entire modern enterprise was grounded.

Critique of Postmodernity

While modernity believed itself to be universal—or at least universalizing—in its scope, postmodernity acknowledges the parochial character not only of modernity but of every human enterprise. While modernity sought after purely objective knowledge, postmodernity knows only that such knowledge is unattainable. As Zygmunt Bauman has put it: "For most of its history, modernity lived in and through self-deception. Concealment of its own parochiality, conviction that whatever is not universal in its particularity is but not-yet-universal, that the project of universality may be incomplete, but remains most definitely on, was the core of that self-deception."[7] There is a sense, however, in which talk about postmodernity remains captive to the same parochial self-deception. Jean-François Lyotard acknowledges as much when he declares, at the very opening of his now-

---

6. José Ortega y Gasset, "Historia como sistema," *Obras*, 6:46.
7. Zygmunt Bauman, *Modernity and Ambivalence* (Ithaca, N.Y.: Cornell University Press, 1991) 232.

famous *The Postmodern Condition*,[8] that he is concerned only with the state of knowledge in the most developed societies. In other words, for Lyotard postmodernity is the outcome of modernity and therefore is to be found primarily in those segments of the world that were also at the center of modernity.

If it is true, as many have stated and as Ashis Nandy has declared in dramatic starkness, that colonialism is the armed version of modernism,[9] it is also true that Lyotard's definition of the postmodern may very well serve as a sort of "Cold War weapon" of neocolonialism. It is significant that, although one of the traits of postmodernity that is most often quoted is the demise of the notion of progress, postmodern scholars and critics such as Lyotard still seem to accept the modern understanding of "development," which served as the ideological grounding for the colonial enterprise. Many insist that Lyotard's "most highly developed" societies are in fact the most highly *mis*developed and that it was only the parochial myopia of modernity that allowed such societies to pose as "developed." Politically speaking, if postmodernity is the state of knowledge in the "most developed" sectors of society, then it is simply the natural outcome of modernity in its aspiration at universal hegemony. This is a point that many Third World and ethnic minority people in the North Atlantic have made. Cornel West, for instance, has underscored the contradiction between postmodernity's "demystification of European cultural predominance" and the fact that "ironically, most First World reflections on 'postmodernism' remain rather parochial and provincial—that is, narrowly Eurocentric."[10]

Many persons whom modernity excluded—or rather, whom modernity included as objects of oppression under the guise of modernization—have cause to rejoice at the news of the demise of modernity. (Or rather, of its impending demise, for it is obvious to any observer that, while literary critics and philosophers of culture may be convinced that postmodernity has arrived, the vast majority of the masses in the so-called developed world still live under the aegis of modernity.) If modernity provided the ideology for colonialism and other forms of exploitation, its obsolescence should not be mourned by those whose oppression it justified.

This is not to say that there is not much in modernity that has proved beneficial to humankind, which we must seek to retain and even to enhance. Modernity, as every human enterprise, is ambiguous and must be

---

8. Jean-François Lyotard, *La condition postmoderne: Rapport sur le savoir* (Paris: Minuit, 1979).

9. Ashis Nandy, *The Intimate Enemy: Loss and Recovery of Self under Colonialism* (Delhi: OUP, 1983) xiv; cited in Stephen Slemon, "Modernism's Last Post," *A Postmodern Reader* (ed. J. Natoli and L. Hutcheon; Albany: State University of New York Press, 1993) 427.

10. Cornel West, "Black Culture and Postmodernism," *A Postmodern Reader, 391.*

seen as such. Thus, while modernity did indeed provide the ideology for colonialism, it also provided the impulse for much of the present rebellion against all forms of oppression: "The famous 'turn to the subject' of modernity can now be seen as both emancipatory and entrapping. ...All of us who speak an emancipatory, liberating language are modern at heart.... As are all of us who will always remain, in our lives as much as in our thoughts, believers in the democratic ideals of liberty and equality."[11]

On the other hand, if postmodernity is, as Lyotard and others rightly point out, the outcome of modernity itself, the new state of knowledge and ideology in the former centers of colonial power, there is ample reason to suspect that it may turn out to be no more liberating than modernity itself. At the same time, much of what postmodernity proposes as an alternative to modernity is what Third World peoples, ethnic minorities, and other marginalized people have been practicing all along—and been dubbed "backward" for it.[12] The following description of postmodern thought sounds strangely familiar to the many oppressed peoples who have been declared incapable of rational modern thought: "Postmodernity's assertion of the value of inclusive 'both/and' thinking deliberately contests the exclusive 'either/or' binary oppositions of modernity. Postmodern paradox, ambiguity, irony, indeterminacy, and contingency are seen to replace modern closure, unity, order, the absolute, and the rational."[13]

A few decades ago, to speak of "both/and," to insist on paradox and irony as essential to understanding, or to believe in a world that was not limited to the mechanical cycle of cause and effect was considered backward and superstitious. Now, things have changed. Now, to think in such terms is postmodern and therefore quite acceptable. For that we must be grateful to those who, in the midst of modern Western culture, have dared announce the demise of modernity, and we must consider them interlocutors whose contribution may prove to be significantly liberating.

At the same time, however, a hermeneutic of suspicion leads us to wonder what hidden agendas lie behind the postmodern critique of modernity. And as soon as we pose this question the suspicion arises that postmodernity may function as a way to keep power in the same—or similar—hands that have held it throughout modernity. If it is true that, as Lyotard and others claim, the "metanarratives" of modernity have lost their power

11. David Tracy, "Theology and the Many Faces of Postmodernity," *Theology Today* 51 (1994) 104–5.

12. See ibid., 104: "For the genuine modern, all history leads by inevitable—indeed clear and distinct—developmental stages from the 'ancients' through the 'medievals' to the secret teleology of all history, us, the moderns. Other cultures often do not possess history at all (indeed, they are 'primitive,' 'archaic,' 'pre-historical')."

13. J. Natoli and L. Hutcheon, "Introduction," *A Postmodern Reader,* ix.

to convince, this means the death of the myths by which the centers of power—colonial, economic, cultural, political, and so on—justified their oppression of others. The aporias or inner contradictions of modernity have brought about its demise—or at least the expectation of such demise. In this we rejoice and join hands with postmodernity. Yet the centers of power remain the same and stubbornly cling to their power. What, then, can those centers do to retain their power? Obviously, they must create a new metanarrative. And, paradoxically enough, this new metanarrative is that there is no metanarrative, that all narratives are partial, contingent to such a degree that they have no power to demand allegiance. The postmodern world of this particular metanarrative is one "without truths, standards, ideals."[14] In such a world, no new metanarrative will have the power to change the status quo, and thus the structures of power that developed under the modern metanarrative will remain.

It is at this point that Hispanics and other oppressed and marginalized groups must part company with the proponents of such postmodernity. There is much in the critique of modernity with which we resonate. Ours has always been a world of irony and paradox. Ours has always been a world of mystery and indeterminacy—mostly because that which was clear and determined was the poverty and systematic exclusion and exploitation of our people. We have always known that truth is something that happens in commitment and in community. Yet for generations we have been told that all of this was not modern; that it was backward; that it was superstitious. And, as most nonmoderns living in the midst of modernity, we have been torn within ourselves, living in two worlds, feeling the oppression of modernity, yet often overwhelmed by its seemingly unassailable rationality. For these reasons, we have cause to rejoice at the postmodern critique of modernity. Yet we have also cause to beware. If postmodernity is the outcome of modernity, and if, as suggested above, it serves agendas that are similar to those of modernity, we must take care, lest we buy into a new system that will turn out to be just as oppressive as the previous one—with the added factor that even the great metanarratives by which we have survived so far will have to be cast aside.

This is no mere theory. As a Protestant Hispanic, I have seen my community torn between its traditional use and understanding of Scripture and the modern reading, which has proven very valuable in helping us understand the process of formation of the text but has also left us not knowing what to do with it. The notion that the world is somehow open to God's action, which is the only ultimate source of hope for oppressed people—and the main source of strength for their action in an otherwise hopeless history—was dubbed "irrational" and premodern. Even more, moderns who did not really understand how such a notion functions in an oppressed community

---

14. Zygmunt Bauman, *Intimations of Postmodernity* (New York: Routledge, 1992) ix.

convinced many of us that we must abandon it, if our action was to be truly effective for the liberation of our people. Meanwhile, no matter how many supposedly objective reasons were given against such a faith, many of our people retained it and continued living and hoping and acting out of it. Now, finally, postmodern criticism of modernity has shown that the supposedly objective and purely rational metanarrative of modernity was not all that objective and rational. In that we rejoice. For that we are grateful to postmodern views and developments, which provide for us the opportunity to be whole once again, no longer torn between a supposedly premodern faith and a modern worldview. At the same time, we must insist that there is much in postmodernity that, precisely because modernity excluded us, we knew all along. We did not need postmodern criticism to tell us that there is truth and life and sense beyond the narrow parameters of modernity. And for that we rejoice.

Furthermore, to the degree that postmodernity is the rediscovery of the radical, irreducible otherness of the other, it can be argued, as David Tracy does, that postmodernity may lead the path away from "religion" as a general abstraction and back toward a theology that takes seriously the otherness of revelation and recovers the prophetic core of the Judeo-Christian tradition.[15]

Metamodernity

It is for these reasons that, when referring to those whom modernity marginalized, I prefer the term "metamodern" rather than "postmodern." This is not just a matter of substituting a Greek for a Latin prefix. Although the two do coincide in many of their meanings, "meta" also has the connotation of "beyond," and it is in that sense that I employ it here. We have always existed at the edges of modernity. We are not those who profited from modernity and who now feel it necessary to promote a postmodernity in which all metanarratives, as well as all principles of truth and justice, are equally powerless to challenge and to transform the status quo. We are those whom modernity colonized, those whom the colonial powers saw as objects of modernization, those whose metanarratives were assaulted and suppressed in the name of the great modern metanarrative. We are those who must still believe in the metanarrative that justice shall prevail and the crooked will be made straight.

What I mean by "metamodern" is similar to what Stephen Slemon means by "post-colonial" when he writes that "post-modernist theory and post-colonial criticism have remained more or less separate in their strategies and their foundational assumptions."[16] Slemon is dealing primarily

---

15. Tracy, "Theology," esp. 108–14.
16. Slemon, "Modernism's Last Post," 427.

with the criticism of texts, with the manner in which modernity dealt with supposedly nonnormative literature, and with the degree to which post-modern criticism leads to a similar attitude of dismissal of such literature. Although his context is different, what he says about the postmodern approach to such texts resonates with some of the concerns of those of us whose metanarratives are based on texts that modernity eviscerated—in the case of Hispanic Protestants, the Bible:

Whereas a post-modernist criticism would want to argue that literary practices such as these [the location of power in the text] expose the constructedness of *all* textuality,...an *interested* post-colonial critical practice would want to allow for the positive production of oppositional truth-claims in these texts. It would retain for post-colonial writing, that is, a mimetic or referential purchase to textuality, and it would recognize in this referential drive the operations of a crucial strategy for survival in marginalized social groups.[17]

Thus, while a postmodern approach would discount the authority of all texts and all metanarratives, a metamodern or "post-colonial" approach would insist on the authority of certain texts that serve to pry open the structures of power created by modernity and allowed to continue standing unchallenged by postmodernity. This has much to do with what elsewhere I have called "reading the Bible in Spanish,"[18] which I believe is one of the pillars of Hispanic theology.

The modern reading of Scripture many of us were taught in seminary, and that dominated biblical studies for generations, sought to eliminate or to explain away anything that did not fit the modern metanarrative. The world was a closed chain of cause and effect, and therefore everything had to be explained by mechanical and physical causes. God did not intervene in history, and therefore any account of divine intervention must be discounted. Science—by which was meant the natural sciences—must have the last word; anything that it could not explain was classified under the category of the "not yet understood." And, even beyond that last word of science, was the great metanarrative of an overpowering cosmic order, which would simply overwhelm any who dared imagine a different world or a different future.

But that is not the reading that takes place Sunday after Sunday in countless churches in poor barrios throughout this hemisphere. Over against that modern reading, the metamodern Hispanic reading has retained a sense of the activity of God, of the openness of the universe, of the possibility of mystery. Such a reading differs from the typical modern reading in ways that the modern mind-set finds difficult to comprehend. For instance, modernity has limited the notion of causality to what the ancients called

---

17. Ibid., 431.
18. Justo González, *Mañana: Christian Theology from a Hispanic Perspective* (Nashville: Abingdon Press, 1990) 75–87.

"efficient cause." The fact is that throughout most of history, and certainly in the Bible, people have thought that "final causes" are at least as important as "efficient causes." In the modern world, things happen "because"; in the Bible, and in most metamodern worldviews, things happen "in order that." In the mechanicist modern worldview, the past controls both the present and the future; in the metamodern worldview, the future pulls the present toward itself. If the past is in control, nothing really surprising may happen—what we call a "surprise" is simply the discovery of something previously unknown. If the future is in control, life must be constantly open to surprise, to astonishment, to real and radical revolution.

Because of a reading that is open to astonishment at God's activity, Hispanics have often been dubbed "fundamentalists." There is a measure of truth in that characterization. But fundamentalism is itself a modern phenomenon—a modern counter-reading of the dominant modern reading—whereas the most typical Hispanic reading is metamodern. It is not, as in the case of fundamentalism, a reading that seeks to preserve the authority of Scripture against the inroads of modernity. It is rather a reading that seeks to empower those whom modernity disempowers and that therefore instinctively sees the weaknesses in modernity itself. It is a reading characterized by what Walter Brueggemann, borrowing a phrase from Martin Buber, would call "abiding astonishment." Commenting on such "abiding astonishment," Brueggemann says:

It is worth considering a "sociology of wonder," and asking who is open to "abiding astonishment," and who might be compelled to overcome, banish, or deny such astonishment? I submit that "abiding astonishment," the celebration of enduring miracle, tends not to occur among those who manage writing, who control the state, who create and transmit proper "facts," who monopolize control, and who explain by cause and effect. The experience and articulation of "wonder" tends to occur in the midst of oral expression, in simpler social units, among those who yearn for and receive miracle, who live by gift since they have little else by which to live, and who are sustained only by slippage (mystery) and gaps in the dominant system of power.[19]

We can read with such "abiding astonishment" precisely because we are "aliens in the promised land"; because modernity excludes us; because postmodernity trivializes our struggles and our hopes; because we are metamodern aliens even in postmodern Jerusalem. It is this openness to astonishment that allows Hispanics today to read Scripture with a profound sense of connection with the people who actually wrote the text. We are well aware of the geographical and cultural distances that stand between us and the original writers and readers. But we leap across that distance by sharing a sense of astonishment, a sense of openness to God's

---

19. Walter Brueggemann, *Abiding Astonishment: Psalms, Modernity, and the Making of History* (Louisville: Westminster/John Knox Press, 1991) 42; see González, *Mañana*, 121.

activity, that was very much part of the writing and the intended reading of the text. Modernity tried to deprive us of such a reading, and we resisted. Postmodernity again, although in a different way, tries to deprive us of the power of such a reading, and once again we must resist. Metamodernity allows us both to claim our identity and to identify with those who in the past were surprised by God—just as we expect to be!

19

Confessing Our Faith in Spanish

Challenge or Promise?

José David Rodríguez

The Significance of a Hispanic Perspective

Recently I had the opportunity of team teaching a course with my father on the Lutheran confessional heritage in Spanish. The course was offered to students enrolled in the Hispanic Ministry Program at the Lutheran School of Theology at Chicago. This course and its English equivalent form part of the core curriculum of the seminary, providing candidates for the ordained ministry and other leadership positions in the church with the content and scope of the Lutheran confessional writings and the manner in which they become normative for Lutheran theology as well as for Lutheran ministry and church life today.[1]

After we had spent eleven weeks studying and reflecting on the subject, the course came to an end. In our evaluation of the course as one of the resources for the preparation of Hispanic leaders for the ministry and mission of the church in the United States and the Caribbean, we became aware that the process of learning had just begun. Courses like these are usually designed by seminaries and other religious educational institutions to ensure that the preaching and teaching of a given denomination's officially recognized leaders will communicate the particular reading and understanding of faith characteristic of that denomination. When candidates from traditionally underrepresented communities are recruited, these courses are redesigned to include the use of the language or other selective elements of the culture and tradition of these communities in order to facilitate their training. Yet the goal remains the same, that is, to ensure that these promising leaders will continue to communicate their denomination's perspectives in their public witness and ministry.

An important finding in the evaluation of these courses by my father, the students, and me was that this design usually becomes not only an ideo-

---

1. This course will be developed into a future publication; in this article I simply wish to highlight some of our most important learning experiences.

logical tool for the assimilation of Eurocentric, middle-class values but also a stumbling block for Hispanics and others who want to make a significant contribution to an understanding of the content and constitutive nature of our faith. However, when taught from a Hispanic perspective, these courses may become provocative educational experiences that not only allow Hispanics to become more active participants in a living tradition of faith but also call the whole church to a more faithful understanding of the gospel.[2] Following Justo L. González's challenge to read the Scriptures in Spanish, my goal in this essay is to examine the implications of correlating faith with the sociocultural history of our communities.[3] I contend that the affirmation of faith from a Hispanic perspective challenges us to recover not only those foundational elements of our sociohistorical reality that give meaning to our identity as a people but also those basic dimensions of the church's faith that have made possible a continuous renewal of our understanding and confession of the gospel.[4]

Hispanic Catholicity

In his introduction to Justo González's book *Mañana,* Virgilio Elizondo makes the provocative claim that when a Hispanic ceases to be "catholic," he or she ceases to be Hispanic.[5] For many this statement would appear to be a reminder that the religious roots of Hispanics and other Latin American peoples lie in the sixteenth-century religio-political conquest of

---

2. Some years ago I published a brief study on the emergence of Hispanic theology in the United States ("De 'apuntes' a 'esbozo': Diez años de reflexión," *Apuntes* 10 [1990] 75–83). In that study I mentioned that an important challenge in the continuous development of this theology was the critical rereading of our denominational traditions, so that in their efforts at evangelization among traditionally marginalized groups of our population those denominations would avoid a conscious or unconscious process of domination. For this task I suggested our engagement in a critical recovery of the theological and ecclesial experience of these denominational traditions, with a focus on those elements that would foster an expression of our witness of faith that would be of help in correcting the mistakes of the past, that would promote a more evangelical expression of faith in the present, and that would enable a stirring up of a vision for the future more in tune with the promise of life of God's reign. This challenge has been addressed by authors such as Edwin Sylvest Jr., "Wesley desde el margen hispano," *Apuntes* 1 (1981) 14–19; Nora Quiroga Boots, "The Wesleyan Tradition and Latin American Theology," *Apuntes* 5 (1985) 9–15; and many others.

3. See Justo L. González, *Mañana: Christian Theology from a Hispanic Perspective* (Nashville: Abingdon Press, 1990) 75–87. On González's notion of "reading the Bible in Spanish," see below.

4. In view of the limits already established for this essay, I will focus my concern in this regard on just two important moments in the historical development of the Christian church: (*a*) the time of its emergence as a minority and persecuted community in the early centuries; and (*b*) the time of its introduction to America by the religious and political conquest of Europeans in the sixteenth century.

5. Virgilio Elizondo, "Foreword" to González, *Mañana,* 9–20.

America by Spanish and Portuguese explorers.[6] Others might falsely assume that the statement reveals the bias of a Roman Catholic theologian and priest, who seizes the opportunity to call back to their original fold those lost Hispanic faithful who have fallen prey to the aggressive proselytism of Protestant missionaries.[7] My own conviction is that with this statement Elizondo points to a very important element of Hispanic and Latin American identity, an element that needs to be taken seriously for a better understanding of the nature of our character and sociohistorical reality.

In recovering our identity we are confronted with the fact that our makeup is much more complex than the traditional stereotypes used to define us. In terms of our religious identity, a kind of catholicity is overwhelmingly present, especially among the most popular sectors of our people, and that goes beyond the traditional dogmatic, cultural, organizational, and programmatic distinctions established in Christendom after the sixteenth century between Protestants and Roman Catholics.[8] For Elizondo this catholicity has constituted the basis for a Latin American style of Christianity in these lands since the early sixteenth century. Indeed, Ada María Isasi-Díaz argues that it is from this catholic perspective that Hispanic Americans develop their understanding of the human and the divine and also try to bring some meaning to their existence.[9]

---

6. One of the most recent and provocative studies of the conquest and evangelization of America is that of Luis N. Rivera Pagán, *Evangelización y violencia: La conquista de América* (San Juan: CEMI, 1990); Eng. trans.: *A Violent Evangelism: The Political and Religious Conquest of the Americas* (Louisville: Westminster/John Knox Press, 1992).

7. Elizondo's foreword will persuade any intelligent reader of the misunderstanding involved in this latter assumption: "Let me be very clear—I do not want to say that every Hispanic has to remain a member of the Roman Catholic church in order to be a Hispanic, but I am saying that when a Hispanic ceases to be catholic (to participate in the religious-cultural expressions of our people), he or she ceases to be a Hispanic" (Elizondo, "Foreword," 17).

8. For Elizondo (ibid., 14) the "catholic" nature of our religious identity is based on a *mestizo* Christianity that is in communion with both the universal church and its traditions as well as our own historical and cultural uniqueness: "It seems to me that quite often the deepest treasures of our Catholic-Iberoamerican culture were too easily identified with the dogmas, rites and rituals of the Roman Catholic church. Likewise, the Bible has been read and interpreted by the Protestants through the eyes of the Nordic European culture that produced Protestantism. Thus, Latin Americans have been asked to abandon their common roots and become Nordic Europeans in the name of the gospel!...I believe that one can convert to Christ without abandoning one's religious-cultural identity." In this regard, it is interesting to point out that in a study of the theological education of Hispanics in the United States and the Caribbean, Justo González (*The Theological Education of Hispanics* [New York: Fund for Theological Education, 1988] 67) argues that, in terms of the mission and ministry of most major Protestant denominations in the United States among Hispanics, "most denominations lack a considered strategy for work among Hispanics, and apparently none has been willing to consider seriously the structural changes that may be necessary for such mission."

9. Ada María Isasi-Díaz, "Apuntes for a Hispanic Women's Theology of Liberation," *Apuntes* 6 (1986) 66–76. In fact, she insists that, although in shaping their theological perspective some Hispanic Americans frequently ignore this cultural and historical reality,

Mestizaje and Marginality: The Collective Social Identity
of Hispanics in North America

In establishing the foundations for a rereading of history from a Hispanic perspective, Justo L. González proposes a definition of the meaning of "Hispanic" in terms of three different but complementary elements: race, culture, and social class. The first of these elements suggests that we are a race in which the different bloodlines of Europe, Africa, and Native America come together. The second element alludes to the language and other significant cultural characteristics that we have in common.[10] The third element indicates that the predominant experience of our communities is one of poverty and exploitation. None of these elements must be abandoned if we are to understand what it means to be Hispanic in the United States. Upon this basis we must make an effort to reread, rewrite, and remake our history.[11]

For Virgilio Elizondo we are a mestizo people, the product of two great invasions and conquests: the Spanish and the Anglo-American. As a biological phenomenon, *mestizaje*—the generation of a new people from disparate parent peoples—has not been uncommon in the evolution of humankind. Yet French biologist J. Ruffie claims that from the birth of Europe thirty-five thousand years ago, when the invading Cro-Magnons integrated with the indigenous Neanderthals, no ethnogenetic event of similar magnitude took place until the birth of Mexico five hundred years ago.[12] It is Elizondo's conviction that a similar event of at least equal magnitude has already begun to take place in the Southwest of the United States with respect to the Hispanic population.[13]

In their efforts to explain the sociological nature of Hispanic minorities in the United States, an increasing number of Hispanic scholars continue to point to the complex nature of our ethnicity.[14] We are a people who cannot

popular religiosity demands that theology give greater consideration to the significance of this *mestizaje* (66).

10. In his description of the cultural identity of Mexicans and other Latin Americans, Virgilio Elizondo (*Galilean Journey: The Mexican American Promise* [Maryknoll, N.Y.: Orbis Books, 1983] 19–46) points to new cultural symbols of resistance and survival, such as group heroes, fiestas, celebrations, and religious observances like *posadas, peregrinaciones,* and so on.

11. Justo L. González, "Towards a New Reading of History," *Apuntes* 1 (1981) 4–14. The article was originally presented at a meeting of Hispanic theologians in San Antonio (April 1981), under the auspices of the Fund for Theological Education. With the intent of making available the content of these presentations to a wider audience, two of the lectures delivered at the event were published in *Apuntes* 1 (1981).

12. J. Ruffie, *De la biologie à la culture* (Paris: Flammarion, 1976) 233.

13. Elizondo, *Galilean Journey,* 5–31.

14. While there is abundant literature in English about this subject, one of the most recent and important publications in Spanish, which tries to bring a global analysis to bear on this subject, is that of Rodolfo J. Cortina and Alberto Moncada, eds., *Hispanos en los Estados Unidos* (Madrid: Ediciones de Cultura Hispánica, Instituto de Cooperación Iberoamericana, 1988).

trace our origins simply back to the Iberian Peninsula or the Latin American countries. The diversity of our cultural, historical, and racial origins as well as the fact that our collective self-identity as a group is in constant development make our ethnicity much more dynamic and complex than that of European ethnic communities whose boundaries are generally well defined and whose ties with their countries of origin are less remote.[15] These studies also indicate the increasing awareness of a collective social identity by Hispanics in North America. For Margarita B. Melville this consists of striving for a consciousness of a pan-ethnic identity with the goal of satisfying common economic and political needs.[16] For others, like Manuel L. Carlos, this consciousness of socioeconomic and political marginalization needs to be complemented by an awareness that the collective social role of Hispanics must be that of an "autonomous cultural enclave," resisting total assimilation by the dominant sectors of society.[17] We are thus led to conclude that in describing the collective identity of Hispanics in North American society two distinctive elements stand out: on the one hand, the rich racial, ethnic, and cultural background of our origins and evolution; on the other, our continuous subjection to subordination and marginality.

There is indeed a sense of *mestizaje* in the anthropological development of our people. We are a cosmic race, a new people generated by a mixture of various races and cultural backgrounds.[18] This new ethnos is the product of two major religious encounters, the Iberian–Roman Catholic colonization of Latin America in the sixteenth century and the later seventeenth-century Protestant colonization of North America. Yet this new

---

15. Alejandro Portes and Cynthia Truelove ("El sentido de la diversidad: Recientes investigaciones sobre las minorías hispanas en los Estados Unidos," *Hispanos en los Estados Unidos*, 31–51) argue that Hispanics in the United States rather than constituting a consolidated minority are a group whose boundaries and self-definition are still in a state of continuous change.

16. Margarita B. Melville, "Los hispanos: ¿Clase, raza, o etnicidad?" *Hispanos en los Estados Unidos*, 133–45. Felix Padilla ("Identidad y movilización latina," ibid., 167–71) argues that the "locus" for the collective unity and identity of diverse Hispanic groups in North America lies in their willingness to transcend their individual national, cultural, and class boundaries through a commitment to seek their common welfare in a society that has marginalized them.

17. Manuel L. Carlos, "Identidad y raíces culturales de los enclaves hispanos en los Estados Unidos," *Hispanos en los Estados Unidos*, 91–97.

18. The most provocative connotations of *mestizaje* were articulated by the Mexican statesman and educator José Vasconcelos in his book *La raza cósmica: La misión de la raza iberoamericana* (Barcelona: Espasa Calpe, 1925). Vasconcelos argued for a close relationship between biology and culture; see in this regard the summary of his thought by Anthony M. Stevens Arroyo: "He held that cultural patterns were preexistent ideas genetically innate in the races. These cultural forces were controlled by the laws of biology. The mixture of all races in Latin America would eventually produce a synthesis of previous world civilizations. And just as the cosmic race is the ultimate expression of biological perfection, the cosmic culture is destined to supersede all other civilizations" (A. M. Stevens Arroyo, ed., *Prophets Denied Honor: An Anthology of the Hispanic Church in the United States* [Maryknoll, N.Y.: Orbis Books, 1980] 32).

collective identity is also the product of suffering and violence.[19] In fact, this subjection to suffering and marginalization continues to be a common denominator among individual Hispanic groups in the United States, as evidenced by numerous sociological studies.[20]

Dominant versus Popular Faith

As a Puerto Rican Hispanic living in the United States, I find that a common denominator in the history of my people and that of the native peoples of these lands has been the marginalization to which we have been subjected by the dominant groups of society. The events that have characterized the missionary enterprise of religious groups with our communities have followed a similar pattern.[21]

Piri Thomas, an African American Puerto Rican who grew up on the streets of New York's Spanish Harlem and survived the anguish of addiction, street combat, and the degradation of prison, provides in his book *Savior, Savior, Hold My Hand* a compelling description of his conversion to Pentecostalism and his continuous struggle against the various institutionalized forms of religion that have contributed to the marginalization of our communities. One of the scenes in the book gives a moving account of Thomas's painful experience within what he calls the "White church." Reacting against the racist and patronizing attitudes of suburban Christians toward the faithful who live in the ghetto, he confronts a man named John, who had spearheaded the efforts of the "White church" among Hispanics in the barrio, with the driving prejudice of these relations. John, reacting defensively, reprimands Piri for showing lack of respect in his comments and proposes that Piri should bring his angry feelings to the Lord in prayer. Piri responds: "Prayer's gotta be strengthened with some kind of action, John. Without disrespect, amigo, if you've read history, too, you'd know many people have been taught to pray and when they finished praying and

---

19. One of the earliest and most influential accounts of the violent conquest and colonization of America was written by the sixteenth-century Dominican historian Bartolomé de Las Casas in his *Brevísima relación de la destrucción de las indias* (ed. André Saint-Lu; Madrid: Ediciones Cátedra, 1991); see also Rivera Pagán, *A Violent Evangelism*.

20. One of the best sources in this regard is Portes and Truelove, "Sentido de la diversidad," especially given the rich bibliographical sources of over ninety entries consulted and provided by the authors.

21. For a more detailed exposition of this thesis and in addition to Rivera Pagán's study (*Evangelización*), see Enrique Dussel, *Hipótesis para una historia de la iglesia en América Latina* (Salamanca: Sígueme, 1964); Jean Pierre Bastian, *Historia del Protestantismo en América Latina* (Mexico City: Casa Unida de Publicaciones, 1990); Moisés Sandoval, *On the Move: A History of the Hispanic Church in the United States* (Maryknoll, N.Y.: Orbis Books, 1990); Ada María Isasi-Díaz, "Ministry among Hispanics," *Vanguard* (September/October 1989) 1–2.

looked around, their land and respect was gone, taken away by the ones who taught them to pray."[22]

Piri's bold resistance and daring response to John's plea for submission to the God of the suburban Christians reveal an important feature of what Luis Rivera Pagán calls the Hispanic American mestizo style of existence and faith.[23] For Víctor Codina, the popular expression of this faith can be traced back to the sixteenth-century "defective" evangelization of America.[24] Contrary to the religion of fear imposed by the conquistadores who took over their lands and enslaved them, the indigenous peoples discerned the presence of a different God—one who led them into the mystery of the Triune God's salvific plan for humanity through the experience of Our Lady of Guadalupe.[25] This conversion experience, supported by the evangelization and personal witness of Spanish religious leaders such as Antonio de Montecinos, Bartolomé de Las Casas, and a host of others,[26] led to the reformulation of faith and a popular creed establishing the basis for the renewal of the church and its theology in the Americas. More importantly, it led to the recovery of the fundamental confessing dimension of Christianity characteristic of both its emergence as a minority and persecuted commu-

---

22. Piri Thomas, *Savior, Savior, Hold My Hand* (New York: Doubleday, 1972) 260.

23. Luis N. Rivera Pagán, "Conquest and Christianization: The Problem of America," *Apuntes* 12 (1992) 47: "The discovery of America led immediately to its conquest, an act of violence performed, from the beginning to end, in the name of Jesus Christ, the Martyr of divine love. In His name, the Antillean Arawaks were extinguished; in His name, Cortés destroyed Tenochtitlán; in His name, Pizarro executed Atahualpa. Truly, however, it also led to one of the most exceptional and exciting chapters in the history of Christian missions, and to the birth of the Hispanic American mestizo style of existence and faith."

24. Víctor Codina, "Credo oficial y credo popular," *Revista Latinoamericana de teología* 26 (1992) 243–52.

25. The true intent of the story is not to bring people to venerate an image of the Virgin but to challenge people then as well as now to join in an ancient biblical tradition that the early Christian community attributed to the Virgin Mary. It is the tradition so eloquently presented in the Magnificat (Luke 1:46–55). It is a tradition of a God who loves all human beings. But for this love to be actualized, God "has scattered the proud in the thoughts of their hearts,... has brought down the powerful from their thrones, and lifted up the lowly" (Luke 1:51–52). For a more detailed account of this foundational religious conversion of the indigenous Latin American peoples to Christianity, see Elizondo, *Galilean Journey,* 11–13, and José D. Rodríguez and Colleen Nelson, "The Virgin of Guadalupe," *Currents in Theology and Mission* 13 (1986) 368–69. Two contemporary Latin American theologians have added significant insights on the meaning of this event for popular religiosity; see María Clara Bingemer and Ivone Gebara, *Mary Mother of God, Mother of the Poor* (Maryknoll, N.Y.: Orbis Books, 1989).

26. While the names of Montecinos and de Las Casas are well known as protectors of the Native Americans, Epifanio de Moirans along with Francisco de Jaca should also be mentioned as protectors of African slaves. See José Tomás López García, "Dos defensores de los esclavos negros," *Raíces de la Teología Latinoamericana* (ed. Pablo Richard; San José: DEI, 1985) 67–71. Among these prophetic witnesses the name of Antonio de Valdivieso needs a special mention as the first great ecclesial martyr, murdered in 1550 due to his compelling preaching in defense of the Native Americans. For an interesting study of sixteenth-century bishops who protected the indigenous people in America, see Enrique Dussel, *El episcopado latinoamericano y la liberación de los pobres 1504–1620* (Mexico City: Centro de Reflexión Teológica, 1979).

nity in the first century and the stance of some of its prophetic leaders who throughout history have challenged this community of faith to remain faithful to God's word in the context of ideological manipulation, oppression, prejudice, and idolatry.[27]

The Confessional Dimension of Faith

Contemporary theologians have helped us understand the foundational confessional nature of Christianity.[28] While their studies of the Christian faith have carefully examined the meaning of its apostolic origins, its trinitarian basis, its evangelical substance, its christological emphasis, and other important and related aspects, they have failed to provide an equally thorough analysis of the sociohistorical implications and significance of those who were actually involved in the act of confession.[29] Part of the problem can be traced to the intention of most theologians to focus their analysis on the confessional writings that record acts of confession and their efforts to avoid a biased perspective in their examination of the subject. Yet all confessional writings point to an act of confession that precedes them, and every theological perspective, no matter how seemingly objective, betrays a bias of which the theologian may not be consciously aware. My intention in the following sections of this essay will be to show how a confession of faith in Spanish, that is, a confession of faith that brings our Hispanic history and perspective to bear on our interpretation of the meaning of the

---

27. According to Codina ("Credo oficial," 251), this popular faith, while indeed at times the expression of religious alienation—false resignation, passivity, and anti-Protestant and anticommunist apologetics—nevertheless constitutes the basis for the renewal of the church's theology and praxis. "Something paradoxical is taking place: the poor, the women of simple faith, are helping to reformulate both the faith and the theology of the church. The popular creed ceases to be an impoverishment and poor assimilation of the official creed and becomes instead a source of life for the whole church. One finds a repetition of both the story of Mary and the history of salvation: God renews the people from the margin. From the *anawim* come the Messiah and the whole spirituality of the New Testament. From the *anawim* of the Third World something new is being born: a spirituality that is of the poor, simple, evangelical, paschal, and martyrial."

28. For a brief analysis of the biblical, historical, and theological origins of this confessional dimension of faith, see Walter Kasper, "The Catholic View of Confessions and Confessional Community," *Confessing One Faith* (ed. G. W. Forell and J. F. McCue; Philadelphia: Augsburg, 1982) 39–62. Carl E. Braaten (*Principles of Lutheran Theology* [Philadelphia: Fortress Press, 1983] 27–28) argues that the confessional principle of Luther and Lutheran theology is a product of the basic act of faith, for a nonconfessional Christianity is a contradiction in terms. He further contends that the confessional datum of faith is most clearly seen in the baptismal formulas and eucharistic hymns that made up the most primitive creed of Christianity.

29. An interesting exception to this trend is Justo L. González's *Christian Thought Revisited* (Nashville: Abingdon Press, 1989), which, along with presenting an interpretation of salient themes in the contribution of major theologians throughout the history of Christianity, provides a chapter where the author investigates the sociopolitical setting of three types of theological perspectives that characterized the early development of Christian theology and how they played a significant role in the theological formulations of their originators.

gospel, provides an insight into the significance of this confessional tradition of Christianity that will prove useful not only to Hispanics but also to others who, along with Hispanics, share in this confessional heritage.

The Political Dimension of the Act of Confession

In his effort to reread theology from a Hispanic perspective, Justo González begins by proposing a reading of the Bible in Spanish. His proposal is not a chauvinistic appeal for Hispanics to do away with serious biblical research grounded on, among other things, the historical-critical method.[30] Nor does he mean the obvious reading of the Bible in Spanish translation. What he does mean is much more than that. His suggestion is to take seriously an emphasis that, since the time of the Reformation, has been a central feature of the Protestant tradition, namely, making the Bible available to the people in their vernacular. It is common to think that the goal of this approach was to allow more people to have direct access to something that was previously reserved for scholars. But there is a more significant and profound dimension to this process. When the Bible becomes a resource accessible to the people and the people discover in the Bible their own particular perspective, then the Bible becomes the people's book, that is, a subversive book no longer under the control of the dominant groups in society:

When the people read the Bible, and read it from their own perspective rather than from the perspective of the powerful, the Bible becomes a mighty political book. This is what I mean by "reading the Bible in Spanish": a reading that includes the realization that the Bible is a political book; a reading in the "vernacular," not only in the cultural, linguistic sense but also in the sociopolitical sense.[31]

The point of departure for such a reading, in contrast to the one characteristic of the dominant culture, is to read the Scriptures as presenting a history of the people of God "beyond innocence," that is, to view biblical history as "responsible remembrance" leading to "responsible action." Indeed, anyone who reads the Bible carefully, going beyond the level of Bible stories, "will have great difficulties in idealizing its heroes/heroines. Biblical characters are not presented as immaculate, but as human beings struggling with ambiguities similar to the ones we have to confront daily."[32] To be sure, biblical history is a history beyond innocence. Its only real heroes are the God of history and history itself, which somehow continues to move forward in spite of the failures of its great protagonists. Since this is also

---

30. He does mention, however, that to someone who had condemned substituting the Revised Standard Version for the "original" King James, he had replied that the Bible had originally been written in Spanish and that God had then translated it into Hebrew and Greek because at that time no one knew Spanish yet (González, *Mañana*, 75).

31. Ibid., 84.

32. Ibid., 75–77.

the nature of Hispanic history,[33] it may well be that on this score we have an interpretative advantage over those whose history is still at the level of guilty innocence and who, therefore, must read Scripture in the same way in which they read their own history, that is, in terms of high ideals and purity in order to justify their privileges and interests.[34]

Confessing the faith in Spanish forces us again to address this political agenda, that is, to deal with issues of power and powerlessness. The fact is that since our confession of faith is the product of a difficult encounter between the word of God and the experience of our communities, it will necessarily be a reflection of the marginality to which this experience is subjected in the social structure. To illustrate this point, González tells the following story: a few years ago, the president of a prestigious seminary in one of the largest cities of the United States commented proudly to him that almost half of the faculty of his seminary had shown so much interest in Latin American theology that they were starting to take Spanish classes. González responded that, indeed, he was happy to know that Latin American theology had created so much enthusiasm among faculty members, but that it was too bad that their decision to learn Spanish was due to the fact that there were so many interesting books to read and not to the fact that this seminary was surrounded by thousands of poor, Spanish-speaking people in need of the gospel.[35]

Confessing the Faith in the Early Centuries

This approach to the act of confession leads us to recover for today some important aspects of the understanding and witness of faith of those who have preceded us and who throughout the centuries have been intentionally displaced and forgotten. From its origins as a community of faith in the early centuries, the Christian church emerged as a confessing community. This community of faith had a core of beliefs that sustained its members. Those sharing these beliefs felt urged to interpret them, live by them, make public confession of them, and record them in writing. This became one of the most important features of the church from the time of the apostles to the present.

---

33. See ibid., 77–78: "We know that we were born out of an act of violence of cosmic proportions in which our Spanish forefathers raped our Indian foremothers. We have no skeletons in our closet. Our skeletons are at the very heart of our history and our reality as a people. Therefore, we are comforted when we read the genealogy of Jesus and find there, not only a Gentile like ourselves, but also an incest, and what amounts to David's rape of Bathsheba. The gospel writer did not hide the skeletons in Jesus' closet, but listed them, so that, we may know that the Savior has really come to be one of us not just one of the high and the mighty, the aristocratic with impeccable blood lines, but one of *us*."

34. Ibid., 75–87.

35. Justo L. González, "Hacia un redescubrimiento de nuestra misión," *Apuntes* 7 (1987) 51–60.

González also reminds us that from its very beginnings and as a consequence of its public witness Christianity was subjected to persecution and martyrdom: "The Lord whom Christians served had died on the cross, condemned as a criminal. Soon thereafter Stephen was stoned to death following his witness before the council of the Jews. Then James was killed at Herod Agrippa's order. Ever since then, and up to our own days, there have been those who have had to seal their witness with their blood."[36]

In the New Testament it is Jews who persecute Christians, since from their perspective the Christians had emerged as a Jewish sect going from town to town tempting good Jews to become heretics.[37] As Jewish nationalism increased and eventually led to rebellion against Rome, Christians, particularly the Gentiles among them, sought to put distance between themselves and that movement. Yet as the Roman authorities acknowledged Christianity as a religion quite different from Judaism, they also began to recognize the threat of this new religious movement in Roman-ruled territories.[38] This new consciousness became the basis for two and one-half centuries of persecution against Christians by the Roman Empire, from the time of Nero to the conversion of Constantine.[39] Scholarly research on the records of this witness shows that they are among the most precious and inspiring testimonies of early Christianity.[40]

This was a time during which the church established a consensus regarding its sacred texts and rule of faith built on the basis of a trinitarian formula.[41] This process also led to the formulation of the "symbols of faith"[42] and the emergence of Christian dogma. However, during the course of the church's historical development and as Christianity became a dominant power in the West, the efforts made by many of the church's leaders to make the church a respectable movement in society led, intentionally or

---

36. Justo L. González, *The Story of Christianity* (3 vols.; San Francisco: Harper and Row, 1984) 1:31.

37. For a more detailed examination of this topic, see Richard A. Horsley, *Sociology and the Jesus Movement* (New York: Crossroad, 1989) 130–32.

38. The rejection of Roman gods and many Roman traditions due to their intimate connection to pagan worship led to the persecution of Christians as haters of humankind and perpetrators of abominations; see González, *Story of Christianity*, 1:33–36, 49–52.

39. Ibid., 1:31–48, 82–90, 102–8.

40. González notes (ibid., 1:39–48) that among the most dramatic documents recording the persecution and attitudes of Christians toward martyrdom are the "acts of the martyrs," which retell the arrest, trial, and death of various martyrs. One of the most informative of these documents is the one that tells of the martyrdom of Felicitas, a woman who, along with other consecrated widows, devoted all her time to work for the church in the early first centuries.

41. Ibid., 58–66. Scholars in the area of the history of the church link these events with the church's struggle against heresy.

42. The reference here is to the public pronouncements of faith made by the church in various creeds, such as the Apostles' Creed, the Nicene Creed, and the Constantinopolitan Creed.

not, to compromise beliefs by interpreting them from the perspective of the dominant sectors of society.[43]

In his critical evaluation of this theological heritage, González challenges us to question the validity of those theological perspectives that dominated the field, to raise the significance of a marginalized perspective that leads to a deeper understanding of the Christian message. González contrasts the omnipotent and impassible god that developed from the appropriation of Greek philosophy by Christian apologists[44] and the "minority God" of the Scriptures who, as an active participant in human history, breaks up the bondage of Israel in Egypt, raises judges to liberate Israel from its enemies, sends prophets to rebuke the people and their rulers, and, incarnated in Jesus Christ, suffers oppression and injustice for our redemption. González writes that this minority status of God is a fact: "This fact, well attested throughout Scripture, finds its clearest expression in Jesus Christ, in whom God is carried to and fro by human beings whose victim God becomes. If being a minority means being subjected and victimized by forces one does not control, God is a minority!"[45]

Surely this was the perspective that inspired the confessing witness of believers who emerged as a minority and persecuted community in the early centuries. It is also the perspective that led to the prophetic stance of those early Christian martyrs and many others whose witness of faith throughout history has challenged the church to remain faithful to God's word in the context of ideological manipulation, oppression, prejudice, and idolatry.[46]

---

43. González (*Christian Thought Revisited*, 77–90) argues that after Christianity became in the fourth century the official religion of the Roman Empire there was an intentional effort by its dominant leaders to interpret the faith in terms of the powerful and intellectual elites in society.

44. González points out (*Mañana*, 98) that while the "idle" philosophers of ancient Greece did not set out to develop an ontology that would justify their personal privileges, the fact remains that most of their intellectual work became an exposition of much of what the Greek aristocracy valued: "Therefore, when Christians, in their eagerness to communicate their faith to the Greco-Roman world, began interpreting their God in Platonic terms, what they introduced into theology was not a sociopolitically neutral idea. What they introduced was an aristocratic idea of God, one which from that point on would serve to support the privilege of the higher classes by sacralizing changelessness as a divine characteristic. Yahweh, whose mighty arm intervened in history on behalf of the oppressed slaves in Egypt and of widows, orphans, and aliens, was set aside in favor of the Supreme Being, the Impassible One, who saw neither the suffering of the children in exile nor the injustices of human societies, and who certainly did not intervene in behalf of the poor and the oppressed."

45. Ibid., 93.

46. For a more detailed examination of this prophetic stance of Christian believers in the early centuries, see González, *Christian Thought Revisited*, 17–109; idem, *Story of Christianity*, 1:7–108; idem, *Historia del pensamiento cristiano*, vol. 1 (Miami: Editorial Caribe, 1992).

Confessing the Faith during the Conquest of America

A significant number of church bodies in the United States declared the 1992 Columbus quincentenary a year for remembrance, repentance, and renewal. Among the goals of this resolution was the willingness to understand more fully the historical context of the coming of Columbus and its impact on the indigenous peoples who populated the Caribbean as well as North and South America. An increasing number of studies show that the initial encounter between Europeans and the American indigenous peoples was characterized by the concurrent act of Christianization and peaceful or violent conquest.[47] It is shocking that the justification for the peaceful or violent seizure of the lands and resources of the indigenous peoples as well as their enslavement, which resulted in the tragic obliteration of various national ethnic groups, had a theological grounding.

In his study of the political and religious Spanish conquest of the Americas, Luis Rivera Pagán mentions two significant examples of the prophetic witness of faith that, in recovering the confessing witness of the faithful in the early centuries, provide a foundation for our present confessing of faith in Spanish. The first of these examples is the work of Bartolomé de Las Casas and a host of other Spanish religious leaders who initiated a prophetic witness for the protection and vindication of the American peoples and nations. To be sure, their critical voice against the cruelty and injustice imposed by the God-fearing Europeans on the indigenous people in America came out of a religious imperative:

> They became convinced that such mistreatment constituted a violation of Pope Alexander's 1493 "donation bulls...." They also came to the conclusion that the European Christians in America were, according to the ecclesiastical norms, in mortal sin on the basis of their cruel conduct.... They felt impelled to protest by their religious vows. It is a religious imperative, not an alternative political or social conception, that promotes the first strong prophetic challenge of the conquest.[48]

Surely, the main exponent of this religious tradition was Bartolomé de Las Casas. From his voluminous writings we learn that his incisive critique of the violent conquest of America emerged from the fact that he was a man educated in the spirit and style of the biblical prophets: "His conversion to the freedom of the American communities was intimately linked, as in Saint Augustine's case, to a biblical text. In the case of de Las Casas the text was Eccl 34:20–21."[49] Yet, like Columbus, Cortés, and many others,

---

47. Among the many important works in this area, see Heinz D. Steffan, *1492–1992: La interminable conquista* (San José: DEI, 1990); Leonardo Boff and Virgilio Elizondo, eds., *1492–1992: The Voice of the Victims* (*Concilium* 232; London: SCM Press, 1990); Giulio Girardi, *La conquista permanente* (Managua: Nicarao, 1992); Guillermo Meléndez, *Sentido histórico del V centenario (1492–1992)* (San José: DEI, 1992).

48. Luis N. Rivera-Pagán, "Prophecy and Patriotism: A Tragic Dilemma," *Apuntes* 12 (1992) 60.

49. Ibid., 63.

Las Casas shared with his rivals a providential and messianic ideology that, ironically, provided the basis for the Spanish conquest.[50] While he strongly repudiated the conquering quest that led to the violent submission of indigenous people to Spanish imperial domain, "he is not aware, though, that the messianic providentialism that prevails in the Catholic Spain of the fifteenth and sixteenth centuries, and which he shares, is truly what propels the bloody subjugation of the infidels."[51]

The second example mentioned by Rivera Pagán comes from another challenging and provocative source, the prophetic witness of the victims of this evangelization and conquest. At the end of his study, Rivera Pagán argues that for Christians faithful to the crucified Lord, a careful examination of the events of this Christianization and conquest should lead to a thoughtful consideration of the witness of the martyrs who offered their lives for the emancipation of the poor and oppressed of the Americas. He challenges the reader to see the blood of Christ shed from the bodies of the American natives and the ill-treated and suffering blacks, offered in sacrifice at the golden altar of mammon. He also shares a very moving story about an initiative taken by an indigenous people of America during a visit of Pope John Paul II to Latin America.[52] Acknowledging the pope as the representative of the Christian faith brought to Latin America in the sixteenth century, the native peoples of Argentina asked for an audience so that they could bring him a gift, in a solemn yet curious expression of thanksgiving. They handed him a Bible, the one brought to them by a bishop back in the sixteenth century. There was no doubt in their minds that the conquest of America had been legitimized with a religious ideology based on the Bible, and they wanted to return this Bible to its rightful owner.

But as these people conveyed their suffering and pain to this Christian leader, they also challenged him to see that even in the most distressing circumstances there is also hope for the manifestation of God's promises. Their experience, based on the blood shed not only by their own people but also by other committed Christians (like Antonio de Valdivieso, bishop of Nicaragua, assassinated in 1550 because of his defense of the Indians, and many other martyrs, men and women from a variety of cultures, races, and social classes who witnessed to a vision of God's redeeming and transforming power in the lives and struggles of God's people), challenged them to discern and appreciate the fact that great blessings can come out of moments of deepest despair through the loving initiative of God's providence. These people challenged the pope then and continue to challenge

---

50. For a more elaborate discussion of this topic, see Rivera Pagán, "Conquest and Christianization," 44–46.

51. Ibid., 46.

52. The reference is to a public message given to Pope John Paul II by twenty-five hundred Native Americans on 8 April 1987 in Salta, Argentina. See Rivera Pagán, A Violent Evangelism, 270.

the church now to participate in witnessing to God's continuous initiative of establishing the conditions for a new relationship between peoples from diverse cultures, races, economic classes, and religious affiliations. The challenge for us today is to become witnesses to this creative, redeeming, and sanctifying activity of God in the present.

One important response to this challenge has come from Hispanic and Latin American women. In her reflection on the impact of the events that took place as a consequence of the European conquest of America, María Pilar Aquino reminds us that, instead of continuing to "cover" the real political and economic intentions of the conquest, we need to engage in a continuous effort of "rediscovering" the truth and God's powerful re-creative activity through the efforts of those who, like Hispanic and Latin American women, are actively engaged in a witness to God's creative, redeeming, and sanctifying activity among us, in order to transform those elements of our sociocultural reality that have maintained oppressive conditions.[53]

The Challenge and Promise of Confessing Our Faith in Spanish

At the beginning of this essay I referred to the experience I recently had of team teaching a course with my father on the Lutheran confessional heritage in Spanish. In our joint evaluation of the course with the students, we realized that, when taught from a Hispanic perspective, this and other courses would challenge us to understand the particular contribution of our communities in recovering some important dimensions of our faith that would prove useful not only to Hispanics but also to others with whom we share in this confessional tradition.

One such important dimension of our faith is the prophetic confessional stance that we traced back to the origins of the church as it emerged as a minority and persecuted community in the early centuries as well as in its introduction to these lands through the courageous witness of its martyrs and prophets. As I reflect on this fundamental dimension of faith, I realize that, while the witness of the Hispanic church in the United States since its emergence in the sixteenth century has been that of prophets denied honor,[54] this witness of faith has nevertheless pointed to a foundational

---

53. In addition to providing a narrative of significant events of this witness in the history of Latin American women, Pilar Aquino recommends the works of other Hispanic and Latin American women who have helped to bring about a better understanding of this process as it takes place in the context of North America. See María Pilar Aquino, "El 'des-cubrimiento' colectivo de la propia fuerza: Perspectivas teológicas desde las mujeres latinoamericanas," *Apuntes* 13 (1993) 86–103. Ada María Isasi-Díaz and Yolanda Tarango have helped me understand some additional theological and ethical dimensions of this witness in their groundbreaking work, *Hispanic Women: Prophetic Voice in the Church* (San Francisco: Harper and Row, 1988).

54. At the same time, I do want to emphasize that a rereading of the history of the church

stance that, throughout history, has been instrumental for challenging the church to remain faithful to God's word in the context of our social reality. Two of the central features of this witness of faith have been its affirmation of our catholic roots and our prophetic vocation. Our faith has its roots in the courageous and continuous efforts of those who have preceded us in a witness of faith that can be traced back to the origins of the Christian community in the early centuries. Yet this witness of faith has also been a costly one, for it calls us to a prophetic stance that for many has entailed suffering as well as martyrdom.[55]

As I mentioned earlier, contemporary theologians have helped us understand the fundamental confessional nature of Christianity. I am confident that, as we reflect on this important aspect of our faith and the witness of those who have tried to recover this prophetic witness of faith throughout history, we will renew our commitment to a faith with catholic roots calling us to a prophetic vocation. This is my belief and hope. It is also an invitation to action for all who take this confession seriously.

---

in the United States since its origins in the sixteenth century from a Hispanic theological perspective has already begun to emerge. Among the most important works of this research are: Stevens Arroyo, *Prophets Denied Honor,* and Moisés Sandoval, *Fronteras: A History of the Latin American Church in the U.S.A. since 1513* (San Antonio: Mexican American Cultural Center, 1983).

55. This is a faith stance that I find closely related to what Paul Tillich and Jaroslav Pelikan have described as the particular contribution of Lutheranism; they do this by characterizing this confessional movement within the Church Catholic as emphasizing a "Catholic substance" and a "Protestant Principle." I part company with them when they make reference to philosophical concepts that may provide a "static" or "essentialist" view of what I consider to be a more dynamic experience of faith, which continues to evolve throughout history. See Jaroslav Pelikan, *Obedient Rebels: Catholic Substance and Protestant Principle in Luther's Reformation* (New York: Harper and Row, 1964).

Strangers No Longer

_____ *Ada María Isasi-Díaz* _____

Latino/Hispanic theology has been developed out of need, commitment, and conviction. The need is that of our communities, which as marginalized and oppressed people in the United States struggle daily to survive at the material and cultural levels. The commitment is that of Hispanic theologians, integral members of our Latino communities where many of us live, where our friends and families live. Our commitment is to the struggle of Hispanic communities all around the United States. The conviction is that of Latino people, including Hispanic theologians, that religion, mainly our Latino expression of Christianity, is at the heart of our culture, at the heart of our daily lives. Need, commitment, and conviction: these are the elements behind the elaboration of Latino/Hispanic theology. We theologians have taken up the task of developing Latino/Hispanic theology because we believe that such a theology makes an important contribution to our Hispanic communities, to the churches, and to theology at large.

The essays in this book present some key theological expositions, which a number of us Latino/Hispanic theologians, though still very few, have been making in the last several years. Reading through these essays one can arrive at three conclusions about our young theology: it is a discourse that has attained a surprising maturity in a very short period of time; it is an ecumenical enterprise; it is a participatory theology, a theology of and by the community. These essays likewise make clear how Latina and Latino Hispanic theologians understand the relationship between Latino/Hispanic theology and theology at large. Let me develop these four points.

Theological Maturity

By theological maturity I mean that Latino/Hispanic theology has gone through a process of development whereby it has acquired certain readily identifiable characteristics because of patient, careful consideration by Hispanic theologians of the goal of our theological task, our methods, our sources, and our theological locus. Of course, I am not suggesting that our theology is totally mature at this point, that it has reached its full development. Our enterprise is young, and much work remains to be done.[1] Besides, there is the fact that since our theological discourse, like all theological discourse, has to do with reflection on the religious experiences and understandings of our people, Latino/Hispanic theology will never be fully mature; it will always be in the process of developing and maturing.

My claim that Latino/Hispanic theology has reached a certain maturity is based on the following five points. First, Latino/Hispanic theological production is precise and specific enough to be identifiable as such. Most of our theology is not unique. On the contrary, we share characteristics with a variety of theologies, most of them rising from other marginalized and oppressed groups. Yet the way in which these characteristics are brought together answers to the specific experience of Latinas and Latinos in the United States, and to our own way of understanding and practicing Christianity. To be able to claim specific characteristics for our theological work necessitates having produced a significant body of material where these characteristics are presented and explored precisely as intrinsic to our theology. It means that the number of Hispanic theologians teaching and writing warrants having a professional association of our own and sponsoring groups in the American Academy of Religion and the Catholic Theological Society of America. It also means that there are enough of us to have a critical mass that makes it possible to elaborate specific theological understandings and to have a body of colleagues who can evaluate and help to refine those understandings in view of our common culture and commitment to our people.

A second characteristic of our theological maturity is the variety of theological perspectives, methods, and disciplines operating in Latino/Hispanic theology. Many of us do Latino/Hispanic theology from a liberation perspective though not all of us agree on what liberation means and what one must do to make it a reality. Some of us have a more traditional perspective, using Latino/Hispanic theology as a way of bringing our perspective to bear on traditional themes and understandings. Some of us use traditional theological methods as we look at the historical development of doctrines

---

1. The production of theological texts, as I will indicate below, is only part of what we call Hispanic/Latino theology, the other part being a praxical component. In the production and publication of Latino/Hispanic theological books (not that I consider articles and pamphlets unimportant, but simply because I have to draw the line somewhere), the forerunner is Virgil Elizondo, *Christianity and Culture* (Huntington, Ind.: Our Sunday Visitor, 1975). It was not until the second half of the 1980s that other texts began to appear. Some of the authors who have published since the mid-1980s are: David Abalos, María Pilar Aquino, Allan Figueroa Deck, Orlando Espín, Roberto Goizueta, Ada María Isasi-Díaz, and Jeanette Rodríguez-Holguín. The work of Justo González in Latino/Hispanic theology began to appear in the 1980s. However, González had already won renown for his earlier books on church history published in several languages. For an extensive Roman Catholic bibliography, see Arturo Bañuelas, "U.S. Hispanic Roman Catholic Theology: A Bibliography," *Apuntes* 11:4 (winter 1991) 93–103. At present a Hispanic Protestant bibliography is being compiled.

and dogmas and try to find ways to include our perspective in the way those doctrines and dogmas are interpreted by official churches. Some of us use methods that start with the religious understandings and practices, the daily experiences, of grassroots Latinas and Latinos. Some of us use more philosophical approaches in our theology, while others use more sociological approaches. Further, Latino/Hispanic theology embraces the main disciplines of theology: biblical criticism, systematic theology, moral theology, pastoral theology, church history, ecclesiology, and liturgical studies. Such heterogeneity within Latino/Hispanic theology is possible only when a certain maturity is present, only when a theology has evolved sufficiently to sustain both similarities and dissimilarities without falling apart.

The third characteristic has to do with the importance of dialogue in our theological task. It is very significant, for example, that our sessions at the American Academy of Religion (and to a large extent at the Catholic Theological Society of America) do not limit the discussion to any one theologian or text. Instead, they have been used as opportunities to dialogue among ourselves and with non-Hispanic theologians. This was also the goal of the conference that resulted in this book: we wanted to dialogue with one another, to read one another's papers and comment on and constructively critique one another's work. Finally, it is significant in this regard that in the last few years there have appeared more edited and coauthored texts on Latino/Hispanic theology than texts by single authors.

The fourth characteristic that points to theological maturity is the insistence on and development of autochthonous elements. Two elements in particular are indigenous to Latino/Hispanic theology, both of them having to do with key sources of Latino/Hispanic theology: the religion of the people (popular religion)[2] and African and Amerindian religious elements present in this religion of the people. The use of these sources in our theology has to do in large part with three understandings that many of us embrace: the ongoing revelation of God in our world today preferentially through the poor and the oppressed; the salvific manifestations of the divine to be found in non-Christian religions; and the fact that, despite very poor pastoral care from the churches, it is precisely thanks to the religion of the people that Christianity is alive in our communities.

A fifth characteristic relates to our ability to recognize the limitations of our theological enterprise and the need to continue to develop further, to clarify and amplify what we say and how we say it. What helps us immensely in this regard is the fact that our theology grows out of the needs in our communities, out of the role that religion plays in the daily struggle

---

2. After some discussion, several of us have started using "the religion of the people" instead of "popular religion" because the word "popular" seems to qualify whatever it modifies as something less important. This was the same reason that a few years ago we stopped using "popular religiosity" and began using "popular religion."

to survive as a marginalized and oppressed group within one of the richest countries in the world. We are proud of what we have accomplished, but because we understand doing theology as a liberative praxis (I will discuss this below), that very understanding drives us to be more concrete and specific as to questions of ultimate meaning intrinsic to our lives. So, as we recognize present limitations, at the same time we look ahead to topics needing further development: What do we clearly understand liberation to be? What is the theological significance of the firm belief of our people that God stands with them against the oppressive forces of society? How do we deal theologically with the ease with which our people participate in different denominational churches without needing to change church affiliation?

Ecumenical Perspective

Hispanic communities in the United States are in themselves heterogeneous communities: while they have much in common, they also harbor great differences. We are a people who come from a great variety of countries and, though we share a certain Hispanic heritage, there are distinct and different elements in the culture of each of our countries of origin. In some of our countries African elements are quite central and play a significant role in music, literature, customs, as well as in religious understandings and practices. In others Amerindian cultural elements are very influential, including religious elements. There are also great differences in the reasons why we have migrated to the United States. Some of us came here out of economic need created by imperialism and neocolonialism. Some of us arrived here fleeing leftist regimes, while others had to run from right-wing governments.

Such multiple elements within our communities have amplified the meaning of the term "mestiza." *Mestizaje* has come to mean much more than the mingling of European and Amerindian races. It certainly includes the mingling of the African black race with both the European and Amerindian races, and perhaps we need to consider subsuming *mulatez,* the mixture of black and white races that is a widespread reality in our communities, under "mestiza." But *mestizaje* and *mulatez* also have become a paradigm not only for our racial diversity but for all the diversity we have in our Latino/Hispanic communities. These terms refer to our ability to sustain a sense of community in spite of religious and political differences, to identify and maintain similarities without ignoring specificities and particularities, to insist on a continuum of differences that not only permits diversity but actually welcomes it.

It is then within this continuum of differences in our communities that we need to understand the ecumenical perspective of Latino/Hispanic theology. Some of us have always done theology from an ecumenical perspective.

For others this is something that needs to be developed. But there is a general conviction among us that we must elaborate an ecumenical theological discourse because many of our people practice what can be called "grassroots ecumenism." Many grassroots Latinas and Latinos attend different churches without seeing any need to change denominations. And many who do change denominations have no difficulty in continuing religious practices officially rejected by those denominations. Religion for Hispanics is not wrapped up in fidelity to a given denomination but rather in the firm belief that God walks with us in our daily struggles and that we are called to live out in very specific ways the strong sense of community that is a fundamental component of our culture. Our Latino/Hispanic theology, therefore, needs to interpret and promote this kind of Christian understanding and practice, which means that it needs to be an ecumenical theology.

But I do not want to overlook the many obstacles we have to overcome if we are to develop truly ecumenical Latino/Hispanic theological discourse. There is much competition among our churches; there are indictments about "sheep stealing" and daily accusations of being "less Christian" or "not really Christian." It seems to me that the only way of overcoming these obstacles is to be faithful to our commitment to our communities, to the understanding that Latino/Hispanic theology is born out of the need of our people. To build not a homogeneous but a really ecumenical Latino/Hispanic theology we need to continue to insist on the possibility of diversity without divisions.

A Community Theology

Latino/Hispanic theology is a discourse, but it is also a praxis: we do not write theology; we do theology. Those of us who do theology are not just those academically trained but also grassroots people who are eminently capable of explaining our religious understandings and practices, people for whom religion is the spark enabling us to continue the daily struggle. Latino/Hispanic theology is elaborated in the books we publish, but it is also carefully laid out in the variety of prayers that our people are always willing to share aloud, prayers that identify what they value and how they see the divine participating in their lives.

I have already talked about the centrality of dialogue to Latino/Hispanic theology. Here I want to comment on the capacity of grassroots Latinos for theological praxis, that is, for liberative, reflective action that has as one of its core elements religious understandings and practices. This means that grassroots Latinas and Latinos can rightly be considered intellectuals as much as those who have academic degrees and publish books. Unfortunately, the word "intellectual" is used in different ways. In common parlance an intellectual is one given to study, speculation, and reflection in academic settings. But "intellectual" also is used to refer to activity requiring the creative use of the intellect. The fact that these two meanings are often consolidated, are not kept apart, means that those who do not study, speculate, and reflect in academic settings are not considered capable of activity requiring the creative use of the intellect. This erroneous collapse of the two meanings of "intellectual" into one serves well the elitism of those with academic degrees who devalue the intellectual capacities and contributions of grassroots people.

The insistence on the religion of the people as the most important source of Latino/Hispanic theology works precisely against this belittling and degrading of the intellectual capacity of grassroots Hispanics. So does our assertion about the ongoing revelation of God preferentially in the lives and struggles of the poor and the oppressed.

Latino/Hispanic theology is a community theology, then, and not solely because of the commitment of academic theologians to the struggles of our people. It is a community theology because it is not only *for* the people but also *by* the people, by the grassroots people who are admirably capable of reflecting theologically. Furthermore, because of our understanding of the preferential option for the oppressed as an intrinsic element of the gospel message, we believe that it is the perspective of grassroots Latinas and Latinos that best can help us be a community committed to liberative praxis.

Latino/Hispanic Theology and Other Theologies

I see Latino/Hispanic theology as a discourse as well as a praxis of transformation produced by the living out of Latino Christian (including Amerindian and African) understandings and practices by Hispanics in the United States.[3] The transformation that is the goal of our work involves a radical liberation that operates at the social and political level, at the psychological level, and at the spiritual-religious level. Ours is not the only theology with this goal. It is also the goal of various liberation theologies throughout the world. The existence of many liberation theologies and of different "official" denominational theologies gives rise to an important question: How do we expect and hope that Latino/Hispanic theology will be regarded and dealt with by non-Hispanic theologians or by those Hispanic theologians working from principles not compatible with the ones the majority of us espouse?

To answer this question I think we need to consider the whole issue of essentialism and otherness, for precisely what the insistence on our own discourse does is denounce and deconstruct theological essentialism. It rejects

---

3. Here I am adapting the insights of Rebecca S. Chopp, *The Power to Speak* (New York: Crossroad, 1989) 7.

the idea that there is only one way to understand the divine, only one way to speak about the divine, only one way of witnessing to the divine. However, the claim that there is more than just "one way" must not and should not result in total relativism, to an "anything goes" attitude, for both of these are based upon and lead to an individualism that is nothing else but the epitome of liberalism. Latino/Hispanic theology has no desire to go it alone, to be left alone. On the contrary, essential to our task of being a significant element in the liberative struggles of our people is the ability of our theology to engage and be engaged by others. Part of our task is to bring to others the religious understandings and practices of Latinas and Latinos.

To do this, first and foremost, we need to insist at all times that Latino/Hispanic theology is not only for Hispanics. It is, of course, a theology done from our perspective and based on our experience, but it is also a theology from which others can learn much. Our theological enterprise has much to contribute to other theologies just as we have much to learn from other theologies. Without denying the need for specificity and particularity, we need to reach beyond, and others need to reach out to us. This stops being a threat, to ourselves and/or to others, once the belief that there is only one theology is no longer operative. Once "the right way" to speak about and witness to the divine is put aside, there is no need to carve out spaces in which only one group of people and their understandings reign supreme. Once we recognize that there are many ways to speak about and witness to the divine, we can all reach out to one another without being afraid that we are going to be exploited or, worse, ignored.

A multiplicity of theologies calls for true dialogue, what I call engagement. Engagement requires a relationship of empathy as well as commitment to a joint search.[4] Of course this means that there can be no real dialogue, no real engagement between Latino/Hispanic theologians and others, unless they take time to know us and the struggle of Latinas and Latinos and we take time to know them and the struggles of their people. In a way, this kind of engagement would change radically the face of theology and theological studies since the point of reference and what everyone is expected to know and to espouse would no longer be "mainline" theology or official theology. Real engagement among theologies and theologians would mean that a multiplicity of methods would be examined, that different social locations would be analyzed, and that the theological praxis of different communities of struggle would become intrinsic to theological education. Engagement among different theologies would prevent us from falling into total relativity and individualism since all engagement is, in a sense, a calling to accountability.

Rules of engagement must be clearly understood and respected, or

---

4. Paulo Freire, *Cultural Action for Freedom* (Cambridge, Mass.: Harvard Educational Review, 1970) 45ff.

engagement could well result in destructive criticism. I am not precluding strong and insightful critique, but constructive critique. Such critique cannot discount what others think, cannot negate the validity of the experiences of others and their right to their own theological discourse. Engagement requires a humble attitude, an attitude of learning, which itself requires me to think the other might be right and I might be wrong. Engagement is not a matter of convincing the other but rather a matter of contributing elements to be considered when reassessment of thinking is going on. Engagement, then, is possible only within an atmosphere of trust, and trust, for those of us struggling to survive, is only possible when true solidarity exists.

Strangers No Longer

We understand Latino/Hispanic theology as an enterprise that has something to say and that should be recognized and engaged. Our sense that we can claim to be no longer strangers is not always a strong one. Many times we make that claim fearfully, afraid of being rejected. Yet, out of the need of our people, out of our commitment to them and our conviction that we have something very worthwhile to contribute, we have been doing and will continue to do Latino/Hispanic theology.

Index